The Linux Cookbook

The Linux Cookbook

Tips and Techniques for Everyday Use

Michael Stutz

An imprint of No Starch Press, Inc.

San Francisco

Printed in the United States of America

2 3 4 5 6 7 8 9 10–04 03 02 01

Trademarked names are used throughout this book. Rather than use a trademark symbol with every occurrence of a trademarked name, we are using the names only in an editorial fashion and to the benefit of the trademark owner, with no intention of infringement of the trademark.

Co-publishers: William Pollock and Phil Hughes
Project Editor: Karol Jurado
Assistant Editor: Nick Hoff
Cover Design: Octopod Studios
Typesetting and Design: Michael Stutz
Technical Editor: Scott Schwartz
Copyeditor: Andy Carroll
Proofreader: Elisabeth Beller

Distributed to the book trade in the United States by Publishers Group West, 1700 Fourth Street, Berkeley, California 94710, phone: 800-788-3123 or 510-528-1444, fax: 510-528-3444

Distributed to the book trade in Canada by Jacqueline Gross & Associates, Inc., 195 Allstate Parkway, Markham, Ontario L3R 4T8 Canada, phone: 905-477-0722, fax: 905-477-8619

For information on translations or book distributors outside the United States, please contact No Starch Press, Inc. directly:

No Starch Press, Inc.
555 De Haro Street, Suite 250, San Francisco, CA 94107
phone: 415-863-9900; fax: 415-863-9950; info@nostarch.com; www.nostarch.com

This official author's edition is published by exclusive arrangement with No Starch Press, Inc.

Library of Congress Cataloging-in-Publication Data

Stutz, Michael.
      The Linux cookbook / Michael Stutz.
            p. cm.
      ISBN 1-886411-48-4 (pbk.)
      1. Linux. 2. Operating systems (Computers) I. Title.

QA76.76.O63 S788 2000
005.4'32--dc21   00-046057

Contents at a glance

Table of Contents

Preface

Because of its robust and stable nature, the Linux-based system is the choice of millions today. But what some may not know is that the free software movement, of which Linux is a part, is very much a counter-cultural phenomenon: the design by which it is produced and published is contrary to the notions of proprietary, intellectual "property" that have dominated mainstream culture so long. While some programmers turn their research into corporate-backed software that you cannot openly change, share, or examine (but only purchase and run on your system), Linux and other free software is the product of many individuals who courageously published and shared their research and work openly, for everyone to benefit from.

I wrote this book because I want everyone to know how to use this software, because I think everyone deserves the freedom that comes with it. I don't willingly use proprietary software—not because it is always *inferior* to free software but because its use precludes freedoms that I find I cannot exist without . . . freedoms that should be everyone's right by default in a free, open society. (See Chapter 1 [Introduction], page 9.)

I know that Linux isn't difficult to use, especially when compared with other software and operating systems, but what was needed was a guide to show people how to use it to get things done: "Oh, you want to do *that*? Here, type this."

That explains the premise of the book—it's a hands-on guide to getting things done on a Linux system, designed for the everyday user who is not necessarily a computer programmer.

The traditional approach to the subject is to either provide laundry lists of all available commands and applications, or focus on their use in a programming or otherwise technical environment. This book takes a different approach, showing how everyday users—be they artists, designers, businessmen, scholars, or scientists—can use these tools and applications to get things done. When I speak of "things," I mean (hopefully) the kind of things that you—the sort of person possibly and partially described above—might want to do with a modern computer system: view text and images, play and record sounds, perform mathematic operations, print to your printer, format text, access the Internet, check your grammar, and so forth.

Like a culinary cookbook, this book presents "recipes" for preparing or accomplishing a particular, specific thing. I've selected what I consider to be the easiest and most effective methods for accomplishing particular tasks, and have arranged these recipes in general sections according to subject matter—the first part of the book is all about getting started, and contains the most essential information you need to know about using Linux; the remaining chapters deal with general categories of usage: Files, Text, Images, Sound, Productivity, and Networking.

Format of Recipes

Each recipe is numbered with at least two figures. These figures are constructed as follows: the first number always corresponds to the chapter number, and the second to the section of the recipe. For example, Chapter 3 is The Shell, and Recipe No. 3.5 is the fifth recipe on shells, Recipe 3.5 [Recording a Shell Session], page 45.

Sometimes recipes are divided into subsections, with a third number specifying the specific recipe—for example, Recipe No. 3.4 is on the subject of command history in the shell, and is divided further into subsections; Recipe No. 3.4.2 is the second recipe on command history, Recipe 3.4.2 [Specifying a Command from Your History], page 44.

Each recipe describes a method for completing a specific task on the system; these tasks require at least one software program. The software programs or files a recipe calls for are its *ingredients*.

The recipes are structured as follows:

1. Recipe number and title of the recipe.

2. Special ingredients, if any. The Debian package(s) and/or or URLs where the program(s) can be obtained are listed, if they are available.

   Debian classifies packages in varying level of importance, from 'required' packages that all systems *must* have in order to run, to 'optional' and 'extra' packages that you only install if you want them. If a described software package is in the first two given categories—'required' and 'important'—then I assume you have it installed, and the package name isn't listed here.

   In the rare case that a software package I describe is not yet available as a Debian package, I just give the URL where to obtain the source packages for that software; have your system administrator install it.

3. Special preparation methods or description, if any. When a configurable program is described, the standard setup as provided by the Debian distribution is assumed, unless otherwise specified here.

4. Description of the recipe and "cooking" method proper.

5. Remarks concerning the results and use.

6. Bulleted example of the method in a specific context.

7. Extra commands or actions you might want to do next.

8. Variations on the recipe, with additional examples.

9. Special notes or references to further information.

Not all of these items may be present in a given recipe.

Assumptions, Scope, and Exclusions

There a few assumptions that this book makes about you, the reader, and about your Linux system.

The *Cookbook* assumes that you have at least minimal understanding of your computer hardware—you don't have to know how to take it apart or anything like that, but you ought to know how to operate the mouse, where the power button is on your computer and monitor, how to load paper in your printer, and so forth. If you need help with any of these tasks or concepts, ask your dealer or the party who set up your computer.

This book also assumes that you have Linux installed and properly set up, and that you have your own user account set up on your system. If you need help with this, please see Recipe 1.3 [If You Need More Help], page 16.

While this book can and should be used by the newcomer to Linux, I like to think that I've presented broad enough coverage of the Linux-based system, and have included enough interesting or obscure material, so that wizards, hackers, and members of the Linux Cabal may find some of it useful—and that said users will not feel ashamed to have a copy of this book on their desk or as part of their library.

Finally, a note about what *isn't* covered in the *Cookbook*.

This book describes only free software (sometimes called "open source" software) that runs on Linux systems.[1] Proprietary software is omitted, as are most software packages that are currently in a "beta" or some other unstable release not yet intended for general use.

Some programs take a number of options that modify the way they work. Sometimes, various options that a tool takes are listed in a table. These lists are not exhaustive; rather, they contain the most popular or useful options, or those options that are relevant to the discussion at hand. Consult the online manual page of a particular tool for the complete listing (see Recipe 2.8.4 [Reading a Page from the System Manual], page 30).

This is a *user* manual; no computer programming activities, such as program compilation, are discussed. Topics related to system administration are also omitted—so you won't find anything in this text on matters such as managing accounts, system maintenance, setting up hardware, and configuring networks.

As with any rule, you can find an exception to this—if you look hard enough for it. If you are running Linux on your home computer as a single user system, you are also the administrator of this system, and are the responsible party for ensuring that any administrative tasks be completed; Appendix A [Administrative Issues], page 359 exists as a reference for those users who will be administrating their own systems.

Typographical Conventions

All recipes have at least one example that demonstrates it.

- The text that describes what the example does appears just before the example itself, and is offset from the text with a bullet, like this.

- A given recipe may have several variations; each is offset with its own bullet.

- The names of documents or users that are used in some recipes may not always reference actual documents or users on your system, but demonstrate the general principles involved. So when I show how to print a file called 'resume', you might not necessarily have a file with that name on your system, but you should understand the idea which the recipe demonstrates.

Sometimes, a terminal screen is shown to illustrate an interactive session:

---

[1] The word "free" in this context refers to freedom or liberty, and not price; this distinction is explained in Chapter 1 [Introduction], page 9.

```
$ Text that you actually type is displayed in a slanted font, like
this. If it is a command to be typed at a shell prompt, the command is
preceded with a '$' character.

Text that denotes program output is displayed in a monospaced Courier
font like this.

$
```

In examples where a shell prompt is displayed, the default current working directory is omitted in the prompt and just a '$' is used; when a command outputs text and then exits, the last line of an example contains a '$' character to denote the return to a shell prompt. Don't worry if this sounds strange to you now; all of this "shell" business is explained in Chapter 3 [The Shell], page 35.

When a command exits and returns to the shell prompt without outputting text, the final shell prompt character is omitted, and a cartouche border is not drawn around the example; this was purely an æsthetic decision.

The names of files or directories appear in the text as 'file'; commands appear as command, and strings of text are typeset like 'some text'.

Text you type is written *like this*, just as in the examples, and when a specific key on the keyboard is mentioned, its conventional name is displayed in a box. For example, (RET) denotes the 'Return' key on the keyboard.[2]

In examples where keys are meant to be pressed and held down together, the keys are separated by hyphens; the hyphens are not meant to be literally pressed. For example, pressing the (CTRL), (ALT), and (DEL) keys and holding them down at the same time is a combination that has meaning in some operating systems (including Linux, where this keystroke means to shut down the system and reboot the computer); it is represented like this:

(CTRL)-(ALT)-(DEL)

The (CTRL) ('Control') key is always used in combination with another key; these combinations are denoted by *C-x*, where *x* is the second key. These combinations are read as 'control-x', where *x* is the name of the second key. To type one of these combinations, press and hold (CTRL), press the second key, and then release both keys.

- For example, to type *C-d* (pronounced 'control d'), press and hold (CTRL), type the (D) key, and then release both keys.

In some applications (notably, the Emacs editor; see Recipe 10.2 [Emacs], page 121), the (META) key is used with another key, in the same way as (SHIFT); these combinations are denoted by *M-x*, where *x* is the second key. Most keyboards today don't have a (META) key, even though the term is still in use; instead, press and release (ESC), and then type the second key.

- To type *M-c*, press and release (ESC), and then press and release the (C) key.

You can sometimes also use the (ALT) key for the (META) key. This often does not work in the X Window System, but in the console you can press and hold (ALT) and then type the second key just as you would with a CTRL key sequence.

---

[2] This key is labelled 'Enter' on some keyboards.

- So to type *M-c* with the (ALT) key, press and hold (ALT), press the (C) key, and then release both keys.

Both (CTRL) and (META) sequences are not case-sensitive; that is, pressing *X* in the last example is the same as pressing *x* (although *x* is certainly easier to type). By convention, the *C-* or *M-* prefix is always given as an uppercase letter, and the key which follows is always given as a lowercase letter.

Menu items in an application are written like **Menu Item**; the names of command functions are written as **Function**.

For aesthetic purposes, a physical space appears in the text between commands and the final (RET) that ends a command line, and should not be literally typed (although nothing bad will happen should you actually type this space). Where explicitly pressing the space bar is called for, that key is represented in examples by (SPC).

Versions, Latest Edition, and Errata

WWW: `http://dsl.org/cookbook/`

The Linux Cookbook is available in both hardcopy and as a machine-readable file. The latest edition of this book in etext ("electronic text") form is always available from its distribution site (`http://dsl.org/cookbook/`) on the World Wide Web. This site includes the most up-to-date complete text (in both HTML and GNU Info formats), and provides a method for purchasing the latest edition of the hardcopy book at a discount.

Every effort has been made to include only the best free software recipes for accomplishing tasks in the easiest and most efficient manner, and they are believed to be correct. Suggestions, comments, and bug reports are always welcome; you can contact the author via email at `stutz@dsl.org`.

Acknowledgments

This is not a book that was borne easily. Conception, took but an idle moment—but once the idea had been implanted, I found resistance and setbacks at every turn. It was only through the help of the following individuals that this book with my name on its cover was finally brought forth, and has now found its way to you.

Everyone involved with this book at No Starch Press (`http://www.nostarch.com/`) deserves a hearty round of thanks. Bill Pollock has published this book precisely according to its author's vision, and had the discernment and foresight to allow that a copylefted edition (with corresponding source data) be made available in conjunction with the hardcopy book. Project manager Karol Jurado worked ceaselessly to keep the production flowing, while dealing with my input files, and giving opinion and advice on all manners of obtuse esoterica whenever the sudden need to know came over me. Both Elisabeth Beller and Andy Carroll contributed improvements to the text.

Steve Turner and the National Writers Union (`http://www.nwu.org/`) played a major role in helping to ensure that this book could be completed, copylefted, and in the hands of Linux users like yourself. Carol Cricow gave invaluable legal assistance, and various advice and assistance came from the NWU's JoAnn Kawell, Philip Mattera, Judy Heim, and Bonnie Britt.

Wendy Seltzer, Fellow, The Berkman Center for Internet & Society at Harvard Law School (`http://cyber.law.harvard.edu/`) assisted with the conception of the Design Science License (DSL), which is used in this book. She gave an initial review of the license draft and provided her expertise and advice throughout the entire process.

Thanks to David Sims, Chris Coleman, and Terrie Schweitzer, who've all been great folks to work with at the O'Reilly Network (`http://oreillynet.com/`), where my "Living Linux" column runs.

I am indebted to Buwei Yang Chao, whose *How To Cook and Eat In Chinese* (John Day Company, 1945) served as much of the inspiration behind the tone and structure of this book. I feel the same regard for two other authors who have come before me, and whose work has had a direct influence in the writing of this book—Dr. Lee Su Jan (*The Fine Art of Chinese Cooking*, Gramercy Publishing 1962) and Andrew Walker (*The UNIX Environment*, Wiley 1984).

Thanks also go out to Kenneth W. Melvin, and to the members of the "Byline" forum on the WELL; both were sources of advice and feedback early in the project. The art-hackers of the `linart` mailing list (`http://linart.net/`) entertained initial discussion of the idea of this book as it first occurred, and the "elders" Ann and Walt gave various support for which I am grateful.

Finally, I must thank Jack Angelotta, Jon Konrath, Steven Snedker, and `mrs` (Marie Stutz), who all listened to the unbelievable as it happened, and stood by—even in moments of terror.

PART ONE: Working with Linux

1 Introduction

Before we get into "cooking" and the recipes proper, this first part of the book deals with preliminaries, explaining the general techniques and methods for working with Linux—including how to get the system ready for use, and how to run commands on the system.

The rest of the book is all recipes, which are sorted in sections by the tasks they perform or the objects they work on—such as text, files, images, and so forth.

1.1 Background and History

In order to understand what Linux is all about, it helps to know a bit about how it all began. So the following is a historical overview, giving a concise background of the software that is the subject of this book.

1.1.1 What's Unix?

WWW: `http://www.bell-labs.com/history/unix/`
WWW: `http://internet-history.org/archives/early.history.of.unix.html`

Unix, the original ancestor of Linux, is an operating system. Or at least it *was* an operating system; the original system known as Unix proper is not the "Unix" we know and use today; there are now many "flavors" of Unix, of which Linux has become the most popular.

A product of the 1960s, Unix and its related software was invented by Dennis Ritchie, Ken Thompson, Brian Kernighan, and other hackers at Bell Labs in 1969; its name was a play on "Multics," another operating system of the time.[1]

In the early days of Unix, any interested party who had the hardware to run it on could get a tape of the software from Bell Labs, with printed manuals, for a very nominal charge. (This was before the era of personal computing, and in practice, mostly only universities and research laboratories did this). Local sites played with the software's source code, extending and customizing the system to their needs and liking.

Beginning in the late 1970s, computer scientists at the University of California, Berkeley, a licensee of the Unix source code, had been making their own improvements and enhancements to the Unix source during the course of their research, which included the development of TCP/IP networking. Their work became known as the BSD ("Berkeley Systems Distribution") flavor of Unix.

The source code of their work was made publicly available under licensing that permitted redistribution, with source or without, provided that Berkeley was credited for their portions of the code. There are many modern variants of the original BSD still actively developed today, and some of them—such as NetBSD and OpenBSD—can run on personal computers.

NOTE: The uppercase word 'UNIX' became a trademark of AT&T (since transferred to other organizations), to mean their particular operating system. But today, when people say "Unix," they usually mean "a Unix-like operating system," a generalization that includes Linux.

---

[1] The name "Unix" was first written as "Unics," which stood for "Uniplex Information and Computing System."

If you'd like further information on this topic, you might be interested in consulting *A Quarter Century of UNIX* by Peter H. Salus (Addison-Wesley 1994), which has become the standard text on the subject.

1.1.2 What's Free Software?

WWW: `http://www.gnu.org/philosophy/free-sw.html`

Over the years, Unix's popularity grew. After the divestiture of AT&T, the tapes of the source code that Bell Labs provided became a proprietary, commercial product: AT&T UNIX. But it was expensive, and didn't come with the source code that made it tick. Even if you paid extra for a copy of the sources, you couldn't share with your programmer colleagues any improvements or discoveries you made.

By the early 1980s, proprietary software development, by only-for-profit corporations, was quickly becoming the norm—even at universities. More software was being distributed without source code than ever before.

In 1984, while at the Massachusetts Institute of Technology in Cambridge, Massachusetts, hacker Richard Stallman saw his colleagues gradually accept and move to this proprietary development model. He did not accept the kind of world such proprietism would offer: no sharing your findings with your fellow man, no freedom for anyone to improve a published work.

So instead of giving in to the world of non-free computing, Stallman decided to start a project to build and assemble a new Unix-like operating system from scratch, and make its source code free for anyone to copy and modify. This was the GNU Project ("GNU's Not Unix").[2]

The GNU Project's software would be licensed in such a way so that everyone was given the freedom to copy, distribute, and modify their copy of the software; as a result, this kind of software became known as *free software*.

Individuals and businesses may charge for free software, but anyone is free to share copies with their neighbors, change it, or look at its source code to see how it works. There are no secrets in free software; it's software that gives all of its users the freedom they deserve.

Proprietary software strictly limits these freedoms—in accordance with copyright law, which was formulated in an age when works were normally set and manipulated in physical form, and not as non-physical data, which is what computers copy and modify.

Free software licensing was developed as a way to work around the failings of copyright law, by permitting anyone to copy and modify a work, though under certain strict terms and conditions. The GNU Project's GNU General Public License (`http://www.gnu.org/copyleft/gpl.txt`), or GNU GPL, is the most widely used of all free software licenses. Popularly called a "copyleft," it permits anyone to copy or modify any software released under its terms—provided all derivatives or modifications are released under the same terms, and all changes are documented.

---

[2] No such "official GNU" operating system has yet been released in its entirety, but most people today consider Linux-based free software systems to be the effective realization of their goals—hence the "GNU" in "Debian GNU/Linux."

1.1.3 What's Open Source?

WWW: http://www.opensource.org/
WWW: http://www.gnu.org/philosophy/free-software-for-freedom.html

The term *open source* was first introduced by some free software hackers in 1998 to be a marketing term for "free software." They felt that some people unfamiliar with the free software movement—namely, large corporations, who'd suddenly taken an interest in the more than ten years' worth of work that had been put into it—might be scared by the word "free." They were concerned that decision-makers in these corporations might confuse free software with things like *freeware*, which is software provided free of charge, and in executable form only. (Free software means nothing of the sort, of course; the "free" in "free software" has always referred to *freedom*, not price.)

The Open Source Initiative (OSI) was founded to promote software that conforms with their public "Open Source Definition," which was derived from the "Debian Free Software Guidelines" (DFSG), originally written by Bruce Perens as a set of software inclusion guidelines for Debian. All free software—including software released under the terms of the GNU General Public License—conforms with this definition.

But some free software advocates and organizations, including the GNU Project, do not endorse the term "open source" at all, believing that it obscures the importance of "freedom" in this movement.[3]

Whether you call it free software, open source software, or something else, there is one fundamental difference between this kind of software and proprietary, non-free software— and that is that free software always ensures that everyone is granted certain fundamental freedoms with respect to that software.

1.1.4 What's Linux?

In the early 1990s, Finnish computer science student Linus Torvalds began hacking on Minix, a small, Unix-like operating system for personal computers then used in college operating systems courses.[4] He decided to improve the main software component underlying Minix, called the *kernel*, by writing his own. (The kernel is the central component of any Unix-like operating system.)

In late 1991, Torvalds published the first version of this kernel on the Internet, calling it "Linux" (a play on both Minix and his own name).[5]

When Torvalds published Linux, he used the copyleft software license published by the GNU Project, the GNU General Public License. Doing so made his software free to use, copy, and modify by anyone—provided any copies or variations were kept equally free. Torvalds also invited contributions by other programmers, and these contributions came; slowly at first but, as the Internet grew, thousands of hackers and programmers

---

[3] You can extend this "free software movement" to be part of a greater "free information" or "free speech" movement, to include all *other* kinds of free works—including works of literature and music.

[4] Presumably, many of these courses use Linux now.

[5] This was not the original name, however. Torvalds had originally called it `freax`, for "'free' + 'freak' + the obligatory '-x'"; while the 1990s were fast becoming the "freaky" alterna decade (at least in fashion), more people seemed to favor "Linux," and the name stuck.

from around the globe contributed to his free software project. The Linux software was immensely extended and improved so that the Linux-based system of today is a complete, modern operating system, which can be used by programmers and non-programmers alike; hence this book.

1.1.5 What's Debian?

WWW: `http://debian.org/`

It takes more than individual software programs to make something that we can use on our computers—someone has to put it all together. It takes time to assemble the pieces into a cohesive, usable collection, and test it all, and then keep up to date with the new developments of each piece of software (a small change in any one of which may introduce a new software dependency problem or conflict with the rest). A Linux *distribution* is such an assemblage. You can do it yourself, of course, and "roll your own" distribution—since it's all free software, *anyone* can add to it or remove from it and call the resulting concoction their own. Most people, however, choose to leave the distribution business to the experts.

For the purposes of this book, I will assume that you are using the Debian GNU/Linux distribution, which, of all the major distributions, is the only one designed and assembled in the same manner that the Linux kernel and most other free software is written—by individuals.

And when I say "Linux" anywhere in this book (including in the title), unless noted, I am not referring to the bare kernel itself, but to the entire working free software system as a whole. This is often called "GNU/Linux."[6]

There are many other distributions, and some of them are quite acceptable—many users swear by Red Hat Linux, for example, which is certainly popular, and reportedly easy to install. The SuSE distribution is very well-received in Europe. So when people speak of Debian, Red Hat, SuSE, and the like in terms of Linux, they're talking about the specific *distribution* of Linux and related software, as assembled and repackaged by these companies or organizations (see Appendix B [Linux Resources on the Web], page 367). The core of the distributions are the same—they're all the Linux kernel, the GNU Project software, and various other free software—but each distribution has its own packaging schemes, defaults, and configuration methods. It is by no means wrong to install and use any of these other distributions, and every recipe in this book should work with all of them (with the exception of variations that are specific to Debian systems, and are labelled as such in the text).

In Debian's early days, it was referred to as the "hacker's distro," because it could be very difficult for a newbie to install and manage. However, that has changed—any Linux newbie can install and use today's Debian painlessly.

NOTE: I recommend Debian because it is non-corporate, openly developed, robust (the standard Debian CD-ROM set comes with more than 2,500 different software packages!), and it is entirely committed to free software by design (yes, there are distributions which are not).

---

[6] The GNU Project's own kernel is called Hurd, and is still in development; Debian's experimental distribution of a Hurd-based free softare system, not yet publicly released, is called Debian GNU/Hurd.

1.1.6 Unix and the Tools Philosophy

WWW: http://cm.bell-labs.com/cm/cs/upe/
WWW: http://www.cs.bell-labs.com/cm/cs/pearls/

To understand the way tasks are performed on Linux, some discussion on the philosophy behind the software that Linux is built upon is in order. A dip in these inviting waters will help clarify the rôle of this book as "cookbook."

The fact that the Unix operating system has survived for more than thirty years should tell us something about the temerity of its design considerations. One of these considerations—perhaps its most endearing—is the "tools" philosophy.

Most operating systems are designed with a concept of files, come with a set of utility programs for handling these files, and then leave it to the large *applications* to do the interesting work: a word processor, a spreadsheet, a presentation designer, a Web browser. (When a few of these applications recognize each other's file formats, or share a common interface, the group of applications is called a "suite.")

Each of these monolithic applications presumably has an "open file" command to read a file from disk and open it in the application; most of them, too, come with commands for searching and replacing text, checking spelling, printing the current document, and so on. The program source code for handling all of these tasks must be accounted for separately, inside each application—taking up extra space both in memory and on disk. This is the anti-Unix approach.

And in the case of proprietary software, all of the actual program source code is kept from the public—so other programmers can't use, build on, or learn from any of it. This kind of closed-source software is presented to the world as a kind of magic trick: if you buy a copy of the program, you may *use* it, but you can never learn how the program actually *works*.

The result of this is that the code to handle essentially the same function inside all of these different applications must be developed by programmers from scratch, separately and independently of the others each time—so the progress of society as a whole is set back by the countless man-hours of time and energy programmers must waste by inefficiently reinventing all the same software functions to perform the same tasks, over and over again.

Unix-like operating systems don't put so much weight on application programs. Instead, they come with many small programs called *tools*. Each tool is generally capable of performing a very simple, specific task, and performing it well—one tool does nothing but output the file(s) or data passed to it, one tool spools its input to the print queue, one tool sorts the lines of its input, and so on.

An important early development in Unix was the invention of "pipes," a way to pass the output of one tool to the input of another. By knowing what the individual tools do and how they are combined, a user could now build powerful "strings" of commands.

Just as the tensile strength of steel is greater than the added strength of its components—nickel, cadmium, and iron—multiple tools could then be combined to perform a task unpre-

dicted by the function of the individual tools. This is the concept of *synergy*, and it forms
the basis of the Unix tools philosophy.[7]

Here's an example, using two tools. The first tool, called `who`, outputs a list of users
currently logged on to the system (see Recipe 2.6.2 [Listing Who Is on the System], page 24).
The second tool is called `wc`, which stands for "word count"; it outputs a count of the number
of words (or lines or characters) of the input you give it (see Recipe 12.1 [Counting Text],
page 149).

By combining these two tools, giving the `wc` command the output of `who`, you can build
a new command to list the number of users currently on the system:

```
$ who | wc -l (RET)
        4
$
```

The output of `who` is piped—via a "pipeline," specified by the vertical bar ('|')
character—to the input of `wc`, which through use of the '`-l`' option outputs the number of
lines of its input.

In this example, the number 4 is shown, indicating that four users are currently logged
on the system. (Incidentally, piping the output of `who` to `wc` in this fashion is a classic tools
example, and was called "the most quoted pipe in the world" by Andrew Walker in *The
UNIX Environment*, a book that was published in 1984.)

Another famous pipeline from the days before spell-check tools goes something like this:

```
$ tr -cs A-Za-z '\012' | tr A-Z a-z | sort -u |
comm -23 - /usr/dict/words (RET)
```

This command (typed all on one line) uses the `tr`, `sort`, and `comm` tools to make a
spelling checker—after you type this command, the lines of text you type (until you interrupt
it) are converted to a single-column list of lowercase words with two calls of `tr`, sorted
in alphabetical order while ferreting out all duplicates, the resultant list which is then
compared with '`/usr/dict/words`', which is the system "dictionary," a list of properly-
spelled words kept in alphabetical order (see Recipe 11.1 [Spelling], page 135).

Collective sets of tools designed around a certain kind of field or concept were called
"workbenches" on older Unix systems; for example, the tools for checking the spelling,
writing style and grammar of their text input were part of the "Writer's Workbench" package
(see Recipe 11.3 [Checking Grammar], page 142).

Today the GNU Project publishes collections of tools under certain general themes,
such as the "GNU text utilities" and "GNU file utilities," but the idea of "workbenches"
is generally not part of the idiom of today's Unix-based systems. Needless to say, we still
use all kinds of tools for all kinds of purposes; the great bulk of this book details various
combinations of tools to obtain the desired results for various common tasks.

You'll find that there's usually one tool or command sequence that works perfectly for
a given task, but sometimes a satisfactory or even identical result can be had by different

---

[7] Because of this approach, and because of its free and open nature, I have come to call Linux a "synergetic"
operating system, in honor of the late R. Buckminster Fuller, who invented a new mathematical system
based on these same principles.

combinations of different tools—especially at the hands of a Unix expert. (Traditionally, such an expert was called a *wizard*.)

Some tasks require more than one tool or command sequence. And yes, there are tasks that require more than what these simple craft or hand tools can provide. Some tasks need more industrial production techniques, which are currently provided for by the application programs. So we still haven't avoided applications entirely; at the turn of the millennium, Linux-based systems still have them, from editors to browsers. But our applications use open file formats, and we can use all of our tools on these data files.

The invention of new tools has been on the rise along with the increased popularity of Linux-based systems. At the time of this writing, there were a total of 1,190 tools in the two primary tool directories ('/bin' and '/usr/bin') on my Linux system. These tools, combined with necessary applications, make free, open source software—for perhaps the first time in its history—a complete, robust system for general use.

1.2 What to Try First

The first four chapters of this book contain all of the introductory matter you need to begin working with Linux. These are the basics.

Beginning Linux users should start with the concepts described in these first chapters. Once you've learned how to start power to the system and log in, you should look over the chapter on the shell, so that you are familiar with typing at the command prompt, and then read the chapter on the graphical windows interface called the X Window System, so that you can start X and run programs from there if you like.

If you are a Linux beginner and are anxious to get up to speed, you might want to skip ahead and read the chapter on files and directories next, to get a sense of what the system looks like and how to maneuver through it. Then, go on to learning how to view text, and how to edit it in an editor (respectively described in the chapters on viewing text and text editing). After this, explore the rest of the book as your needs and interests dictate.

So, to recapitulate, here is what I consider to be the essential material to absorb for familiarizing yourself with the basic usage of a Linux system:

1. Chapter 1 [Introduction], page 9 (this current chapter).
2. Chapter 2 [What Every Linux User Knows], page 17.
3. Chapter 3 [The Shell], page 35 (ignoring the section on customization for now).
4. Chapter 4 [The X Window System], page 51 (ignoring the section on configuration for now).
5. Chapter 5 [Files and Directories], page 65.
6. Chapter 9 [Viewing Text], page 111 (mostly the first section, Recipe 9.1 [Perusing Text], page 111).
7. Chapter 10 [Text Editing], page 119 (enough to select a text editor and begin using it).

If you have a question about a tool or application in particular, look it up in the *program* index (see [Program Index], page 373). The index proper, listing recipe names and the general concepts involved, is called the *concept* index (see [Concept Index], page 379).

1.3 If You Need More Help

If you need more help than this book can give, remember that you do have other options. Try these steps for getting help:

- Chances are good that you are not alone in your question, and that someone else has asked it before; therefore, the compendiums of "Frequently Asked Questions" just might have the answer you need: the Debian FAQ (`http://www.debian.org/doc/FAQ/`) and the Linux FAQ (`http://mainmatter.com/`).

- The Linux Documentation Project (`http://linuxdoc.org/`) is the center of the most complete and up-to-date Linux-related documentation available; see if there is a document related to the topic you need help with.

- The Usenet newsgroups `news:comp.os.linux.help` and `news:linux.debian.user` are often an excellent place to discuss issues with other Linux users. (Usenet is described in Recipe 32.3 [Reading Usenet], page 348).

- Check `http://linux.com/lug/` to find the Linux User Group ("LUG") nearest you— people involved with LUGs can be great sources of hands-on help, and it can be fun and rewarding to get involved with other Linux and free software enthusiasts in your local area.

- Finally, you can hire a consultant. This may be a good option if you need work done right away and are willing to pay for it.

  The *Linux Consultants HOWTO* is a list of consultants around the world who provide various support services for Linux and open source software in general (see Recipe 2.8.6 [Reading System Documentation and Help Files], page 32). Consultants have various interests and areas of expertise, and they are listed in that document with contact information.

2 What Every Linux User Knows

This chapter concerns those concepts and commands that every Linux user knows—how to start and stop the system, log in and out from it, change your password, see what is happening on the system, and use the system help facilities. Mastery of these basic concepts is essential for using Linux with any degree of success.

Some of these recipes make reference to files and directories; these concepts are explained in Chapter 5 [Files and Directories], page 65.

2.1 Controlling Power to the System

These recipes show how to start and stop power to the system—how to turn it on and turn it off. It's more than just pressing the button on the case; in particular, there is a right way to turn off the system, and doing it wrong can result in losing some of your work. Fortunately, there isn't any black magic involved, as we soon shall see—properly shutting down the system is easy!

2.1.1 Powering Up the System

The first thing you do to begin using the system is start power to it. To power up the system, just turn it on. This is called *booting* the system.

As the Linux kernel boots there will be many messages on the screen. After a while, the system will display a `login:` prompt. You can now log in. See Recipe 2.2.1 [Logging In to the System], page 18.

Some systems are configured to start `xdm` at boot time (see Recipe 4.1.1 [Starting X], page 53). If your system is configured like this, instead of the `login:` prompt described above, you'll see a graphical screen with a box in the middle containing both `login:` and `Password:` prompts. Type (CTRL)-(ALT)-(F1) to switch to the first virtual console, where you can log in to the system in the usual way (see Recipe 2.3 [Console Basics], page 20).

2.1.2 Shutting Down the System

You can't just flip the power switch when you are done using the computer, because Linux is constantly writing data to disk. (It also keeps data in memory, even when it may have appeared to have written that data to disk.) Simply turning off the power could result in the loss or corruption of some of your work.

To turn off a single user system, first log out of all consoles (discussed in Recipe 2.3 [Console Basics], page 20). Then, type (CTRL)-(ALT)-(DEL) (press and hold these three keys at once).[1]

The system will print some messages as it shuts down, and when you see the line, 'Rebooting...', it's safe to turn the power to machine off.

NOTE: You don't want to wait *too* long after you see this message; if left untouched, the system will reboot and you'll be back to the beginning!

---

[1] If you keyboard has two (ALT) and (CTRL) keys, use the *left* set of these keys.

2.2 Accounts and Privileges

Linux is a multi-user system, meaning that many users can use one Linux system simultaneously, from different terminals. So to avoid confusion (and to maintain a semblance of privacy), each user's workspace must be kept separate from the others.

Even if a particular Linux system is a stand-alone personal computer with no other terminals physically connected to it, it can be shared by different people at different times, making the separation of user workspace still a valid issue.

This separation is accomplished by giving each individual user an *account* on the system. You need an account in order to use the system; with an account you are issued an individual workspace to use, and a unique *username* that identifies you to the system and to other users. It is the name that the system (and those who use it) will then forever know you as; it's a single word, in all lowercase letters.

During the installation process, the system administrator should have created an account for you. (The system administrator has a special account whose username is `root`; this account has total access to the entire system, so it is often called the *superuser*.)

Until the mid-1990s it was widely common for usernames to be the first letter of your first name followed by your entire surname, up to 12 characters total. So for example, user Samuel Clemens would have a username of `sclemens` by this convention; this, however, is not a hard and fast rule, especially on home systems where you may be the only user. Sometimes, a middle initial may be used ("`dkjohnson`"), or sometimes even nicknames or initials are used ("`zenboy`," "`xibo`"). But whatever username you pick for yourself, make sure it's one you can live with, and one you can stand being called by both the system and other users (your username also becomes part of your email address, as we'll see in Chapter 30 [Email], page 315).

In addition to your username, you should also have a *password* that you can keep secret so that only you can use your account. Good passwords are strings of text that nobody else is likely to guess (i.e., not obvious words like '`secret`', or identifying names like '`Ruski`', if that happens to be your pet cat). A good password is one that is highly memorable to you so that you don't have to write it down, but is complex enough in construction so that anyone else couldn't ever guess it. For example, '`t39sAH`' might be a fine password for someone whose first date was to see the movie *The 39 Steps* directed by Alfred Hitchcock.

NOTE: While usernames are always in lowercase, passwords are case sensitive; the passwords '`Secret`', '`secret`', and '`SECRET`' are all considered different.

2.2.1 Logging In to the System

To begin a session on a Linux system, you need to *log in*. Do this by entering your username at the `login:` prompt on your terminal, and then entering your password when asked.

The `login:` prompt appears on the terminal after the system boots. If your system is configured to start the X Window System at boot time, you'll be presented with an X login screen instead of the standard login prompt. If that happens, press (CTRL)-(ALT)-(F1) to switch to the text login screen; this is explained further in Recipe 2.3 [Console Basics], page 20.

A typical `login:` prompt looks like this:

```
Debian GNU/Linux 2.2 bardo tty1

bardo login:
```

Every Linux system has its own name, called the system's *hostname*; a Linux system is sometimes called a *host*, and it identifies itself with its hostname at the **login:** prompt. It's important to name your system—like a username for a user account, a hostname gives name to the system you are using (and it becomes especially important when putting the system on a network). The system administrator usually names the system when it is being initially configured (the hostname can always be changed later; its name is kept in the file '/etc/hostname'). Like usernames, hostnames are one word in all lowercase letters. People usually give their system a name they like, such as **darkstar** or **shiva**.

In this example, '**bardo**' is the hostname of this particular Linux system.

The name of the terminal you are connecting from is displayed just after the hostname. In this example, the terminal is '**tty1**', which means that this is the first terminal on this particular system. (Incidentally, '**tty**' is short for "teletype," which historically was the kind of terminal hardware that most Unix-based systems used by default.)

To log in to the system, type your username (followed by (RET)) at the **login:** prompt, and then type your password when asked (also followed by (RET)); for security purposes, your password is not displayed on the screen when you type it.

- To log in to the system with a username of '**kurt**' and a password of '**empathy**', type:

```
Debian GNU/Linux 2.2 bardo tty1

bardo login: kurt (RET)
Password: empathy (RET)
Linux bardo 2.0.30 #1 Tue Jul 29 10:01:26 EDT 1997 i586 unknown

Copyright (C) 1993-1998 Software in the Public Interest, and others

Most of the programs included with the Debian Linux system are
freely redistributable; the exact distribution terms for each
program are described in the individual files in
/usr/doc/*/copyright

Debian GNU/Linux comes with ABSOLUTELY NO WARRANTY, to the extent
permitted by applicable law.
Last login: Tue Apr  5 12:03:47 on tty1.
No mail.
~ $
```

Once you've entered your username and password, you are "logged in" to the system. You can then use the system and run commands.

As soon as you log in, the system displays the contents of '/etc/motd', the "Message of the Day" file. The system then displays the time and date of your last login, and reports whether or not you have electronic mail waiting for you (see Chapter 30 [Email], page 315). Finally, the system puts you in a *shell*—the environment in which you interact with the system and give it commands. Use of the default shell on most Linux systems, `bash`, is discussed in Chapter 3 [The Shell], page 35.

The dollar sign ('$') displayed to the left of the cursor is called the *shell prompt*; it means that the system is ready and waiting for input. (You can change this prompt to any text of your liking; to learn how, see Recipe 3.6.1 [Changing the Shell Prompt], page 46.) By default, the shell prompt includes the name of the current directory, which it places to the left of the '$' character. The tilde character ('~'), is a shell symbol that denotes the user's home directory—when you log in, you are in your home directory (these terms are defined in Chapter 5 [Files and Directories], page 65).

2.2.2 Logging Out of the System

To end your session on the system, type *logout* at the shell prompt. This command logs you out of the system, and a new `login:` prompt appears on your terminal.

- To log out of the system, type:

```
$ logout (RET)


Debian GNU/Linux 2.2 bardo tty1

bardo login:
```

What works equally well to typing the `logout` command is to just type *C-d* (hold down (CTRL) and press (D)). You don't even have to type (RET) afterwards. Many users prefer this quick shortcut.

Logging out of the system frees the terminal you were using—and ensures that nobody can access your account from this terminal.

If you are the only person using your system and have just ended a session by logging out, you might want to power down the system. See Recipe 2.1.2 [Shutting Down the System], page 17, earlier in this chapter.

2.3 Console Basics

A Linux *terminal* is a place to put input and get output from the system, and usually has at least a keyboard and monitor.

When you access a Linux system by the keyboard and monitor that are directly connected to it, you are said to be using the *console* terminal. (Linux systems can be accessed in other ways, such as through a network or via another terminal connected to a serial line; see Chapter 29 [Communications], page 307).

Linux systems feature *virtual consoles*, which act as separate console displays that can run separate login sessions, but are accessed from the same physical console terminal. Linux systems are configured to have seven virtual consoles by default. When you are at the console terminal, you can switch between virtual consoles at any time, and you can log in and use the system from several virtual consoles at once.

The following recipes explain the basic things you will need to do with virtual consoles.

2.3.1 Switching between Consoles

To switch to a different virtual console, press (ALT)-(F*n*), where *n* is the number of the console to switch to.

- To switch to the fourth virtual console, press (ALT)-(F4).

This command switches to the fourth virtual console, denoted by '**tty4**':

```
Debian GNU/Linux 2.2 bardo tty4

bardo login:
```

You can also cycle through the different virtual consoles with the left and right arrow keys. To switch to the next-lowest virtual console (or wrap around to the highest virtual console, if you're at the first virtual console), press (ALT)-(←). To switch to the next-highest virtual console, press (ALT) (→).

- To switch from the fourth to the third virtual console, press:

    (ALT)-(←)

This keystroke switches to the third virtual console, '**tty3**':

```
Debian GNU/Linux 2.2 bardo tty3

bardo login:
```

The seventh virtual console is reserved for the X Window System. If X is installed, this virtual terminal will never show a **login:** prompt, but when you are using X, this is where your X session appears. If your system is configured to start X immediately, this virtual console will show an X login screen.

You can switch to a virtual console from the X Window System using (CTRL) in conjunction with the usual (ALT) and function keys. This is the only console manipulation keystroke that works in X.

- To switch from X to the first virtual console, press:

    (CTRL)-(ALT)-(F1)

2.3.2 Scrolling the Console Text

When you are logged in at a virtual console, new lines of text appear at the bottom of the console screen, while older lines of text scroll off the top of the screen.

- To view this older text, press (SHIFT)-(PgUp) to scroll back through it.
- Once you have scrolled back, press (SHIFT)-(PgDn) to scroll *forward* through the text toward the most recent text displayed on the console.

The amount of text you can scroll back through depends on system memory.

NOTE: This technique is for scrolling through text displayed in your shell session (see Chapter 3 [The Shell], page 35). It does not work for scrolling through text in a tool or application in the console—in other words, you can't use this technique to scroll through text that is displayed by a tool for perusing text files. To scroll through text in an application, use its own facilities for scrolling, if it has any.

2.3.3 Keys for Console Manipulation

Some keystrokes for manipulating the console display, including those for switching between virtual consoles, are described below. It's a good idea to experiment with these commands until you are comfortable with them, because knowing how to use virtual consoles is basic to using Linux.

KEYSTROKE	DESCRIPTION
(ALT)-(F*n*)	Switch to virtual console *n*, where *n* is a number from 1 to 7 (the default maximum).
(CTRL)-(ALT)-(F*n*)	When in X, switch to virtual console *n*, where *n* is a number from 1 to 6.
(ALT)-(←)	Switch to the next-lowest virtual console. For example, typing this while in virtual console 4 switches to virtual console 3. Pressing this keystroke in the lowest console wraps around to the highest console.
(ALT)-(→)	Switch to the next-highest virtual console. For example, typing this while in virtual console 4 switches to virtual console 5. Pressing this keystroke in the highest console wraps around to the lowest console.
(SHIFT)-(PgUp)	Scroll back one screen to view previously displayed text.
(SHIFT)-(PgDn)	When viewing previously displayed text, scroll forward one screen.

2.4 Running a Command

A *tool* is a software program that performs a certain function—usually a specialized, simple task. For example, the `hostname` tool outputs the system's hostname, and the `who` tool outputs a listing of the users who are currently logged in. An *application* is the name given to larger, usually interactive, programs for completing broader kinds of tasks—such as programs for image editing or word processing.

A tool or application may take any number of *options* (sometimes called "flags"), which specify a change in its default behavior. It may also take *arguments*, which specify a file or some other text to operate on. Arguments are usually specified after any options.

A *command* is the name of a tool or application along with the options and arguments you want to use, if any. Since typing the name of a tool itself is often sufficient to accomplish a desired task, tools alone are often called commands.

Commands are case sensitive; the names of tools and applications are usually in all lowercase letters.

To run (or "execute") a tool or application without giving any options or arguments, type its name at a shell prompt followed by (RET).

- To run the `hostname` tool, type:

```
$ hostname (RET)
bardo
$
```

The hostname of the system in the example is '`bardo`'.

Options always begin with a hyphen character, ' ', which is usually followed by one alphanumeric character. To include an option in a command, follow the name of the tool or application with the option. Always separate the tool name, each option, and each argument with a space character.

Long-style options (sometimes called "GNU-style" options) begin with two hyphen characters ('`--`') and are usually one English word.

For example, many tools have an option, '`--version`', to output the version number of the tool. (Many tools also have a '`--help`' option, which outputs a list of options the tool takes; see Recipe 2.8.3 [Listing the Usage of a Tool], page 29.)

- To output the version of the `hostname` tool, type:

```
$ hostname --version (RET)
hostname 2.10
$
```

This command outputs the text '`hostname 2.10`', indicating that this is version 2.10 of the `hostname` tool.

Sometimes, an option itself may may take an argument. For example, `hostname` has an option for specifying a file name to use to read the hostname from, '`-F`'; it takes as an argument the name of the file that `hostname` should read from.

- To run `hostname` and specify that the file '`host.info`' is the file to read from, type:

```
$ hostname -F host.info (RET)
```

2.5 Changing Your Password

To change your password, use the **passwd** tool. It prompts you for your current password and a new password to replace it with. For security purposes, neither the old nor the new password is echoed to the screen as you type it. To make sure that you type the new password correctly, **passwd** prompts you for your new password twice. You must type it exactly the same way both times, or **passwd** will not change your password.

- To change your password, type:

```
$ passwd (RET)
Changing password for kurt
Old password: your current password (RET)
Enter the new password (minimum of 5, maximum of 8 characters)
Please use a combination of upper and lower case letters and numbers.
New password: your new password (RET)
Re-enter new password: your new password (RET)
Password changed.
$
```

NOTE: Passwords can contain uppercase and lowercase letters, the digits 0 through 9, and punctuation marks; they should be between five and eight characters long. See Recipe 2.2 [Accounts and Privileges], page 18, for suggestions on choosing a good password.

2.6 Listing User Activity

The recipes in this section describe some of the simple commands for finding out who you are currently sharing the system with and what they are doing.

2.6.1 Listing Your Username

Use **whoami** to output the username of the user that is logged in at your terminal. This is not as inutile a command as one might first think—if you're at a shared terminal, it's useful to determine whether or not it is your account that you're messing in, and for those with multiple accounts on a system, it's useful to see which of them you're currently logged in with.

- To output your username, type:

```
$ whoami (RET)
kurt
$
```

In this example, the username of the user logged in at this terminal is 'kurt'.

2.6.2 Listing Who Is on the System

Use **who** to output a list of all the users currently logged in to the system. It outputs a minimum of three columns, listing the username, terminal location, and time of login for all users on the system. A fourth column is displayed if a user is using the X Window System; it lists the window location of the user's session (see Chapter 4 [The X Window System], page 51).

- To see who is currently logged in, type:

```
$ who (RET)
murky     tty1      Oct 20 20:09
dave      tty2      Oct 21 14:37
kurt      tty3      Oct 21 15:04
kurt      ttyp1     Oct 21 15:04 (:0.0)
$
```

The output in this example shows that the user `murky` is logged in on `tty1` (the first virtual console on the system), and has been on since 20:09 on 20 October. The user `dave` is logged in on `tty2` (the second virtual console), and has been on since 14:37 on 21 October. The user `kurt` is logged in twice—on `tty3` (the third virtual console), and `ttyp1`, which is an X session with a window location of '(:0.0)'.

NOTE: This command is for listing the users on the local system; to list the users connected to a different system on the network, or to see more detailed information that a user may have made public about himself, see Recipe 32.4.2 [Checking Whether a User Is Online], page 351.

2.6.3 Listing Who Is on and What They're Doing

The `w` tool is similar to `who`, but it displays more detail. It outputs a header line that contains information about the current system status, including the current time, the amount of time the system has been up and running, and the number of users on the system. It then outputs a list of users currently logged in to the system, giving eight columns of information for each. These columns include username, terminal location, X session (if any), the time of login, the amount of time the user has been idle, and what command the user is running. (It also gives two columns showing the amount of time the system's CPU has spent on all of the user's current jobs ("JCPU") and foreground process ("PCPU"); processes are discussed in Recipe 2.7 [Listing System Activity], page 26, and jobs in Recipe 3.3 [Managing Jobs], page 40.)

- To see who is currently logged in and what they are doing, type:

```
$ w (RET)
  5:27pm  up 17:53,   4 users,  load average: 0.12, 0.06, 0.01
USER     TTY      FROM       LOGIN    IDLE   JCPU   PCPU   WHAT
murky    tty1              Oct 20 20:09 17:22m  0.32s  0.32s  -bash
dave     tty2                 14:37  13.00s   2:35   0.07s  less foo
kurt     tty3                 15:04   1:00m  0.41s  0.09s  startx
kurt     ttyp1    :0.0        15:04   0:00s 21.65s 20.96s  emacs
$
```

In this example, the command's output shows that the current system time is 5:27 p.m., the system has been up for 17 hours and 53 minutes, and there are four users currently logged in: `murky` is logged in at `tty1`, has been idle for 17 hours and 22 minutes, and is at a `bash` shell prompt; `dave` is logged in at `tty2`, has been idle for 13 seconds, and is using `less` to peruse a file called 'foo' (see Recipe 9.1 [Perusing Text], page 111); and `kurt` is logged in at two terminals—`tty3` and `ttyp1`, which is an X session. He ran the `startx` command on `tty3` to start his X session, and within his X session, he is currently using Emacs.

2.6.4 Listing the Last Times a User Logged In

Use `last` to find out who has recently used the system, which terminals they used, and when they logged in and out.

- To output a list of recent system use, type:

  $ *last* (RET)

To find out when a particular user last logged in to the system, give his username as an argument.

- To find out when user `kurt` last logged in, type:

  $ *last kurt* (RET)

NOTE: The `last` tool gets its data from the system file '`/var/log/wtmp`'; the last line of output tells how far this file goes back. Sometimes, the output will go back for several weeks or more.

2.7 Listing System Activity

When you run a command, you are starting a *process* on the system, which is a program that is currently executing. Every process is given a unique number, called its *process ID*, or "PID."

Use `ps` to list processes on the system. Some of the information it can display about a process includes process ID, name of command being run, username running the command, and how long the process has been running. By default, `ps` outputs 5 columns: process ID, the name of the terminal from which the process was started, the current status of the process (including 'S' for *sleeping*, meaning that it is on hold at the moment, 'R' meaning that it is running, and 'Z' meaning that it is a *zombie* process, or a process that has already died), the total amount of time the CPU has spent on the process since the process started, and finally the name of the command being run.

The following recipes describe popular usage of `ps`.

2.7.1 Listing Your Current Processes

Type *ps* with no arguments to list the processes you have running in your current shell session.

- To list the processes in your current shell session, type:

```
$ ps (RET)
  PID TTY STAT TIME COMMAND
  193   1 S   0:01 -bash
  204   1 S   0:00 ps
$
```

In this example, `ps` shows that two processes are running: the `bash` and `ps` commands.

2.7.2 Listing All of a User's Processes

To list all the processes of a specific user, use `ps` and give the username to list as an argument to the '-u' option. While you can't snoop on the actual activities of other users, you can list the commands they are running at a given moment.

- To list all the processes that user `hst` has running on the system, type:

    `$ ps -u hst (RET)`

NOTE: This command is useful for listing all of your own processes, across all terminals and shell sessions; give your *own* username as an argument.

2.7.3 Listing All Processes on the System

To list all processes by all users on the system, use the '**aux**' options.

- To list all of the processes and give their usernames, type:

    `$ ps aux (RET)`

NOTE: There could be a lot of output—even single-user Linux systems typically have fifty or more processes running at one time—so you may want to pipe the output of this command through `less` for perusal (see Recipe 9.1 [Perusing Text], page 111).

Additionally, use `top` to show a display of all processes on the system, sorted by their demand on the system resources. The display is continually updated with current process information; press *Q* to stop the display and exit the program. This tool also displays the information about system runtime and memory that can be output with the `uptime` and `free` commands.

- To display a continually updated display of the current system processes, type:

    `$ top (RET)`

2.7.4 Listing Processes by Name or Number

To list processes whose output contains a name or other text to match, list all processes and pipe the output to `grep`. This is useful for when you want to see which users are running a particular program or command.

- To list all the processes whose commands contain reference to an 'sbin' directory in them, type:

    `$ ps aux | grep sbin (RET)`

- To list any processes whose process IDs contain a 13 in them, type:

    `$ ps aux | grep 13 (RET)`

To list the process (if any) which corresponds to a process ID, give that PID as an argument to the '-p' option.

- To list the process whose PID is 344, type:

    $ *ps -p 344* (RET)

2.8 Help Facilities

Linux systems come with a lot of help facilities, including complete manuals in etext form. In fact, the foremost trouble with Linux documentation isn't that there is not enough of it, but that you have to sift through the mounds of it, trying to find the precise information you're looking for!

I describe the help facilities in the following sections; their relative usefulness for the particular kind of information you're looking for is noted.

If you find that you need more help, don't panic—other options are available. They're described in Recipe 1.3 [If You Need More Help], page 16.

2.8.1 Finding the Right Tool for the Job

When you know what a particular tool or application *does*, but you can't remember it's name, use `apropos`. This tool takes a keyword as an argument, and it outputs a list of installed software whose one-line descriptions contain that keyword. This is also useful for finding software on your system related to, say, "audio" or "sound" or "sort" or some other such general concept.

- To output a list of programs that pertain to consoles, type:

```
$ apropos consoles (RET)
console (4)            - console terminal and virtual consoles
gpm (1)                - a cut and paste utility and mouse server for
                         virtual consoles
$
```

NOTE: The `apropos` tool only finds exact matches, so a search for the keyword '`console`' might not list the programs that a search for the keyword '`consoles`' would yield, and vice versa.

Another way to find tools by keyword is to search the system manual pages (see Recipe 2.8.4 [Reading a Page from the System Manual], page 30). To do this, use `man` and give the text to search for as an argument to the '-k' option. This searches the short descriptions and manual page names for the given text, and outputs a list of those tools that match in the same format as the `apropos` tool.

- To output a list of all tools whose pages in the system manual contain a reference to consoles, type:

    $ *man -k consoles* (RET) .

On Debian systems, yet another way to find installed software by keyword is to use `dpkg`, the Debian package tool. Use the '-l' option to list all of the installed packages, which are each output on a line of their own with their package name and a brief description.

You can output a list of packages that match a keyword by piping the output to **grep**. Use the '**-i**' option with **grep** to match keywords regardless of case (**grep** is discussed in Chapter 14 [Searching Text], page 165).

Additionally, you can directly peruse the file '**/var/lib/dpkg/available**'; it lists all available packages and gives a description of them.

- To list all of the packages on the system, type:

      $ *dpkg -l* (RET)

- To list all of the packages whose name or description contains the text "edit," regardless of case, type:

      $ *dpkg -l | grep -i edit* (RET)

- To peruse descriptions of the packages that are available, type:

      $ *less /var/lib/dpkg/available* (RET)

2.8.2 Listing a Description of a Program

Use **whatis** to list a one-line description of a program. Give the name of the tool or application to list as an argument.

- To get a description of the **who** tool, type:

      $ *whatis who* (RET)

NOTE: The **whatis** tool gets its descriptions from the *manual page* of a given program; manual pages are described later in this section, in Recipe 2.8.4 [Reading a Page from the System Manual], page 30.

2.8.3 Listing the Usage of a Tool

Many tools have a long-style option, '**--help**', that outputs usage information about the tool, including the options and arguments the tool takes.

- To list the possible options for **whoami**, type:

```
$ whoami --help (RET)
Usage: whoami [OPTION]...
Print the user name associated with the current effective user id.
Same as id -un.

  --help      display this help and exit
  --version   output version information and exit

Report bugs to sh-utils-bugs@gnu.ai.mit.edu
$
```

This command outputs some usage information about the **whoami** tool, including a short description and a list of possible options.

NOTE: Not all tools take the '**--help**' option; some tools take a '**-h**' or '**-?**' option instead, which performs the same function.

2.8.4 Reading a Page from the System Manual

In the olden days, the hardcopy reference manual that came with most Unix systems also existed electronically on the system itself; each software program that came with the system had its own *manual page* (often called a "man page") that described it. This is still true on Linux-based systems today, except they don't always come with a hardcopy manual.

Use the `man` tool to view a page in the system manual. As an argument to `man`, give the name of the program whose manual page you want to view (so to view the manual page for `man`, you would type *man man*).

- To view the manual page for `w`, type:

    $ *man w* (RET)

This command displays the manual page for `w`:

```
    W(1)                    Linux Programmer's Manual                W(1)

    NAME
           w - Show who is logged on and what they are doing.

    SYNOPSIS
           w - [husfV] [user]

    DESCRIPTION
           w  displays  information  about the users currently on the
           machine, and their processes.  The header shows,  in  this
           order,   the  current  time,  how long the system has been
           running, how many users are currently logged on,  and  the
           system load averages for the past 1, 5, and 15 minutes.

           The  following  entries are displayed for each user: login
           name, the tty name, the  remote  host,  login  time,  idle
           time,  JCPU,  PCPU,  and the command line of their current
           process.

           The JCPU time is the time used by all  processes  attached
    Manual page w(1) line 1
```

Use the up and down arrow keys to move through the text. Press ⓠ to stop viewing the manual page and exit `man`. Since `man` uses `less` to display the text, you can use any of the `less` keyboard commands to peruse the manual page (see Recipe 9.1 [Perusing Text], page 111).

Despite its name, a manual page does not always contain the complete documentation to a program, but it's more like a quick reference. It usually gives a short description of the program, and lists the options and arguments it takes; some manual pages also include an example or a list of related commands. (Sometimes, commands have very complete, extensive manual pages, but more often, their complete documentation is found either in other help files that come with it or in its Info documentation; these are subjects of the following two recipes.)

To prepare a man page for printing, see Recipe 25.3.4 [Preparing a Man Page for Printing], page 278.

2.8.5 Using the GNU Info System

The GNU Info System is an online hypertext reference system for documentation prepared in the Info format. This documentation tends to be more complete than a typical man page, and often, the Info documentation for a given software package will be an entire book or manual. All of the manuals published by the Free Software Foundation are released in Info format; these manuals contain the same text (*sans* illustrations) as the paper manuals that you can purchase directly from the Free Software Foundation.

There are different ways to peruse the Info documentation: you can use the standalone info tool, read Info files in the Emacs editor (see Recipe 10.2 [Emacs], page 121), or use one of the other tools designed for this purpose. Additionally, tools exist for converting Info documentation to HTML that you can read in a Web browser (see Recipe 5.9 [Browsing Files], page 81).

To read the Info manual for a tool or application with the info tool, give its name as an argument. With no arguments, info opens your system's Top Info menu, which lists all of the available manuals that are installed on the system.

- To view all of the Info manuals on the system, type:

      $ info (RET)

This command starts info at the system's Top menu, which shows some of the info key commands and displays a list of available manuals:

```
File: dir,      Node: Top,      This is the top of the INFO tree

    This (the Directory node) gives a menu of major topics.
    Typing "q" exits, "?" lists all Info commands, "d" returns here,
    "h" gives a primer for first-timers,
    "mEmacs<Return>" visits the Emacs manual, etc.

    In Emacs, you can click mouse button 2 on a menu item or cross reference
    to select it.

* Menu:

Texinfo documentation system
* Info: (info).                     Documentation browsing system.
* Texinfo: (texinfo).               The GNU documentation format.
* install-info: (texinfo)Invoking install-info. Updating info/dir entries.
* texi2dvi: (texinfo)Format with texi2dvi.      Printing Texinfo documentation.
* texindex: (texinfo)Format with tex/texindex.  Sorting Texinfo index files.
* makeinfo: (texinfo)makeinfo Preferred.        Translate Texinfo source.
-----Info: (dir)Top, 211 lines --Top-------------------------------------
Welcome to Info version 2.18. "C-h" for help, "m" for menu item.
```

Use the arrow keys to move through each "page" of information, called an Info *node*. Nodes are the base unit of information in Info, and are arranged hierarchically—a manual's Top node will contain an Info *menu* containing links to its various chapters, and a chapter node will contain a menu with links for its sections, and so on. Links also appear as cross references in the text.

Links look the same in both menu items and cross references: an asterisk ('*'), the name of the node it links to, and either one or two colon characters (':'). To follow a link to the node it points to, move the cursor over any part of the node name in the link and press (RET).

To run a tutorial that describes how to use `info`, press the (H) key. Press (Q) at any time to stop reading the documentation and exit `info`.

To read Info documentation for a tool or application, give its name as an argument to `info`; if no Info manual exists for that tool, `info` displays the `man` page for that tool instead.

- To read the Info documentation for the `tar` tool, type:

      $ info tar (RET)

This command opens a copy of *The GNU tar Manual* in `info`.

To read the contents of a file written in Info format, give the name of the file to read with the '-f' option. This is useful for reading an Info file that you have obtained elsewhere, and is not in the '/usr/info' directory with the rest of the installed Info files. Info can automatically recognize and expand Info files that are compressed and have a '.gz' file name extension (see Recipe 8.5 [Compressed Files], page 102).

- To read 'faq.info', an Info file in the current directory, type:

      $ info -f faq.info (RET)

This command starts `info` and opens the Info file 'faq.info', beginning at the top node in the file.

To read a specific *node* in an Info file, give the name of the node to use in quotes as an argument to the '-n' option.

- To read 'faq.info', an Info file in the current directory, beginning with the node **Text**, type:

      $ info -n 'Text' -f faq.info (RET)

NOTE: You can also read Info documentation directly from the Emacs editor; you type `C-h i` from Emacs to start the Info reader, and then use the same commands as in the standalone `info` tool (see Recipe 10.2.1 [Getting Acquainted with Emacs], page 121).

The Emacs "incremental" search command, `C-s`, also works in `info`; it's a very fast, efficient way to search for a word or phrase in an entire Info text (like this entire book); see Recipe 14.6.1 [Searching Incrementally in Emacs], page 173.

2.8.6 Reading System Documentation and Help Files

Debian: 'doc-linux-text'
WWW: http://linuxdoc.org/

The '/usr/doc' directory is for miscellaneous documentation: HOWTOs, FAQs, Debian-specific documentation files and documentation files that come with commands. (To learn

more about files and directories, see Chapter 5 [Files and Directories], page 65.) To peruse
any of these files, use `less`, described in full in Recipe 9.1 [Perusing Text], page 111.

When a software package is installed, any additional documentation files it might have
beyond a manual page and Info manual are placed here, in a subdirectory with the name
of that package. For example, additional documentation for the `hostname` package is in
'`/usr/doc/hostname`', and documentation for the `passwd` package is in '`/usr/doc/passwd`'.
Most packages have a file called '`README`', which usually contains relevant information. Often
this file is compressed as '`README.gz`', in which case you can use `zless` instead of `less`.

The Linux Documentation Project (LDP) has overseen the creation of more than 100
"HOWTO" files, each of which covers a particular aspect of the installation or use of Linux-
based systems.

The LDP HOWTOs are compressed text files stored in the '`/usr/doc/HOWTO`' directory; to view them, use `zless`. The file '`/usr/doc/HOWTO/HOWTO-Index.gz`' contains an
annotated index of all the HOWTO documents installed on the system.[2]

Finally, the '`/usr/doc/FAQ`' directory contains a number of FAQ ("Frequently Asked
Questions") files on various subjects, and the files that make up the Debian FAQ are in the
'`/usr/doc/debian/FAQ`' directory. The Debian FAQ is available both in HTML format,
which you can view in a Web browser (see Recipe 5.9 [Browsing Files], page 81), and as a
compressed text file, which you can view in `zless`.

- To view the HTML version of the Debian FAQ in the `lynx` Web browser, type:
    ```
    $ lynx /usr/doc/debian/FAQ/debian-faq.html (RET)
    ```
- To view the compressed text version of the Debian FAQ in `zless`, type:
    ```
    $ zless /usr/doc/debian/FAQ/debian-faq.txt.gz (RET)
    ```

NOTE: It's often very useful to use a Web browser to browse through the documentation
files in these directories—see Recipe 5.9 [Browsing Files], page 81.

On some systems, '`/usr/doc`' is superseded by the '`/usr/share/doc`' directory.

---

[2] LDP documents are available in other formats as well, including HTML and DVI.

3 The Shell

The subject of this chapter is the *shell*, the program that reads your command input and runs the specified commands. The shell environment is the most fundamental way to interact with the system—you are said to be "in" a shell from the very moment you've successfully logged in to the system.

The '$' character preceding the cursor is called the *shell prompt*; it tells you that the system is ready and waiting for input. On Debian systems, the default shell prompt also includes the name of the current directory (see Chapter 5 [Files and Directories], page 65). A tilde character ('~') denotes your home directory, which is where you'll find yourself when you log in.

For example, a typical user's shell prompt might look like this:

```
~ $ _
```

If your shell prompt shows a number sign ('#') instead of a '$', this means that you're logged in with the superuser, or **root**, account. Beware: the **root** account has complete control over the system; one wrong keystroke and you might accidentally break it something awful. You need to have a different user account for yourself, and use that account for your regular use (see Recipe A.3.1 [Making a User Account], page 363).

Every Linux system has at least one shell program, and most have several. We'll cover **bash**, which is the standard shell on most Linux systems. (Its name stands for "Bourne again shell"—a pun on the name of Steve Bourne, who was author of the traditional Unix shell, the Bourne shell.)

NOTE: See Info file 'bashref.info', node 'Top', for more information on using **bash**.

3.1 Keys for Command Line Editing

In Recipe 2.4 [Running a Command], page 22, you learned how to run commands by typing them in at the shell prompt. The text you type at a shell prompt is called the *command line* (it's also called the *input line*).

The following table describes the keystrokes used for typing command lines.

KEYSTROKES	DESCRIPTION
text	Insert *text* at the point where the cursor is at; if there is text to the right of the cursor, it is shifted over to the right.
(BKSP)	Delete the character to the left of the cursor.
(DEL)	Delete the character the cursor is underneath.
(RET)	Send the command line to **bash** for execution (in other words, it runs the command typed at the shell prompt). You don't have to be at the far right end of the command line to type (RET); you can type it when the cursor is anywhere on the command line.

C-a	Move the cursor to the beginning of the input line.
C-d	Same as (DEL) (this is the Emacs equivalent).
C-e	Move the cursor to the end of the input line.
C-k	Kill, or "cut," all text on the input line, from the character the cursor is underneath to the end of the line.
C-l	Clear the terminal screen.
C-u	Kill the entire input line.
C-y	Yank, or "paste," the text that was last killed. Text is inserted at the point where the cursor is.
C-_	Undo the last thing typed on this command line.
(←)	Move the cursor to the left one character.
(→)	Move the cursor to the right one character.
(↑) and (↓)	Cycle through the command history (see Recipe 3.4 [Command History], page 43).

NOTE: These keyboard commands are the same as those used by the Emacs editor (see Recipe 10.2 [Emacs], page 121). Many other Emacs keyboard commands also work on the command line (see Recipe 10.2.2 [Basic Emacs Editing Keys], page 123). And, for Vi aficionados, it is possible to configure `bash` to recognize Vi-style bindings instead.

The following sections describe some important features of command line editing, such as quoting special characters and strings, letting the shell complete your typing, re-running commands, and running multiple commands. See Info file 'bashref.info', node 'Command Line Editing' for more information on `bash`'s command line editing features.

3.1.1 Passing Special Characters to Commands

Some characters are *reserved* and have special meaning to the shell on their own. Before you can pass one of these characters to a command, you must *quote* it by enclosing the entire argument in single quotes ('').

For example, here's how to pass 'Please Stop!' to a command:

        'Please Stop!'

When the argument you want to pass has one or more single quote characters in it, enclose it in double quotes, like so:

        "Please Don't Stop!"

To pass special characters as a string, give them as:

        $'string'

where *string* is the string of characters to be passed. Special backslash escape sequences for certain characters are commonly included in a string, as listed in the following table.

ESCAPE SEQUENCE	DESCRIPTION
\a	Alert (rings the system bell).
\b	Backspace.
\e	Escape.
\f	Form feed.
\n	Newline.
\r	Carriage return.
\t	Horizontal tab.
\v	Vertical tab.
\\	Backslash.
NNN	Character whose ASCII code is *NNN* in octal (base 8).

To demonstrate the passing of special character sequences to tool, the following examples will use the `figlet` tool, which displays the text you give as an argument in a "font" made up of text characters (see Recipe 16.3.1 [Horizontal Text Fonts], page 202).

- To pass a backslash character as an argument to `figlet`, type:

      $ figlet $'\\' (RET)

- To pass a form feed character followed by a pilcrow sign character (octal character code 266) to `figlet`, type:

      $ echo $'\f\266' (RET)

3.1.2 Letting the Shell Complete What You Type

Completion is where `bash` does its best to finish your typing. To use it, press (TAB) on the input line and the shell will *complete* the word to the left of the cursor to the best of its ability. Completion is one of those things that, once you begin to use it, you will wonder how you ever managed to get by without.

Completion works on both file names and command names, depending on the context of the cursor when you type (TAB).

For example, suppose you want to specify, as an argument to the `ls` command, the '/usr/lib/emacs/20.4/i386-debian-linux-gnu/' directory—that's a lot to type. So instead of typing out the whole directory name, you can type (TAB) to complete it for you. Notice how our first attempt, typing only the letter 'e' in '/e', brings up a series of files— while the second attempt, typing 'em', further refines our search:

      $ ls /usr/lib/e(TAB)
      elm-me+   emacs   emacsen-common   entity-map   expect5.30
      $ ls /usr/lib/em(TAB)

At this point, the system beeps[1] and the shell completes the word 'emacs', since all options in this directory beginning with the letters 'em' complete to at least that word.

---

[1] The Unix way of saying it is that the command "rings the system bell."

Press /(TAB) to access this word and go on, and the shell completes the subdirectory '20.4' since that is the only file or directory in the 'emacs' subdirectory:

    $ ls /usr/lib/emacs/(TAB) 20.4/

Press (TAB) again to have the shell complete the only subdirectory in '20.4':

    $ ls /usr/lib/emacs/20.4/(TAB) i386-debian-linux-gnu/

NOTE: Many applications also support command and/or file name completion; the most famous example of this is the Emacs text editor (see Recipe 10.2 [Emacs], page 121).

3.1.3 Repeating the Last Command You Typed

Type (↑) to put the last command you typed back on the input line. You can then type (RET) to run the command again, or you can edit the command first.

- To repeat the last command entered, type:

      $ (↑) (RET)

The (↑) key moves the last command you typed back to the input line, and (RET) executes it.

By typing (↑) more than once, you can go back to earlier commands you've typed; this is a function of your command *history*, which is explained in full in Recipe 3.4 [Command History], page 43.

Additionally, you can use the **bash** reverse-incremental search feature, *C-r*, to *search*, in reverse, through your command history. You'll find this useful if you remember typing a command line with 'foo' in it recently, and you wish to repeat the command without having to retype it. Type *C-r* followed by the text *foo*, and the last command you typed containing 'foo' appears on the input line.

Like the Emacs command of the same name (see Recipe 14.6.1 [Searching Incrementally in Emacs], page 173), this is called an *incremental* search because it builds the search string in character increments as you type. Typing the string 'cat' will first search for (and display) the last input line containing a 'c', then 'ca', and finally 'cat', as you type the individual characters of the search string. Typing *C-r* again retrieves the next previous command line that has a match for the search string.

- To put the last command you entered containing the string 'grep' back on the input line, type:

      $ C-r
      (reverse-i-search)'': grep

- To put the third-to-the-last command you entered containing the string grep back on the input line, type:

      $ C-r
      (reverse-i-search)'': grep
      C-r C-r

When a command is displayed on the input line, type (RET) to run it. You can also edit the command line as usual.

3.1.4 Running a List of Commands

To run more than one command on the input line, type each command in the order you want them to run, separating each command from the next with a semicolon (';'). You'll sometimes find this useful when you want to run several non-interactive commands in sequence.

- To clear the screen and then log out of the system, type:

      $ clear; logout (RET)

- To run the `hostname` command three times, type:

```
$ hostname; hostname; hostname (RET)
figaro
figaro
figaro
$
```

3.2 Redirecting Input and Output

The shell moves text in designated "streams." The *standard output* is where the shell streams the text output of commands—the screen on your terminal, by default. The *standard input*, typically the keyboard, is where you input data for commands. When a command reads the standard input, it usually keeps reading text until you type *C-d* on a new line by itself.

When a command runs and exits with an error, the error message is usually output to your screen, but as a separate stream called the *standard error*.

You redirect these streams—to a file, or even another command—with *redirection*. The following sections describe the shell redirection operators that you can use to redirect standard input and output.

3.2.1 Redirecting Input to a File

To redirect standard input to a file, use the '<' operator. To do so, follow a command with < and the name of the file it should take input from. For example, instead of giving a list of keywords as arguments to `apropos` (see Recipe 2.8.1 [Finding the Right Tool for the Job], page 28), you can redirect standard input to a file containing a list of keywords to use.

- To redirect standard input for `apropos` to file '`keywords`', type:

      $ apropos < keywords (RET)

3.2.2 Redirecting Output to a File

Use the '>' operator to redirect standard output to a file. To use it, follow a command with > and the name of the file the output should be written to.

- To redirect standard output of the command *apropos shell bash* to the file '`commands`', type:

      $ apropos shell bash > commands (RET)

If you redirect standard output to an existing file, it will overwrite the file, unless you use the '>>' operator to *append* the standard output to the contents of the existing file.

- To append the standard output of **apropos shells** to an existing file 'commands', type:

      $ apropos shells >> commands (RET)

3.2.3 Redirecting Error Messages to a File

To redirect the standard error stream to a file, use the '>' operator preceded by a '2'. Follow a command with **2>** and the name of the file the error stream should be written to.

- To redirect the standard error of **apropos shell bash** to the file 'command.error', type:

      $ apropos shell bash 2> command.error (RET)

As with the standard output, use the '>>' operator instead of '>' to *append* the standard error to the contents of an existing file.

- To append the standard error of **apropos shells** to an existing file 'command.error', type:

      $ apropos shells 2>> command.error (RET)

To redirect *both* standard output and standard error to the same file, use '&>' instead.

- To redirect the standard output *and* the standard error of **apropos shells** to the file 'commands', type:

      $ apropos shells &> commands (RET)

3.2.4 Redirecting Output to Another Command's Input

Piping is when you connect the standard output of one command to the standard input of another. You do this by specifying the two commands in order, separated by a vertical bar character, '|' (sometimes called a "pipe"). Commands built in this fashion are called *pipelines*.

For example, it's often useful to pipe commands that display a lot of text output to **less**, a tool for perusing text (see Recipe 9.1 [Perusing Text], page 111).

- To pipe the output of **apropos bash shell shells** to **less**, type:

      $ apropos bash shell shells | less (RET)

This redirects the standard output of the command **apropos bash shell shells** to the standard input of the command **less**, which displays it on the screen.

3.3 Managing Jobs

The processes you have running in a particular shell are called your *jobs*. You can have more than one job running from a shell at once, but only one job can be active at the terminal, reading standard input and writing standard output. This job is the *foreground* job, while any other jobs are said to be running in the *background*.

The shell assigns each job a unique *job number*. Use the job number as an argument to specify the job to commands. Do this by giving the job number preceded by a '%' character.

To find the job number of a job you have running, list your jobs (see Recipe 3.3.4 [Listing Your Jobs], page 42).

The following sections describe the various commands for managing jobs.

3.3.1 Suspending a Job

Type `C-z` to suspend or stop the foreground job—useful for when you want to do something else in the shell and return to the current job later. The job stops until you either bring it back to the foreground or make it run in the background (see Recipe 3.3.3 [Putting a Job in the Foreground], page 42 and see Recipe 3.3.2 [Putting a Job in the Background], page 41).

For example, if you are reading a document in `info`, typing `C-z` will suspend the `info` program and return you to a shell prompt where you can do something else (see Recipe 2.8.5 [Using the GNU Info System], page 31). The shell outputs a line giving the job number (in brackets) of the suspended job, the text '`Stopped`' to indicate that the job has stopped, and the command line itself, as shown here:

```
[1]+  Stopped                 info -f cookbook.info
```

In this example, the job number is 1 and the command that has stopped is '`info -f cookbook.info`'. The '`+`' character next to the job number indicates that this is the most recent job.

If you have any stopped jobs when you log out, the shell will tell you this instead of logging you out:

```
$ logout (RET)
There are stopped jobs.
$
```

At this point you can list your jobs (see Recipe 3.3.4 [Listing Your Jobs], page 42), stop any jobs you have running (see Recipe 3.3.5 [Stopping a Job], page 43), and then log out.

3.3.2 Putting a Job in the Background

New jobs run in the foreground unless you specify otherwise. To run a job in the background, end the input line with an ampersand ('`&`'). This is useful for running non-interactive programs that perform a lot of calculations.

- To run the command `apropos shell > shell-commands` as a background job, type:

```
$ apropos shell > shell-commands & (RET)
[1] 6575
$
```

The shell outputs the job number (in this case, 1) and process ID (in this case, 6575), and then returns to a shell prompt. When the background job finishes, the shell will list the job number, the command, and the text '`Done`', indicating that the job has completed successfully:

```
[1]+  Done                       apropos shell >shell-commands
```

To move a job from the foreground to the background, first suspend it (see Recipe 3.3.1 [Suspending a Job], page 41) and then type *bg* (for "background").

- For example, to start the command *apropos shell > shell-commands* in the foreground, suspend it, and then specify that it finish in the background, you would type:

```
$ apropos shell > shell-commands (RET)
C-z

[1]+  Stopped                    apropos shell >shell-commands
$ bg (RET)
[1]+ apropos shell &
$
```

If you have suspended multiple jobs, specify the job to be put in the background by giving its job number as an argument.

- To run job 4 in the background, type:
  ```
  $ bg %4 (RET)
  ```

NOTE: Running a job in the background is sometimes called "backgrounding" or "amping off" a job.

3.3.3 Putting a Job in the Foreground

Type **fg** to move a background job to the foreground. By default, **fg** works on the most recent background job.

- To bring the most recent background job to the foreground, type:
  ```
  $ fg (RET)
  ```

To move a specific job to the foreground when you have multiple jobs in the background, specify the job number as an option to **fg**.

- To bring job 3 to the foreground, type:
  ```
  $ fg %3 (RET)
  ```

3.3.4 Listing Your Jobs

To list the jobs running in the current shell, type *jobs*.

- To list your jobs, type:

```
$ jobs (RET)
[1]-  Stopped                    apropos shell >shell-commands
[2]+  Stopped                    apropos bash >bash-commands
$
```

This example shows two jobs—*apropos shell > shell-commands* and *apropos bash > bash-commands*. The '+' character next to a job number indicates that it's the most recent job, and the '-' character indicates that it's the job *previous* to the most recent job. If you have no current jobs, `jobs` returns nothing.

To list all of the *processes* you have running on the system, use `ps` instead of `jobs`—see Recipe 2.7 [Listing System Activity], page 26.

3.3.5 Stopping a Job

Typing *C-c* interrupts the foreground job before it completes, exiting the program.

- To interrupt `cat`, a job running in the foreground, type:

```
$ cat (RET)
C-c (RET)
$
```

Use `kill` to interrupt ("kill") a background job, specifying the job number as an argument.

- To kill job number 2, type:

   `$ kill %2` (RET)

3.4 Command History

Your command *history* is the sequential list of commands you have typed, in the current or previous shell sessions. The commands in this history list are called *events*.

By default, `bash` remembers the last 500 events, but this number is configurable (see Recipe 3.6.4 [Customizing Future Shells], page 47).

Your command history is stored in a text file in your home directory called '`.bash_history`'; you can view this file or edit it like you would any other text file.

Two very useful things that having a command history lets you do is to repeat the last command you typed, and (as explained earlier in this chapter) to do an incremental backwards search through your history.

The following sections explain how to view your history and specify events from it on the command line. See Info file '`bashref.info`', node '`Bash History Facilities`', for more information on command history.

3.4.1 Viewing Your Command History

Use `history` to view your command history.

- To view your command history, type:

```
$ history (RET)
1 who
2 apropos shell >shell-commands
3 apropos bash >bash-commands
4 history
$
```

This command shows the contents of your command history file, listing one command per line prefaced by its *event number*. Use an event number to specify that event in your history (see Recipe 3.4.2 [Specifying a Command from Your History], page 44).

If your history is a long one, this list will scroll off the screen, in which case you may want to pipe the output to `less` in order to peruse it. It's also common to search for a past command by piping the output to `grep` (see Recipe 3.2.4 [Redirecting Output to Another Command's Input], page 40 and Recipe 14.1 [Searching for a Word or Phrase], page 165).

- To search your history for the text 'apropos', type:

```
$ history | grep apropos (RET)
2 apropos shell >shell-commands
3 apropos bash >bash-commands
5 history | grep apropos
$
```

This command will show the events from your history containing the text 'apropos'. (The last line of output is the command you just typed.)

3.4.2 Specifying a Command from Your History

You can specify a past event from your history on the input line, in order to run it again.

The simplest way to specify a history event is to use the up and down arrow keys at the shell prompt to browse your history. The up arrow key (⇧) takes you back through past events, and the down arrow key (⇩) moves you forward into recent history. When a history event is on the input line, you can edit it as normal, and type (RET) to run it as a command; it will then become the newest event in your history.

- To specify the second-to-the-last command in your history, type:

  $ (⇧) (⇧)

To run a history event by its event number, enter an exclamation point ('!', sometimes called "bang") followed by the event number. (Get the event number by viewing your history; see Recipe 3.4.1 [Viewing Your Command History], page 43).

- To run history event number 1, type:

  $ *!1* (RET)

3.5 Recording a Shell Session

Use `script` to create a typescript, or "capture log," of a shell session—it writes a verbatim copy of your session to a file, including commands you type and their output. The first and last lines of the file show the beginning and ending time and date of the capture session. To stop recording the typescript, type `exit` at a shell prompt. By default, typescripts are saved to a file called '`typescript`' in the current directory; specify the file name to use as an argument.

- To create a typescript of a shell session and save it to the file '`log.19990817`', type:

```
$ script log.19990817 (RET)
Script started, output file is log.19990817
$ hostname (RET)
erie
$ apropos bash > bash.commands (RET)
$ exit (RET)
exit
Script done, output file is log.19990817
$
```

In this example, the typescript records a shell session consisting of two commands (hostname and apropos) to a file called '`log.19990817`'. The typescript looks like this:

```
Script started on Tue May 25 14:21:52 1999
$ hostname
erie
$ apropos bash > bash.commands
$ exit
exit

Script done on Tue May 25 14:22:30 1999
```

NOTE: It's possible, but usually not desirable, to run `script` from within another `script` session. This usually happens when you've forgotten that you are running it, and you run it again inside the current typescript, even multiple times—as a result, you may end up with multiple sessions "nested" inside each other like a set of Russian dolls.

3.6 Customizing Your Shell

The following sections describe the most common ways to customize the shell—including changing the text of the shell prompt and creating aliases for other commands. These customizations will apply to the rest of your current shell session, unless you change them again. Eventually, you will want to make them work all the time, like whenever you log in or start a new shell—and how to do this is discussed below.

3.6.1 Changing the Shell Prompt

A shell *variable* is a symbol that stores a text string, and is referenced by a unique name. `bash` keeps one special variable, named `PS1`, for the text of the shell prompt. To change the text of the shell prompt, you need to change the contents of the `PS1` variable.

To change a variable's contents, type its name followed by an equal sign ('`=`') character and the string that should replace the variable's existing contents.

- To change your shell prompt to '`Your wish is my command:` ', type:

```
$ PS1='Your wish is my command: ' (RET)
Your wish is my command:
```

Since the replacement text has spaces in it, we've quoted it (see Recipe 3.1.1 [Passing Special Characters to Commands], page 36).

You can put special characters in the prompt variable in order to output special text. For example, the characters '`\w`' in the value of `PS1` will list the current working directory at that place in the shell prompt text.

- To change your prompt to the default `bash` prompt—the current working directory followed by a '`$`' character—type:

```
$ PS1='\w $ ' (RET)
~ $
```

The following table lists some special characters and their text output at the shell prompt.

SPECIAL CHARACTER	TEXT OUTPUT
\a	Inserts a *C-g* character, which makes the internal speaker beep. (It "rings the system bell"; *C-g* is sometimes called the *bell character*.)
\d	The current date.
\h	The hostname of the system.
\n	A newline character.
\t	The current system time, in 24-hour format.
\@	The current system time, in 12-hour a.m./p.m. format.
\w	The current working directory.
\u	Your username.
\!	The history number of this command.

You can combine any number of these special characters with regular characters when creating a value for `PS1`.

- To change the prompt to the current date followed by a space character, the hostname
of the system in parenthesis, and a greater-than character, type:

  $ *PS1='\d (\h)>'* (RET)
  14 Dec 1999 (ithaca)>

3.6.2 Making a Command Alias

Use `alias` to assign an *alias*, a name that represents another command or commands.
Aliases are useful for creating short command names for lengthy and frequently used commands.

- To make an alias of **bye** for the **exit** command, type:

  $ *alias bye="exit"* (RET)

This command makes 'bye' an alias for 'exit' in the current shell, so typing *bye* would
then run *exit*.

  You can also include options and arguments in an alias.

- To make an alias of 'ap' for the command **apropos shell bash shells**, type:

  $ *alias ap="apropos shell bash shells"* (RET)

This command makes 'ap' an alias for 'apropos shell bash shells' in the current shell,
so typing *ap* would run *apropos shell bash shells*.

3.6.3 Adding to Your Path

To add or remove a directory in your path, use a text editor to change the shell variable
'PATH' in the '.bashrc' file in your home directory (see Chapter 10 [Text Editing], page 119).

  For example, suppose the line that defines the 'PATH' variable in your '.bashrc' file looks
like this:

  PATH="/usr/bin:/bin:/usr/bin/X11:/usr/games"

You can add the directory '/home/nancy/bin' to this path, by editing this line like so:

  PATH="/usr/bin:/bin:/usr/bin/X11:/usr/games:/home/nancy/bin"

NOTE: See Chapter 5 [Files and Directories], page 65 for a complete description of directories and the path.

3.6.4 Customizing Future Shells

There are a number of configuration startup files in your home directory that you can edit
to make your configurations permanent. You can also edit these files to specify commands
to be run whenever you first log in, log out, or start a new shell. These configuration files are
text files that can be edited with any text editor (see Chapter 10 [Text Editing], page 119).

  When you log in, **bash** first checks to see if the file '/etc/profile' exists, and if so, it
executes the commands in this file. This is a generic, system-wide startup file that is run
for all users; only the system administrator can add or delete commands to this file.

  Next, **bash** reads and executes the commands in '.bash_profile', a "hidden" file in
your home directory (see Recipe 5.3.4 [Listing Hidden Files], page 73). Thus, to make a
command run every time you log in, add the command to this file.

For all new shells after you've logged in (that is, all but the "login shell"), bash reads and executes the commands in the '.bashrc' file in your home directory. Commands in this file run whenever a new shell is started *except* for the login shell.

There are separate configuration files for login and all other shells so that you can put specific customizations in your '.bash_profile' that only run when you first log in to the system. To avoid having to put commands in both files when you want to run the same ones for all shells, append the following to the end of your '.bash_profile' file:

```
if [ -f ~/.bashrc ]; then . ~/.bashrc; fi
```

This makes bash run the '.bashrc' file in your home directory when you log in. In this way, you can put *all* of your customizations in your '.bashrc' file, and they will be run *both* at log in and for all subsequent shells. Any customizations before this line in '.bash_profile' run only when you log in.

For example, a simple '.bash_profile' might look like this:

```
# "Comment" lines in shell scripts begin with a # character.
# They are not executed by bash, but exist so that you may
# document your file.

# You can insert blank lines in your file to increase readability;
# bash will not mind.

# Generate a welcome message when you log in.
figlet 'Good day, '$USER'!'

# Now run the commands in .bashrc
if [ -f ~/.bashrc ]; then . ~/.bashrc; fi
```

This '.bash_profile' prints a welcome message with the **figlet** text font tool (see Recipe 16.3.1 [Horizonal Text Fonts], page 202), and then runs the commands in the '.bashrc' file.

A simple .bashrc file might look like this:

```
# Make color directory listings the default.
alias ls="ls --color=auto"

# Make "l" give a verbose directory listing.
alias l="ls -l"

# Set a custom path.
PATH="/usr/local/bin:/usr/bin:/bin:/usr/bin/X11:/usr/games:~/bin:."

# Set a custom shell prompt.
PS1="[\w] $ "

# Make a long history list and history file.
HISTSIZE=20000
HISTFILESIZE=20000
```

```
# Export the path and prompt variables for all
# variables you define.
export HISTSIZE HISTFILESIZE PATH PS1
```

This '.bashrc' sets a few useful command aliases and uses a custom path and shell prompt whenever a new shell is run; with the preceding '.bash_profile', this '.bashrc' is also run at login.

When you log out, bash reads and executes the commands in the '.bash_logout' file in your home directory, if it exists. To run commands when you log out, put them in this file.

- To clear the screen every time you log out, your '.bash_logout' would contain the following line:

```
clear
```

This executes the clear command, which clears the screen of the current terminal, such as in the xterm window where you type it, or in a virtual console.

NOTE: Some distributions come with default shell startup files filled with all kinds of interesting stuff. Debian users might want to look at the example startup files in '/usr/share/doc/bash/examples/startup-files'.

4 The X Window System

Debian: 'xserver-common'
WWW: http://www.xfree86.org/

The X Window System, commonly called "X,"[1] is a graphical windowing interface that comes with all popular Linux distributions. X is available for many Unix-based operating systems; the version of X that runs on Linux systems with x86-based CPUs is called "XFree86." The current version of X is 11, Revision 6—or "X11R6."

All the command-line tools and most of the applications that you can run in the console can run in X; also available are numerous applications written specifically for X.

This chapter shows you how to get around in X: how to start it and stop it, run programs within it, manipulate windows, and customize X to your liking. See *The Linux XFree86 HOWTO* for information on installing X (see Recipe 2.8.6 [Reading System Documentation and Help Files], page 32).

4.1 Running X

WWW: http://www.afterstep.org/
WWW: http://www.fvwm.org/
WWW: http://www.windowmaker.org/
WWW: http://www.gnome.org/
WWW: http://www.kde.org/

When you start X, you should see a mouse pointer appear on the screen as a large, black "X." If your X is configured to start any tools or applications, they should each start and appear in individual windows. A typical X session looks like this:

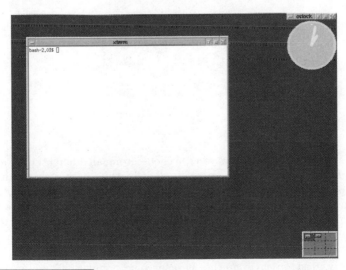

---

[1] Sometimes you might see it referred to as "X Windows," but this term is incorrect.

The *root window* is the background behind all of the other windows. It is usually set to a color, but you can change it (see Recipe 4.6.3 [Changing the Root Window Parameters], page 60). Each program or application in X runs in its own window. Each window has a decorative border on all four sides, called the *window border*; L-shaped corners, called *frames*; a top window bar, called the *title bar*, which displays the name of the window; and several title bar buttons on the left and right sides of the title bar (described in Recipe 4.3 [Manipulating X Client Windows], page 57).

The entire visible work area, including the root window and any other windows, is called the *desktop*. The box in the lower right-hand corner, called the *pager*, allows you to move about a large desktop (see Recipe 4.4 [Moving around the Desktop], page 58).

A *window manager* controls the way windows look and are displayed—the window dressing, as it were—and can provide some additional menu or program management capabilities. There are many different window managers to choose from, with a variety of features and capabilities. (See Recipe 4.6.4 [Choosing a Window Manager], page 61, for help in choosing a window manager that's right for you.)

Window managers typically allow you to customize the colors and borders that are used to display a window, as well as the type and location of buttons that appear on the window (see Recipe 4.2 [Running a Program in X], page 54). For example, in the image above, the clock image itself is the `oclock` program; the blue outline around it is the window border, as drawn by the `fvwm2` window manager. With the `afterstep` window manager, the window border would look quite different:

There are many window managers you can choose from, all different; instead of describing only one, or describing all of them only superficially, this chapter shows the *basics* of X, which are common to all window managers. I try to make no assumptions as to which window manager you are using; while the `fvwm` family of window managers has long been a popular choice on most Linux-based systems, today other window managers—including WindowMaker (the binary itself is called `wmaker`), Enlightenment, AfterStep, and others— have all gained in popularity.

And recently, *desktop environments* have become popular. These are a collection of applications that run on top of the window manager (and X), with the purpose of giving your X session a standardized "look and feel"; these suites normally come with a few basic tools such as clocks and file managers. The two popular ones are GNOME and KDE, and while they generate a lot of press these days because of their graphical nature, both are changing very quickly and at the time of this writing are not yet ready for widespread, general use (and they can cause your system to crash).

If you have a recent Linux distribution and chose the default install, chances are good that you have either GNOME or KDE installed, with either the **fvwm2** or **wmaker** window manager assigned as the default. (While you can have more than one window manager installed on your system, you can only run one at a time.)

4.1.1 Starting X

There are two ways to start X. Some systems run the X Display Manager, **xdm**, when the system boots, at which point a graphical **xdm** login screen appears; you can use this to log in directly to an X session. On systems not running **xdm**, the virtual console reserved for X will be blank until you start X by running the **startx** command.

- To start X from a virtual console, type:

      $ *startx* (RET)

- To run **startx** and redirect its output to a log file, type:

      $ *startx >$HOME/startx.log 2>&1* (RET)

Both of these examples start X on the seventh virtual console, regardless of which console you are at when you run the command—your console switches to X automatically. You can always switch to another console during your X session (see Recipe 2.3 [Console Basics], page 20). The second example writes any error messages or output of **startx** to a file called 'startx.log' in your home directory.

On some systems, X starts with 8-bit color depth by default. Use **startx** with the special '-bpp' option to specify the color depth. Follow the option with a number indicating the color depth to use, and precede the option with two hyphen characters ('--'), which tells **startx** to pass the options which follow it to the X server itself.

- To start X from a virtual console, and specify 16-bit color depth, type:

      $ *startx -- -bpp 16* (RET)

NOTE: If your system runs **xdm**, you can always switch to the seventh virtual console (or whichever console **xdm** is running on), and then log in at the **xdm** login screen.

4.1.2 Stopping X

To end an X session, you normally choose an **exit X** option from a menu in your window manager.

- To end your X session if you are running the **fvwm2** window manager, click the left mouse button in the root window to pull up the start menu, and then choose **Really quit?** from the **Exit Fvwm** submenu.
- To end your X session if you are running the **afterstep** window manager, click the left mouse button in the root window to pull up the start menu, and then choose **Really quit?** from the **Exit Fvwm** submenu.

If you started your X session with `startx`, these commands will return you to a shell prompt in the virtual console where the command was typed. If, on the other hand, you started your X session by logging in to `xdm` on the seventh virtual console, you will be logged out of the X session and the `xdm` login screen will appear; you can then switch to another virtual console or log in to X again.

To exit X immediately and terminate all X processes, press the (CTRL)-(ALT)-(BKSP) combination (if your keyboard has two (ALT) and (CTRL) keys, press the left ones). You'll lose any unsaved application data, but this is useful when you cannot exit your X session normally—in the case of a system freeze or other problem.

- To exit X immediately, type:

     (CTRL) - (ALT) - (BKSP)

4.2 Running a Program in X

Programs running in an X session are called X *clients*. (The X Window System itself is called the X *server*). To run a program in X, you start it as an X client—either by selecting it from a menu, or by typing the command to run in an `xterm` shell window (see Recipe 4.5 [Running a Shell in X], page 59). Most window managers have a "start menu" of some kind; it's usually accessed by clicking the left mouse button anywhere on the root window. To run an X client from the start menu, click the left mouse button to select the client's name from the submenus.

For example, to start a square-shaped, analog-face clock from the start menu, click the left mouse button on the root window to make the menu appear, and click the left mouse button through the application menus and on 'Xclock (analog)'. This starts the `xclock` client, specifying the option to display an analog face:

You can also start a client by running it from a shell window—useful for starting a client that isn't on the menu, or for when you want to specify options or arguments. When you run an X client from a shell window, it opens in its own window; run the client in the background to free the shell prompt in the shell window (see Recipe 3.3.2 [Putting a Job in the Background], page 41).

- To run a digital clock from a shell window, type:

      $ *xclock -digital &* (RET)

This command runs `xclock` in the background from a shell window; the '`digital`' option specifies a digital clock.

The following sections explain how to specify certain command-line options common to most X clients—such as window layout, colors, and fonts.

4.2.1 Specifying Window Size and Location

Specify a window's size and location by giving its *window geometry* with the '`geometry`' option. Four fields control the width and height of the windows, and the window's distance ("offset") from the edge of the screen. It is specified in the form:

      `-geometry WIDTHxHEIGHT+XOFF+YOFF`

The values in these four fields are usually given in pixels, although some applications measure `WIDTH` and `HEIGHT` in characters. While you must give these values in order, you can omit either pair. For example, to specify just the size of the window, give values for `WIDTH` and `HEIGHT` only.

- To start a small `xclock`, 48 pixels wide and 48 pixels high, type:

      $ *xclock -geometry 48x48* (RET)

- To start a large `xclock`, 480 pixels wide and 500 pixels high, type:

      $ *xclock -geometry 480x500* (RET)

- To start an `xclock` with a width of 48 pixels and the default height, type:

      $ *xclock -geometry 48* (RET)

- To start an `xclock` with a height of 48 pixels and the default width, type:

      $ *xclock -geometry x48* (RET)

You can give positive or negative numbers for the `XOFF` and `YOFF` fields. Positive `XOFF` values specify a position from the left of the screen; negative values specify a position from the right. If `YOFF` is positive, it specifies a position from the top of the screen; if negative, it specifies a position from the bottom of the screen. When giving these offsets, you must specify values for both `XOFF` and `YOFF`.

To place the window in one of the four corners of the desktop, use zeroes for the appropriate `XOFF` and `YOFF` values, as follows:

XOFF AND YOFF VALUES	WINDOW POSITION
+0+0	Upper left corner.
+0-0	Lower left corner.
-0+0	Upper right corner.
-0-0	Lower right corner.

- To start a default size `xclock` in the lower left-hand corner, type:

      $ *xclock -geometry +0-0* (RET)

Or, to put it all together, you can specify the size and location of a window with one geometry line that includes all four values.

- To start an `xclock` with a width of 120 pixels, a height of 100 pixels, an x offset of 250 pixels from the right side of the screen, and a y offset of 25 pixels from the top of the screen, type:

      $ xclock -geometry 120x100-250+25 (RET)

4.2.2 Specifying Window Colors

The window colors available in your X session depend on your display hardware and the X server that is running. The `xcolors` tool will show all colors available on your X server and the names used to specify them. (Color names are not case sensitive.)

- To list the available colors, type:

      $ xcolors (RET)

Press ⓠ to exit `xcolors`.

To specify a color to use for the window background, window border, and text or graphics in the window itself, give the color name as an argument to the appropriate option: '`-bg`' for background color, '`-bd`' for window border color, and '`-fg`' for foreground color.

- To start an `xclock` with a light blue window background, type:

      $ xclock -bg lightblue (RET)

You can specify any combination of these attributes.

- To start an `xclock` with a sea green window background and a turquoise window foreground, type:

      $ xclock -bg seagreen -fg turquoise (RET)

4.2.3 Specifying Window Font

To get an X font name, use `xfontsel` (see Recipe 16.1 [X Fonts], page 199). To specify a font for use in a window, use the '`-fn`' option followed by the X font name to use.

- To start an `xclock` with a digital display, and specify that it use a 17-point Helvetica font for text, type:

      $ xclock -digital -fn -*-helvetica-*-r-*-*-17-*-*-*-*-*-*-* (RET)

This command starts an `xclock` that looks like this:

Thu Jan 25 11:15:23 2001

NOTE: If you specify the font for a shell window, you can resize it after it's running, as described in Recipe 16.1.4 [Resizing the Xterm Font], page 201.

4.2.4 Specifying Additional Window Attributes

X applications often have up to three special menus with options for changing certain attributes. To see these menus, hold (CTRL) and click one of the three mouse buttons.[2] The following table lists and describes various window attributes common to most X-aware applications.

WINDOW OPTIONS	DESCRIPTION
-bd *color* -bordercolor *color*	Use *color* for the window border color.
-bg *color* -background *color*	Use *color* for the window background color.
-bw *number* -borderwidth *number*	Specify the window border width in pixels.
-fg *color* -foreground *color*	Use *color* for the window foreground text or graphics.
-fn *font* -font *font*	Use *font* for the font to use.
-geometry *geometry*	Specify window geometry.
-iconic	Immediately iconify the program (see Recipe 4.3.4 [Minimizing a Window], page 58).
-title *string*	Use *string* for the window title.

4.3 Manipulating X Client Windows

Only one X client can accept keyboard and mouse input at a time, and that client is called the *active client*. To make a client active, move the mouse over the client's window. When a client is the active client, it is said to be "in focus." Depending on the window manager, the shape of the mouse pointer may change, or the window border and title bar of the active client may be different (a common default is steel blue for the active client color and gray for all other windows).

Each window has its own set of controls to manipulate that window. Here's how to perform basic window operations with the mouse.

4.3.1 Moving a Window

To move a window, click and hold the left mouse button on the window's title bar, then drag its *window outline* to a new position. When the outline is in place, release the left mouse button, and the window will move to the position held by the window outline.

---

[2] If you have a mouse with only two buttons, click both buttons simultaneously to emulate the middle button.

4.3.2 Resizing a Window

To resize a window, click and hold the left mouse button on any one of the window's four frames, and move the mouse to shrink or grow the window outline. Release the left mouse button to resize the window to the size of the window outline.

4.3.3 Destroying a Window

To destroy a window and stop the program it displays, click the left mouse button on the 'X' button in the upper right-hand corner of the title bar. This is useful for when the program running in the window has stopped responding. (Of course, if a program in a window has an option to stop it normally, you can always use it to stop the program and close its window.)

4.3.4 Minimizing a Window

To *minimize* a window, so that it disappears and an icon representing the running program is placed on the desktop, click the left mouse button on the '_' button in the upper right-hand corner of the title bar. This is also called *iconifying* a window.

4.3.5 Maximizing a Window

To *maximize* an icon to a window (or "deiconify" it), double-click the left mouse button on the icon name, directly beneath the icon itself. The icon will disappear and the window will return to its prior position.

4.4 Moving around the Desktop

Many window managers (including `afterstep` and `fvwm2`) allow you to use a *virtual desktop*, which lets you use more screen space than your monitor can display at one time. A virtual desktop can be larger than the display, in which case you can scroll though it with the mouse. The view which fills the display is called the *viewport*. When you move the mouse off the screen in a direction where the current (virtual) desktop extends, the view scrolls in that direction. Virtual desktops are useful for running many clients full screen at once, each in its own separate desktop.

Some configurations disallow scrolling between desktops; in that case, switch between them with a *pager*, which shows a miniature view of your virtual desktop, and allows you to switch between desktops. It is a *sticky window* (it "sticks to the glass" above all other windows), and is always in the lower right-hand corner of your screen, even when you scroll across a virtual desktop. Both your current desktop and active X client are highlighted in the pager.

The default `fvwm2` virtual desktop size is nine desktops in a 3x3 grid:

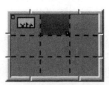

In the preceding illustration, the current desktop is the second one in the top row. The first desktop contains two X client windows—a small one and a large one—but there are no windows in any other desktop (including the current one).

To switch to another desktop, click the left mouse button on its corresponding view in the pager, or use a keyboard shortcut. In `fvwm2`, the default keys for switching between desktops are (ALT) in conjunction with the arrow keys; in `afterstep`, use the (CTRL) key in place of (ALT).

- To switch to the desktop to the left of the current one while running `fvw2`, type (ALT)-(←).

- To switch to the desktop directly to the left of the current one while running `afterstep`, type (CTRL)-(←).

4.5 Running a Shell in X

Use `xterm` to run a shell in a window. You can run commands in an `xterm` window just as you would in a virtual console; a shell in an `xterm` acts the same as a shell in a virtual console (see Chapter 3 [The Shell], page 35).

Unlike a shell in a console, you can cut and paste text from an `xterm` to another X client (see Recipe 10.4 [Selecting Text], page 128).

To scroll through text that has scrolled past the top of the screen, type (Shift)-(PgUp). The number of lines you can scroll back to depends on the value of the scrollback buffer, specified with the '`-sl`' option; its default value is 64.

There are many options for controlling `xterm`'s emulation characteristics; consult the `xterm` **man** page for a complete listing (see Recipe 2.8.4 [Reading a Page from the System Manual], page 30).

NOTE: `xterm` is probably the most popular terminal emulator X client, but it is not the only one; others to choose from include `wterm` and `rxvt`, all with their own special features—try them all to find one you like.

4.6 Configuring X

There are some aspects of X that people usually want to configure right away. This section discusses some of the most popular, including changing the video mode, automatically running clients at startup, and choosing a window manager. You'll find more information on this subject in both *The X Window User HOWTO* and *The Configuration HOWTO* (for how to read them, see Recipe 2.8.6 [Reading System Documentation and Help Files], page 32).

4.6.1 Switching between Video Modes

A *video mode* is a display resolution, given in pixels, such as 640x480. An X server can switch between the video modes allowed by your hardware and set up by the administrator; it is not uncommon for a machine running X to offer several video modes, so that 640x480, 800x600, and 1024x768 display resolutions are possible.

To switch to another video mode, use the ⊕ and ⊖ keys on the numeric keypad with the left (CTRL) and (ALT) keys. The ⊕ key switches to the next mode with a lower resolution, and the ⊖ key switches to the next mode with a higher resolution.

- To switch to the next-lowest video mode, type:

    (CTRL)-(ALT)-⊕

- To switch to the next-highest video mode, type:

    (CTRL)-(ALT)-⊖

Type either of the above key combinations repeatedly to cycle through all available modes.

NOTE: For more information on video modes, see *The XFree86 Video Timings HOWTO* (see Recipe 2.8.6 [Reading System Documentation and Help Files], page 32).

4.6.2 Running X Clients Automatically

The '.xsession' file, a hidden file in your home directory, specifies the clients that are automatically run when your X session first starts ("hidden" files are explained in Chapter 5 [Files and Directories], page 65). It is just a shell script, usually containing a list of clients to run. You can edit your '.xsession' file in a text editor, and if this file doesn't exist, you can create it.

Clients start in the order in which they are listed, and the last line should specify the window manager to use. The following example '.xsession' file starts an **xterm** with a black background and white text, puts an 'oclock' (a round clock) window in the upper left-hand corner, starts the Emacs text editor, and then starts the **fvwm2** window manager:

```
#! /bin/sh
#
# A sample .xsession file.

xterm -bg black -fg white &
oclock -geometry +0+0 &
emacs &
exec /usr/bin/X11/fvwm2
```

All clients start as background jobs, with the exception of the window manager on the last line, because when this file runs, the X session is running in the foreground (see Recipe 3.3 [Managing Jobs], page 40). Always put an ampersand ('&') character at the end of any command line you put in your '.xsession' file, except for the line giving the window manager on the last line.

4.6.3 Changing the Root Window Parameters

By default, the root window background is painted gray with a weaved pattern. To draw these patterns, X tiles the root window with a *bitmap*, which is a black-and-white image stored in a special file format. X comes with some bitmaps installed in the '/usr/X11R6/include/bitmaps/' directory; the default bitmap file is 'root_weave' (you can make your own patterns with the **bitmap** tool; see Recipe 18.4 [Interactive Image Editors and Tools], page 226).

Use `xsetroot` to change the color and bitmap pattern in the root window.

To change the color, use the '`-solid`' option, and give the name of the color to use as an argument. (Use `xcolors` to get a list of possible color names; see Recipe 4.2.2 [Specifying Window Colors], page 56.)

- To change the root window color to blue violet, type:

      $ *xsetroot -solid blueviolet* (RET)

To change the root window pattern, use the '`-bitmap`' option, and give the name of the bitmap file to use.

- To tile the root window with a star pattern, type:

      $ *xsetroot -bitmap /usr/X11R6/include/bitmaps/star* (RET)

When specifying a pattern, use the '`-fg`' and '`-bg`' options to specify the foreground and background colors.

- To tile the root window with a light slate gray star pattern on a black background, type (all on one line):

      $ *xsetroot -fg slategray2 -bg black -bitmap*
      /usr/X11R6/include/bitmaps/star (RET)

Use `xsetroot` with the special '`-gray`' option to change the root window to a shade of gray designed to be easy on the eyes, with no pattern.

- To make the root window a gray color with no pattern, type:

      $ *xsetroot -gray* (RET)

NOTE: You can also put an image in the window (although this consumes memory that could be spared for a memory-hogging Web browser instead; but see Recipe 17.2.2 [Putting an Image in the Root Window], page 211, for how to do it).

4.6.4 Choosing a Window Manager

Yes, there are *many* window managers to choose from. Some people like the flashiness of Enlightenment, running with KDE or GNOME, while others prefer the spartan `wm2`—the choice is yours.

The following table describes some of the more popular window managers currently available.

WINDOW MANAGER	DESCRIPTION
9wm	9wm is a simple window manager inspired by AT&T's Plan 9 window manager—it does not use title bars or icons. It should appeal to those who like the `wily` text editor (see Recipe 10.1 [Choosing the Perfect Text Editor], page 119). Debian: '9wm' WWW: `ftp://ftp.cs.su.oz.au/dhog/9wm/`
afterstep	AfterStep is inspired by the look and feel of the NeXTSTEP interface. Debian: 'afterstep' WWW: `http://www.afterstep.org/`

enlightenment   Enlightenment is a graphics-intensive window manager that
                     uses desktop "themes" for decorating the various controls of
                     the X session.
                     Debian: 'enlightenment'
                     WWW: http://www.enlightenment.org/

fvwm95   fvwm95 makes X look like a certain proprietary, corporate OS
                     from circa 1995.
                     Debian: 'fvwm95'
                     WWW: http://www.foxproject.org/xclass/fvwm95.html

twm   The Tab Window Manager is an older, simple window man-
                     ager that is available on almost every system. (It's also some-
                     times called Tom's Window Manager, named after its primary
                     author, Tom LaStrange.)
                     Debian: 'twm'

wm2   wm2 is a minimalist, configuration-free window manager.
                     Debian: 'wm2'
                     WWW: http://www.all-day-breakfast.com/wm2/

PART TWO: Files

5 Files and Directories

This chapter discusses the basic tools for manipulating files and directories—tools that are among the most essential on a Linux system.

A *file* is a collection of data that is stored on disk and that can be manipulated as a single unit by its name.

A *directory* is a file that acts as a folder for other files. A directory can also contain other directories (*subdirectories*); a directory that contains another directory is called the *parent* directory of the directory it contains.

A *directory tree* includes a directory and all of its files, including the contents of all subdirectories. (Each directory is a "branch" in the "tree.") A slash character alone ('/') is the name of the *root directory* at the base of the directory tree hierarchy; it is the trunk from which all other files or directories branch.

The following image shows an abridged version of the directory hierarchy.

```
                                    /
                                   / dict
                                  /
                                 / bin
                                /
                        usr    /
                          /  / jon
                           / /    /
                            / play
                           / /
                          /  / work
                         / /
                          / joe
                         /
                 home   /
                   /   /
                    / /
                     / bin
                    /
                   / etc
                  /
                 / (root)
```

To represent a directory's place in the file hierarchy, specify all of the directories between it and the root directory, using a slash ('/') as the delimiter to separate directories. So the directory 'dict' as it appears in the preceding illustration would be represented as '/usr/dict'.

Each user has a branch in the '/home' directory for their own files, called their *home directory*. The hierarchy in the previous illustration has two home directories: 'joe' and 'jon', both subdirectories of '/home'.

When you are in a shell, you are always in a directory on the system, and that directory is called the *current working directory*. When you first log in to the system, your home directory is the current working directory.

Whenever specifying a file name as an argument to a tool or application, you can give the slash-delimited *path name* relative to the current working directory. For example, if '/home/joe' is the current working directory, you can use *work* to specify the directory '/home/joe/work', and *work/schedule* to specify 'schedule', a file in the '/home/joe/work' directory.

Every directory has two special files whose names consist of one and two periods: '..' refers to the parent of the current working directory, and '.' refers to the current working directory itself. If the current working directory is '/home/joe', you can use '.' to specify '/home/joe' and '..' to specify '/home'. Furthermore, you can specify the '/home/jon' directory as *../jon*.

Another way to specify a file name is to specify a slash-delimited list of all of the directory branches from the root directory ('/') down to the file to specify. This unique, specific path from the root directory to a file is called the file's *full path name*. (When referring to a file that is not a directory, this is sometimes called the *absolute file name*).

You can specify any file or directory on the system by giving its full path name. A file can have the same name as other files in different directories on the system, but no two files or directories can share a full path name. For example, user joe can have a file 'schedule' in his '/home/joe/work' directory and a file 'schedule' in his '/home/joe/play' directory. While both files have the same name ('schedule'), they are contained in different directories, and each has a unique full path name—'/home/joe/work/schedule' and '/home/joe/play/schedule'.

However, you don't have to type the full path name of a tool or application in order to start it. The shell keeps a list of directories, called the *path*, where it searches for programs. If a program is "in your path," or in one of these directories, you can run it simply by typing its name.

By default, the path includes '/bin' and '/usr/bin'. For example, the who command is in the '/usr/bin' directory, so its full path name is /usr/bin/who. Since the '/usr/bin' directory is in the path, you can type *who* to run /usr/bin/who, no matter what the current working directory is.

The following table describes some of the standard directories on Linux systems.

DIRECTORY	DESCRIPTION
/	The ancestor of all directories on the system; all other directories are subdirectories of this directory, either directly or through other subdirectories.
/bin	Essential tools and other programs (or *binaries*).
/dev	Files representing the system's various hardware *devices*. For example, you use the file '/dev/cdrom' to access the CD-ROM drive.
/etc	Miscellaneous system configuration files, startup files, *etcetera*.
/home	The *home* directories for all of the system's users.
/lib	Essential system *library* files used by tools in '/bin'.
/proc	Files that give information about current system *processes*.

/root	The superuser's home directory, whose username is root. (In the past, the home directory for the superuser was simply '/'; later, '/root' was adopted for this purpose to reduce clutter in '/'.)
/sbin	Essential system administrator tools, or *system binaries*.
/tmp	*Temporary* files.
/usr	Subdirectories with files related to *user* tools and applications.
/usr/X11R6	Files relating to the X Window System, including those programs (in '/usr/X11R6/bin') that run only under X.
/usr/bin	Tools and applications for users.
/usr/dict	*Dictionaries* and word lists (slowly being outmoded by '/usr/share/dict').
/usr/doc	Miscellaneous system *documentation*.
/usr/games	*Games* and amusements.
/usr/info	Files for the GNU *Info* hypertext system.
/usr/lib	*Libraries* used by tools in '/usr/bin'.
/usr/local	*Local* files—files unique to the individual system—including local documentation (in '/usr/local/doc') and programs (in '/usr/local/bin').
/usr/man	The online *manuals*, which are read with the man command (see Recipe 2.8.4 [Reading a Page from the System Manual], page 30).
/usr/share	Data for installed applications that is architecture-independent and can be *shared* between systems. A number of subdirectories with equivalents in '/usr' also appear here, including '/usr/share/doc', '/usr/share/info', and '/usr/share/icons'.
/usr/src	Program *source* code for software compiled on the system.
/usr/tmp	Another directory for *temporary* files.
/var	*Variable* data files, such as spool queues and log files.

NOTE: For more information on the directory structure of Linux-based systems, view the compressed files in the '/usr/doc/debian-policy/fsstnd/' directory (see Recipe 9.1 [Perusing Text], page 111).

5.1 Naming Files and Directories

File names can consist of upper- and lowercase letters, numbers, periods ('.'), hyphens
('-'), and underscores ('_').[1] File names are also case sensitive—'foo', 'Foo' and 'FOO' are
all different file names. File names are almost always all lowercase letters.

Linux does not force you to use file extensions, but it is convenient and useful to give
files proper extensions, since they will help you to identify file types at a glance. You can
have files with multiple extensions, such as 'long.file.with.many.extensions', and you
can have files with none at all, such as 'myfile'. A JPEG image file, for example, does
not have to have a '.jpg' or '.jpeg' extension, and program files do not need a special
extension to make them work.

The file name before any file extensions is called the *base file name*. For example, the
base file name of 'house.jpeg' is 'house'.

Some commonly used file extensions are shown in the following table, including extensions for text and graphics files. (See Recipe 18.2 [Converting Images between Formats],
page 223, for more extensions used with image files, and see Recipe 21.3 [Playing a Sound
File], page 245, for extensions used with sound files.)

EXTENSION	DESCRIPTION
.txt *or* .text	Plain, unformatted text.
.tex	Text formatted in the TEX or LaTeX formatting language.
.ltx *or* .latex	Text formatted in the LaTeX formatting language (neither are as common as just using '.tex').
.gz	A compressed file.
.sgml	SGML ("Standardized General Markup Language") format.
.html	HTML ("Hypertext Markup Language") format.
.xml	XML ("Extended Markup Language") format.

The following sections show how to make new files; to rename an existing file, move it
to a file with the new name—see Recipe 5.5 [Moving Files and Directories], page 76.

5.1.1 Making an Empty File

You may sometimes want to create a new, empty file as a kind of "placeholder." To do so,
give the name that you want to use for the file as an argument to touch.

- To create the file 'a_fresh_start' in the current directory, type:

      $ *touch a_fresh_start* (RET)

- To create the file 'another_empty_file' in the 'work/completed' subdirectory of the
  current directory, type:

      $ *touch work/completed/another_empty_file* (RET)

---

[1] Technically, there *are* other characters that you can use—but doing so may get you into trouble later on.

This tool "touches" the files you give as arguments. If a file does not exist, it creates it; if the file already exists, it changes the modification timestamp on the file to the current date and time, just as if you had used the file.

NOTE: Often, you make a file when you edit it, such as when in a text or image or sound editor; in that case, you don't need to make the file first.

5.1.2 Making a Directory

Use `mkdir` ("make directory") to make a new directory, giving the path name of the new directory as an argument. Directory names follow the same conventions as used with other files—that is, no spaces, slashes, or other unusual characters are recommended.

- To make a new directory called '`work`' in the current working directory, type:

      $ *mkdir work* (RET)

- To make a new directory called '`work`' in the '`/tmp`' directory, type:

      $ *mkdir /tmp/work* (RET)

5.1.3 Making a Directory Tree

Use `mkdir` with the '`-p`' option to make a subdirectory and any of its parents that do not already exist. This is useful when you want to make a fairly complex directory tree from scratch, and don't want to have to make each directory individually.

- To make the '`work/completed/2001`' directory—a subdirectory of the '`completed`' directory, which in turn is a subdirectory of the '`work`' directory in the current directory, type:

      $ *mkdir -p work/completed/2001* (RET)

This makes a '`2001`' subdirectory in the directory called '`completed`', which in turn is in a directory called '`work`' in the current directory; if the '`completed`' or the '`work`' directories do not already exist, they are made as well (if you know that '`work`' and '`completed`' both exist, the above command works fine without the '`-p`' option).

5.2 Changing Directories

Use `cd` to change the current working directory; give the name of the new directory as an argument.

- To change the current working directory to '`work`', a subdirectory in the current directory, type:

      $ *cd work* (RET)

- To change to the current directory's parent directory, type:

      $ *cd ..* (RET)

You can also give the full path name of a directory.

- To change the current working directory to '`/usr/doc`', type:

      $ *cd /usr/doc* (RET)

This command makes '`/usr/doc`' the current working directory.

5.2.1 Changing to Your Home Directory

With no arguments, `cd` makes your home directory the current working directory.

- To make your home directory the current working directory, type:

      $ *cd* (RET)

5.2.2 Changing to the Last Directory You Visited

To return to the last directory you were in, use `cd` and give '`-`' as the directory name. For example, if you are in the '`/home/mrs/work/samples`' directory, and you use `cd` to change to some other directory, then at any point while you are in this other directory you can type *cd* - to return the current working directory to '`/home/mrs/work/samples`'.

- To return to the directory you were last in, type:

      $ *cd* - (RET)

5.2.3 Getting the Name of the Current Directory

To determine what the current working directory is, use `pwd` ("print working directory"), which lists the full path name of the current working directory.

- To determine what the current working directory is, type:

```
$ pwd (RET)
/home/mrs
$
```

In this example, `pwd` output the text '`/home/mrs`', indicating that the current working directory is '`/home/mrs`'.

5.3 Listing Directories

Debian: 'mc'
Debian: 'mozilla'
WWW: http://www.gnome.org/mc/
WWW: http://www.mozilla.org/

Use `ls` to *list* the contents of a directory. It takes as arguments the names of the directories to list. With no arguments, `ls` lists the contents of the current working directory.

- To list the contents of the current working directory, type:

```
$ ls (RET)
apple    cherry  orange
$
```

In this example, the current working directory contains three files: '`apple`', '`cherry`', and '`orange`'.

- To list the contents of 'work', a subdirectory in the current directory, type:

  $ ls work (RET)

- To list the contents of the '/usr/doc' directory, type:

  $ ls /usr/doc (RET)

You cannot discern file types from the default listing; directories and executables are indistinguishable from all other files. Using the '-F' option, however, tells ls to place a '/' character after the names of subdirectories and a '*' character after the names of executable files.

- To list the contents of the directory so that directories and executables are distinguished from other files, type:

```
$ ls -F (RET)
repeat* test1    test2    words/
$
```

In this example, the current directory contains an executable file named 'repeat', a directory named 'words', and some other files named 'test1' and 'test2'.

Another way to list the contents of directories—and one I use all the time, when I'm in X and when I also want to look at image files in those directories—is to use Mozilla or some other Web browser as a local file browser. Use the prefix[2] file:/ to view local files. Alone, it opens a directory listing of the root directory; file:/home/joe opens a directory listing of user joe's home directory, file:/usr/local/src opens the local source code directory, and so on. Directory listings will be rendered in HTML on the fly in almost all browsers, so you can click on subdirectories to traverse to them, and click on files to open them in the browser.

Yet another way to list the contents of directories is to use a "file manager" tool, of which there are at least a few on Linux; the most popular of these is probably the "Midnight Commander," or mc.

The following subsections describe some commonly used options for controlling which files ls lists and what information about those files ls outputs. It is one of the most often used file commands on Unix-like systems.

5.3.1 Listing File Attributes

Use ls with the '-l' ("long") option to output a more extensive directory listing—one that contains each file's size in bytes, last modification time, file type, and ownership and permissions (see Recipe 6.2 [File Ownership], page 84).

- To output a verbose listing of the '/usr/doc/bash' directory, type:

---

[2] Called a URN, or "Uniform Resource Name."

```
$ ls -l /usr/doc/bash (RET)
total 72
-rw-r--r--   1 root     root     13744 Oct 19 22:57 CHANGES.gz
-rw-r--r--   1 root     root      1816 Oct 19 22:57 COMPAT.gz
-rw-r--r--   1 root     root     16398 Oct 19 22:57 FAQ.gz
-rw-r--r--   1 root     root      2928 Oct 19 22:57 INTRO.gz
-rw-r--r--   1 root     root      4751 Oct 19 22:57 NEWS.gz
-rw-r--r--   1 root     root      1588 Oct 19 22:57 POSIX.NOTES.gz
-rw-r--r--   1 root     root      2718 Oct 19 22:57 README.Debian.gz
-rw-r--r--   1 root     root     19596 Oct 19 22:57 changelog.gz
-rw-r--r--   1 root     root      1446 Oct 19 22:57 copyright
drwxr-xr-x   9 root     root      1024 Jul 25  1997 examples
$
```

This command outputs a verbose listing of the files in '/usr/doc/bash'. The first line of output gives the total amount of disk space, in 1024-byte blocks, that the files take up (in this example, 72). Each subsequent line displays several columns of information about one file.

The first column displays the file's type and permissions. The first character in this column specifies the file type; the hyphen ('-') is the default and means that the file is a regular file. Directories are denoted by 'd', and symbolic links (see Recipe 5.7 [Giving a File More than One Name], page 79) are denoted by 'l'. The remaining nine characters of the first column show the file permissions (see Recipe 6.3 [Controlling Access to Files], page 85). The second column lists the number of hard links to the file. The third and fourth columns give the names of the user and group that the file belongs to. The fifth column gives the size of the file in bytes, the sixth column gives the date and time of last modification, and the last column gives the file name.

5.3.2 Listing Directories Recursively

Use the '-R' option to list a directory *recursively*, which outputs a listing of that directory and all of its subdirectories.

- To output a recursive directory listing of the current directory, type:

```
$ ls -R (RET)
play    work

play:
notes

work:
notes
$
```

In this example, the current working directory contains two subdirectories, 'work' and 'play', and no other files. Each subdirectory contains a file called 'notes'.

- To list all of the files on the system, type:

```
$ ls -R / (RET)
```

This command recursively lists the contents of the root directory, '/', and all of its subdirectories. It is common to combine this with the attribute option, '-l', to output a verbose listing of all the files on the system:

```
$ ls -lR / (RET)
```

NOTE: You can't list the contents of some directories on the system if you don't have permission to do so (see Recipe 6.3 [Controlling Access to Files], page 85).

5.3.3 Listing Newest Files First

Use the '-t' option with ls to sort a directory listing so that the newest files are listed first.

- To list all of the files in the '/usr/tmp' directory sorted with newest first, type:

  ```
  $ ls -t /usr/tmp (RET)
  ```

5.3.4 Listing Hidden Files

By default, ls does not output files that begin with a period character ('.'). To reduce clutter, many applications "hide" configuration files in your home directory by giving them names that begin with a period; these are called *dot files*, or sometimes "hidden" files. As mentioned earlier, every directory has two special dot files: '..', the parent directory, and '.', the directory itself.

To list *all* contents of a directory, including these dot files, use the '-a' option.

- To list all files in the current directory, type:

  ```
  $ ls -a (RET)
  ```

Use the '-A' option to list *almost* all files in the directory: it lists all files, including dot files, with the exception of '..' and '.'.

- To list all files in the current directory except for '..' and '.', type:

  ```
  $ ls -A (RET)
  ```

5.3.5 Listing Directories in Color

Use ls with the '--color' option to list the directory contents in color; files appear in different colors depending on their content. Some of the default color settings include displaying directory names in blue, text files in white, executable files in green, and links in turquoise.

- To list the files in the root directory in color, type:

```
$ ls --color /
System.map    etc          man          usr
System.old    floppy       mnt          var
bin           home         proc         vmlinuz
boot          initrd       root         vmlinuz.old
cdrom         lib          sbin
dev           lost+found   tmp
$
```

NOTE: It's common practice to create a command alias that substitutes 'ls --color' for 'ls', so that typing just *ls* outputs a color listing. To learn more about making aliases, see Recipe 3.6.2 [Making a Command Alias], page 47.

5.3.6 Listing Directory Tree Graphs

Debian: 'tree'
WWW: ftp://mama.indstate.edu/linux/tree/

Use **tree** to output an ASCII text tree graph of a given directory tree.

- To output a tree graph of the current directory and all its subdirectories, type:

```
$ tree (RET)
.
|-- projects
|    |-- current
|    '-- old
|         |-- 1
|         '-- 2
'-- trip
     '-- schedule.txt

4 directories, 3 files
$
```

In the preceding example, a tree graph is drawn showing the current directory, which contains the two directories 'projects' and 'trip'; the 'projects' directory in turn contains the directories 'current' and 'old'.

To output a tree graph of a specific directory tree, give the name of that directory tree as an argument.

- To output a tree graph of your home directory and all its subdirectories, type:

    ```
    $ tree ~ (RET)
    ```

To output a graph of a directory tree containing directory names only, use the '-d' option. This is useful for outputting a directory tree of the entire system, or for getting a picture of a particular directory tree.

- To output a tree graph of the entire system to the file '**tree**', type:

```
        $ tree -d / > tree (RET)
```
- To peruse a tree graph of the '/usr/local' directory tree, type:
```
        $ tree -d /usr/local |less (RET)
```

NOTE: Another tool for outputting directory trees is described in Recipe 24.2 [Listing a File's Disk Usage], page 266.

5.3.7 Additional Directory Listing Options

The ls tool has many options to control the files listed and the information given for each file; the following table describes some of them. (The options are case sensitive.)

OPTION	DESCRIPTION
--color	Colorize the names of files depending on their type.
-R	Produce a recursive listing.
-a	List all files in a directory, including hidden, or "dot," files.
-d	List directories by name instead of listing their contents.
-f	Do not sort directory contents; list them in the order they are written on the disk.
-l	Produce a verbose listing.
-r	Sort directory contents in reverse order.
-s	Output the size—as an integer in 1K blocks—of each file to the left of the file name.
-t	Sort output by timestamp instead of alphabetically, so the newest files are listed first.

NOTE: You can combine any of these options; for example, to list the contents of a directory sorted newest first, and display all attributes, use '-lt'. To recursively list all hidden files and display all attributes, use '-lRa'. It doesn't matter what order you put the options in—so '-lRa' is the same as, say, '-alR'.

5.4 Copying Files and Directories

Use cp ("copy") to copy files. It takes two arguments: the source file, which is the existing file to copy, and the target file, which is the file name for the new copy. cp then makes an identical copy of the source file, giving it the specified target name. If a file with the target name already exists, cp overwrites it. It does not alter the source file.

- To copy the file 'my-copy' to the file 'neighbor-copy', type:
```
        $ cp my-copy neighbor-copy (RET)
```

This command creates a new file called 'neighbor-copy' that is identical to 'my-copy' in every respect except for its name, owner, group, and timestamp—the new file has a timestamp that shows the time when it was copied. The file 'my-copy' is not altered.

Use the '-p' ("preserve") option to preserve all attributes of the original file, including its timestamp, owner, group, and permissions.

- To copy the file 'my-copy' to the file 'neighbor-copy', preserving all of the attributes of the source file in the target file, type:

    $ *cp -p my-copy neighbor-copy* (RET)

This command copies the file 'my-copy' to a new file called 'neighbor-copy' that is identical to 'my-copy' in every respect except for its name.

To copy a directory along with the files and subdirectories it contains, use the -R option— it makes a *recursive* copy of the specified directory and its entire contents.

- To copy the directory 'public_html', and all of its files and subdirectories, to a new directory called 'private_html', type:

    $ *cp -R public_html private_html* (RET)

The '-R' option does not copy files that are symbolic links (see Recipe 5.7 [Giving a File More than One Name], page 79), and it does not retain all original permissions. To recursively copy a directory including links, and retain all of its permissions, use the '-a' ("archive") option. This is useful for making a backup copy of a large directory tree.

- To make an archive copy of the directory tree 'public_html' to the directory 'private_html', type:

    $ *cp -a public_html private_html* (RET)

5.5 Moving Files and Directories

Use the mv ("move") tool to move, or rename, a file or directory to a different location. It takes two arguments: the name of the file or directory to move followed by the path name to move it to. If you move a file to a directory that contains a file of the same name, the file is overwritten.

- To move the file 'notes' in the current working directory to '../play', type:

    $ *mv notes ../play* (RET)

This command moves the file 'notes' in the current directory to 'play', a subdirectory of the current working directory's parent. If a file 'notes' already exists in 'play', that file is overwritten. If the subdirectory 'play' does not exist, this command moves 'notes' to its parent directory and renames it 'play'.

To move a file or directory that is not in the current directory, give its full path name as an argument.

- To move the file '/usr/tmp/notes' to the current working directory, type:

    $ *mv /usr/tmp/notes .* (RET)

This command moves the file '/usr/tmp/notes' to the current working directory.

To move a directory, give the path name of the directory you want to move and the path name to move it to as arguments.

- To move the directory 'work' in the current working directory to 'play', type:

    $ *mv work play* (RET)

This command moves the directory 'work' in the current directory to the directory 'play'. If the directory 'play' already exists, mv puts 'work' inside 'play'—it does not overwrite directories.

Renaming a file is the same as moving it; just specify as arguments the file to rename followed by the new file name.

- To rename the file 'notes' to 'notes.old', type:

      $ mv notes notes.old (RET)

5.5.1 Changing File Names to Lowercase

WWW: http://eternity.2y.net/chcase

To change the uppercase letters in a file name to lowercase (or vice versa), use chcase. It takes as arguments the files whose names it should change.

- To change the file names of all of the files in the current directory to lowercase letters, type:

      $ chcase * (RET)

Use the '-u' option to change file names to all uppercase letters.

- To change file names of all of the files with a '.dos' extension in the '~/tmp' directory to all uppercase letters, type:

      $ chcase -u ~/tmp/*.dos (RET)

By default, chcase does not rename directories; use the '-d' option to rename directories as well as other files. The '-r' option recursively descends into any subdirectories and renames those files, too.

- To change all of the files and subdirectory names in the current directory to all lowercase letters, type:

      $ chcase -d * (RET)

- To change all of the files and subdirectory names in the current directory to all uppercase letters, and descend recursively into all subdirectories, type:

      $ chcase -d -r -u * (RET)

- To change all of the files in the current directory to all lowercase letters, and descend recursively into all subdirectories (but do not change any directory names), type:

      $ chcase -r * (RET)

5.5.2 Renaming Multiple Files with the Same Extension

WWW: http://eternity.2y.net/chcase

To give a different file name extension to a group of files that share the same file name extension, use chcase with the '-x' option for specifying a Perl expression; give the patterns to match the source and target files as a quoted argument.

For example, you can rename all file names ending in '.htm' to end in '.html' by giving 's/htm/html/' as the expression to use.

- To rename all of the files in the current directory with a '.htm' extension to '.html', type:

      $ chcase -x 's/htm/html/' '*.htm' (RET)

By default, chcase will not overwrite files; so if you want to rename 'index.htm' to 'index.html', and both files already exist in the current directory, the above example will do nothing. Use the '-o' option to specify that existing files may be *overwritten*.

- To rename all of the files in the current directory with a '.htm' extension to '.html' and overwrite any existing files, type:

      $ chcase -o -x 's/htm/html/' '*.htm' (RET)

NOTE: Renaming multiple files at once is a common request.

5.6 Removing Files and Directories

Use rm ("remove") to delete a file and remove it from the system. Give the name of the file to remove as an argument.

- To remove the file 'notes' in the current working directory, type:

      $ rm notes (RET)

To remove a directory and all of the files and subdirectories it contains, use the '-R' ("recursive") option.

- To remove the directory 'waste' and all of its contents, type:

      $ rm -R waste (RET)

To remove an empty directory, use rmdir; it removes the empty directories you specify. If you specify a directory that contains files or subdirectories, rmdir reports an error.

- To remove the directory 'empty', type:

      $ rmdir empty (RET)

5.6.1 Removing a File with a Strange Name

Files with strange characters in their names (like spaces, control characters, beginning hyphens, and so on) pose a problem when you want to remove them. There are a few solutions to this problem.

One way is to use tab completion to complete the name of the file (see Recipe 3.1.2 [Letting the Shell Complete What You Type], page 37). This works when the name of the file you want to remove has enough characters to uniquely identify it so that completion can work.

- To use tab completion to remove the file 'No Way' in the current directory, type:

      $ rm No(TAB) Way (RET)

In the above example, after (TAB) was typed, the shell filled in the rest of the file name (' Way').

When a file name begins with a control character or other strange character, specify the file name with a file name pattern that uniquely identifies it (see Recipe 5.8 [Specifying File Names with Patterns], page 80, for tips on building file name patterns). Use the '-i' option to verify the deletion.

- To delete the file '^Acat' in a directory that also contains the files 'cat' and 'dog', type:

```
$ rm -i ?cat (RET)
rm: remove '^Acat'? y (RET)
$
```

In the above example, the expansion pattern '?cat' matches the file '^Acat' and no other files in the directory. The '-i' option was used because, in some cases, no unique pattern can be made for a file—for example, if this directory also contained a file called '1cat', the above rm command would also attempt to remove it; with the '-i' option, you can answer **n** to it.

These first two methods will not work with files that begin with a hyphen character, because rm will interpret such a file name as an option; to remove such a file, use the '--' option—it specifies that what follows are arguments and not options.

- To remove the file '-cat' from the current directory, type:

    $ rm -- -cat (RET)

5.6.2 A Safe Way to Remove a File

WWW: ftp://ftp.wg.omron.co.jp/pub/unix-faq/docs
WWW: http://dsl.org/comp/tinyutils/

Once a file is removed, it is permanently deleted and there is no command you can use to restore it; you cannot "undelete" it. (Although if you can unmount the filesystem that contained the file immediately after you deleted the file, a wizard might be able to help reconstruct the lost file by using grep to search the filesystem device file.)

A safer way to remove files is to use del, which is simply an alias to rm with the '-i' option. This specifies for rm to run in *interactive* mode and confirm the deletion of each file. It may be good practice to get in the habit of using del all the time, so that you don't make an accidental slip and rm an important file.

NOTE: Question 3.6 in the Unix FAQ (see '/usr/doc/FAQ/unix-faq-part3') discusses this issue, and gives a shell script called can that you can use in place of rm—it puts files in a "trashcan" directory instead of removing them; you then periodically empty out the trashcan with rm.

5.7 Giving a File More than One Name

Links are special files that point to other files; when you act on a file that is a link, you act on the file it points to. There are two kinds of links: hard links and symbolic links. A *hard link* is another name for an existing file; there is no difference between the link and the original file. So if you make a hard link from file 'foo' to file 'bar', and then remove file 'bar', file 'foo' is also removed. Each file has at least one hard link, which is the original file name itself. Directories always have at least *two* hard links—the directory name itself (which appears in its parent directory) and the special file '.' inside the directory. Likewise, when you make a new subdirectory, the parent directory gains a new hard link for the special file '..' inside the new subdirectory.

A *symbolic link* (sometimes called a "symlink" or "soft link") passes most operations—such as reading and writing—to the file it points to, just as a hard link does. However, if you remove a symlink, you remove only the symlink itself, and *not* the original file.

Use `ln` ("link") to make links between files. Give as arguments the name of the source file to link from and the name of the new file to link to. By default, `ln` makes hard links.

- To create a hard link from 'seattle' to 'emerald-city', type:

    $ *ln seattle emerald-city* (RET)

This command makes a hard link from an existing file, 'seattle', to a new file, 'emerald-city'. You can read and edit file 'emerald-city' just as you would 'seattle'; any changes you make to 'emerald-city' are also written to 'seattle' (and vice versa). If you remove the file 'emerald-city', file 'seattle' is also removed.

To create a symlink instead of a hard link, use the '-s' option.

- To create a symbolic link from 'seattle' to 'emerald-city', type:

    $ *ln -s seattle emerald-city* (RET)

After running this command, you can read and edit 'emerald-city'; any changes you make to 'emerald-city' will be written to 'seattle' (and vice versa). But if you remove the file 'emerald-city', the file 'seattle' will not be removed.

5.8 Specifying File Names with Patterns

The shell provides a way to construct patterns, called file name *expansions*, that specify a group of files. You can use them when specifying file and directory names as arguments to any tool or application.

The following table lists the various file expansion characters and their meaning.

CHARACTER	DESCRIPTION
*	The asterisk matches a series of zero or more characters, and is sometimes called the "wildcard" character. For example, * alone matches all file names, a* matches all file names that consist of an 'a' character followed by zero or more characters, and a*b matches all file names that begin with an 'a' character and end with a 'b' character, with any (or no) characters in between.
?	The question mark matches exactly one character. Therefore, ? alone matches all file names with exactly one character, ?? matches all file names with exactly *two* characters, and a? matches any file name that begins with an 'a' character and has exactly one character following it.
[*list*]	Square brackets match one character in *list*. For example, [ab] matches exactly two file names: 'a' and 'b'. The pattern c[io] matches 'ci' and 'co', but no other file names.
~	The tilde character expands to your home directory. For example, if your username is joe and therefore your home directory is '/home/joe', then '~' expands to '/home/joe'. You can follow the tilde with a path to specify a file in your home directory—for example, '~/work' expands to '/home/joe/work'.

Brackets also have special meaning when used in conjunction with other characters, as described by the following table.

CHARACTER	DESCRIPTION
-	A hyphen as part of a bracketed *list* denotes a *range* of characters to match—so `[a-m]` matches any of the lowercase letters from 'a' through 'm'. To match a literal hyphen character, use it as the first or last character in the list. For example, `a[-b]c` matches the files 'a-c' and 'abc'.
!	Put an exclamation point at the beginning of a bracketed list to match all characters *except* those listed. For example, `a[!b]c` matches all files that begin with an 'a' character, end with a 'c' character, and have any one character, *except* a 'b' character, in between; it matches 'aac', 'a-c', 'adc', and so on.

You can combine these special expansion characters in any combination, and you can specify more than one pattern as multiple arguments. The following examples show file expansion in action using commands described in this chapter.

- To list all files in the '/usr/bin' directory that have the text 'tex' anywhere in their name, type:

  `$ ls /usr/bin/*tex*` (RET)

- To copy all files whose names end with '.txt' to the 'doc' subdirectory, type:

  `$ cp *.txt doc` (RET)

- To output a verbose listing of all files whose names end with either a '.txt' or '.text' extension, sorting the list so that newer files are listed first, type:

  `$ ls -lt *.txt *.text` (RET)

- To move all files in the '/usr/tmp' directory whose names consist of the text 'song' followed by an integer from 0 to 9 and a '.cdda' extension, placing them in a directory 'music' in your home directory, type:

  `$ mv /usr/tmp/song[0-9].cdda ~/music` (RET)

- To remove all files in the current working directory that begin with a hyphen and have the text 'out' somewhere else in their file name, type:

  `$ rm -- -*out*` (RET)

- To concatenate all files whose names consist of an 'a' character followed by two or more characters, type:

  `$ cat a??*` (RET)

5.9 Browsing Files

You can view and peruse local files in a Web browser, such as the text-only browser `lynx` or the graphical Mozilla browser for X.

The `lynx` tool is very good for browsing files on the system—give the name of the directory to browse, and `lynx` will display a listing of available files and directories in that directory.

You can use the cursor keys to browse and press (RET) on a subdirectory to traverse to that directory; `lynx` can display plain text files, compressed text files, and files written in HTML; it's useful for browsing system documentation in the '/usr/doc' and '/usr/share/doc' directories, where many software packages come with help files and manuals written in HTML.

- To browse the system documentation files in the '/usr/doc' directory, type:

      $ lynx /usr/doc (RET)

For more about using `lynx`, see Recipe 31.3 [Reading Text from the Web], page 330.

With Mozilla and some other browsers you must precede the full path name with the 'file:/' URN—so the '/usr/doc' directory would be 'file://usr/doc'. With `lynx`, just give a local path name as an argument.

- To browse the system documentation files in the '/usr/doc' directory in Mozilla, type the following in Mozilla's Location window:

      file://usr/doc

6 Sharing Files

Groups, file ownership, and access permissions are Linux features that enable users to share files with one another. But even if you don't plan on sharing files with other users on your system, familiarity with these concepts will help you understand how file access and security work in Linux.

6.1 Groups and How to Work in Them

A *group* is a set of users, created to share files and to facilitate collaboration. Each member of a group can work with the group's files and make new files that belong to the group. The system administrator can add new groups and give users membership to the different groups, according to the users' organizational needs. For example, a system used by the crew of a ship might have groups such as `galley`, `deck`, `bridge`, and `crew`; the user `captain` might be a member of all the groups, but user `steward` might be a member of only the `galley` and `crew` groups.

On a Linux system, you're always a member of at least one group: your *login group*. You are the only member of this group, and its group name is the same as your username.

Let's look at how to manage your group memberships.

6.1.1 Listing the Groups a User Belongs To

To list a user's group memberships, use the `groups` tool. Give a username as an argument, and `groups` outputs a line containing that username followed by all of the groups the user is a member of. With no arguments, `groups` lists your own username and group memberships.

- To list your group memberships, type:

```
$ groups (RET)
steward galley crew
$
```

In this example, three groups are output: `steward` (the user's login group), `galley`, and `crew`.

- To list the group memberships of user `blackbeard`, type:

```
$ groups blackbeard (RET)
blackbeard : blackbeard
$
```

In this example, the command outputs the given username, `blackbeard`, followed by the name of one group, `blackbeard`, indicating that user `blackbeard` belongs to only one group: his login group.

6.1.2 Listing the Members of a Group

Debian: 'members'

To list the members of a particular group, use the **members** tool, giving the name of the particular group as an argument.

- To output a list of the members of the **galley** group, type:

```
$ members galley (RET)
captain steward pete
$
```

In this example, three usernames are output, indicating that these three users are the members of the **galley** group.

6.2 File Ownership

Every file belongs to both a user and a group—usually to the user who created it and to the group the user was working in at the time (which is almost always the user's login group). File ownership determines the type of access users have to particular files (see Recipe 6.3 [Controlling Access to Files], page 85).

6.2.1 Determining the Ownership of a File

To find out which user and group own a particular file, use **ls** with the '-l' option to list the file's attributes (see Recipe 5.3.1 [Listing File Attributes], page 71). The name of the user who owns the file appears in the third column of the output, and the name of the group that owns the file appears in the fourth column.

For example, suppose the verbose listing for a file called 'cruise' looks like this:

```
-rwxrw-r--     1 captain   crew        8,420 Jan 12 21:42 cruise
```

The user who owns this file is **captain**, and the group that owns it is **crew**.

NOTE: When you create a file, it normally belongs to you and to your login group, but you can change its ownership, as described in the next recipe. You normally own all of the files in your home directory.

6.2.2 Changing the Ownership of a File

You can't give away a file to another user, but other users can make copies of a file that belongs to you, provided they have read permission for that file (see Recipe 6.3 [Controlling Access to Files], page 85). When you make a copy of another user's file, you own the copy.

You can also change the group ownership of any file you own. To do this, use **chgrp**; it takes as arguments the name of the group to transfer ownership to and the names of the files to work on. You must be a member of the group you want to give ownership to.

- To change the group ownership of file 'cruise' to **bridge**, type:

```
$ chgrp bridge cruise (RET)
```

This command transfers group ownership of 'cruise' to bridge; the file's group access permissions (see Recipe 6.3 [Controlling Access to Files], page 85) now apply to the members of the bridge group.

Use the '-R' option to *recursively* change the group ownership of directories and all of their contents.

- To give group ownership of the 'maps' directory and all the files it contains to the bridge group, type:

      $ *chgrp -R bridge maps* (RET)

6.3 Controlling Access to Files

Each file has *permissions* that specify what type of access to the file users have. There are three kinds of permissions: read, write, and execute. You need *read* permission for a file to read its contents, *write* permission to write changes to or remove it, and *execute* permission to run it as a program.

Normally, users have write permission only for files in their own home directories. Only the superuser has write permission for the files in important directories, such as '/bin' and '/etc'—so as a regular user, you never have to worry about accidentally writing to or removing an important system file.

Permissions work differently for directories than for other kinds of files. Read permission for a directory means that you can see the files in the directory; write permission lets you create, move, or remove files in the directory; and execute permission lets you use the directory name in a path (see Chapter 5 [Files and Directories], page 65).

If you have read permission but not execute permission for a directory, you can only read the names of files in that directory—you can't read their other attributes, examine their contents, write to them, or execute them. With execute but not read permission for a directory, you can read, write to, or execute any file in the directory, provided that you know its name and that you have the appropriate permissions for that file.

Each file has separate permissions for three categories of users: the user who owns the file, all other members of the group that owns the file, and all other users on the system. If you are a member of the group that owns a file, the file's group permissions apply to you (unless you are the owner of the file, in which case the user permissions apply to you).

When you create a new file, it has a default set of permissions—usually read and write for the user, and read for the group and all other users. (On some systems, the default permissions are read and write for both the user and group, and read for all other users.)

The file access permissions for a file are collectively called its *access mode*. The following sections describe how to list and change file access modes, including how to set the most commonly used access modes.

NOTE: The superuser, root, can always access any file on the system, regardless of its access permissions.

See Info file 'fileutils.info', node 'File permissions', for more information on file permissions and access modes.

6.3.1 Listing the Permissions of a File

To list a file's access permissions, use `ls` with the '`-l`' option (see Recipe 5.3.1 [Listing File Attributes], page 71). File access permissions appear in the first column of the output, after the character for file type.

For example, consider the verbose listing of the file '`cruise`':

```
-rwxrw-r--        1 captain    crew          8,420 Jan 12 21:42 cruise
```

The first character ('`-`') is the file type; the next three characters ('`rwx`') specify permissions for the user who owns the file; and the next three ('`rw-`') specify permissions for all members of the group that owns the file *except* for the user who owns it. The last three characters in the column ('`r--`') specify permissions for all other users on the system.

All three permissions sections have the same format, indicating from left to right, read, write, and execute permission with '`r`', '`w`', and '`x`' characters. A hyphen ('`-`') in place of one of these letters indicates that permission is not given.

In this example, the listing indicates that the user who owns the file, `captain`, has read, write, and execute permission, and the group that owns the file, `crew`, has read and write permission. All other users on the system have only read permission.

6.3.2 Changing the Permissions of a File

To change the access mode of any file you own, use the `chmod` ("change mode") tool. It takes two arguments: an *operation*, which specifies the permissions to grant or revoke for certain users, and the names of the files to work on.

To build an operation, first specify the category or categories of users as a combination of the following characters:

CHARACTER	CATEGORY
u	The user who owns the file.
g	All other members of the file's group.
o	All other users on the system.
a	All users on the system; this is the same as '`ugo`'.

Follow this with the operator denoting the action to take:

OPERATOR	ACTION
+	Add permissions to the user's existing permissions.
-	Remove permissions from the user's existing permissions.
=	Make these the *only* permissions the user has for this file.

Finally, specify the permissions themselves:

CHARACTER	PERMISSION
r	Set read permission.
w	Set write permission.
x	Set execute permission.

For example, use 'u+w' to add write permission to the existing permissions for the user who owns the file, and use 'a+rw' to add both read and write permissions to the existing permissions of all users. (You could also use 'ugo+rw' instead of 'a+rw'.)

6.3.3 Write-Protecting a File

If you revoke users' write permissions for a file, they can no longer write to or remove the file. This effectively "write-protects" a file, preventing accidental changes to it. A write-protected file is sometimes called a "read only" file.

To write-protect a file so that no users other than yourself can write to it, use `chmod` with 'go-w' as the operation.

- To write-protect the file 'cruise' so that no other users can change it, type:

        $ chmod go-w cruise (RET)

6.3.4 Making a File Private

To make a file private from all other users on the system, use `chmod` with 'go=' as the operation. This revokes all **group** and **other** access permissions.

- To make the file 'cruise' private from all users but yourself, type:

        $ chmod go= cruise (RET)

6.3.5 Making a File Public

To allow anyone with an account on the system to read and make changes to a file, use `chmod` with 'a+rw' as the operation. This grants read and write permission to all users, making the file "public." When a file has read permission set for all users, it is called *world readable*, and when a file has write permission set for all users, it is called *world writable*.

- To make the file 'cruise' both world readable and world writable, type:

        $ chmod a+rw cruise (RET)

6.3.6 Making a File Executable

An *executable file* is a file that you can run as a program. To change the permissions of a file so that all users can run it as a program, use `chmod` with 'a+x' as the operation.

- To give execute permission to all users for the file 'myscript', type:

        $ chmod a+x myscript (RET)

NOTE: Often, shell scripts that you obtain or write yourself do not have execute permission set, and you'll have to do this yourself.

7 Finding Files

Sometimes you will need to find files on the system that match given criteria, such as name and file size. This chapter will show you how to find a file when you know only part of the file name, and how to find a file whose name matches a given pattern. You will also learn how to list files and directories by their size and to find the locations of commands.

NOTE: When you want to find files in a directory whose *contents* match a particular pattern, search through the files with `grep`—see Chapter 14 [Searching Text], page 165. A method of searching for a given pattern in the contents of files in different directories is given in Recipe 7.2.5 [Running Commands on the Files You Find], page 93.

See Info file '`find.info`', node 'Top', for more information on finding files.

7.1 Finding All Files That Match a Pattern

The simplest way to find files is with GNU `locate`. Use it when you want to list all files on the system whose full path name matches a particular pattern—for example, all files with the text 'audio' somewhere in their full path name, or all files ending with 'ogg'; `locate` outputs a list of all files on the system that match the pattern, giving their full path name. When specifying a pattern, you can use any of the file name expansion characters (see Recipe 5.8 [Specifying File Names with Patterns], page 80).

- To find all the files on the system that have the text 'audio' anywhere in their name, type:

      $ *locate audio* (RET)

- To find all the files on the system whose file names end with the text 'ogg', type:

      $ *locate *ogg* (RET)

- To find all hidden "dotfiles" on the system, type:

      $ *locate /.* (RET)

NOTE: `locate` searches are not case sensitive.

Sometimes, a `locate` search will generate a lot of output. Pipe the output to `less` to peruse it (see Recipe 9.1 [Perusing Text], page 111).

7.2 Finding Files in a Directory Tree

Use `find` to find specific files in a particular directory tree, specifying the name of the directory tree to search, the criteria to match, and—optionally—the action to perform on the found files. (Unlike most other tools, you must specify the directory tree argument *before* any other options.)

You can specify a number of search criteria, and format the output in various ways; the following sections include recipes for the most commonly used `find` commands, as well as a list of `find`'s most popular options.

7.2.1 Finding Files in a Directory Tree by Name

Use `find` to find files in a directory tree by name. Give the name of the directory tree to search through, and use the '-name' option followed by the name you want to find.

- To list all files on the system whose file name is 'top', type:

    $ *find / -name top* (RET)

This command will search all directories on the system to which you have access; if you don't have `execute` permission for a directory, `find` will report that permission is denied to search the directory.

The '-name' option is case sensitive; use the similar '-iname' option to find name regardless of case.

- To list all files on the system whose file name is 'top', regardless of case, type:

    $ *find / -iname top* (RET)

This command would match any files whose name consisted of the letters 'top', regardless of case—including 'Top', 'top', and 'TOP'.

Use file expansion characters (see Recipe 5.8 [Specifying File Names with Patterns], page 80) to find files whose names match a pattern. Give these file name patterns between single quotes.

- To list all files on the system whose names begin with the characters 'top', type:

    $ *find / -name 'top*'* (RET)

- To list all files whose names begin with the three characters 'top' followed by exactly three more characters, type:

    $ *find / -name 'top???'* (RET)

- To list all files whose names begin with the three characters 'top' followed by five or more characters, type:

    $ *find / -name 'top?????*'* (RET)

- To list all files in your home directory tree that end in '.tex', regardless of case, type:

    $ *find ~ -iname '*.tex'* (RET)

- To list all files in the '/usr/share' directory tree with the text 'farm' somewhere in their name, type:

    $ *find /usr/share -name '*farm*'* (RET)

Use '-regex' in place of '-name' to search for files whose names match a *regular expression*, or a pattern describing a set of strings (see Recipe 14.2 [Regular Expressions—Matching Text Patterns], page 166).

- To list all files in the current directory tree whose names have either the string 'net' or 'comm' anywhere in their file names, type:

    $ *find . -regex '.*\(net\|comm\).*'* (RET)

NOTE: The '-regex' option matches the whole path name, relative to the directory tree you specify, and not just file names.

7.2.2 Finding Files in a Directory Tree by Size

To find files of a certain size, use the '-size' option, following it with the file size to match. The file size takes one of three forms: when preceded with a plus sign ('+'), it matches all files *greater* than the given size; when preceded with a hyphen or minus sign ('-'), it matches all files *less* than the given size; with neither prefix, it matches all files whose size is *exactly* as specified. (The default unit is 512-byte blocks; follow the size with 'k' to denote kilobytes or 'b' to denote bytes.)

- To list all files in the '/usr/local' directory tree that are greater than 10,000 kilobytes in size, type:

    ```
    $ find /usr/local -size +10000k RET
    ```

- To list all files in your home directory tree less than 300 bytes in size, type:

    ```
    $ find ~ -size -300b RET
    ```

- To list all files on the system whose size is exactly 42 512-byte blocks, type:

    ```
    $ find / -size 42 RET
    ```

Use the '-empty' option to find empty files—files whose size is 0 bytes. This is useful for finding files that you might not need, and can remove.

- To find all empty files in your home directory tree, type:

    ```
    $ find ~ -empty RET
    ```

NOTE: To find the largest or smallest files in a given directory, output a sorted listing of that directory (see Recipe 7 3 [Finding Files in Directory Listings], page 96).

7.2.3 Finding Files in a Directory Tree by Modification Time

To find files last modified during a specified time, use find with the '-mtime' or '-mmin' options; the argument you give with '-mtime' specifies the number of 24-hour periods, and with '-mmin' it specifies the number of minutes.

- To list the files in the '/usr/local' directory tree that were modified *exactly* 24 hours ago, type:

    ```
    $ find /usr/local -mtime 1 RET
    ```

- To list the files in the '/usr' directory tree that were modified *exactly* five minutes ago, type:

    ```
    $ find /usr -mmin 5 RET
    ```

To specify a range of time, precede the number you give with either a plus sign ('+') to match times that are equal to or greater than the given argument, or a hyphen or minus sign ('-') to match times that are equal to or less than the given argument.

- To list the files in the '/usr/local' directory tree that were modified *within* the past 24 hours, type:

    ```
    $ find /usr/local -mtime -1 RET
    ```

- To list the files in the '/usr' directory tree that were modified *within* the past five minutes, type:

    ```
    $ find /usr -mmin -5 RET
    ```

Include the '-daystart' option to measure time from the beginning of the current day instead of 24 hours ago.

- To list all of the files in your home directory tree that were modified yesterday, type:

      $ find ~ -mtime 1 -daystart (RET)

- To list all of the files in the '/usr' directory tree that were modified one year or longer ago, type:

      $ find /usr -mtime +356 -daystart (RET)

- To list all of the files in your home directory tree that were modified from two to four days ago, type:

      $ find ~ -mtime 2 -mtime -4 -daystart (RET)

In the preceding example, the combined options '-mtime 2' and '-mtime -4' matched files that were modified between two and four days ago.

To find files newer than a given file, give the name of that file as an argument to the '-newer' option.

- To find files in the '/etc' directory tree that are newer than the file '/etc/motd', type:

      $ find /etc -newer /etc/motd (RET)

To find files newer than a given date, use the trick described in the find Info documentation: create a temporary file in '/tmp' with touch whose timestamp is set to the date you want to search for, and then specify that temporary file as the argument to '-newer'.

- To list all files in your home directory tree that were modified after May 4 of the current year, type:

      $ touch -t 05040000 /tmp/timestamp (RET)
      $ find ~ -newer /tmp/timestamp (RET)

In this example, a temporary file called '/tmp/timestamp' is written; after the search, you can remove it (see Recipe 5.6 [Removing Files and Directories], page 78).

NOTE: You can also find files that were last accessed a number of days after they were modified by giving that number as an argument to the '-used' option. This is useful for finding files that get little use—files matching '-used +100', say, were accessed 100 or more days after they were last modified.

7.2.4 Finding Files in a Directory Tree by Owner

To find files owned by a particular user, give the username to search for as an argument to the '-user' option.

- To list all files in the '/usr/local/fonts' directory tree owned by the user warwick, type:

      $ find /usr/local/fonts -user warwick (RET)

The '-group' option is similar, but it matches group ownership instead of user ownership.

- To list all files in the '/dev' directory tree owned by the audio group, type:

      $ find /dev -group audio (RET)

7.2.5 Running Commands on the Files You Find

You can also use **find** to execute a command you specify on each found file, by giving the command as an argument to the '-exec' option. If you use the string ''{}'' in the command, this string is replaced with the file name of the current found file when the command executes. Mark the end of the command with the string '';''.

- To find all files in the '~/html/' directory tree with an '.html' extension, and output lines from these files that contain the string 'organic', type:

      $ find ~/html/ -name '*.html' -exec grep organic '{}' ';' (RET)

In this example, the command **grep organic** *file* is executed for each file that **find** finds, with *file* being the name of each file in turn.

To have **find** pause and confirm execution for each file it finds, use '-ok' instead of '-exec'.

- To remove files from your home directory tree that were accessed more than one year after they were last modified, pausing to confirm before each removal, type:

      $ find ~ -used +365 -ok rm '{}' ';' (RET)

7.2.6 Finding Files by Multiple Criteria

You can combine many of **find**'s options to find files that match multiple criteria.

- To list files in your home directory tree whose names begin with the string 'top', and that are newer than the file '/etc/motd', type:

      $ find ~ -name 'top*' -newer /etc/motd (RET)

- To compress all the files in your home directory tree that are two megabytes or larger, and that are not already compressed with **gzip** (having a '.gz' file name extension), type:

      $ find ~ -size +2000000c -regex '.*[^gz]' -exec gzip '{}' ';' (RET)

The following tables describe many other options you can use with **find**. The first table lists and describes **find**'s general options for specifying its behavior. As you will see, **find** can take many different options; see its **man** page or its **info** documentation for all of them.

OPTION	DESCRIPTION
-daystart	Use the beginning of today rather than 24 hours previous for time criteria.
-depth	Search the subdirectories before each directory.
-help	Output a help message and exit.
-maxdepth *levels*	Specify the maximum number of directory levels to descend in the specified directory tree.
-mount *or* -xdev	Do not descend directories that have another disk mounted on them.
-version	Output the version number and exit.

The following table lists and describes **find**'s options for specifying which files to find.

Specify the numeric arguments to these options in one of three ways: preceded with a plus sign ('+') to match values equal to or greater than the given argument; preceded with a hyphen or minus sign ('-') to match values equal to or less than the given argument; or give the number alone to match exactly that value.

OPTION	DESCRIPTION
-amin *minutes*	Time in minutes since the file was last accessed.
-anewer *file*	File was accessed more recently than *file*.
-atime *days*	Time in days since the file was last accessed.
-cmin *minutes*	Time in minutes since the file was last changed.
-cnewer *file*	File was changed more recently than *file*.
-ctime *days*	Days since the file was last changed.
-empty	File is empty.
-group *group*	Name of the group that owns file.
-iname *pattern*	Case-insensitive file name pattern to match ('report' matches the files 'Report', 'report', 'REPORT', etc.).
-ipath *pattern*	Full path name of file matches the pattern *pattern*, regardless of case ('./r*rt' matches './records/report' and './Record-Labels/ART').
-iregex *regexp*	Path name of file, relative to specified directory tree, matches the regular expression *regexp*, regardless of case ('t?p' matches 'TIP' and 'top').
-links *links*	Number of links to the file (see Recipe 5.7 [Giving a File More than One Name], page 79).
-mmin *minutes*	Number of minutes since the file's data was last changed.
-mtime *days*	Number of days since the file's data was last changed.
-name *pattern*	Base name of the file matches the pattern *pattern*.
-newer *file*	File was modified more recently than *file*.
-path *pattern*	Full path name of file matches the pattern *pattern* ('./r*rt' matches './records/report').
-perm *access mode*	File's permissions are exactly *access mode* (see Recipe 6.3 [Controlling Access to Files], page 85).
-regex *regexp*	Path name of file, relative to specified directory tree, matches the regular expression *regexp*.
-size *size*	File uses *size* space, in 512-byte blocks. Append *size* with 'b' for bytes or 'k' for kilobytes.

-type *type*	File is type *type*, where *type* can be 'd' for directory, 'f' for regular file, or 'l' for symbolic link.
-user *user*	File is owned by *user*.

The following table lists and describes find's options for specifying what to do with the files it finds.

OPTION	DESCRIPTION
-exec *commands*	Specifies commands, separated by semicolons, to be executed on matching files. To specify the current file name as an argument to a command, use '{}'.
-ok *commands*	Like '-exec' but prompts for confirmation before executing *commands*.
-print	Outputs the name of found files to the standard output, each followed by a newline character so that each is displayed on a line of its own. On by default.
-printf *format*	Use "C-style" output (the same as used by the printf function in the C programming language), as specified by string *format*.

The following table describes the variables may be used in the *format* string used by the '-printf' option.

VARIABLE	DESCRIPTION
\a	Ring the system bell (called the "alarm" on older systems).
\b	Output a backspace character.
\f	Output a form feed character.
\n	Output a newline character.
\r	Output a carriage return.
\t	Output a horizontal tab character.
\\	Output a backslash character.
%%	Output a percent sign character.
%b	Output file's size, rounded up in 512-byte blocks.
%f	Output base file name.
%h	Output the leading directories of file's name.
%k	Output file's size, rounded up in 1K blocks.
%s	Output file's size in bytes.

7.3 Finding Files in Directory Listings

The following recipes show how to find the largest and smallest files and directories in a given directory or tree by listing them by size. They also show how to find the number of files in a given directory.

7.3.1 Finding the Largest Files in a Directory

To find the largest files in a given directory, use `ls` to list its contents with the '-S' option, which sorts files in descending order by their size (normally, `ls` outputs files sorted alphabetically). Include the '-l' option to output the size and other file attributes.

- To list the files in the current directory, with their attributes, sorted with the largest files first, type:

      $ ls -lS (RET)

NOTE: Pipe the output to `less` to peruse it (see Recipe 9.1 [Perusing Text], page 111).

7.3.2 Finding the Smallest Files in a Directory

To list the contents of a directory with the smallest files first, use `ls` with both the '-S' and '-r' options, which *reverses* the sorting order of the listing.

- To list the files in the current directory and their attributes, sorted from smallest to largest, type:

      $ ls -lSr (RET)

7.3.3 Finding the Smallest Directories

To output a list of *directories* sorted by their size—the size of all the files they contain—use `du` and `sort`. The `du` tool outputs directories in ascending order with the smallest first; the '-S' option puts the size in kilobytes of each directory in the first column of output. Give the directory tree you want to output as an option, and pipe the output to `sort` with the '-n' option, which sorts its input numerically.

- To output a list of the subdirectories of the current directory tree, sorted in ascending order by size, type:

      $ du -S . | sort -n (RET)

7.3.4 Finding the Largest Directories

Use the '-r' option with `sort` to *reverse* the listing and output the largest directories first.

- To output a list of the subdirectories in the current directory tree, sorted in descending order by size, type:

      $ du -S . | sort -nr (RET)

- To output a list of the subdirectories in the '/usr/local' directory tree, sorted in descending order by size, type:

      $ du -S /usr/local | sort -nr (RET)

7.3.5 Finding the Number of Files in a Listing

To find the number of files in a directory, use `ls` and pipe the output to '`wc -l`', which outputs the number of lines in its input (see Recipe 12.1 [Counting Text], page 149).

- To output the number of files in the current directory, type:

```
$ ls | wc -l (RET)
     19
$
```

In this example, the command outputs the text '**19**', indicating that there are 19 files in the current directory.

Since `ls` does not list hidden files by default (see Recipe 5.3.4 [Listing Hidden Files], page 73), the preceding command does not count them. Use `ls`'s '**-A**' option to count dot files as well.

- To count the number of files—including dot files—in the current directory, type:

```
$ ls -A | wc -l (RET)
     81
$
```

This command outputs the text '**81**', indicating that there are 81 files, including hidden files, in the current directory.

To list the number of files in a given directory *tree*, and not just a single directory, use `find` instead of `ls`, giving the special `find` predicate '`\! -type d`' to exclude the listing (and therefore, counting) of directories.

- To list the number of files in the '`/usr/share`' directory tree, type:
    ```
    $ find /usr/share \! -type d | wc -l (RET)
    ```
- To list the number of files *and* directories in the '`/usr/share`' directory tree, type:
    ```
    $ find /usr/share | wc -l (RET)
    ```
- To list the number of *directories* in the '`/usr/share`' directory tree, type:
    ```
    $ find /usr/share \! -type f | wc -l (RET)
    ```

7.4 Finding Where a Command Is Located

Use `which` to find the full path name of a tool or application from its base file name; when you give the base file name as an option, `which` outputs the absolute file name of the command that would have run had you typed it. This is useful when you are not sure whether or not a particular command is installed on the system.

- To find out whether `perl` is installed on your system, and, if so, where it resides, type:

```
$ which perl (RET)
/usr/bin/perl
```

In this example, `which` output '`/usr/bin/perl`', indicating that the `perl` binary is installed in the '`/usr/bin`' directory.

NOTE: This is also useful for determining "which" binary would execute, should you type the name, since some systems may have different binaries of the same file name located in different directories. In that case, you can use `which` to find which one would execute.

8 Managing Files

File management tools include those for splitting, comparing, and compressing files, making backup archives, and tracking file revisions. Other management tools exist for determining the contents of a file, and for changing its timestamp.

8.1 Determining File Type and Format

When we speak of a file's *type*, we are referring to the kind of data it contains, which may include text, executable commands, or some other data; this data is organized in a particular way in the file, and this organization is called its *format*. For example, an image file might contain data in the JPEG image format, or a text file might contain unformatted text in the English language or text formatted in the TEX markup language.

The `file` tool analyzes files and indicates their type and—if known—the format of the data they contain. Supply the name of a file as an argument to `file` and it outputs the name of the file, followed by a description of its format and type.

- To determine the format of the file '`/usr/doc/HOWTO/README.gz`', type:

```
$ file /usr/doc/HOWTO/README.gz (RET)
/usr/doc/HOWTO/README.gz: gzip compressed data, deflated, original
filename, last modified: Sun Apr 26 02:51:48 1998, os: Unix
$
```

This command reports that the file '`/usr/doc/HOWTO/README.gz`' contains data that has been compressed with the `gzip` tool.

To determine the original format of the data in a compressed file, use the '`-z`' option.

- To determine the format of the compressed data contained in the file '`/usr/doc/HOWTO/README.gz`', type:

```
$ file -z /usr/doc/HOWTO/README.gz (RET)
/usr/doc/HOWTO/README.gz: English text (gzip compressed data, deflated,
original filename, last modified: Sun Apr 26 02:51:48 1998, os: Unix)
$
```

This command reports that the data in '`/usr/doc/HOWTO/README.gz`', a compressed file, is English text.

NOTE: Currently, `file` differentiates among more than 100 different data formats, including several human languages, many sound and graphics formats, and executable files for many different operating systems.

8.2 Changing File Modification Time

Use `touch` to change a file's timestamp without modifying its contents. Give the name of the file to be changed as an argument. The default action is to change the timestamp to the current time.

- To change the timestamp of file 'pizzicato' to the current date and time, type:

  $ *touch pizzicato* (RET)

To specify a timestamp other than the current system time, use the '-d' option, followed by the date and time that should be used enclosed in quote characters. You can specify just the date, just the time, or both.

- To change the timestamp of file 'pizzicato' to '17 May 1999 14:16', type:

  $ *touch -d '17 May 1999 14:16' pizzicato* (RET)

- To change the timestamp of file 'pizzicato' to '14 May', type:

  $ *touch -d '14 May' pizzicato* (RET)

- To change the timestamp of file 'pizzicato' to '14:16', type:

  $ *touch -d '14:16' pizzicato* (RET)

NOTE: When only the date is given, the time is set to '0:00'; when no year is given, the current year is used.

See Info file 'fileutils.info', node 'Date input formats', for more information on date input formats.

8.3 Splitting a File into Smaller Ones

It's sometimes necessary to split one file into a number of smaller ones. For example, suppose you have a very large sound file in the near-CD-quality MPEG2, level 3 ("MP3") format. Your file, 'large.mp3', is 4,394,422 bytes in size, and you want to transfer it from your desktop to your laptop, but your laptop and desktop are not connected on a network—the only way to transfer files between them is by floppy disk. Because this file is much too large to fit on one floppy, you use split.

The split tool copies a file, chopping up the copy into separate files of a specified size. It takes as optional arguments the name of the input file (using standard input if none is given) and the file name prefix to use when writing the output files (using 'x' if none is given). The output files' names will consist of the file prefix followed by a group of letters: 'aa', 'ab', 'ac', and so on—the default output file names would be 'xaa', 'xab', and so on.

Specify the number of *lines* to put in each output file with the '-l' option, or use the '-b' option to specify the number of *bytes* to put in each output file. To specify the output files' sizes in kilobytes or megabytes, use the '-b' option and append 'k' or 'm', respectively, to the value you supply. If neither '-l' nor '-b' is used, split defaults to using 1,000 lines per output file.

- To split 'large.mp3' into separate files of one megabyte each, whose names begin with 'large.mp3.', type:

  $ *split -b1m large.mp3 large.mp3.* (RET)

This command creates five new files whose names begin with 'large.mp3.'. The first four files are one megabyte in size, while the last file is 200,118 bytes—the remaining portion of the original file. No alteration is made to 'large.mp3'.

You could then copy these five files onto four floppies (the last file fits on a floppy with one of the larger files), copy them all to your laptop, and then reconstruct the original file with cat (see Recipe 10.6 [Concatenating Text], page 130).

- To reconstruct the original file from the split files, type:

      $ *cat large.mp3.* > large.mp3* (RET)
      $ *rm large.mp3.** (RET)

In this example, the `rm` tool is used to delete all of the split files after the original file has been reconstructed.

8.4 Comparing Files

There are a number of tools for comparing the contents of files in different ways; these recipes show how to use some of them. These tools are especially useful for comparing passages of text in files, but that's not the only way you can use them.

8.4.1 Determining Whether Two Files Differ

Use `cmp` to determine whether or not two text files differ. It takes the names of two files as arguments, and if the files contain the same data, `cmp` outputs nothing. If, however, the files differ, `cmp` outputs the byte position and line number in the files where the first difference occurs.

- To determine whether the files 'master' and 'backup' differ, type:

      $ *cmp master backup* (RET)

8.4.2 Finding the Differences between Files

Use `diff` to compare two files and output a *difference report* (sometimes called a "diff") containing the text that *differs* between two files. The difference report is formatted so that other tools (namely, `patch`—see Recipe 8.4.3 [Patching a File with a Difference Report], page 102) can use it to make a file identical to the one it was compared with.

To compare two files and output a difference report, give their names as arguments to `diff`.

- To compare the files 'manuscript.old' and 'manuscript.new', type:

      $ *diff manuscript.old manuscript.new* (RET)

The difference report is output to standard output; to save it to a file, redirect the output to the file to save to:

      $ *diff manuscript.old manuscript.new > manuscript.diff* (RET)

In the preceding example, the difference report is saved to a file called 'manuscript.diff'.

The difference report is meant to be used with commands such as `patch`, in order to apply the differences to a file. See Info file '`diff.info`', node 'Top', for more information on `diff` and the format of its output.

To better see the difference between two files, use `sdiff` instead of `diff`; instead of giving a difference report, it outputs the files in two columns, side by side, separated by spaces. Lines that differ in the files are separated by '|'; lines that appear only in the first file end with a '<', and lines that appear only in the second file are preceded with a '>'.

- To peruse the files 'laurel' and 'hardy' side by side on the screen, with any differences indicated between columns, type:

        `$ sdiff laurel hardy | less` (RET)

To output the difference between *three* separate files, use `diff3`.

- To output a difference report for files 'larry', 'curly', and 'moe', and output it in a file called 'stooges', type:

      `$ diff3 larry curly moe > stooges` (RET)

8.4.3 Patching a File with a Difference Report

To apply the differences in a difference report to the original file compared in the report, use `patch`. It takes as arguments the name of the file to be patched and the name of the difference report file (or "patchfile"). It then applies the changes specified in the patchfile to the original file. This is especially useful for distributing different versions of a file—small patchfiles may be sent across networks easier than large source files.

- To update the original file 'manuscript.new' with the patchfile 'manuscript.diff', type:

      `$ patch manuscript.new manuscript.diff` (RET)

8.5 Compressed Files

File compression is useful for storing or transferring large files. When you *compress* a file, you shrink it and save disk space. File compression uses an algorithm to change the data in the file; to use the data in a compressed file, you must first *uncompress* it to restore the original data (and original file size).

    The following recipes explain how to compress and uncompress files.

8.5.1 Compressing a File

Use the `gzip` ("GNU zip") tool to compress files. It takes as an argument the name of the file or files to be compressed; it writes a compressed version of the specified files, appends a '.gz' extension to their file names, and then deletes the original files.

- To compress the file 'war-and-peace', type:

      `$ gzip war-and-peace` (RET)

    This command compresses the file 'war-and-peace', putting it in a new file named 'war-and-peace.gz'; `gzip` then deletes the original file, 'war-and-peace'.

8.5.2 Decompressing a File

To access the contents of a compressed file, use `gunzip` to decompress (or "uncompress") it.

    Like `gzip`, `gunzip` takes as an argument the name of the file or files to work on. It expands the specified files, writing the output to new files without the '.gz' extensions, and then deletes the compressed files.

- To expand the file 'war-and-peace.gz', type:

      `$ gunzip war-and-peace.gz` (RET)

This command expands the file 'war-and-peace.gz' and puts it in a new file called 'war-and-peace'; gunzip then deletes the compressed file, 'war-and-peace.gz'.

NOTE: You can view a compressed text file without uncompressing it by using zless. This is useful when you want to view a compressed file but do not want to write changes to it. (For more information about zless, see Recipe 9.1 [Perusing Text], page 111).

8.6 File Archives

An *archive* is a single file that contains a collection of other files, and often directories. Archives are usually used to transfer or make a backup copy of a collection of files and directories—this way, you can work with only one file instead of many. This single file can be easily compressed as explained in the previous section, and the files in the archive retain the structure and permissions of the original files.

Use the **tar** tool to create, list, and extract files from archives. Archives made with **tar** are sometimes called "tar files," "tar archives," or—because all the archived files are rolled into one—"tarballs."

The following recipes show how to use **tar** to create an archive, list the contents of an archive, and extract the files from an archive. Two common options used with all three of these operations are '-f' and '-v': to specify the name of the archive file, use '-f' followed by the file name; use the '-v' ("verbose") option to have **tar** output the names of files as they are processed. While the '-v' option is not necessary, it lets you observe the progress of your **tar** operation.

NOTE: The name of this tool comes from "tape archive," because it was originally made to write the archives directly to a magnetic tape device. It is still used for this purpose, but today, archives are almost always saved to a file on disk.

See Info file 'tar.info', node 'Top', for more information about managing archives with **tar**.

8.6.1 Creating a File Archive

To create an archive with **tar**, use the '-c' ("create") option, and specify the name of the archive file to create with the '-f' option. It's common practice to use a name with a '.tar' extension, such as 'my-backup.tar'.

Give as arguments the names of the files to be archived; to create an archive of a directory and all of the files and subdirectories it contains, give the directory's name as an argument.

- To create an archive called 'project.tar' from the contents of the 'project' directory, type:

      $ tar -cvf project.tar project (RET)

This command creates an archive file called 'project.tar' containing the 'project' directory and all of its contents. The original 'project' directory remains unchanged.

Use the '-z' option to compress the archive as it is being written. This yields the same output as creating an uncompressed archive and then using **gzip** to compress it, but it eliminates the extra step.

- To create a compressed archive called 'project.tar.gz' from the contents of the 'project' directory, type:

    $ tar -zcvf project.tar.gz project (RET)

This command creates a compressed archive file, 'project.tar.gz', containing the 'project' directory and all of its contents. The original 'project' directory remains unchanged.

NOTE: When you use the '-z' option, you should specify the archive name with a '.tar.gz' extension and not a '.tar' extension, so the file name shows that the archive is compressed. This is not a requirement, but it serves as a reminder and is the standard practice.

8.6.2 Listing the Contents of an Archive

To list the contents of a tar archive without extracting them, use tar with the '-t' option.

- To list the contents of an archive called 'project.tar', type:

    $ tar -tvf project.tar (RET)

This command lists the contents of the 'project.tar' archive. Using the '-v' option along with the '-t' option causes tar to output the permissions and modification time of each file, along with its file name—the same format used by the ls command with the '-l' option (see Recipe 5.3.1 [Listing File Attributes], page 71).

Include the '-z' option to list the contents of a compressed archive.

- To list the contents of a compressed archive called 'project.tar.gz', type:

    $ tar -ztvf project.tar (RET)

8.6.3 Extracting Files from an Archive

To extract (or *unpack*) the contents of a tar archive, use tar with the '-x' ("extract") option.

- To extract the contents of an archive called 'project.tar', type:

    $ tar -xvf project.tar (RET)

This command extracts the contents of the 'project.tar' archive into the current directory.

If an archive is compressed, which usually means it will have a '.tar.gz' or '.tgz' extension, include the '-z' option.

- To extract the contents of a compressed archive called 'project.tar.gz', type:

    $ tar -zxvf project.tar.gz (RET)

NOTE: If there are files or subdirectories in the current directory with the same name as any of those in the archive, those files will be overwritten when the archive is extracted. If you don't know what files are included in an archive, consider listing the contents of the archive first (see Recipe 8.6.2 [Listing the Contents of an Archive], page 104).

Another reason to list the contents of an archive before extracting them is to determine whether the files in the archive are contained in a directory. If not, and the current directory contains many unrelated files, you might confuse them with the files extracted from the archive.

To extract the files into a directory of their own, make a new directory, move the archive to that directory, and change to that directory, where you can then extract the files from the archive.

8.7 Tracking Revisions to a File

The Revision Control System (RCS) is a set of tools for managing multiple revisions of a single file.

To store a revision of a file so that RCS can keep track of it, you *check in* the file with RCS. This deposits the revision of the file in an RCS *repository*—a file that RCS uses to store all changes to that file. RCS makes a repository file with the same file name as the file you are checking in, but with a ',v' extension appended to the name. For example, checking in the file 'foo.text' with RCS creates a repository file called 'foo.text,v'.

Each time you want RCS to remember a revision of a file, you check in the file, and RCS writes to that file's RCS repository the *differences* between the file and the last revision on record in the repository.

To access a revision of a file, you *check out* the revision from RCS. The revision is obtained from the file's repository and is written to the current directory.

Although RCS is most often used with text files, you can also use it to keep track of revisions made to other kinds of files, such as image files and sound files.

Another revision control system, Concurrent Versions System (CVS), is used for tracking collections of multiple files whose revisions are made concurrently by multiple authors. While much less simple than RCS, it is very popular for managing free software projects on the Internet. See Info file 'cvs.info', node 'Top', for information on using CVS.

8.7.1 Checking In a File Revision

When you have a version of a file that you want to keep track of, use ci to check in that file with RCS.

Type ci followed by the name of a file to deposit that file into the RCS repository. If the file has never before been checked in, ci prompts for a description to use for that file; each subsequent time the file is checked in, ci prompts for text to include in the file's revision log (see Recipe 8.7.3 [Viewing a File's Revision Log], page 107). Log messages may contain more than one line of text; type a period ('.') on a line by itself to end the entry.

For example, suppose the file 'novel' contains this text:

```
This is a tale about many things, including a long voyage across
America.
```

- To check in the file 'novel' with RCS, type:

```
$ ci novel (RET)
novel,v  <--  novel
enter description, terminated with single '.' or end of file:
NOTE: This is NOT the log message!
>> The Great American Novel. (RET)
>> . (RET)
$
```

This command deposits the file in an RCS repository file called 'novel,v', and the original file, 'novel', is removed. To edit or access the file again, you must check out a revision of the file from RCS with which to work (see Recipe 8.7.2 [Checking Out a File Revision], page 106).

Whenever you have a new revision that you want to save, use `ci` as before to check in the file. This begins the process all over again.

For example, suppose you have checked out the first revision of 'novel' and changed the file so that it now looks like this:

```
This is a very long tale about a great many things, including my long
voyage across America, and back home again.
```

- To deposit this revision in RCS, type:

```
$ ci novel (RET)
novel,v  <--  novel
new revision: 1.2; previous revision: 1.1
enter log message, terminated with single '.' or end of file:
>> Second draft. (RET)
>> . (RET)
$
```

If you create a subdirectory called 'RCS' (in all uppercase letters) in the current directory, RCS recognizes this specially named directory instead of the current directory as the place to store the ',v' revision files. This helps reduce clutter in the directory you are working in.

If the file you are depositing is a text file, you can have RCS insert a line of text, every time the file is checked out, containing the name of the file, the revision number, the date and time in the UTC (Coordinated Universal Time) time zone, and the user ID of the author. To do this, put the text 'Id' at a place in the file where you want this text to be written. You only need to do this once; each time you check the file out, RCS replaces this string in the file with the header text.

For example, this chapter was written to a file, 'managing-files.texinfo', whose revisions were tracked with RCS; the 'Id' string in this file currently reads:

```
$Id: managing-files.texinfo,v 1.32 2001/05/16 16:57:58 m Exp m $
```

8.7.2 Checking Out a File Revision

Use `co` to check out a revision of a file from an RCS repository.

To check out the latest revision of a file that you intend to edit (and to check in later as a new revision), use the `-l` (for "lock") option. Locking a revision in this fashion prevents overlapping changes being made to the file should another revision be accidentally checked out before this revision is checked in.

- To check out the latest revision of the file 'novel' for editing, type:

    $ *co -l novel* (RET)

This command checks out the latest revision of file 'novel' from the 'novel,v' repository, writing it to a file called 'novel' in the current directory. (If a file with that name already exists in the current directory, `co` asks whether or not to overwrite the file.) You can make changes to this file and then check it in as a new revision (see Recipe 8.7.1 [Checking In a File Revision], page 105).

You can also check out a version of a file as *read only*, where changes cannot be written to it. Do this to check out a version to view only and not to edit.

To check out the current version of a file for examination, type *co* followed by the name of the file.

- To check out the current revision of file 'novel', but not permit changes to it, type:

    $ *co novel* (RET)

This command checks out the latest revision of the file 'novel' from the RCS repository 'novel,v' (either from the current directory or in a subdirectory named 'RCS').

To check out a version other than the most recent version, specify the version number to check out with the '-r' option. Again, use the '-l' option to allow the revision to be edited.

- To check out revision 1.14 of file 'novel', type:

    $ *co -l -r1.14 novel* (RET)

NOTE: Before checking out an old revision of a file, remember to check in the latest changes first, or they may be lost.

8.7.3 Viewing a File's Revision Log

Use `rlog` to view the RCS revision log for a file—type *rlog* followed by the name of a file to list all of the revisions of that file.

- To view the revision log for file 'novel', type:

```
$ rlog novel (RET)

RCS file: novel,v
Working file: novel
head: 1.2
branch:
locks: strict
access list:
symbolic names:
keyword substitution: kv
total revisions: 2;    selected revisions: 2
description:
The Great American Novel.
----------------------------
revision 1.2
date: 1991/06/20 15:31:44;  author: leo;  state: Exp;  lines: +2 -2
Second draft.
----------------------------
revision 1.1
date: 1991/06/21 19:03:58;  author: leo;  state: Exp;
Initial revision
=====================================================================
$
```

This command outputs the revision log for the file 'novel'; it lists information about the RCS repository, including its name ('novel,v') and the name of the actual file ('novel'). It also shows that there are two revisions—the first, which was checked in to RCS on 20 June 1991, and the second, which was checked in to RCS the next day, on 21 June 1991.

PART THREE: Text

9 Viewing Text

Dealing with textual matter is the meat of Linux (and of most computing), so there are going to be many chapters about the various aspects of text. This first chapter in this part of the book shows how to *view* text on your display screen.

There are many ways to view or otherwise output text. When your intention is to edit the text of a file, open it in a text editor, as described in Chapter 10 [Text Editing], page 119.

Some kinds of files—such as PostScript, DVI, and PDF files—often contain text in them, but they are technically not text files. These are image format files, and I describe methods for viewing them in Recipe 17.1 [Previewing Print Files], page 207.

NOTE: To learn how to browse files and their contents in a Web browser, see Recipe 5.9 [Browsing Files], page 81.

9.1 Perusing Text

Use `less` to peruse text, viewing it one screen (or "page") at a time. The `less` tool works on either files or standard output—it is popularly used as the last command on a pipeline so that you can page through the text output of some commands. For an example, see Recipe 3.2.4 [Redirecting Output to Another Command's Input], page 40.

`zless` is identical to `less`, but you use it to view compressed text files; it allows you to read a compressed text file's contents without having to uncompress it first (see Recipe 8.5 [Compressed Files], page 102). Most of the system documentation in the '`/usr/doc`' and '`/usr/share/doc`' directories, for example, consists of compressed text files.

You may, on occasion, be confronted with a reference to a command for paging text called `more`. It was the standard tool for paging text until it gave way to `less` in the early to mid-1990s; `less` comes with many more options—its most notable advantage being the ability to scroll *backward* through a file—but at the expense of being almost exactly three times the size of `more`. Hence there are two meanings to the saying, "less is more."

9.1.1 Perusing a Text File

To peruse or page through a text file, give the name of the file as an argument to `less`.

- To page through the text file '`README`', type:

      $ *less README* (RET)

This command starts `less` and displays the file '`README`' on the screen.

You can more forward through the document a line at a time by typing (↓), and you can move forward through the document a screenful at a time by typing (PgDn). To move backward by a line, type (↑), and type (PgUp) to move backward by a screenful.

You can also search through the text you are currently perusing—this is described in Recipe 14.7 [Searching Text in Less], page 175.

To stop viewing and exit `less`, press (Q).

9.1.2 Perusing Multiple Text Files

You can specify more than one file to page through with `less`, and you can specify file patterns in order to open all of the files that match that pattern.

- To page through all of the Unix FAQ files in '`/usr/doc/FAQ`', type:

  $ *less /usr/doc/FAQ/unix-faq-part** (RET)

This command starts `less`, opens in it all of the files that match the given pattern '`/usr/doc/FAQ/unix-faq-part*`', and begins displaying the first one:

```
            Path: senator-bedfellow.mit.edu!faqserv
            From: tmatimar@isgtec.com (Ted Timar)
            Newsgroups: comp.unix.questions,comp.unix.shell,comp.answers,news.answers
            Subject: Unix - Frequently Asked Questions (1/7) [Frequent posting]
            Supersedes: <unix-faq/faq/part1_869650053@rtfm.mit.edu>
            Followup-To: comp.unix.questions
            Date: 31 Jul 1997 07:55:27 GMT
            Organization: ISG Technologies, Inc
            Lines: 413
            Approved: news-answers-request@MIT.Edu
            Distribution: world
            Expires: 28 Aug 1997 07:55:05 GMT
            Message-ID: <unix-faq/faq/part1_870335705@rtfm.mit.edu>
            References: <unix-faq/faq/contents_870335705@rtfm.mit.edu>
            NNTP-Posting-Host: penguin-lust.mit.edu
            X-Last-Updated: 1996/06/11
            Originator: faqserv@penguin-lust.MIT.EDU
            Xref: senator-bedfellow.mit.edu comp.unix.questions:131651 comp.unix.shell:52166
             comp.answers:27315 news.answers:108512

            Archive-name: unix-faq/faq/part1
            Version: $Id: part1,v 2.9 1996/06/11 13:07:56 tmatimar Exp $

/usr/doc/FAQ/unix-faq-part1 (file 1 of 7)
```

NOTE: When you specify more than one file to page, `less` displays each file in turn, beginning with the first file you specify or the first file that matches the given pattern. To move to the next file, press (N); to move to the previous file, press (P).

9.1.3 Commands Available While Perusing Text

The following table gives a summary of the keyboard commands that you can use while paging through text in `less`. It lists the keystrokes and describes the commands.

KEYSTROKE	COMMAND
(↑)	Scroll back through the text ("up") one line.
(↓)	Scroll forward through the text ("down") one line.
(←) *or* (→)	Scroll horizontally (left or right) one tab stop; useful for perusing files that contain long lines.
(PgUp) *or* (SPC)	Scroll forward through the text by one screenful.
(PgDn)	Scroll backward through the text by one screenful.
C-l	Redraw the screen.

/pattern	Search forward through the file for lines containing *pattern*.
?pattern	Search backward through the file for lines containing *pattern*.
<	Move to beginning of the file.
>	Move to end of the file.
h	Display a help screen.
q	Quit viewing the file and exit less.

9.2 Outputting Text

The simplest way to view text is to output it to standard output. This is useful for quickly looking at part of a text, or for passing part of a text to other tools in a command line.

Many people still use cat to view a text file, especially if it is a very small file. To output all of a file's contents on the screen, use cat and give the file name as an argument.

This isn't always the best way to peruse or read text—a very large text will scroll off the top of the screen, for example—but sometimes the simple outputting of text is quite appropriate, such as when you just want to output one line of a file, or when you want to output several files into one new file.

This section describes the tools used for such purposes. These tools are best used as filters, often at the end of a pipeline, outputting the standard input from other commands.

NOTE: Tools and methods for outputting text for printing, such as outputting text in a font, are described in Recipe 15.2 [Converting Plain Text for Output], page 179.

9.2.1 Showing Non-printing Characters

Use cat with the '-v' option to output non-printing characters, such as control characters, in such a way so that you can see them. With this option, cat outputs those characters in *hat notation*, where they are represented by a '^' and the character corresponding to the actual control character (for example, a bell character would be output as '^G').

- To peruse the file 'translation' with non-printing characters displayed in hat notation, type:

    $ cat -v translation | less (RET)

In this example, the output of cat is piped to less for viewing on the screen; you could have piped it to another command, or redirected it to a file instead.

To visually display the end of each line, use the '-E' option; it specifies that a '$' should be output after the end of each line. This is useful for determining whether lines contain trailing space characters.

Also useful is the '-T' option, which outputs tab characters as '^I'.

The '-A' option combines all three of these options—it is the same as specifying '-vET'.

9.2.2 Outputting a Beginning Part of a Text

Use **head** to output the beginning of a text. By default, it outputs the first ten lines of its input.

- To output the first ten lines of file 'placement-list', type:

    $ *head placement-list* (RET)

You can specify as a numeric option the number of lines to output. If you specify more lines than a file contains, **head** just outputs the entire text.

- To output the first line of file 'placement-list', type:

    $ *head -1 placement-list* (RET)

- To output the first sixty-six lines of file 'placement-list', type:

    $ *head -66 placement-list* (RET)

To output a given number of *characters* instead of lines, give the number of characters to output as an argument to the '-c' option.

- To output the first character in the file 'placement-list', type:

    $ *head -c1 placement-list* (RET)

9.2.3 Outputting an Ending Part of a Text

The **tail** tool works like **head**, but outputs the last part of its input. Like **head**, it outputs ten lines by default.

- To output the last ten lines of file 'placement-list', type:

    $ *tail placement-list* (RET)

- To output the last fourteen lines of file 'placement-list', type:

    $ *tail -14 placement-list* (RET)

It is sometimes useful to view the end of a file on a continuing basis; this can be useful for a "growing" file, a file that is being written to by another process. To keep viewing the end of such a file, use **tail** with the '-f' ("follow") option. Type *C-c* to stop viewing the file.

- To follow the end of the file 'access_log', type:

    $ *tail -f access_log* (RET)

NOTE: You can achieve the same result with **less**; to do this, type *F* while perusing the text (see Recipe 9.1 [Perusing Text], page 111).

9.2.4 Outputting a Middle Part of a Text

There are a few ways to output only a middle portion of a text.

To output a particular line of a file, use the **sed** tool (see Recipe 10.5 [Editing Streams of Text], page 129). Give as a quoted argument the line number to output followed by '!d'. Give the file name as the second argument.

- To output line 47 of file 'placement-list', type:

    $ *sed '47!d' placement-list* (RET)

To output a region of more than one line, give the starting and ending line numbers, separated by a comma.

- To output lines 47 to 108 of file 'placement-list', type:

    ```
    $ sed '47,108!d' placement-list (RET)
    ```

You can also combine multiple **head** or **tail** commands on a pipeline to get the desired result (see Recipe 3.2.4 [Redirecting Output to Another Command's Input], page 40).

- To output the tenth line in the file 'placement-list', type:

    ```
    $ head placement-list | tail -1 (RET)
    ```

- To output the fifth and fourth lines from the bottom of file 'placement-list', type:

    ```
    $ tail -5 placement-list | head -2 (RET)
    ```

- To output the 500th character in 'placement-list', type:

    ```
    $ head -c500 placement-list | tail -c1 (RET)
    ```

- To output the first character on the fifth line of the file 'placement-list', type:

    ```
    $ head -5 placement-list | tail -1 | head -c1 (RET)
    ```

In the preceding example, three commands were used: the first five lines of the file 'placement-list' are passed to tail, which outputs the last line in the output (the fifth line in the file); then, the last **head** command outputs the first character in that last line, which achieves the desired result.

9.2.5 Outputting the Text between Strings

Use **sed** to select lines of text between strings and output either just that section of text, or all of the lines of text *except* that section. The strings can be words or even regular expressions (see Recipe 14.2 [Regular Expressions—Matching Text Patterns], page 166).

Use the '-n' option followed by ''/*first*/,/*last*/p'' to output just the text between the strings *first* and *last*, inclusive. This is useful for outputting, say, just one chapter or section of a text file when you know the text used to begin the sections with.

- To output all the text from file 'book-draft' between 'Chapter 3' and 'Chapter 4', type:

    ```
    $ sed -n '/Chapter 3/,/Chapter 4/p' book-draft (RET)
    ```

To output all of the lines of text *except* those between two patterns, omit the '-n' option.

- To output all the text from file 'book-draft', except that which lies between the text 'Chapter 3' and 'Chapter 4', type:

    ```
    $ sed '/Chapter 3/,/Chapter 4/p' book-draft (RET)
    ```

NOTE: For a more thorough introduction to **sed**, see Recipe 10.5 [Editing Streams of Text], page 129.

9.2.6 Outputting Text in a Dialect

Debian: 'filters'
WWW: http://www.princeton.edu/~mkporwit/pub_links/davido/slang/
WWW: http://www.mathlab.sunysb.edu/~elijah/src.html

There are all kinds of tools that work as filters on text; this recipe describes a specific group of filters—those that filter their standard input to give the text an accent or dialect, and are intended to be humorous.

Generally speaking, a *filter* is a tool that works on standard input, changing it in some way, and then passing it to standard output.

- To apply the `kraut` filter to the text in the file '/etc/motd', type:

    $ *cat /etc/motd | kraut* (RET)

These commands pass the contents of the file '/etc/motd' to the `kraut` filter, whose output is then sent to standard output. The contents of '/etc/motd' are not changed.

Some of the dialect filters available include `nyc`, which gives a "New Yawker" dialect to text, and `newspeak`, which translates text into the approved language of the thought police, as described in George Orwell's novel, *1984*. Hail Big Brother!

9.3 Streaming Text

WWW: http://www.maurer-it.com/open-source/sview/

It's been demonstrated that people read and comprehend printed text faster than they read and comprehend text displayed on a computer display screen. Rapid serial visual presentation, or RSVP, is a technique that aims to increase reading speed and comprehension with the use of computer display screens. With this technique, text is displayed *streamed* on the screen, one word at a time, with pauses between words and punctuation. The average reading time is lowered and comprehension is increased significantly with this technique.

GNOME `sview` is a "streaming viewer" for X; it streams text a word at a time on the screen, at a default rate of 450 words per minute. Use it to read text files and the X selection, which is text you have selected with the mouse (see Recipe 10.4 [Selecting Text], page 128).

To open a file in `sview`, either specify it as an argument to the command, or choose `Open` from the `File` menu in `sview`, and select the file from there.

- To view the contents of the text file 'alice-in-wonderland' in `sview`, type:

    $ *sview alice-in-wonderland* (RET)

To start streaming the text, either press Ⓢ once, or left-click on the button marked RSVP. Both Ⓢ and the RSVP button toggle the streaming; the left and right arrow keys control the speed.

Text being streamed with `sview` looks like this:

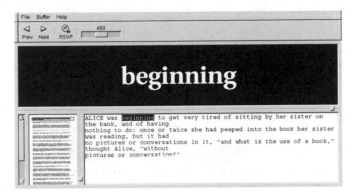

The large area with the word 'beginning' in it is where the text is being streamed. The text in the lower-left window is a shrunken view of the entire file, the text in the lower-right window is the paragraph from which the current word comes from.

To open another file, choose it from the menu; you can have many files open in `sview` at once. `sview` places each file in its own buffer. You can also paste the X selection into a buffer of its own—to switch to a different buffer, choose its name from the `Buffer` menu.

Type ⟨Q⟩ to quit reading and exit `sview`.

The following table lists the keyboard commands used in `sview` and describes their meaning.

KEYSTROKE	DESCRIPTION
⟨←⟩	Decrease the stream speed.
⟨→⟩	Increase the stream speed.
C-o	Open a file.
C-q	Quit viewing text and exit `sview`.
C-w	Erase the current text buffer.
M-n	Move forward to the next word.
M-p	Move backward to the previous word.
⟨S⟩	Toggle the streaming of text.
⟨X⟩	Display the X selection in its own buffer.
⟨N⟩	Move forward to the next paragraph.
⟨P⟩	Move backward to the previous paragraph.

9.4 Viewing a Character Chart

To view a character chart containing a list of all the valid characters in the ASCII character set and the character codes to use to type them, view the `ascii man` page.

- To view an ASCII character set, type:

    $ `man ascii` (RET)

You can use the octal codes listed for each character to type them in Emacs—see Recipe 10.2.5 [Inserting Special Characters in Emacs], page 126.

The default Linux character set, the ISO 8859-1 ("Latin 1") character set, contains all of the standard ASCII character set plus an additional 128 characters.

To view the ISO 8859-1 character set, which contains an extended set of characters above the standard 127 ASCII characters, view the `iso_8859_1` `man` page.

- To view the ISO 8859-1 character set, type:

    $ `man iso_8859_1` (RET)

You can use this page to see all of the characters in this character set and how to input them.

NOTE: There's a special way to "quote" these characters in Emacs; this technique is described in Recipe 10.2.5 [Inserting Special Characters in Emacs], page 126.

The '`miscfiles`' package also contains charts for these character sets, as explained in Recipe 11.4 [Word Lists and Reference Files], page 145.

10 Text Editing

Text editing is one of the most fundamental activities of computing on Linux-based systems, or most any computer for that matter. We edit text when writing a document, sending email, making a Web page, posting an article for Usenet, programming—and the list goes on. Most people spend a good deal of their computing time editing text with a text editor application.

There are a lot of text editors to choose from on Linux systems, as the first recipe in this chapter shows, but the majority of editors fit in one of two families of editor: Emacs and Vi. Most users prefer one or the other; rarely is one adept at both. I give more coverage to Emacs, and not only because it's my preferred editor—its keystroke commands are used by default in many other tools and applications, including the `bash` shell (see Chapter 3 [The Shell], page 35).

10.1 Choosing the Perfect Text Editor

The following table describes some of the more interesting text editors available, and includes information about their special traits and characteristics.

TEXT EDITOR	DESCRIPTION
ae	Anthony's Editor, ae, is a simple, easy-to-use text editor. It has modes to emulate the behavior of other text editors. Debian: 'ae' WWW: http://dmoz.org/Computers/Software/Editors/Vi/
cooledit	Cooledit is a popular, fast text editor for use in X; its features include anti-aliased fonts, Unicode support, and extensibility via the Python programming language. Debian: 'cooledit' WWW: http://cooledit.sourceforge.net/
dedit	DEdit is a simple editor for use in X with GNOME installed. It can read compressed files and display Japanese characters. Debian: 'dedit'
ee	Intended to be an editor that novices can begin using immediately, the Easy Editor features pop-up menus. Debian: 'ee' WWW: http://mahon.cwx.net/
elvis	Elvis is a modern implementation of Vi that comes with many new features and extensions. Debian: 'elvis' WWW: http://www.fh-wedel.de/elvis/
emacs	Emacs is one of the two most-popular text editors. I've devoted an entire section to it in this book: Recipe 10.2 [Emacs], page 121. Debian: 'emacsen-common' Debian: 'emacs20' WWW: 'http://www.emacs.org/'

jed John E. Davis's `jed` offers many of the conveniences of Emacs and is geared specifically toward programmers. It loads quickly, and makes editing files at a shell prompt easy and fast.
Debian: 'jed'
WWW: `http://space.mit.edu/~davis/jed.html`

joe Joe's Own Editor, `joe`, is a full-screen editor with a look and feel reminiscent of old DOS text editors like EDIT.
Debian: 'joe'
WWW: `ftp://ftp.std.com/src/editors/`

nano Nano is a free software editor inspired by Pico, the editor that is included with the University of Washington's proprietary Pine email program. It's also faster than Pico, and comes with more features.
Debian: 'nano'
WWW: `http://www.nano-editor.org/`

ted Ted is a WYSIWYG text editor for use in X which reads and writes '.rtf' files in Microsoft's "Rich Text Format."
Debian: 'ted'
WWW: `http://www.nllgg.nl/Ted/`

the The Hessling Editor is a configurable editor that uses the Rexx macro language. It was inspired by the XEDIT editor for VM/CMS and the Kedit editor for DOS.
Debian: 'the'
Debian: 'the-doc'
WWW: `http://www.lightlink.com/hessling/THE/`

vi Vi (pronounced "vye," or sometimes "vee-eye") is a *visual*, or full-screen, editor. Touch typists often find its keystroke commands enable very fast editing.
Together with Emacs, Vi shares the spotlight for most popular editor on Linux and Unix-based systems in general. Both were initially written in the same period, and both have their staunch adherents. To run a hands-on tutorial, see Recipe 10.3 [Running a Vi Tutorial], page 128.
Debian: 'nvi'
WWW: `ftp://mongoose.bostic.com/pub/nvi.tar.gz`

vim Like the Elvis editor, Vim ("Vi improved") is a modern implementation of Vi whose new features include syntax coloring, scrollbars and menus, mouse support, and built-in help.
Debian: 'vim'
WWW: `http://www.vim.org/`

wily Wily, an interesting mouse-centric editor, is inspired by the Acme editor from AT&T's Plan 9 experimental operating system. Wily commands consist of various combinations of the three mouse buttons, called *chords*, which can be tricky to master.
Debian: 'wily'
WWW: `http://www.cs.su.oz.au/~gary/wily/`

xedit   Xedit is a simple text editor that comes with, and works in, X. It
                        lets you insert, delete, copy and paste text as well as open and save
                        files—the very basics.
                        Debian: 'xcontrib'

xemacs   XEmacs is a version of Emacs with advanced capabilities for use in X,
                        including the ability to display images.
                        Debian: 'emacsen-common'
                        Debian: 'xemacs'
                        WWW: http://www.xemacs.org/

10.2 Emacs

Debian: 'emacsen-common'
WWW: 'http://www.emacs.org/'

To call Emacs a text editor does not do it justice—it's a large application capable of performing many functions, including reading email and Usenet news, browsing the World
Wide Web, and even perfunctory psychoanalysis.

There is more than one version of Emacs. GNU Emacs is the Emacs released under
the auspices of Richard Stallman, who wrote the original Emacs predecessor in the 1970s.
XEmacs (formerly Lucid Emacs) offers essentially the same features GNU Emacs does, but
also contains its own features for use with the X Window System (it also behaves differently
from GNU Emacs in some minor ways).

GNU Emacs and XEmacs are by far the most popular emacsen (as they are referred to
in number); other flavors include jed (described in the previous section) and Chet's Emacs,
ce, developed by a programmer at Case Western Reserve University.

Following is a brief introduction to using Emacs, interspersed with the necessary Emacs
jargon; following that are recipes that describe how to use some of Emacs's advanced editing
features.

10.2.1 Getting Acquainted with Emacs

Start Emacs in the usual way, either by choosing it from the menu supplied by your window
manager in X, or by typing its name (in lowercase letters) at a shell prompt.

- To start GNU Emacs at a shell prompt, type:

    $ *emacs* (RET)

- To start XEmacs at a shell prompt, type:

    $ *xemacs* (RET)

Upon startup in X, a typical GNU Emacs window looks like this (the window frame will differ depending on your window manager):

The welcome message appears when Emacs first starts, and it tells you, among other things, how to run a tutorial (which we'll look at in just a minute).

The top bar is called the *menu bar*, and you can pull down its menus with the mouse (or, in the console, with *C*-F10).

A file or other text open in Emacs is held in its own area called a *buffer*. By default, the current buffer appears in the large area underneath the menu bar. To write text in the buffer, just type it. The place in the buffer where the cursor is at is called *point*, and is referenced by many Emacs commands.

The horizontal bar near the bottom of the Emacs window and directly underneath the current buffer is called the *mode line*; it gives information about the current buffer, including its name, what percentage of the buffer fits on the screen, what line point is on, and whether or not the buffer is saved to a file.

The mode line also lists the modes active in the buffer. Emacs *modes* are general states that control the way Emacs behaves—for example, when `Overwrite` mode is set, text you type *overwrites* the text at point; in `Insert` mode (the default), text you type is *inserted* at point. Usually, either `Fundamental` mode (the default) or `Text` mode will be listed.

The *echo area* is where Emacs writes brief status messages, such as error messages; it is the last line in the Emacs window. When you type a command that requires input, that input is requested in this area (and when that happens, the place you type your input, in the echo area, is then called the *minibuffer*).

Emacs commands usually begin with a Control or Meta (Escape) key sequence; many commands begin with the *C*-*x* sequence, which you type by pressing and holding the CTRL key and then pressing the X key (see [Typographical Conventions], page 3).

Because Emacs is different in culture from the editors and approach of the Microsoft Windows and Apple MacOS world, it has gotten a rather unfounded reputation in those corners that it is odd and difficult to use. This is not so. The keyboard commands to run its various functions are designed for ease of use and easy recall.

For example, the `find-file` function prompts for the name of a file and opens a copy of the file in a new buffer; its keyboard accelerator is `C-x C-f` (you can keep (CTRL) depressed while you press and release the (X) and (F) keys).

You can run any Emacs function by typing `M-x` followed by the function name and pressing (RET).

- To run the `find-file` function, type:

    `M-x find-file` (RET)

This command runs the `find-file` function, which prompts for the name of a file and opens a copy of the file in a new buffer.

Type `C-g` in Emacs to quit a function or command; if you make a mistake when typing a command, this is useful to cancel and abort the keyboard input.

Now that we have run through the essential Emacs terminology, I'll show you how to exit the program—just type `C-x C-c`.

Emacs can have more than one buffer open at once. To switch between buffers, type `C-x C-b`. Then, give the name of the buffer to switch to, followed by (RET); alternatively, type (RET) without a buffer name to switch to the last buffer you had visited. (Viewing a buffer in Emacs is called *visiting* the buffer.)

- To switch to a buffer called 'rolo', type:

    `C-x C-b rolo` (RET)

A special buffer called '*scratch*' is for notes and things you don't want to save; it always exists in Emacs.

- To switch to the '*scratch*' buffer, type:

    `C-x C-b *scratch*` (RET)

Any file names you give as an argument to `emacs` will open in separate buffers:

    `$ emacs todo rolo /usr/local/src/nirvarna/README` (RET)

(You can also make new buffers and open files in buffers later, of course.)

Emacs comes with an interactive, self-paced tutorial that teaches you how to use the basics. In my experience, setting aside 25 minutes to go through the tutorial is one of the best things you can do in your computing career—even if you decide that you don't like Emacs very much, a great many other applications use Emacs-like keyboard commands and heuristics, so familiarizing yourself with them will always pay off.

To start the tutorial at any time when you are in Emacs, type `C-h t`.

Incidentally, `C-h` is the Emacs help key; all help-related commands begin with this key. For example, to read the *Emacs FAQ*, type `C-h F`, and to run the Info documentation browser (which contains *The GNU Emacs Manual*), type `C-h i`.

10.2.2 Basic Emacs Editing Keys

The following table lists basic editing keys and describes their function. Where two common keystrokes are available for a function, both are given.

KEYS	DESCRIPTION
(↑) *or* C-p	Move point up to the previous line.
(↓) *or* C-n	Move point down to the next line.
(←) *or* C-b	Move point *back* through the buffer one character to the left.
(→) *or* C-f	Move point *forward* through the buffer one character to the right.
(PgUp) *or* C-v	Move point forward through the buffer one screenful.
(PgDn) *or* M-v	Move point backward through the buffer one screenful.
(BKSP) *or* C-h	Delete character to the left of point.
(DEL) *or* C-d	Delete character to the right of point.
(INS)	Toggles between **Insert** mode and **Overwrite** mode.
(Shift)-(INS) *or* C-y	Yank text in the kill ring at point (see Recipe 10.4.2 [Pasting Text], page 129).
C-(SPC)	Set mark (see Recipe 10.4.1 [Cutting Text], page 129).
C-_	Undo the last action (control-underscore).
C-a	Move point to the beginning of the current line.
C-e	Move point to the end of the current line.
C-g	Cancel the current command.
C-h F	Open a copy of the *Emacs FAQ* in a new buffer.
C-h a *function* (RET)	List all Emacs commands related to *function*.
C-h i	Start Info.
C-h k *key*	Describe key.
C-h t	Start the Emacs tutorial.
C-k	Kill text from point to end of line.
C-l	Re-center the text in the Emacs window, placing the line where point is in the middle of the screen.
C-t	Transpose the character at point with the character to the left of point.
C-u *number*	Repeat the next command or keystroke you type *number* times.
C-w	Kill text from mark to point.
C-x C-c	Save all buffers open in Emacs, and then exit the program.

C-x C-f *file* (RET)	Open *file* in a new buffer for editing. To create a new file that does not yet exist, just specify the file name you want to give it. To browse through your files, type (TAB) instead of a file name.
C-*left-click*	Display a menu of all open buffers, sorted by major mode (works in X only).
(SHIFT)-*left-click*	Display a font selection menu (works in X only).

10.2.3 Making Abbreviations in Emacs

An *abbrev* is a word that is an *abbreviation* of a (usually) longer word or phrase. Abbrevs exist as a convenience to you—you can define abbrevs to expand to a long phrase that is inconvenient to type, or you can define a misspelling that you tend to make to expand to its correct spelling. Abbrevs only expand when you have **Abbrev** mode enabled.

- To turn on **Abbrev** mode, type:

     M-x abbrev-mode (RET)

To define an abbrev, type the abbrev you want to use and then type *C-x aig*. Emacs will prompt in the minibuffer for the text you want the abbrev to expand to; type that text and then type (RET).

- To define 'rbf' as an abbrev for 'R. Buckminster Fuller', do the following:
    - First, type the abbrev itself:

         rbf
    - Next, specify that this text is to be an abbrev; type:

         C-x aig
    - Now type the text to expand it to:

         Global expansion for "rbf": *R. Buckminster Fuller* (RET)

Now, whenever you type 'rbf' followed by a whitespace or punctuation character in the current buffer, that text will expand to the text 'R. Buckminster Fuller'.

To save the abbrevs you have defined so that you can use them later, use the **write-abbrev-file** function. This saves all of the abbrevs currently defined to a file that you can read in a future Emacs session. (You can also open the file in a buffer and edit the abbrevs if you like.)

- To save the abbrevs you have currently defined to a file '~/.misspelling-abbrevs', type:

     M-x write-abbrev-file (RET) *~/.misspelling-abbrevs* (RET)

Then, in a future Emacs session, you can use the **read-abbrev-file** function to define those abbrevs for that session.

- To read the abbrevs from the file '~/.misspelling-abbrevs', and define them for the current session, type:

     M-x read-abbrev-file (RET) *~/.misspelling-abbrevs* (RET)

NOTE: Emacs mode commands are toggles. So to turn off **Abbrev** mode in a buffer, just type *M-x abbrev-mode* (RET) again. If you turn **Abbrev** mode on in that buffer later on during the Emacs session, the abbrevs will be remembered and will expand again.

10.2.4 Recording and Running Macros in Emacs

A *macro* is like a recording of a sequence of keystrokes—when you run a macro, Emacs executes that key sequence as if you had typed them.

To begin recording a macro, type *C-x (*. Then, everything you type is recorded as the macro until you stop recording by typing *C-x)*. After you have recorded a macro, you can play it back at any time during the Emacs session by typing *C-x e*. You can precede it with the `universal-argument` command, *C-u*, to specify a number of times to play it back.

- To record a macro that capitalizes the first word of the current line (*M-c* capitalizes the word to the right of point) and then advances to the next line, type:

    C-x (C-a M-c C-n C-x)

- To play the macro back 20 times, type:

    C-u 20 C-x e

Macros are primary to how Emacs works—in fact, the name Emacs is derived from 'Editing MACroS', because the first version of Emacs in 1976 was actually a collection of such macros written for another text editor.

10.2.5 Inserting Special Characters in Emacs

There are some characters that you cannot normally type into an Emacs buffer. For example, in a text file, you can specify a page break by inserting the formfeed character, ASCII *C-l* or octal code 014; when you print a file with formfeeds, the current page is ejected at this character and printing is resumed on a new page.

However, *C-l* has meaning as an Emacs command. To insert a character like this, use the `quoted-insert` function, *C-q*. It takes either a literal keystroke to insert, or the octal code of the character to insert. It inserts that character at point.

- To insert a formfeed character at point by specifying its actual keystroke (*C-l*), type:

    C-q C-l

- To insert a formfeed character at point by specifying its octal character code, type:

    C-q 014 (RET)

The preceding examples both do the same thing: they insert a formfeed character at point.

An interesting use of *C-q* is to underline text. To do this, insert a literal *C-h* character followed by an underscore ('_') after each character you want to underline.

- To underline the character before point, type:

    C-q C-h _

You can then use `ul` to output the text to the screen (see Recipe 13.3 [Underlining Text], page 160).

Another kind of special character insert you might want to make is for accented characters and other characters used in various languages.

To insert an accented character, use `ISO Accents` mode. When this mode is active, you can type a special accent character followed by the character to be accented, and the proper accented character will be inserted at point.

The following table shows the special accent characters and the key combinations to use.

PREFIX...	PLUS THIS LETTER	YIELDS THIS RESULT
"	a	ä
"	e	ë
"	i	ï
"	o	ö
"	u	ü
"	s	ß
'	a	á
'	e	é
'	i	í
'	o	ó
'	u	ú
`	a	à
`	e	è
`	i	ì
`	o	ò
`	u	ù
~	a	ã
~	c	ç
~	d	đ
~	n	ñ
~	t	ŧ
~	u	ũ
~	<	«
~	>	»
~	!	¡
~	?	¿
^	a	â
^	e	ê
^	i	î
^	o	ô
^	u	û
/	a	å
/	e	æ
/	o	ø

When a buffer contains accented characters, it can no longer be saved as plain ASCII text, but must instead be saved as text in the ISO-8859-1 character set (see Recipe 9.4 [Viewing a Character Chart], page 117). When you save a buffer, Emacs will notify you that it must do this.

- To type the line 'Emacs ist spaß!' in the current buffer, type:

  ```
  M-x iso-accents-mode (RET)
  Emacs ist spa"ss!
  ```

In the event that you want to type the literal key combinations that make up an accented character in a buffer where you have ISO Accents mode on, type the prefix character twice.

- To type the text `''o` (and not the accent character ó) in a buffer while ISO Accents mode is on, type:

      ''o

NOTE: GNU Emacs has recently added a number of internationalization functions. A complete discussion of their use is out of the scope of this book; for more information on this topic, see recipe "International Character Set Support" in *The GNU Emacs Manual*.

10.3 Running a Vi Tutorial

Debian: 'nvi'
WWW: `ftp://mongoose.bostic.com/pub/nvi.tar.gz`
WWW: `http://www.cs.cmu.edu/~vaschelp/Editors/Vi/`

The Vi editor comes with a hands-on, self-paced tutorial, which you can use in vi to learn how to use it. It's stored as a compressed file in the '/usr/doc/nvi' directory; copy this file to your home directory, uncompress it, and open it with vi to start the tutorial.

- To run the vi tutorial, type the following from your home directory:

```
$ cp /usr/doc/nvi/vi.beginner.gz .  RET
$ gunzip vi.beginner  RET
$ vi vi.beginner  RET
```

NOTE: An advanced tutorial is also available in '/usr/doc/nvi'.

10.4 Selecting Text

In X, you can cut and paste text between other windows, including xterm and Emacs windows. The most recently selected text is called the *X selection*.

In the console, you can cut and paste text in the same virtual console or into a different virtual console. To do this, you need the gpm package installed and set up for your mouse (it's a default, recommended package).

The operations described in this section work the same both in X and in virtual consoles. You cannot presently cut and paste text between X and a virtual console.

Three buttons on the mouse are used for cutting and pasting. If you have a two-button mouse, your administrator can set it to emulate three buttons—to specify the middle button, press the left and right buttons simultaneously.

Click the left mouse button and drag the mouse over text to select it. You can also double-click the left mouse button on a word to select that word, and triple-click the left mouse button on a line to select that line. Furthermore, you can click the left mouse button at one end of a portion of text you want to select, and then click the right mouse button at the other end to select all of the text between the points.

NOTE: In an `xterm` window, when you're running a tool or application locally in a shell (such as the `lynx` Web browser), the left mouse button alone won't work. When this happens, press and hold the (SHIFT) key while using the mouse to select text.

10.4.1 Cutting Text

You don't have to select text to cut it. At a shell prompt or in Emacs, type *C-k* to cut the text from the cursor to the end of the line.

In Emacs parlance, cutting text is known as *killing* text. Emacs has additional commands for killing text:

- When you have selected an area of text with the mouse as described previously, you can type (Shift)-(DEL) to delete it.

- You can also click the left mouse button at one end of an area of text and then double-click the right mouse button at the other end of the area to kill the area of text.

- Finally, to kill a large portion of text in an Emacs buffer, set the *mark* at one end of the text by moving point to that end and typing *C-*(SPC). Then, move point to the other end of the text, and type *C-w* to kill it.

10.4.2 Pasting Text

Debian: 'xpaste'

To paste the text that was last selected with the mouse, click the middle mouse button at the place you want to paste to. You can also use the keyboard by moving the cursor to where you want to paste and then typing (Shift)-(INS). These commands work both in X and in the console.

In X, to display the contents of the X selection in its own window, run the `xpaste` X client; its only purpose in life is to display this text in its window.

In Emacs, pasting text is called *yanking* the text. Emacs offers the additional key, *C-y* ("yank"), to yank the text that was last selected or killed. This key also works in the `bash` shell, where it pastes the last text that was killed with *C-k* in that shell session, if any.

10.5 Editing Streams of Text

Some of the recipes in this book that work on text use `sed`, the "stream editor." It is not a text editor in the usual sense— you don't open a file in `sed` and interactively edit it; instead, it performs editing operations on a *stream* of text sent to its standard input, and it writes the results to the standard output. This is more like a filter than an editor, and `sed` is a useful tool for formatting and searching through text.

"The seder's grab-bag" (`http://seders.icheme.org/`) is a useful collection of `sed` information including a FAQ and many example scripts.

The `sed` "one-liners" (`http://www-h.eng.cam.ac.uk/help/tpl/unix/sed.html`) are useful commands for editing and processing text.

See Info file '`sed.info`', node '`Top`', for more information on `sed` usage.

Other tools that are good for stream editing include the AWK and Perl programming languages; to learn more about using these powerful languages, I recommend the following books:

- *The GNU Awk User's Guide* (`http://www.gnu.org/manual/gawk-3.0.3/gawk.html`)
- *Picking Up Perl* (`http://www.ebb.org/PickingUpPerl/`)

10.6 Concatenating Text

The `cat` tool gets its name because it con*cat*enates all of the text given to it, outputting the result to the standard output. It is useful for concatenating files of text together.

For example, suppose you have two files, '`early`' and '`later`'. The file '`early`' contains this text:

```
This Side of Paradise
The Beautiful and Damned
```

And the file '`later`' contains this text:

```
The Great Gatsby
Tender is the Night
The Last Tycoon
```

- To concatenate these files into a new file, '`novels`', type:

    `$ cat early later > novels` (RET)

This command redirects the standard output to a new file, '`novels`', which would then contain the following text:

```
This Side of Paradise
The Beautiful and Damned
The Great Gatsby
Tender is the Night
The Last Tycoon
```

The files '`early`' and '`later`' are not altered.

Had you typed `cat later early > novels` instead, the files would be concatenated in that reversed order instead, beginning with '`later`'; so the file '`novels`' would contain the following:

```
The Great Gatsby
Tender is the Night
The Last Tycoon
This Side of Paradise
The Beautiful and Damned
```

The following sections give other recipes for concatenating text.

NOTE: You can also use `cat` to concatenate files that are *not* text, but its most popular usage is with text files. Another way to concatenate files of text in an automated way is to use file *inclusion*—see Recipe 10.7 [Including Text Files], page 132.

A similar tool, `zcat`, reads the contents of compressed files.

10.6.1 Writing Text to Files

Sometimes, it's too much trouble to call up a text editor for a particular job—you just want
to write a text file with two lines in it, say, or you just want to append a text file with one
line. There are ways of doing these kind of micro-editing jobs without a text editor.

To write a text file without using a text editor, redirect the standard output of `cat` to
the file to write. You can then type your text, typing *C-d* on a line of its own to end the
file. This is useful when you want to quickly create a small text file, but that is about it;
usually, you open or create a text file in a text editor, as described in the previous sections
in this chapter.

- To make a file, 'novels', with some text in it, type:

```
$ cat > novels (RET)
This Side of Paradise (RET)
The Beautiful and Damned (RET)
The Great Gatsby (RET)
Tender is the Night (RET)
C-d
$
```

In this example, the text file 'novels' was created and contains four lines of text (the
last line with the *C-d* is never part of the file).

Typing text like this without an editor will sometimes do in a pinch but, if you make a
mistake, there is not much recourse besides starting over—you can type *C-u* to erase the
current line, and *C-c* to abort the whole thing and not write the text to a file at all, but
that's about it.

10.6.2 Appending Text to a File

To add text to a text file without opening the file in a text editor, use `cat` with the append
operator, '>>'. (Using '>' instead would overwrite the file.)

- To add a line of text to the bottom of file 'novels', type:

```
$ cat >> novels (RET)
The Last Tycoon (RET)
C-d
```

In this example, no files were specified to `cat` for input, so `cat` used the standard input;
then, one line of text was typed, and this text was appended to file 'novels', the file used
in the example of the previous recipe. So now this file would contain the following:

```
This Side of Paradise
The Beautiful and Damned
The Great Gatsby
Tender is the Night
The Last Tycoon
```

10.6.3 Inserting Text at the Beginning of a File

WWW: `http://dsl.org/comp/tinyutils/`

Inserting text at the *beginning* of a text file without calling up a text editor is a bit trickier than appending text to a file's end—but it *is* possible.

To insert one or more lines of text at the beginning of a file, use `ins`. Give the name of the file in which to insert text as an argument; `ins` will read lines of text from the standard input and insert them at the beginning of the file. (It works by opening the file in `ed`, a simple line editor.)

Give the EOF—that is, type `C-d` on a line by itself—to signify the end of the lines of text to insert.

- To insert several lines of text at the beginning of the file '**novels**', type:

```
$ ins novels (RET)
The Novels of F. Scott Fitzgerald (RET)
-------------------------------- (RET)
C-d
$
```

This command inserts two lines of text at the beginning of **novels**, the file used in the previous examples in this section. This file would now contain the following:

```
The Novels of F. Scott Fitzgerald
--------------------------------
This Side of Paradise
The Beautiful and Damned
The Great Gatsby
Tender is the Night
The Last Tycoon
```

10.7 Including Text Files

Debian: 'm4'

File *inclusion* is where the contents of a file can be included at a particular place within some other file, just by specifying the file's name at that place in the other file.

This is useful if you want or need to frequently rearrange divisions or sections of a document, if you need to keep a document in more than one arrangement, or if you have some sections of text that you frequently insert in more than one document. For these situations, you can keep each section in a separate file and build an *include file* that contains the file names for the various sections in the order you want to generate that file.

To include a file in a text file, specify the file to be included on a line of its own, like this:

```
include(file)
```

When you process this file for inclusion, the line with the 'include' statement is replaced with the contents of the file *file* (whose path is relative to the current directory of the include file).

Use the m4 tool, the GNU macro processor, to process an include file. It takes as an argument the name of the include file, and it outputs the inclusion to the standard output. You can use redirection to redirect the output to a file.

For example, suppose the file 'soups' contains this text:

```
Clam Chowder
Lobster Bisque
Vegetable
```

And suppose the file 'sandwiches' contains this text:

```
BLT
Ham on Rye
Roast Beef
```

And finally, suppose the file 'menu' contains this text:

```
Diner Menu For Today


Soups
-----

include(soups)


Sandwiches
----------

include(sandwiches)
```

- To process the file and write to the file 'monday.txt', type:

      $ m4 menu > monday.txt (RET)

This command writes a new file, 'monday.txt', which looks like this:

```
Diner Menu For Today


Soups
-----

Clam Chowder
Lobster Bisque
Vegetable



Sandwiches
----------

BLT
Ham on Rye
Roast Beef
```

NOTE: You can write more than one include file that will use your files—and the files themselves can have include files of their own.

This is a fairly simple use of `m4`; it can do much more, including run commands, manipulate text, and run custom macros. See Info file '`m4.info`', node '`Top`' for more information on this tool.

11 Grammar and Reference

The tools and resources for writing and editing on Linux-based systems include spell checkers, dictionaries, and reference files. This chapter shows methods for using them.

11.1 Spelling

There are several ways to spell check text and files on Linux; the following recipes show how to find the correct spellings of particular words and how to perform batch, interactive, and Emacs-based spell checks.

The system dictionary file, '`/usr/dict/words`',[1] is nothing more than a word list (albeit a very large one), sorted in alphabetical order and containing one word per line. Words that are correct regardless of case are listed in lowercase letters, and words that rely on some form of capitalization in order to be correct (such as proper nouns) appear in that form. All of the Linux spelling tools use this text file to check spelling; if a word does not appear in the dictionary file, it is considered to be misspelled.

NOTE: None of the computerized spell-check tools will correct your writing if you are using the wrong word to begin with—for example, if you have '`there`' when you mean '`their`', the computer will not catch it (yet!).

11.1.1 Finding the Correct Spelling of a Word

If you're unsure whether or not you're using the correct spelling of a word, use `spell` to find out. `spell` reads from the standard input and outputs any words not found in the system dictionary—so if a word is misspelled, it will be echoed back on the screen after you type it.

- For example, to check whether the word '`occurance`' is misspelled, type:

```
$ spell ⟨RET⟩
occurance ⟨RET⟩
occurance
C-d
$
```

In the example, `spell` echoed the word '`occurance`', meaning that this word was not in the system dictionary and therefore was quite likely a misspelling. Then, `C-d` was typed to exit `spell`.

11.1.2 Listing the Misspellings in a Text

To output a list of misspelled words in a file, give the name of the file to check as an argument to `spell`. Any misspelled words in the file are output, each on a line of its own and in the order that they appear in the file.

---

[1] On an increasing number of systems, this file is being replaced with '`/usr/share/dict/words`'; administrators should make a symbolic link from this to the shorter, preferred form.

- To spell check the file 'fall-lecture.draft', type:

```
$ spell fall-lecture.draft (RET)
occurance
willl
occurance
$
```

In this example, three words are output: 'occurance', 'willl' and 'occurance' again, meaning that these three words were found in 'fall-lecture.draft', in that order, and were not in the system dictionary (and so were probably misspelled). Note that the misspelling 'occurance' appears twice in the file.

To correct the misspellings, you could then open the file in your preferred text editor and edit it. Later in this section I'll describe an interactive spell checker that allows you to correct misspellings as they are found. Still another option is to use a text editor with spell-checking facilities built in, such as Emacs.

- To spell check the file 'fall-lecture.draft', and output any possibly misspelled words to a file 'fall-lecture.spelling', type:

   `$ spell fall-lecture.draft > fall-lecture.spelling (RET)`

In this example, the standard output redirection character, '>', is used to redirect the output to a file (see Recipe 3.2.2 [Redirecting Output to a File], page 39).

To output an *alphabetical* list of the misspelled words, pipe the output to `sort`; then pipe the sorted output to the `uniq` filter to remove duplicates from the list (`uniq` removes duplicate adjacent lines from its input, outputting the "unique" lines).

- To output a sorted list of the misspelled words that are in the file 'fall-lecture.draft', type:

   `$ spell fall-lecture.draft | sort | uniq (RET)`

11.1.3 Keeping a Spelling Word List

The stock American English dictionary installed with Linux-based systems includes over 45,000 words. However large that number may seem, a lot of words are invariably left out—including slang, jargon, and some proper names.

You can view the system dictionary as you would any other text file, but users never edit this file to add words to it.[2] Instead, you add new words to your own *personal dictionary*, a file in the same format as the system dictionary, but kept in your home directory as the file '~/.ispell_default'.

Users can have their own personal dictionary; the spelling commands discussed in this chapter automatically use your personal dictionary, if you have one, in addition to the system dictionary.

You build your personal dictionary using the *i* and *u* options of `ispell`, which insert words into your personal dictionary. Use these options either with the stand-alone tool or

---

[2] If a word is reasonably universal, you may, of course, contact the global maintainers of `wenglish` or other appropriate packages and try to convince them that said word ought to be included.

with the various `ispell` Emacs functions (see Recipe 11.1.4 [Interactive Spell Checking], page 137 and Recipe 11.1.5 [Spell Checking in Emacs], page 139).

NOTE: You can also add (or remove) words by manually editing the file with a text editor, but take care so that the list is kept in alphabetical order!

Over time, personal dictionaries begin to look very personal, as a reflection of their owners; Gregory Cosmo Haun made a work of art by photographing the portraits of a dozen users superimposed with listings of their personal dictionaries (accessible online at `http://www.reed.edu/~cosmo/art/DictPort.html`).

11.1.4 Interactive Spell Checking

Use `ispell` to spell check a file *interactively*, so that every time a misspelling is found, you're given a chance to replace it then and there.

- To interactively spell check 'fall-lecture.notes', type:

      $ *ispell fall-lecture.notes* (RET)

When you type this, `ispell` begins checking the file. It stops at the first misspelling it finds:

```
        lecutres              File: fall-lecture.notes

The focus of my series of [lecutres] this fall are the aspects of the novel.

0: lectures












        [SP] <number> R)epl A)ccept I)nsert L)ookup U)ncap Q)uit e(X)it or ? for help
```

On the top line of the screen, `ispell` displays the misspelled word, followed by the name of the file. Underneath this is the sentence in which the misspelling appears, with the word in question highlighted. Following this is a list of suggested words, each offset by a number—in this example, `ispell` has only one suggestion: 'lectures'.

To replace a misspelling with a suggested word, type the number that corresponds to the suggested word (in this example, you would type *0* to replace the misspelling with 'lectures'). You only need to type the number of your selection—a (RET) is not required.

You can also type a correction yourself; this is useful when `ispell` either offers no suggestions, or when it does and the word you want is not one of them. To do this, type *r* (for "replace") and then type the replacement word, followed by (RET).

Sometimes, `ispell` will question a word that you may not want to count as a misspelling, such as proper names and the like—words that don't appear in the system dictionary. There are a few things you can do in such cases, as follows.

To accept a misspelled word as correct for the current `ispell` session only, type a; from then on during the current session, this word will be considered correct.

If, however, you want `ispell` (and `spell`, and all other tools that access the system dictionary) to remember this word as being correct for this and all future sessions, insert the word in your own personal dictionary. Type u to insert a copy of the word *uncapitalized*, in all lowercase letters—this way, even if the word is capitalized at the beginning of a sentence, the lowercase version of the word is saved. From then on, in the current `ispell` session and in future sessions, this word, regardless of case, will be considered correct.

When case is important to the spelling—for example, in a word that is a proper name such as 'Seattle', or a word with mixed case, such as 'LaTeX'—type i to insert a copy of the word in your personal dictionary with its case *just as it appears*; this way, words spelled with the same letters but with different case will be considered misspellings.

When `ispell` finishes spell checking a file, it saves its changes to the file and then exits. It also makes a copy of the original file, without the changes applied; this file has the same name as the original but with '.bak' added to the end—so in our example, the backup file is called 'fall-lecture.notes.bak'. This is useful if you regret the changes you've made and want to restore the file to how it was before you mucked it up—just remove the spell-checked file and then rename the '.bak' file to its original name.

The following table is a reference to the `ispell` key commands.

KEY	COMMAND
(SPC)	Accept misspelled word as correct, but only for this particular instance.
number	Replace the misspelled word with the suggestion that corresponds to the given number.
?	Display a help screen.
a	Accept misspelled word as correct for the remainder of this `ispell` session.
i	Accept misspelled word as correct and add it to your private dictionary with the capitalization as it appears.
l	Look up words in the system dictionary according to a pattern you then give.
q	Quit checking and restore the file to how it was before this session.
r	Replace misspelled word with a word you type.
u	Accept misspelled word as correct and add it to your private dictionary in all lowercase letters.
x	Save the changes thus made, and then stop checking this file.

11.1.5 Spell Checking in Emacs

Emacs has several useful commands for spell checking. The `ispell-word`, `ispell-region`, and `ispell-buffer` functions, as you might guess from their names, use the `ispell` command inside Emacs to check portions of the current buffer.

The first command, `ispell-word`, checks the spelling of the word at point; if there is no word at point, it checks the first word to the left of point. This command has a keyboard shortcut, `M-$`. The second command, `ispell-region`, checks the spelling of all words in the currently selected region of text. The third command, `ispell-buffer`, checks the spelling of the entire buffer.

- To check the spelling of the word at point, type:

    `M-x ispell-word` (RET)

- To check the spelling of all words in the currently selected region of text, type:

    `M-x ispell-region` (RET)

- To check the spelling of all words in the current buffer, type:

    `M-x ispell-buffer` (RET)

Flyspell mode is another useful Emacs spelling command that, when set in a buffer, highlights misspelled words. This function is useful when you are writing a first draft in a buffer, because it lets you catch misspellings as you type them.

- To turn on **Flyspell** mode in a buffer, type:

    `M-x flyspoll-mode` (RET)

NOTE: This command is a toggle; run it again to turn it off.

To correct a word in **Flyspell** mode, click and release the middle mouse button on the word to pull up a menu of suggestions; you then use the mouse to select the replacement word or add it to your personal dictionary.

If there are words you frequently misspell, you can define abbrevs for them (see Recipe 10.2.3 [Making Abbreviations in Emacs], page 125). Then, when you type the misspelled word, Emacs will automatically replace it with the correct spelling.

Finally, if you prefer the sparse, non-interactive interface of `spell`, you can use the Emacs interfaces to that command instead: **Spell word**, **Spell region**, and **Spell buffer**. When any of these commands find a misspelling, they prompt for a replacement in the minibuffer but do not offer suggestions or provide any of `ispell`'s other features.

11.2 Dictionaries

Debian: 'wordnet-dev'
WWW: http://www.cogsci.princeton.edu/~wn/

The term *dictionary* on Linux systems generally refers to one of two things: the traditional Unix-style dictionary, which is an alphabetically sorted word list containing no actual definitions, and the newer database-style dictionary that contains the headwords as well as their definitions. The latter is the kind of thing most people mean when they talk about dictionaries. (When most Unix folk talk about dictionaries, however, they almost always mean the former.)

WordNet is a lexical reference system in the form of a database containing thousands of words arranged in synonym sets. You can search the database and output the results in text with the **wn** tool or the **wnb** X client (the "WordNet browser").

Use of the X client is fairly straightforward—type a word in the dialog box near the top of the screen, followed by (RET), to get its definition(s), which are displayed in the large output window underneath the dialog box.

For example, this is what appears when you do a search for the definition of the word 'browse':

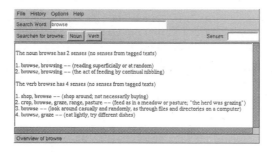

Between the dialog box and the output window, there are menus for searching for synonyms and other word senses. A separate menu is given for each part of speech a word may have; in the preceding example, the word 'browse' can be either a noun or a verb, so two menus are shown.

To get a list of all word sense information available for a given word, run **wn** with the name of the word as an argument. This outputs a list of all word sense information available for the word, with each possible sense preceded with the name of the option to use to output it.

- To output a list of word senses available for the word 'browse', type:

    $ *wn browse* (RET)

The following sections show how to use **wn** on the command line.

NOTE: For more information on WordNet, consult the **wnintro man** page (see Recipe 2.8.4 [Reading a Page from the System Manual], page 30).

11.2.1 Listing Words that Match a Pattern

There are several ways to search for and output words from the system dictionary.

Use **look** to output a list of words in the system dictionary that begin with a given string—this is useful for finding words that begin with a particular phrase or prefix. Give the string as an argument; it is not case sensitive.

- To output a list of words from the dictionary that begin with the string 'homew', type:

    $ *look homew* (RET)

This command outputs words like 'homeward' and 'homework'.

Since the system dictionary is an ordinary text file, you can also use **grep** to search it for words that match a given pattern or regular expression (see Recipe 14.2 [Regular Expressions—Matching Text Patterns], page 166).

- To list all words in the dictionary that contain the string 'dont', regardless of case, type:

    $ *grep -i dont /usr/dict/words* (RET)

- To list all words in the dictionary that end with 'ing', type:

    $ *grep ingˆ /usr/dict/words* (RET)

- To list all of the words that are composed only of vowels, type:

    $ *grep -i 'ˆ[aeiou]*$' /usr/dict/words* (RET)

To find some words that rhyme with a given word, use grep to search '/usr/dict/words' for words ending in the same last few characters as the word they should rhyme with (see Recipe 14.2.2 [Matching Lines Ending with Certain Text], page 168).

- To output a list of words that rhyme with 'friend', search '/usr/dict/words' for lines ending with 'end':

    $ *grep 'end$' /usr/dict/words* (RET)

Finally, to do a search on the WordNet dictionary, use wn with one of the '-grep' options. When you give some text to search for as an argument, this command does the equivalent search as look, except only the particular kind of word sense you specify is searched: '-grepn' searches nouns, '-grepv' searches verbs, '-grepa' searches adjectives, and '-grepr' searches adverbs. You can combine options to search multiple word senses.

- To search the WordNet dictionary for nouns that begin with 'homew', type:

    $ *wn homew -grepn* (RET)

- To search the WordNet dictionary for both nouns and adjectives that begin with 'homew', type:

    $ *wn homew -grepn -grepa* (RET)

11.2.2 Listing the Definitions of a Word

To list the definitions of a word, give the word as an argument to wn, followed by the '-over' option.

- To list the definitions of the word 'slope', type:

    $ *wn slope -over* (RET)

11.2.3 Listing the Synonyms of a Word

A *synonym* of a word is a different word with a similar meaning that can be used in place of the first word in some context. To output synonyms for a word with wn, give the word as an argument, followed by one of the following options: '-synsn' for nouns, '-synsv' for verbs, '-synsa' for adjectives, and '-sysnr' for adverbs.

- To output all of the synonyms for the noun 'break', type:

    $ *wn break -synsn* (RET)

- To output all of the synonyms for the verb 'break', type:

    $ *wn break -synsv* (RET)

11.2.4 Listing the Antonyms of a Word

An *antonym* of a word is a different word that has the opposite meaning of the first in some context. To output antonyms for a word with **wn**, give the word as an argument, followed by one the following options: '`-antsv`' for verbs, '`-antsa`' for adjectives, and '`-antsr`' for adverbs.

- To output all of the antonyms for the adjective '`sad`', type:

    $ `wn sad -antsa` (RET)

11.2.5 Listing the Hypernyms of a Word

A *hypernym* of a word is a related term whose meaning is more general than the given word. (For example, the words '`mammal`' and '`animal`' are hypernyms of the word '`cat`'.)

To output hypernyms for a word with **wn**, use one of the following options: '`-hypen`' for nouns and '`-hypev`' for verbs.

- To output all of the hypernyms for the noun '`cat`', type:

    $ `wn cat -hypen` (RET)

11.2.6 Online Dictionaries

Debian '`dict`'
WWW: http://www.dict.org/

The DICT Development Group has a number of free dictionaries on their Web site at http://www.dict.org/. On that page, you can look up the definitions of words (including thesaurus and other searches) from a dictionary that contains over 300,000 headwords, or make a copy of their dictionary for use on your own system. A **dict** client exists for accessing DICT servers and outputting definitions locally; this tool is available in the '`dict`' package.

DICT also has a number of specialized dictionaries that are plain text files (including the author's *Free Journalism Dictionary*, containing jargon and terms used in the journalism and publishing professions). Their *FILE* project, *The Free Internet Lexicon and Encyclopedia*, is an effort to build a free, open source collection of modern-word, idiom, and jargon dictionaries. FILE is a volunteer effort and depends on the support of scholars and lexicographers; the DICT pages contain information on how to help contribute to this worthy project.

11.3 Checking Grammar

WWW: http://www.gnu.org/software/diction/diction.html

Two venerable Unix tools for checking writing have recently been made available for Linux-based systems: **style** and **diction**.

Old-timers probably remember these names—the originals came with AT&T UNIX as part of the much-loved "Writer's Workbench" (WWB) suite of tools back in the late 1970s and early 1980s.[3]

AT&T "unbundled" the Writer's Workbench from their UNIX version 7 product, and as the many flavors of Unix blossomed over the years, these tools were lost by the wayside— eventually becoming the stuff of Unix lore.

In 1997, Michael Haardt wrote new Linux versions of these tools from scratch. They support both the English and German languages, and they're now part of the GNU Project.

Two additional commands that were part of the Writer's Workbench have long been standard on Linux: `look` and `spell`, described previously in this chapter.

11.3.1 Checking Text for Misused Phrases

Use `diction` to check for wordy, trite, clichéd, or misused phrases in a text. It checks for all the kind of expressions William Strunk warned us about in his *Elements of Style* (`http://coba.shsu.edu/help/strunk/`).

According to *The UNIX Environment*, by Andrew Walker, the `diction` tool that came with the old Writer's Workbench just *found* the phrases, and a separate command called `suggest` would output suggestions. In the GNU version that works for Linux systems, both functions have been combined in the single `diction` command.

In GNU `diction`, the words or phrases are enclosed in brackets '`[like this]`'. If `diction` has any suggested replacements, it gives them preceded by a right arrow, '`->` like this'.

When checking more than just a screenful of text, you'll want to pipe the output to `less` so that you can peruse it on the screen (see Recipe 9.1 [Perusing Text], page 111), or pipe the output to a file for later examination.

- To check file '`dissertation`' for clichés or other misused phrases, type:

    `$ diction dissertation | less` (RET)

- To check file '`dissertation`' for clichés or other misused phrases, and write the output to a file called '`dissertation.diction`', type:

    `$ diction dissertation > dissertation.diction` (RET)

If you don't specify a file name, `diction` reads text from the standard input until you type `C-d` on a line by itself. This is especially useful when you want to check a single sentence:

```
$ diction (RET)
Let us ask the question we wish to state. (RET)
(stdin):1: Let us [ask the question -> ask]
[we wish to state -> (cliche, avoid)].
C-d
$
```

---

[3] There was also a set of tools for formatting text called the "Documenter's Workbench" (DWB), and there was a planned "Reader's Workbench"; we can only guess at what that might have been, but today we do have Project Gutenbook (`http://www.gutenbook.org/`), a new etext reader.

To check the text of a Web page, use the text-only Web browser `lynx` with the '`-dump`' and '`-nolist`' options to output the plain text of a given URL, and pipe this output to `diction`. (If you expect there to be a lot of output, add another pipe at the end to `less` so you can peruse it.)

> To peruse a copy of the text of `http://example.org/1.html` with markings for possible wordy and misused phrases, type:
>
> `$ lynx -dump -nolist http://example.org/1.html | diction | less` (RET)

11.3.2 Checking Text for Doubled Words

One of the things that `diction` looks for is doubled words—words repeated twice in a row. If it finds such a sequence, it encloses the second member of the doubled pair in brackets, followed by a right arrow and the text '`Double word`', like '`this [<i>this -> Double word.]`'.

To check a text file for doubled words *only*, and not for any of the other things `diction` checks, use `grep` to find only those lines in `diction`'s output that contain the text '`Double word`', if any.

- To output all lines containing double words in the file '`dissertation`', type:

    `$ diction dissertation | grep 'Double word'` (RET)

11.3.3 Checking Text for Readability

The `style` command analyzes the writing style of a given text. It performs a number of readability tests on the text and outputs their results, and it gives some statistical information about the sentences of the text. Give as an argument the name of the text file to check.

- To check the readability of the file '`dissertation`', type:

    `$ style dissertation` (RET)

Like `diction`, `style` reads text from the standard input if no text is given—this is useful for the end of a pipeline, or for checking the writing style of a particular sentence or other text you type.

The sentence characteristics of the text that `style` outputs are as follows:

- Number of characters
- Number of words, their average length, and their average number of syllables
- Number of sentences and average length in words
- Number of short and long sentences
- Number of paragraphs and average length in sentences
- Number of questions and imperatives

The various readability formulas that `style` uses and outputs are as follows:

- Kincaid formula, originally developed for Navy training manuals; a good readability for technical documentation
- Automated Readability Index (ARI)
- Coleman-Liau formula

- Flesch Reading Ease Score, which gives an approximation of readability from 0 (difficult) to 100 (easy)
- Fog Index, which gives a school-grade reading level
- WSTF Index, a readability indicator for German documents
- Wheeler-Smith Index, Lix formula, and SMOG-Grading tests, all readability indicators that give a school-grade reading level

11.3.4 Checking Text for Difficult Sentences

To output just the "difficult" sentences of a text, use **style** with the '**-r**' option followed by a number; **style** will output only those sentences whose Automated Readability Index (ARI) is greater than the number you give.

- To output all sentences in the file '**dissertation**' whose ARI is greater than a value of 20, type:

      $ style -r 20 dissertation (RET)

11.3.5 Checking Text for Long Sentences

Use **style** to output sentences longer than a certain length by giving the minimum number of words as an argument to the '**-l**' option.

- To output all sentences longer than 14 words in the file '**dissertation**', type:

      $ style -l 14 dissertation (RET)

11.4 Word Lists and Reference Files

Debian: 'miscfiles'
WWW: ftp://ftp.gnu.org/pub/gnu/miscfiles/miscfiles-1.1.tar.gz

The GNU Miscfiles are a collection of text files containing various facts and reference material, such as common abbreviations, telephone area codes, and English connective phrases.

The files are stored in the '**/usr/share/misc**' directory, and they are all compressed; use **zless** to peruse them (see Recipe 9.1 [Perusing Text], page 111).

The following table lists the files in '**/usr/share/misc**' and describes their contents.

FILE	DESCRIPTION
GNU-manifesto.gz	The GNU Manifesto.
abbrevs.talk.gz abbrevs.gen.gz	Collections of common abbreviations used in electronic communication. (This is the place to look to find the secrets of 'TTYL' and 'LOL'.)
airport.gz	List of three-letter city codes for some of the major airports. The city code is useful for querying the National Weather Service computers to get the latest weather report for your region.
ascii.gz	A chart of the ASCII character set.

`birthtoken.gz`	The traditional stone and flower tokens for each month.
`cities.dat.gz`	The population, political coordinates (nation, region), and geographic coordinates (latitude, longitude) of many major cities.
`inter.phone.gz`	International country and city telephone codes.
`languages.gz`	Two-letter codes for languages, from ISO 639.
`latin1.gz`	A chart of the extended ASCII character set, also known as the ISO 8859 ("Latin-1") character set.
`mailinglists.gz`	Description of all the public Project GNU-related mailing lists.
`na.phone.gz`	North American (+1) telephone area codes.
`operator.gz`	Precedence table for operators in the C language.
`postal.codes.gz`	Postal codes for U.S. and Mexican states and Canadian provinces.
`us-constitution.gz`	*The Constitution of the United States of America* (no *Bill of Rights*, though). (On Debian systems, this file is placed in '`/usr/share/state`'.)
`us-declaration.gz`	*The Declaration of Independence of the Thirteen Colonies.* (On Debian systems, this file is placed in '`/usr/share/state`'.)
`rfc-index.txt`	Indexes of Internet standardization Request For Comments (RFC) documents. (On Debian systems, this file is placed in '`/usr/share/rfc`').
`zipcodes.gz`	U.S. five-digit Zip codes.

'`miscfiles`' is not the only reference package available for Debian systems, though; other related packages include the following:

PACKAGE	DESCRIPTION
`doc-iana`	Internet protocol parameter registry documents, as published by the Internet Assigned Numbers Authority.
`doc-rfc`	A collection of important RFCs, stored in '`/usr/share/rfc`'.
`jargon`	The "Jargon file," which is the definitive dictionary of hacker slang.
`vera`	List of computer acronyms.

NOTE: The official GNU `miscfiles` distribution also includes the Jargon file and the '/usr/dict/words' dictionary file, which are available in separate packages for Debian, and are removed from the Debian '`miscfiles`' distribution. '/usr/dict/words' is part of the standard spelling packages, and the Jargon file comes in the optional '`jargon`' package, and installs in '/usr/share/jargon'.

12 Analyzing Text

There are many ways to use command-line tools to analyze text in various ways, such as counting the number of words in a text, creating a concordance, and comparing texts to see if (and where) they differ. There are also other tricks you can do with text that count as analysis, such as finding anagrams and palindromes, or cutting up text to generate unexpected combinations of words. This chapter covers all these topics.

12.1 Counting Text

Use the "word count" tool, `wc`, to count characters, words, and lines in text.

Give the name of a file as an argument; if none is given, `wc` works on standard input. By default, `wc` outputs three columns, displaying the counts for lines, words, and characters in the text.

- To output the number of lines, words, and characters in file 'outline', type:

      $ wc outline (RET)

The following subsections describe how to specify just one kind of count with `wc`, and how to count text in Emacs.

NOTE: You can get a count of how many *different* words are in a text, too—see Recipe 12.2 [Making a Concordance of a Text], page 150. To count the average *length* of words, sentences, and paragraphs, use `style` (see Recipe 11.3.3 [Checking Text for Readability], page 144).

12.1.1 Counting the Characters in a Text

Use `wc` with the '-c' option to specify that just the number of characters be counted and output.

- To output the number of characters in file 'classified.ad', type:

      $ wc -c classified.ad (RET)

12.1.2 Counting the Words in a Text

Use `wc` with the '-w' option to specify that just the number of words be counted and output.

- To output the number of words in the file 'story', type:

      $ wc -w story (RET)

To output counts for several files, first concatenate the files with `cat`, and then pipe the output to `wc`.

- To output the combined number of words for all the files with a '.txt' file name extension in the current directory, type:

      $ cat *.txt | wc -w (RET)

NOTE: To read more about concatenation with `cat`, see Recipe 10.6 [Concatenating Text], page 130.

12.1.3 Counting the Lines in a Text

Use `wc` with the '-l' option to specify that just the number of lines be counted and output.

- To output the number of lines in the file '`outline`', type:

      $ wc -l outline (RET)

12.1.4 Counting the Occurrences of Something

To find the number of occurrences of some text string or pattern in a file or files, use `grep` to search the file(s) for the text string, and pipe the output to `wc` with the '-l' option.

- To find the number of lines in the file '`outline`' that contain the string '`chapter`', type:

      $ grep chapter outline | wc -l (RET)

NOTE: For more recipes for searching text, and more about `grep`, see Chapter 14 [Searching Text], page 165.

12.1.5 Counting Lines per Page in Emacs

The `count-lines-page` function in Emacs outputs in the minibuffer the number of lines on the current *page* (as delimited by pagebreak characters, if any—see Recipe 13.2 [Paginating Text], page 158), followed by the number of lines in the buffer before the line that point is on, and the number of lines in the buffer after point.

- To count the number of lines per page in the current buffer in Emacs, type:

      C-x l

Emacs outputs the number of lines per page of the current buffer in the echo area.

For example, if the output in the minibuffer is

    Page has 351 lines (69 + 283)

this means that the current page contains 351 lines, and point is on line number 70—there are 69 lines before this line, and 283 lines after this line.

12.2 Making a Concordance of a Text

A *concordance* is an index of all the words in a text, along with their contexts. A concordance-like functionality—an alphabetical listing of all words in a text and their frequency—can be made fairly easily with some basic shell tools: `tr`, `sort`, and `uniq`.

- To output a word-frequency list of the text file '`naked_lunch`', type:

      $ tr ' ' ' ' (RET)
      > ' < naked_lunch | sort | uniq -c (RET)

These commands *translate* all space characters to newline characters, outputting the text with each word on its own line; this is then sorted alphabetically, and that output is passed to `uniq`, which outputs only the *unique* lines—that is, all non-duplicate lines—while the '-c' option precedes each line with its *count* (the number of times it occurs in the text).

To get a word frequency count—that is, the total number of *different* words in a text—just pipe the output of the frequency list to `wc` with the '-l' option. This counts all the lines of its input, which in this case will be the list of unique words, one per line.

- To output a count of the number of unique words in the text file '`naked_lunch`', type:

```
$ tr ' ' ' RET
> ' < naked_lunch | sort | uniq -c | wc -l RET
```

12.3 Text Relevance

The following recipes show how to analyze a given text for its relevancy to other text, either to keywords or to whole files of text.

You can also use the `diff` family of tools to analyze differences in text; those tools are especially good for comparing different revisions of the same file (see Recipe 8.4 [Comparing Files], page 101).

12.3.1 Sorting Text in Order of Relevance

Debian: '`rel`'
WWW: http://www.johncon.com/

Use `rel` to analyze text files for relevance to a given set of keywords. It outputs the names of those files that are relevant to the given keywords, ranked in order of relevance; if a file does not meet the criteria, it is not output in the relevance listing.

`rel` takes as an option the keyword to search for in quotes; you can build a boolean expression by grouping multiple keywords in parentheses and using any of the following operators between them:

OPERATOR	DESCRIPTION
|	Logical "or."
&	Logical "and."
!	Logical "not."

Give as arguments the names of the files to rank.

- To rank the files '`report.a`', '`report.b`', and '`report.c`' in order of relevance to the keywords '`saving`' and '`profit`', type:

```
$ rel "(saving & profit)" report.a report.b report.c RET
```

Give the name of a directory tree to analyze all files in the directory tree.

- To output a list of any files containing either '`invitation`' or '`request`' in the '`~/mail`' directory, ranked in order of relevancy, type:

```
$ rel "(invitation | request)" ~/mail RET
```

- To output a list of any files containing '`invitation`' and not '`wedding`' in the '`~/mail`' directory, ranked in order of relevancy, type:

```
$ rel "(invitation ! wedding)" ~/mail RET
```

- To output a list of any files containing '`invitation`' and '`party`' in the '`~/mail`' directory, ranked in order of relevancy, type:

```
$ rel "(invitation & party)" ~/mail RET
```

12.3.2 Listing Relevant Files in Emacs

Debian: 'remembrance-agent'
WWW: http://www.media.mit.edu/~rhodes/RA/

The purpose of the Remembrance Agent is to analyze the text you type in an Emacs session and, in the background, find similar or relevant passages of text within your other files. It then outputs in a smaller window a list of suggestions—those files that it has found—which you can open in a new buffer.

When installing the Remembrance Agent, you create three databases of the files to use when making relevance suggestions; when `remembrance-agent` is running, it searches these three databases in parallel, looking for relevant text. You could create, for example, one database of saved email, one of your own writings, and one of saved documents.

- To toggle the Remembrance Agent in the current buffer, type:

    `C-c r t`

When `remembrance-agent` is running, suggested buffers will be displayed in the small '`*Remembrance*`' buffer at the bottom of the screen. To open a suggestion in a new buffer, type `C-c r number`, where *number* is the number of the suggestion.

- To open the second suggested file in a new buffer, type:

    `C-c r 2`

12.4 Finding Anagrams in Text

Debian: 'an'

An *anagram* is a word or phrase whose characters consist entirely of all the characters of a given word or phrase—for example, '`stop`' and '`tops`' are both anagrams of '`pots`'.

Use **an** to find and output anagrams. Give as an argument the word or quoted phrase to use; **an** writes its results to the standard output.

- To output all anagrams of the word '`lake`', type:

    `$ an lake` (RET)

- To output all anagrams of the phrase '`lakes and oceans`', type:

    `$ an 'lakes and oceans'` (RET)

To limit the anagrams output to those containing a given string, specify that string with the '`-c`' option.

- To output only anagrams of the phrase '`lakes and oceans`' which contain the string '`seas`', type:

    `$ an -c seas 'lakes and oceans'` (RET)

To print all of the words that some or all letters in a given word or phrase can make, use the '`-w`' option. This outputs words that are not anagrams, since anagrams must contain *all* of the letters of the other word or phrase.

- To output all of the words that can be made from the letters of the word '`seas`', type:

    `$ an -w seas` (RET)

This command outputs all of the words that can be formed from all or some of the characters in 'seas', including 'see' and 'as'.

12.5 Finding Palindromes in Text

A *palindrome* is a word that reads the same both forwards and backwards; for example, "Mom," "madam," and "nun" are all palindromes.

To find palindromes in a file, use this simple Perl "one-liner," and substitute *file* for the name of the file to check:

```
perl -lne 'print if $_ eq reverse' file
```

To check for palindromes in the standard input, specify '-' as the file name to check. This is useful for putting at the end of a pipeline.

- To output all of the palindromes in the system dictionary, type:

  ```
  $ perl -lne 'print if $_ eq reverse' /usr/dict/words (RET)
  ```

12.6 Text Cut-Ups

A *cut-up* is a random rearrangement of a physical layout of text, made with the intention of finding unique or interesting phrases in the rearrangement. Software for rearranging text in random ways has existed since the earliest text-processing tools; the popularity of these tools will never die.

The cut-up technique in literature was discovered by painter Brion Gysin and American writer William S. Burroughs in 1959; they believed it brought the montage technique of painting to the written word.

"All writing is in fact cut-ups," Burroughs wrote.[1] "A collage of words read heard overheard ... [u]se of scissors renders the process explicit and subject to extension and variation."

These recipes describe a few of the common ways to make text cut-ups; more free software tools for making cut-ups are listed at http://dsl.org/comp/cutups.shtml.

12.6.1 Making Simple Text Cut-Ups

WWW: http://dsl.org/comp/tinyutils/

To perform a simple cut-up of a text, use cutup. It takes the name of a file as input and cuts it both horizontally and vertically along the middle, rearranges the four sections to their diagonally opposite corners, and then writes that cut-up to the standard output. The original file is not modified.

- To make a cut-up from a file called 'nova', type:

  ```
  $ cutup nova (RET)
  ```

---

[1] In *The Third Mind*, by William S. Burroughs and Brion Gysin.

12.6.2 Making Random Word Cut-Ups

Debian: 'dadadodo'
WWW: http://www.jwz.org/dadadodo/

No simple cut-up filter, Jamie Zawinski's `dadadodo` uses the computer to go one step beyond—it generates passages of random text whose structure and characters are similar to the text input you give it. The program works better on larger texts, where more subtleties can be analyzed and hence more realistic-looking text is output.

Give as an argument the name of the text file to be used; by default, `dadadodo` outputs text to standard output until you interrupt it by typing *C-c*.

- To output random text based on the text in the file 'nova', type:

      $ *dadadodo nova* (RET)

This command will output passages of random text based on the text in the file 'nova' until it is interrupted by the user.

You can analyze a text and save the analysis to a file of compiled data; this analysis can then be used to generate random text when the original input text is not present. The following table describes this and other `dadadodo` options.

OPTION	DESCRIPTION
-c *integer*	Generate *integer* sentences (default is 0, meaning "generate an infinite amount until interrupted").
-l *file*	Load compiled data in *file* and use it to generate text.
-o *file*	Output compiled data to file *file* for later use.
-p *integer*	Pause for *integer* seconds between paragraphs.

12.6.3 Making Cut-Ups in Emacs

The `dissociated-press` function in Emacs makes random cut-ups of the current buffer in a new buffer called '`*Dissociation*`'; the original buffer is not modified. The text in the new buffer is generated by combining random portions of the buffer by overlapping characters or words, thus (usually) creating plausible-sounding sentences. It pauses occasionally and asks whether or not you want to continue the dissociation.

- To generate a Dissociated Press cut-up from the current buffer, type:

      M-x dissociated-press (RET)

Give a positive argument to the `dissociated-press` function to specify the number of characters to use for overlap; give a negative argument to specify the number of *words* for overlap.

- To generate a Dissociated Press cut-up from the current buffer, always overlapping by three characters, type:

      C-u 3 M-x dissociated-press (RET)

- To generate a Dissociated Press cut-up from the current buffer, always overlapping by one word, type:

      C-u -1 M-x dissociated-press (RET)

13 Formatting Text

Methods and tools for changing the arrangement or presentation of text are often useful for preparing text for printing. This chapter discusses ways of changing the spacing of text and setting up pages, of underlining and sorting and reversing text, and of numbering lines of text.

13.1 Spacing Text

These recipes are for changing the *spacing* of text—the whitespace that exists between words, lines, and paragraphs.

The filters described in this section send output to standard output by default; to save their output to a file, use shell redirection (see Recipe 3.2.2 [Redirecting Output to a File], page 39).

13.1.1 Eliminating Extra Spaces in Text

To eliminate extra whitespaces **within** lines of text, use the `fmt` filter; to eliminate extra whitespace *between* lines of text, use `cat`.

Use `fmt` with the '-u' option to output text with "uniform spacing," where the space between words is reduced to one space character and the space between sentences is reduced to two space characters.

- To output the file 'term-paper' with uniform spacing, type:

      $ fmt -u term-paper (RET)

Use `cat` with the '-s' option to "squeeze" multiple adjacent blank lines into one.

- To output the file 'term-paper' with multiple blank lines output as only one blank line, type:

      $ cat -s term-paper (RET)

You can combine both of these commands to output text with multiple adjacent lines removed *and* give it a unified spacing between words. The following example shows how the output of the combined commands is sent to `less` so that it can be perused on the screen.

- To peruse the text file 'term-paper' with multiple blank lines removed and giving the text unified spacing between words, type:

      $ cat -s term-paper | fmt -u | less (RET)

Notice that in this example, both `fmt` and `less` worked on their standard input instead of on a file—the standard output of `cat` (the contents of 'term-paper' with extra blank lines squeezed out) was passed to the standard input of `fmt`, and its standard output (the space-squeezed 'term-paper', now with uniform spacing) was sent to the standard input of `less`, which displayed it on the screen.

13.1.2 Single-Spacing Text

There are many methods for single-spacing text. To remove all empty lines from text output, use `grep` with the regular expression '.', which matches any character, and therefore matches any line that isn't empty (see Recipe 14.2 [Regular Expressions—Matching Text Patterns], page 166). You can then redirect this output to a file, or pipe it to other commands; the original file is not altered.

- To output all non-empty lines from the file 'term-paper', type:

      $ grep . term-paper (RET)

  This command outputs all lines that are not empty—so lines containing only non-printing characters, such as spaces and tabs, will still be output.

  To remove from the output all empty lines, and all lines that consist of only space characters, use '[^].' as the regexp to search for. But this regexp will still output lines that contain only tab characters; to remove from the output all empty lines and lines that contain only a combination of tab or space characters, use '[^[:space:]].' as the regexp to search for. It uses the special predefined '[:space:]' regexp class, which matches any kind of space character at all, including tabs.

- To output only the lines from the file 'term-paper' that contain more than just space characters, type:

      $ grep '[^].' term-paper (RET)

  To output only the lines from the file 'term-paper' that contain more than just space or tab characters, type:

      $ grep '[^[:space:]].' term-paper (RET)

  If a file is already double-spaced, where all even lines are blank, you can remove those lines from the output by using `sed` with the 'n;d' expression.

- To output only the odd lines from file 'term-paper', type:

      $ sed 'n;d' term-paper (RET)

13.1.3 Double-Spacing Text

To double-space text, where one blank line is inserted between each line in the original text, use the `pr` tool with the '-d' option. By default, `pr` paginates text and puts a header at the top of each page with the current date, time, and page number; give the '-t' option to omit this header.

- To double-space the file 'term-paper' and write the output to the file 'term-paper.print', type:

      $ pr -d -t term-paper > term-paper.print (RET)

  To send the output directly to the printer for printing, you would pipe the output to `lpr`:

      $ pr -d -t term-paper | lpr (RET)

NOTE: The `pr` ("print") tool is a text pre-formatter, often used to paginate and otherwise prepare text files for printing; there is more discussion on the use of this tool in Recipe 13.2 [Paginating Text], page 158.

13.1.4 Triple-Spacing Text

To triple-space text, where two blank lines are inserted between each line of the original text, use `sed` with the ''`G;G`'' expression.

- To triple-space the file '`term-paper`' and write the output to the file '`term-paper.print`', type:

      $ sed 'G;G' term-paper > term-paper.print (RET)

The '`G`' expression appends one blank line to each line of `sed`'s output; using '`;`' you can specify more than one blank line to append (but you must quote this command, because the semicolon ('`;`') has meaning to the shell—see Recipe 3.1.1 [Passing Special Characters to Commands], page 36). You can use multiple '`G`' characters to output text with more than double or triple spaces.

- To quadruple-space the file '`term-paper`', and write the output to the file '`term-paper.print`', type:

      $ sed 'G;G;G' term-paper > term-paper.print (RET)

The usage of `sed` is described in Recipe 10.5 [Editing Streams of Text], page 129.

13.1.5 Adding Line Breaks to Text

Sometimes a file will not have line breaks at the end of each line (this commonly happens during file conversions between operating systems). To add line breaks to a file that does not have them, use the text formatter `fmt`. It outputs text with lines arranged up to a specified width; if no length is specified, it formats text up to a width of 75 characters per line.

- To output the file '`term-paper`' with lines up to 75 characters long, type:

      $ fmt term-paper (RET)

Use the '`-w`' option to specify the maximum line width.

- To output the file '`term-paper`' with lines up to 80 characters long, type:

      $ fmt -w 80 term-paper (RET)

13.1.6 Adding Margins to Text

Giving text an extra left margin is especially good when you want to print a copy and punch holes in it for use with a three-ring binder.

To output a text file with a larger left margin, use `pr` with the file name as an argument; give the '`-t`' option (to disable headers and footers), and, as an argument to the '`-o`' option, give the number of spaces to offset the text. Add the number of spaces to the page width (whose default is 72) and specify this new width as an argument to the '`-w`' option.

- To output the file '`owners-manual`' with a five-space (or five-*column*) margin to a new file, '`owners-manual.pr`', type:

      $ pr -t -o 5 -w 77 owners-manual > owners-manual.pr (RET)

This command is almost always used for printing, so the output is usually just piped to `lpr` instead of saved to a file. Many text documents have a width of 80 and not 72 columns; if you are printing such a document and need to keep the 80 columns across the page, specify a new width of 85. If your printer can only print 80 columns of text, specify a width of 80; the text will be reformatted to 75 columns after the 5-column margin.

- To print the file 'owners-manual' with a 5-column margin and 80 columns of text, type:

    $ pr -t -o 5 -w 85 owners-manual | lpr (RET)

- To print the file 'owners-manual' with a 5-column margin and 75 columns of text, type:

    $ pr -t -o 5 -w 80 owners-manual | lpr (RET)

13.1.7 Swapping Tab and Space Characters

Use the **expand** and **unexpand** tools to swap tab characters for space characters, and to swap space characters with tabs, respectively.

Both tools take a file name as an argument and write changes to the standard output; if no files are specified, they work on the standard input.

To convert tab characters to spaces, use **expand**. To convert only the *initial* or leading tabs on each line, give the '-i' option; the default action is to convert *all* tabs.

- To convert all tab characters to spaces in file 'list', and write the output to 'list2', type:

    $ expand list > list2 (RET)

- To convert only initial tab characters to spaces in file 'list', and write the output to the standard output, type:

    $ expand -i list (RET)

To convert multiple space characters to tabs, use **unexpand**. By default, it only converts leading spaces into tabs, counting eight space characters for each tab. Use the '-a' option to specify that *all* instances of eight space characters be converted to tabs.

- To convert every eight leading space characters to tabs in file 'list2', and write the output to 'list', type:

    $ unexpand list2 > list (RET)

- To convert all occurrences of eight space characters to tabs in file 'list2', and write the output to the standard output, type:

    $ unexpand -a list2 (RET)

To specify the number of spaces to convert to a tab, give that number as an argument to the '-t' option.

- To convert every leading space character to a tab character in 'list2', and write the output to the standard output, type:

    $ unexpand -t 1 list2 (RET)

13.2 Paginating Text

The formfeed character, ASCII *C-l* or octal code 014, is the delimiter used to paginate text. When you send text with a formfeed character to the printer, the current page being printed is ejected and a new page begins—thus, you can paginate a text file by inserting formfeed characters at a place where you want a page break to occur.

To insert formfeed characters in a text file, use the **pr** filter.

Give the '-f' option to omit the footer and separate pages of output with the formfeed character, and use '-h ""' to output a blank header (otherwise, the current date and time, file name, and current page number are output at the top of each page).

- To paginate the file 'listings' and write the output to a file called 'listings.page', type:

      $ *pr -f -h "" listings > listings.page* (RET)

By default, **pr** outputs pages of 66 lines each. You can specify the page length as an argument to the '-l' option.

- To paginate the file 'listings' with 43-line pages, and write the output to a file called 'listings.page', type:

      $ *pr -f -h "" -l 43 listings > listings.page* (RET)

NOTE: If a page has more lines than a printer can fit on a physical sheet of paper, it will automatically break the text at that line as well as at the places in the text where there are formfeed characters.

You can paginate text in Emacs by manually inserting formfeed characters where you want them—see Recipe 10.2.5 [Inserting Special Characters in Emacs], page 126.

13.2.1 Placing Headers on Each Page

The **pr** tool is a general-purpose page formatter and print-preparation utility. By default, **pr** outputs text in pages of 66 lines each, with headers at the top of each page containing the date and time, file name, and page number, and footers containing five blank lines.

- To print the file 'duchess' with the default **pr** preparation, type:

      $ *pr duchess | lpr* (RET)

13.2.2 Placing Text in Columns

You can also use **pr** to put text in columns—give the number of columns to output as an argument. Use the '-t' option to omit the printing of the default headers and footers.

- To print the file 'news.update' in four columns with no headers or footers, type:

      $ *pr -4 -t news.update | lpr* (RET)

13.2.3 Options Available When Paginating Text

The following table describes some of **pr**'s options; see the **pr** info for a complete description of its capabilities (see Recipe 2.8.5 [Using the GNU Info System], page 31).

OPTION	DESCRIPTION
+*first*:*last*	Specify the first and last page to process; the last page can be omitted, so +7 begins processing with the seventh page and continues until the end of the file is reached.

-column	Specify the number of columns to output text in, making all columns fit the page width.
`-a`	Print columns across instead of down.
`-c`	Output control characters in hat notation and print all other unprintable characters in "octal backslash" notation.
`-d`	Specify double-spaced output.
`-f`	Separate pages of output with a formfeed character instead of a footer of blank lines (63 lines of text per 66-line page instead of 53).
`-h` *header*	Specify the header to use instead of the default; specify *-h* `""` for a blank header.
`-l` *length*	Specify the page length to be *length* lines (default 66). If page length is less than 11, headers and footers are omitted and existing form feeds are ignored.
`-m`	Use when specifying multiple files; this option merges and outputs them in parallel, one per column.
`-o` *spaces*	Set the number of spaces to use in the left margin (default 0).
`-t`	Omit the header and footer on each page, but retain existing formfeeds.
`-T`	Omit the header and footer on each page, as well as existing formfeeds.
`-v`	Output non-printing characters in "octal backslash" notation.
`-w` *width*	Specify the page width to use, in characters (default 72).

NOTE: It's also common to use `pr` to change the spacing of text (see Recipe 13.1 [Spacing Text], page 155).

13.3 Underlining Text

In the days of typewriters, text that was meant to be set in an italicized font was denoted by underlining the text with underscore characters; now, it's common practice to denote an italicized word in plain text by typing an underscore character, '_', just before and after a word in a text file, like '_this_'.

Some text markup languages use different methods for denoting italics; for example, in TEX or LaTeX files, italicized text is often denoted with brackets and the '\it' command, like '{\it this}'. (LaTeX files use the same format, but '\emph' is often used in place of '\it'.)

You can convert one form to the other by using the Emacs `replace-regular-expression` function and specifying the text to be replaced as a regexp (see Recipe 14.2 [Regular Expressions—Matching Text Patterns], page 166).

- To replace plaintext-style italics with TeX '\it' commands, type:

      M-x replace-regular-expression (RET)
      *_\([^_]+\)_* (RET)
      \{\\it \1} (RET)

- To replace TeX-style italics with plaintext _underscores_, type:

      M-x replace-regular-expression (RET)
      \{\\it \{\([^\}]+\)\} (RET)
      *_\1_* (RET)

Both examples above used the special regexp symbol '\1', which matches the same text matched by the first '\(... \)' construct in the previous regexp. See Info file 'emacs-e20.info', node 'Regexps' for more information on regexp syntax in Emacs.

To put a literal underline under text, you need to use a text editor to insert a C-h character followed by an underscore ('_') immediately after each character you want to underline; you can insert the C-h in Emacs with the *C-q* function (see Recipe 10.2.5 [Inserting Special Characters in Emacs], page 126).

When a text file contains these literal underlines, use the ul tool to output the file so that it is viewable by the terminal you are using; this is also useful for printing (pipe the output of ul to lpr).

- To output the file 'term-paper' so that you can view underbars, type:

      $ *ul term-paper* (RET)

To output such text without the backspace character, *C-h*, in the output, use col with the '-u' option.

- To output the file 'term-paper' with all backspace characters stripped out, type:

      $ *col -u term-paper* (RET)

13.4 Sorting Text

You can sort a list in a text file with sort. By default, it outputs text in ascending alphabetical order; use the '-r' option to reverse the sort and output text in descending alphabetical order.

For example, suppose a file 'provinces' contains the following:

      Shantung
      Honan
      Szechwan
      Hunan
      Kiangsu
      Kwangtung
      Fukien

- To sort the file 'provinces' and output all lines in ascending order, type:

```
$ sort provinces (RET)
Fukien
Honan
Hunan
Kiangsu
Kwangtung
Shantung
Szechwan
$
```

- To sort the file 'provinces' and output all lines in descending order, type:

```
$ sort -r provinces (RET)
Szechwan
Shantung
Kwangtung
Kiangsu
Hunan
Honan
Fukien
$
```

The following table describes some of sort's options.

OPTION	DESCRIPTION
-b	Ignore leading blanks on each line when sorting.
-d	Sort in "phone directory" order, with only letters, digits, and blanks being sorted.
-f	When sorting, *fold* lowercase letters into their uppercase equivalent, so that differences in case are ignored.
-i	Ignore all spaces and all non-typewriter characters when sorting.
-n	Sort numerically instead of by character value.
-o *file*	Write output to *file* instead of standard output.

13.5 Numbering Lines of Text

There are several ways to number lines of text.

One way to do it is to use the nl ("number lines") tool. Its default action is to write its input (either the file names given as an argument, or the standard input) to the standard output, with an indentation and all non-empty lines preceded with line numbers.

- To peruse the file 'report' with each line of the file preceded by line numbers, type:

    ```
    $ nl report | less (RET)
    ```

You can set the numbering style with the '-b' option followed by an argument. The following table lists the possible arguments and describes the numbering style they select.

ARGUMENT	NUMBERING STYLE
a	Number all lines.
t	Number only non-blank lines. This is the default.
n	Do not number lines.
p*regexp*	Only number lines that contain the regular expression *regexp* (see Recipe 14.2 [Regular Expressions—Matching Text Patterns], page 166).

The default is for line numbers to start with one, and increment by one. Set the initial line number by giving an argument to the '-v' option, and set the increment by giving an argument to the '-i' option.

- To output the file 'report' with each line of the file preceded by line numbers, starting with the number two and counting by fours, type:

      $ nl -v 2 -i 4 report (RET)

- To number only the lines of the file 'cantos' that begin with a period ('.'), starting numbering at zero and using a numbering increment of five, and to write the output to 'cantos.numbered', type:

      $ nl -i 5 -v 0 -b p'^\.' cantos > cantos.numbered (RET)

The other way to number lines is to use cat with one of the following two options: the '-n' option numbers each line of its input text, while the '-b' option only numbers non-blank lines.

- To peruse the text file 'report' with each line of the file numbered, type:

      $ cat -n report | less (RET)

- To peruse the text file 'report' with each non-blank line of the file numbered, type:

      $ cat -b report | less (RET)

In the preceding examples, output from cat is piped to less for perusal; the original file is not altered.

To take an input file, number its lines, and then write the line-numbered version to a new file, send the standard output of the cat command to the new file to write.

- To write a line-numbered version of file 'report' to file 'report.lines', type:

      $ cat -n report > report.lines (RET)

13.6 Reversing Text

The tac command is similar to cat, but it outputs text in reverse order. There is another difference—tac works on *records*, sections of text with separator strings, instead of lines of text. Its default separator string is the linebreak character, so by default tac outputs files in line-for-line reverse order.

- To output the file 'prizes' in line-for-line reverse order, type:

      $ tac prizes (RET)

Specify a different separator with the '-s' option. This is often useful when specifying non-printing characters such as formfeeds. To specify such a character, use the ANSI-C method of quoting (see Recipe 3.1.1 [Passing Special Characters to Commands], page 36).

- To output 'prizes' in page-for-page reverse order, type:

  ```
  $ tac -s $'\f' prizes (RET)
  ```

The preceding example uses the formfeed, or page break, character as the delimiter, and so it outputs the file 'prizes' in page-for-page reverse order, with the last page output first.

Use the '-r' option to use a regular expression for the separator string (see Recipe 14.2 [Regular Expressions—Matching Text Patterns], page 166). You can build regular expressions to output text in word-for-word and character-for-character reverse order:

- To output 'prizes' in word-for-word reverse order, type:

  ```
  $ tac -r -s '[^a-zA-z0-9\-]' prizes (RET)
  ```

- To output 'prizes' in character-for-character reverse order, type:

  ```
  $ tac -r -s '.\| (RET)
  ' prizes (RET)
  ```

To reverse the characters on each *line*, use **rev**.

- To output 'prizes' with the characters on each line reversed, type:

  ```
  $ rev prizes (RET)
  ```

14 Searching Text

It's quite common to search through text for a given sequence of characters (such as a word or phrase), called a *string*, or even for a pattern describing a *set* of such strings; this chapter contains recipes for doing these kind of things.

14.1 Searching for a Word or Phrase

The primary command used for searching through text is the rather froglike-sounding tool called `grep` (the origin of its name is explained in Recipe 14.2 [Regular Expressions— Matching Text Patterns], page 166, where its advanced usage is discussed). It outputs lines of its input that contain a given string or pattern.

To search for a word, give that word as the first argument. By default, `grep` searches standard input; give the name of a file to search as the second argument.

- To output lines in the file 'catalog' containing the word 'CD', type:

  `$ grep CD catalog` (RET)

To search for a phrase, specify it in quotes.

- To output lines in the file 'catalog' containing the word 'Compact Disc', type:

  `$ grep 'Compact Disc' catalog` (RET)

The preceding example outputs all lines in the file 'catalog' that contain the exact string 'Compact Disc', it will not match, however, lines containing 'compact disc' or any other variation on the case of letters in the search pattern. Use the '-i' option to specify that matches are to be made regardless of case.

- To output lines in the file 'catalog' containing the string 'compact disc' regardless of the case of its letters, type:

  `$ grep -i 'compact disc' catalog` (RET)

This command outputs lines in the file 'catalog' containing any variation of the pattern 'compact disc', including 'Compact Disc', 'COMPACT DISC', and 'comPact dIsC'.

One thing to keep in mind is that `grep` only matches patterns that appear on a single line, so in the preceding example, if one line in 'catalog' ends with the word 'compact' and the next begins with 'disc', `grep` will not match either line. There is a way around this with `grep` (see Recipe 14.2.8 [Finding Phrases Regardless of Spacing], page 170), or you can search the text in Emacs (see Recipe 14.6.2 [Searching for a Phrase in Emacs], page 174).

You can specify more than one file to search. When you specify multiple files, each match that `grep` outputs is preceded by the name of the file it's in (and you can suppress this with the '-h' option.)

- To output lines in all of the files in the current directory containing the word 'CD', type:

  `$ grep CD *` (RET)

- To output lines in all of the '.txt' files in the '~/doc' directory containing the word 'CD', suppressing the listing of file names in the output, type:

  `$ grep -h CD ~/doc/*.txt` (RET)

Use the '-r' option to search a given directory *recursively*, searching all subdirectories it contains.

- To output lines containing the word 'CD' in all of the '.txt' files in the '~/doc' directory and in all of its subdirectories, type:

  $ *grep -r CD ~/doc/*.txt* (RET)

NOTE: There are more complex things you can search for than simple strings, as will be explained in the next section.

14.2 Regular Expressions—Matching Text Patterns

In addition to word and phrase searches, you can use grep to search for complex text patterns called *regular expressions*. A regular expression—or "regexp"—is a text string of special characters that specifies a *set* of patterns to match.

Technically speaking, the word or phrase patterns described in the previous section are regular expressions—just very simple ones. In a regular expression, most characters—including letters and numbers—represent themselves. For example, the regexp pattern *1* matches the string '1', and the pattern *bee* matches the string 'bee'.

There are a number of reserved characters called *metacharacters* that don't represent themselves in a regular expression, but have a special meaning that is used to build complex patterns. These metacharacters are as follows: ., *, [,], ^, $, and \.

To specify one of these literal characters in a regular expression, precede the character with a '\'.

- To output lines in the file 'catalog' that contain a '$' character, type:

  $ *grep '\$' catalog* (RET)

- To output lines in the file 'catalog' that contain the string '$1.99', type:

  $ *grep '\$1\.99' catalog* (RET)

- To output lines in the file 'catalog' that contain a '\' character, type:

  $ *grep '\\' catalog* (RET)

The following table describes the special meanings of the metacharacters and gives examples of their usage.

METACHARACTER	MEANING
.	Matches any one character, with the exception of the newline character. For example, . matches 'a', '1', '?', '.' (a literal period character), and so forth.
*	Matches the preceding regexp zero or more times. For example, -* matches '-', '--', '---', '----------', and so forth. Now imagine a line of text with a million '-' characters somewhere in it, all marching off across the horizon, up into the blue sky, and through the clouds. A million '-' characters in a row. This pattern would match it. Now think of the same long parade, but it's a million and one '-' characters—it matches that, too.

[ ]   Encloses a *character set*, and matches any member of the
                              set—for example, [abc] matches either 'a', 'b', or 'c'. In ad-
                              dition, the hyphen ('-') and caret ('^') characters have special
                              meanings when used inside brackets:

              -               The hyphen specifies a range of characters, ordered according
                              to their ASCII value (see Recipe 9.4 [Viewing a Character
                              Chart], page 117). For example, [0-9] is synonymous with
                              [0123456789]; [A-Za-z] matches one uppercase or lowercase
                              letter. To include a literal '-' in a list, specify it as the last
                              character in a list: so [0-9-] matches either a single digit
                              character or a '-'.x

              ^   As the first character of a list, the caret means that any char-
                              acter *except* those in the list should be matched. For example,
                              [^a] matches any character except 'a', and [^0-9] matches
                              any character except a numeric digit.

    ^   Matches the beginning of the line. So ^a matches 'a' only
                              when it is the first character on a line.

    $ Matches the end of the line. So a$ matches 'a' only when it
                              is the last character on a line.

    \   Use \ before a metacharacter when you want to specify that
                              literal character. So \$ matches a dollar sign character ('$'),
                              and \\ matches a single backslash character ('\').

                              In addition, use \ to build *new* metacharacters, by using it
                              before a number of other characters:

            \| Called the 'alternation operator'; it matches *either* regexp
                              it is between— use it to join two separate regexps to match
                              either of them. For example, a\|b matches either 'a' or 'b'.

            \+   Matches the preceding regexp as many times as possible, but
                              at least once. So a\+ matches one or more 'a' adjacent char-
                              acters, such as 'aaa', 'aa', and 'a'.

            \?   Matches the regexp preceding it either zero or one times. So
                              a\? matches 'a' or an empty string—which matches every
                              line.

    \{*number*\}   Matches the previous regexp (one specified to the left of
                              this construction) that number of times—so a\{4\} matches
                              'aaaa'. Use \{*number*,\} to match the preceding regexp
                              number or more times, \{,*number*\} to match the preceding
                              regexp zero to *number* times, and \{*number1*,*number2*\} to
                              match the preceding regexp from *number1* to *number2* times.

\(*regexp*\)   Group *regexp* together for an *alternative*; useful for combination regexps. For example, while *moo*\? matches 'mo' or 'moo', \(*moo*\)\? matches 'moo' *or* the empty set.

NOTE: The name 'grep' derives from a command in the now-obsolete Unix ed line editor tool—the ed command for searching *globally* through a file for a *regular expression* and then *printing* those lines was *g/re/p*, where *re* was the regular expression you'd use. Eventually, the grep command was written to do this search on a file when not using ed.[1]

The following sections describe some regexp recipes for commonly searched-for patterns.

14.2.1 Matching Lines Beginning with Certain Text

Use '^' in a regexp to denote the beginning of a line.

- To output all lines in '/usr/dict/words' beginning with 'pre', type:

  $ *grep '^pre' /usr/dict/words* (RET)

- To output all lines in the file 'book' that begin with the text 'in the beginning', regardless of case, type:

  $ *grep -i '^in the beginning' book* (RET)

NOTE: These regexps were quoted with ' characters; this is because some shells otherwise treat the '^' character as a special "metacharacter" (see Recipe 3.1.1 [Passing Special Characters to Commands], page 36).[2]

14.2.2 Matching Lines Ending with Certain Text

Use '$' as the last character of quoted text to match that text only at the end of a line.

- To output lines in the file 'sayings' ending with an exclamation point, type:

  $ *grep '!$' sayings* (RET)

NOTE: To use '$' in a regexp to find words that rhyme with a given word, see Recipe 11.2.1 [Listing Words that Match a Pattern], page 140.

14.2.3 Matching Lines of a Certain Length

To match lines of a particular length, use that number of '.' characters between '^' and '$'—for example, to match all lines that are two characters (or columns) wide, use '^..$' as the regexp to search for.

- To output all lines in '/usr/dict/words' that are exactly two characters wide, type:

  $ *grep '^..$' /usr/dict/words* (RET)

For longer lines, it is more useful to use a different construct: '^.\{*number*\}$', where *number* is the number of lines to match. Use ',' to specify a range of numbers.

- To output all lines in '/usr/dict/words' that are exactly seventeen characters wide, type:

---

[1] The ed command is still available on virtually all unices, Linux inclusive, and the old 'g/re/p' still works.

[2] The default shell on most Linux systems, bash, doesn't—but it's still probably good practice to quote a regexp with a caret in it.

```
$ grep '^.\{17\}$' /usr/dict/words (RET)
```

- To output all lines in '/usr/dict/words' that are twenty-five or more characters wide, type:

```
$ grep '^.\{25,\}$' /usr/dict/words (RET)
```

14.2.4 Matching Lines That Contain Any of Some Regexps

To match lines that contain any of a number of regexps, specify each of the regexps to search for between alternation operators ('\|') as the regexp to search for. Lines containing any of the given regexps will be output.

- To output all lines in 'playlist' that contain either the patterns 'the sea' or 'cake', type:

```
$ grep 'the sea\|cake' playlist (RET)
```

This command outputs any lines in 'playlist' that match the patterns 'the sea' or 'cake', including lines matching *both* patterns.

14.2.5 Matching Lines That Contain All of Some Regexps

To output lines that match *all* of a number of regexps, use grep to output lines containing the first regexp you want to match, and pipe the output to a grep with the second regexp as an argument. Continue adding pipes to grep searches for all the regexps you want to search for.

- To output all lines in 'playlist' that contain both patterns 'the sea' and 'cake', regardless of case, type:

```
$ grep -i 'the sea' playlist | grep -i cake (RET)
```

NOTE: To match lines containing some regexps in a particular order, see Recipe 14.2.11 [Regexps for Common Situations], page 171.

14.2.6 Matching Lines That Don't Contain a Regexp

To output all lines in a text that *don't* contain a given pattern, use grep with the '-v' option—this option reverts the sense of matching, selecting all non-matching lines.

- To output all lines in '/usr/dict/words' that are not three characters wide, type:

```
$ grep -v '^...$' (RET)
```

- To output all lines in 'access_log' that do not contain the string 'http', type:

```
$ grep -v http access_log (RET)
```

14.2.7 Matching Lines That Only Contain Certain Characters

To match lines that only contain certain characters, use the regexp '^[*characters*]*$', where *characters* are the ones to match.

- To output lines in '/usr/dict/words' that only contain vowels, type:

```
$ grep -i '^[aeiou]*$' /usr/dict/words (RET)
```

The '-i' option matches characters regardless of case; so, in this example, all vowel characters are matched regardless of case.

14.2.8 Finding Phrases Regardless of Spacing

One way to search for a phrase that might occur with extra spaces between words, or across a line or page break, is to remove all linefeeds and extra spaces from the input, and then **grep** that.

To do this, pipe the input[3] to **tr** with ''\r\n:\>\|-'' as an argument to the '-d' option (removing all linebreaks from the input); pipe that to the **fmt** filter with the '-u' option (outputting the text with uniform spacing); and pipe that to **grep** with the pattern to search for.

- To search across line breaks for the string 'at the same time as' in the file 'notes', type:

      $ cat notes | tr -d '\r\n:\>\|-' | fmt -u | grep 'at the same time
      as' (RET)

NOTE: The Emacs editor has its own special search for doing this—see Recipe 14.6.2 [Searching for a Phrase in Emacs], page 174.

14.2.9 Finding Patterns in Certain Contexts

To search for a pattern that only occurs in a particular context, **grep** for the context in which it should occur, and pipe the output to another **grep** to search for the actual pattern.

For example, this can be useful to search for a given pattern only when it is quoted with an '>' character in an email message.

- To list lines from the file 'email-archive' that contain the word 'narrative' only when it is quoted, type:

      $ grep '^>' email-archive | grep narrative (RET)

You can also reverse the order and use the '-v' option to output all lines containing a given pattern that are *not* in a given context.

- To list lines from the file 'email-archive' that contain the word 'narrative', but not when it is quoted, type:

      $ grep narrative email-archive | grep -v '^>' (RET)

14.2.10 Using a List of Regexps to Match From

You can keep a list of regexps in a file, and use **grep** to search text for any of the patterns in the file. To do this, specify the name of the file containing the regexps to search for as an argument to the '-f' option.

This can be useful, for example, if you need to search a given text for a number of words—keep each word on its own line in the regexp file.

- To output all lines in '/usr/dict/words' containing any of the words listed in the file 'forbidden-words', type:

      $ grep -f forbidden-words /usr/dict/words (RET)

- To output all lines in '/usr/dict/words' that do *not* contain any of the words listed in 'forbidden-words', regardless of case, type:

      $ grep -v -i -f forbidden-words /usr/dict/words (RET)

---

[3] If the input is a file, use **cat** to do this, as in the example.

14.2.11 Regexps for Common Situations

The following table lists sample regexps and describes what they match. You can use these regexps as boilerplate when building your own regular expressions for searching text. Remember to enclose regexps in quotes.

TO MATCH LINES THAT ...	USE THIS REGEXP
contain nine zeroes in a row	0\{9\}
are exactly four characters long	^....$ *or* ^.\{4\}$
are exactly seventy characters long	^.\{70\}$
begin with an asterisk character	^*
begin with 'tow' and end with 'ing'	^tow.*ing$
contain a number	[0-9]
do not contain a number	^[^0-9]*$
contain a year from 1991 through 1995	199[1-5]
contain a year from 1957 through 1969	\(195[7-9]\)|\(196[0-9]\)
contain either '.txt' or '.text'	\.te\?xt
contain 'cat' then 'gory' in the same word	cat\.\+gory
contain 'cat' then 'gory' in the same line	cat\.\+\?gory
contain a 'q' not followed by a 'u'	q[^u]
contain any ftp, gopher, or 'http' URLs	\(ftp|gopher|http|\)://.*\..*
contain 'N', 'T', and 'K', with zero or more characters between each	N.*T.*K

14.3 Searching More than Plain Text Files

The following recipes are for searching data other than in plain text files.

14.3.1 Matching Lines in Compressed Files

Use **zgrep** to search through text in files that are *compressed*. These files usually have a '.gz' file name extension, and can't be searched or otherwise read by other tools without uncompressing the file first (for more about compressed files, see Recipe 8.5 [Compressed Files], page 102).

The **zgrep** tool works just like **grep**, except it searches through the text of compressed files. It outputs matches to the given pattern as if you'd searched through normal, uncompressed files. It leaves the files compressed when it exits.

- To search through the compressed file 'README.gz' for the text 'Linux', type:

      $ zgrep Linux README.gz (RET)

14.3.2 Matching Lines in Web Pages

You can `grep` a Web page or other URL by giving the URL to `lynx` with the '`-dump`' option, and piping the output to `grep`.

- To search the contents of the URL `http://example.com/` for lines containing the text '`gonzo`' or '`hunter`', type:

  ```
  $ lynx -dump http://example.com/ | grep 'gonzo\|hunter' (RET)
  ```

14.4 Outputting the Context of a Search

It is sometimes useful to see a matched line in its context in the file—that is, to see some of the lines that surround it.

Use the '`-C`' option with `grep` to output results in *context*—it outputs matched lines with two lines of "context" both before and after each match. To specify the number of context lines output both before and after matched lines, use that number as an option instead of '`-C`'.

- To search '`/usr/dict/words`' for lines matching '`tsch`' and output two lines of context before and after each line of output, type:

  ```
  $ grep -C tsch /usr/dict/words (RET)
  ```

- To search '`/usr/dict/words`' for lines matching '`tsch`' and output six lines of context before and after each line of output, type:

  ```
  $ grep -6 tsch /usr/dict/words (RET)
  ```

To output matches and the lines *before* them, use '`-B`'; to output matches and the lines *after* them, use '`-A`'. Give a numeric option with either of these options to specify that number of context lines.

- To search '`/usr/dict/words`' for lines matching '`tsch`' and output two lines of context *before* each line of output, type:

  ```
  $ grep -B tsch /usr/dict/words (RET)
  ```

- To search '`/usr/dict/words`' for lines matching '`tsch`' and output six lines of context *after* each line of output, type:

  ```
  $ grep -A6 tsch /usr/dict/words (RET)
  ```

- To search '`/usr/dict/words`' for lines matching '`tsch`' and output ten lines of context before and three lines of context after each line of output, type:

  ```
  $ grep -B10 -A3 tsch /usr/dict/words (RET)
  ```

14.5 Searching and Replacing Text

A quick way to search and replace some text in a file is to use the following one-line `perl` command:

```
$ perl -pi -e "s/oldstring/newstring/g;" filespec (RET)
```

In this example, *oldstring* is the string to search, *newstring* is the string to replace it with, and *filespec* is the name of the file or files to work on. You can use this for more than one file.

- To replace the string 'helpless' with the string 'helpful' in all files in the current directory, type:

    $ *perl -pi -e "s/helpless/helpful/g;" ** (RET)

You can also search and replace text in an Emacs buffer; to do this, use the **replace-regexp** function and give both the expression to search for and the expression to replace it with.

- To replace the text 'helpless' with the text 'helpful' in the current buffer, type:

    M-x replace-regexp (RET) *helpless* (RET) *helpful* (RET)

NOTE: You can also search and replace text in most text editors, including Emacs; see Recipe 14.6.4 [Searching and Replacing in Emacs], page 174.

14.6 Searching Text in Emacs

The following sections show ways of searching for text in Emacs—incrementally, for a word or phrase, or for a pattern—and for searching and then replacing text.

14.6.1 Searching Incrementally in Emacs

Type *C-s* to use the Emacs incremental search function. It takes text as input in the minibuffer and it searches for that text from point toward the end of the current buffer. Type *C-s* again to search for the next occurrence of the text you're searching for; this works until no more matches occur. Then, Emacs reports 'Failing I-search' in the minibuffer; type *C-s* again to wrap to the beginning of the buffer and continue the search from there.

It gets its name "incremental" because it begins searching immediately when you start to type text, and so it builds a search string in *increments*—for example, if you want to search for the word 'sunflower' in the current buffer, you start to type

    C-s s

At that point Emacs searches forward through the buffer to the first 's' character, and highlights it. Then, as you type u, it searches forward to the first 'su' in the buffer and highlights that (if a 'u' appears immediately after the 's' it first stopped at, it stays where it's at, and highlights the 's' and the 'u'). It continues to do this as long as you type and as long as there is a match in the current buffer. As soon as what you type does not appear in the buffer, Emacs beeps and a message appears in the minibuffer stating that the search has failed.

To search for the next instance of the last string you gave, type *C-s* again; if you keep (CTRL) held down, every time you press the (S) key, Emacs will advance to the next match in the buffer.

This is generally the fastest and most common type of search you will use in Emacs.

You can do an incremental search through the buffer in *reverse*—that is, from point to the beginning of the buffer—with the **isearch-backward** function, *C-r*.

- To search for the text 'moon' in the current buffer from point in reverse to the beginning of the buffer, type:

    C-r moon

14.6.2 Searching for a Phrase in Emacs

Like **grep**, the Emacs incremental search only works on lines of text, so it only finds phrases on a single line. If you search for 'hello, world' with the incremental search and the text 'hello,' appears at the end of a line and the text 'world' appears at the beginning of the next line, it won't find it.

To find a multi-word phrase across line breaks, use the **word-search-forward** function. It searches for a phrase or words regardless of punctuation or spacing.

- To search forward through the current buffer for the phrase 'join me', type:

  M-x word-search-forward (RET) *join me* (RET)

NOTE: The **word-search-backward** function does the same as **word-search-forward**, except it searches *backward* through the buffer, from point to the beginning of the buffer.

14.6.3 Searching for a Regexp in Emacs

Use the **search-forward-regexp** function to search for a regular expression from point to the end of the current buffer.

- To search forward through the current buffer for the regexp '@.*\.org', type:

  M-x search-forward-regexp (RET) *@.*\.org* (RET)

The keyboard accelerator for this command is *M-C-s*—on most keyboards, you press and release (ESC) and then hold down (CTRL) while you type *s*. To repeat the last regexp search you made, type *M-C-s C-s*; then, as long as you have (CTRL) held down, you can keep typing *s* to advance to the next match, just as you would with an incremental search.

NOTE: There is a **search-backward-regexp** function that is identical but searches backward, from point to the top of the buffer.

14.6.4 Searching and Replacing in Emacs

To search for and replace text in Emacs, use the **replace-regexp** function. When you run this function, Emacs will ask for both the text or regexp to search for and the text to replace it with.

- To replace the text 'day' with the text 'night' in the current buffer, type:

  M-x replace-regexp (RET) *day* (RET) *night* (RET)

This function is especially useful for replacing control characters with text, or for replacing text with control characters, which you can specify with *C-q*, the **quoted-insert** function (see Recipe 10.2.5 [Inserting Special Characters in Emacs], page 126).

- To replace all the '^M' characters in the current buffer with regular linefeeds, type:

  M-x replace-regexp (RET) *C-q C-m* (RET) *C-q 012* (RET) (RET)

14.7 Searching Text in Less

There are two useful commands in **less** for searching through text: / and ?. To search *forward* through the text, type / followed by a regexp to search for; to search *backward* through the text, use ?.

When you do a search, the word or other regexp you search for appears highlighted throughout the text.

- To search forward through the text you are perusing for the word 'cat', type:

      /cat (RET)

  To search backward through the text you are perusing for the regexp '[ch]at', type:

      ?[ch]at (RET)

15 Typesetting and Word Processing

If you're coming to Linux with a Microsoft Windows or Apple MacOS background, or from some other non-Unix computing environment, you are likely used to one approach to "word processing." In these environments, most writing is done in word processors—large programs that offer a vast array of formatting options and that store their output in proprietary file formats. Most people use word processors no matter where the intended output will go (even if it's just your diary).

Word processors, from complete suites like StarOffice to commercial favorites like Word-Perfect, are available for Linux—and have been for years. However, the standard personal-computing paradigm known as "word processing" has never really taken off on Linux—or, for that matter, on Unix-like operating systems in general. With Linux, most writing is done in a text editor, and files are kept in plain text.

When you keep a file in plain text, you can use command-line tools to format the pages and paragraphs; add page numbers and headers; check the spelling, style, and usage; count the lines, words, and characters it contains; convert it to HTML and other formats; and even print the text in a font of your choosing—all of which are described in the recipes in this book. The text can be formatted, analyzed, cut, chopped, sliced, diced, and otherwise processed by the vast array of Linux command-line tools that work on text—over 750 in an average installation.

This approach may seem primitive at first—especially to those weaned in a computing environment that dictates that all writing must be set in a typeface from the moment of creation—but the word-processing approach can be excessive compared to what Linux provides. You can, if you like, view or print plain text in a font, with a single command—which is what ninety percent of people want to do with a word processor ninety percent of the time, anyway; to do this, see Recipe 15.2 [Converting Plain Text for Output], page 179.

It's my opinion that word processing is not a forward-thinking direction for the handling of text, especially on Linux systems and especially now that text is not always destined for printed output: text can end up on a Web page, in an "eBook," in an email message, or possibly in print. The best common source for these formats is plain text. Word processing programs, and the special file formats they require, are anathema to the generalized, tools-based and plain-text philosophy of Unix and Linux (see Recipe 1.1.6 [Unix and the Tools Philosophy], page 13). "Word processing" itself may be an obsolete idea of the 1980s personal computing environment, and it may no longer be a necessity in the age of the Web and email—mediums in which plain text content is more native than proprietary word processor formats.

If you do need to design a special layout for hardcopy, you can *typeset* the text. One could write a book on the subject of Linux typesetting; unfortunately, no such book has yet been written, but this chapter contains recipes for producing typeset text. They were selected as being the easiest to prepare or most effective for their purpose.

NOTE: For more information on this subject, I recommend Christopher B. Browne's excellent overview, "Word Processors for Linux" (`http://www.hex.net/~cbbrowne/wp.html`).

15.1 Choosing the Right Typesetting System for the Job

Choosing the proper typesetting system to use when you are about to begin a project can be daunting: each has its own drawbacks and abilities, and to the less experienced it may not be immediately clear which is most appropriate for a particular document or project.

The following table can help you determine which system is best for a particular task. There isn't one way of doing such things, of course—these are only my recommendations. The first column lists the kind of output you intend, the second gives examples of the kind of documents, and the third suggests the typesetting system(s) to use. These systems are described in the remaining sections of this chapter.

INTENDED OUTPUT	EXAMPLES	TYPESETTING SYSTEM
Printed, typeset output *and* electronic HTML or text file	Internet FAQ, white paper, dissertation	`enscript`; Texinfo; SGMLtools
Printed, typeset output *and* text file	`man` page, command reference card	`groff`
Printed, typeset output	Letter or other correspondence, report, book manuscript	LaTeX or LyX
Printed, typeset output	Brochure or newsletter with multiple columns and images	LyX
Printed, typeset output	Envelope, mailing label, other specialized document	TeX
Printed text output in a font	Grocery list, saved email message, to-do list	`enscript`
Printed, typeset output	Poster, sign	`enscript`; HTML; LyX; TeX
Large printed text output	Long banners for parties or other occasions	`banner`

NOTE: If you really don't need a document to be typeset, then don't bother! Just keep it a plain text file, and use a text editor to edit it (see Chapter 10 [Text Editing], page 119). Do this for writing notes, email messages, Web pages, Usenet articles, and so forth. If you ever do need to typeset it later, you will still be able to do so. And you can, if you like, view or print plain text in nice fonts (see Recipe 15.2.1 [Outputting Text in a Font], page 180).

15.2 Converting Plain Text for Output

Debian: 'enscript'
WWW: http://www.iki.fi/~mtr/genscript/

The simplest way to typeset plain text is to convert it to PostScript. This is often done to prepare text for printing; the original source text file remains as unformatted text, but the text of the printed output is formatted in basic ways, such as being set in a font.

The main tool for converting text to PostScript is called enscript; it converts the text file that is specified as an argument into PostScript, making any number of formatting changes in between. It's great for quickly making nice output from a plain text file—you can use it to do things such as output text in a font of your choosing, or paginate text with graphical headers at the top of each page.

By default, enscript paginates its input, outputs it in a 10-point Courier font, and puts a simple header at the top of each page containing the file name, date and time, and page number in bold. Use the '-B' option to omit this header.

If you have a PostScript printer connected to your system, enscript can be set up to spool its output right to the printer. You can verify if your system is set up this way by looking at the enscript configuration file, '/etc/enscript.cfg'. The line

        DefaultOutputMethod: printer

specifies that output is spooled directly to the printer; changing it to 'stdout' instead of 'printer' sends the output to the standard output instead.

Even if your default printer does not natively understand PostScript, it may be able to take enscript output, anyway. Most Linux installations these days have print filters set up so that PostScript spooled for printing is automatically converted to a format the printer understands (if your system doesn't have this setup for some reason, convert the PostScript to a format recognized by your printer with the gs tool, and then print that—see Recipe 20.3 [Converting PostScript], page 239).

- To convert the text file 'saved-mail' to PostScript, with default formatting, and spool the output right to the printer, type:

        $ enscript saved-mail (RET)

To write the output to a file instead of spooling it, give the name of the file you want to output as an argument to the '-p' option. This is useful when you don't have a PostScript printer and you need to convert the output first, or for when you just want to make a PostScript image file from some text, or for previewing the output before you print it. In the latter case, you can view it on the display screen with a PostScript viewer application such as ghostview (see Recipe 17.1.2 [Previewing a PostScript File], page 207).

- To write the text file 'saved-mail' to a PostScript file, 'saved-mail.ps', and then preview it in X, type:

        $ enscript -p report.ps saved-mail (RET)
        $ ghostview saved-mail.ps (RET)

The following recipes show how to use enscript to output text with different effects and properties.

NOTE: Once you make a PostScript file from text input, you can use any of the tools to format this new PostScript file, including rearranging and resizing its pages (see Chapter 20 [PostScript], page 235).

15.2.1 Outputting Text in a Font

To output text in a particular PostScript font, use `enscript` and give the name of the font you want to use as a quoted argument to the '`-f`' option.

Specify both the font family and size in points: give the capitalized name of the font family (with hyphens to indicate spaces between words) followed by the the size in points. For example, '`Courier14`' outputs text in the Courier font at 14 points, and '`Times-Roman12.2`' outputs text in the Times Roman font at 12.2 points. Some of the available font names are listed in the file '`/usr/share/enscript/afm/font.map`'; the `enscript man` page describes how to use additional fonts that might be installed on your system.

- To print the contents of the text file '`saved-mail`' on a PostScript printer, with text set in the Helvetica font at 12 points, type:

    $ *enscript -B -f "Helvetica12" saved-mail* (RET)

- To make a PostScript file called '`saved-mail.ps`' containing the contents of the text file '`saved-mail`', with text set in the Helvetica font at 12 points, type:

    $ *enscript -B -f "Helvetica12" -p saved-mail.ps saved-mail* (RET)

The '`-B`' option was used in the preceding examples to omit the output of a header on each page. When headers are used, they're normally output in 10-point Courier Bold; to specify a different font for the text in the header, give its name as an argument to the '`-F`' option.

- To print the contents of the text file '`saved-mail`' to a PostScript printer, with text set in 10-point Times Roman and header text set in 18-point Times Bold, type:

    $ *enscript -f "Times-Roman10" -F "Times-Bold18" saved-mail* (RET)

- To make a PostScript file called '`saved-mail.ps`' containing the contents of the text file '`saved-mail`', with text and headers both set in 16-point Palatino Roman, type:

    $ *enscript -f "Palatino-Roman16" -F "Palatino-Roman16" -p saved-mail.ps saved-mail* (RET)

15.2.2 Outputting Text as a Poster or Sign

You can output any text you type directly to the printer (or to a PostScript file) by omitting the name of the input file; `enscript` will read the text on the standard input until you type *C-d* on a new line.

This is especially useful for making a quick-and-dirty sign or poster—to do this, specify a large font for the text, such as Helvetica Bold at 72 points, and omit the display of default headers.

- To print a sign in 72-point Helvetica Bold type to a PostScript printer, type:

```
$ enscript -B -f "Helvetica-Bold72" (RET)
(RET)
CAUTION (RET)
(RET)
WET PAINT! (RET)
C-d
```

72-point type is very large; use the '--word-wrap' option with longer lines of text to wrap lines at word boundaries if necessary. You might need this option because at these larger font sizes, you run the risk of making lines that are longer than could fit on the page. You can also use the '-r' option to print the text in landscape orientation, as described in Recipe 15.2.5 [Outputting Text in Landscape Orientation], page 184.

- To print a sign in 63-point Helvetica Bold across the long side of the page, type:

```
$ enscript -B -r --word-wrap -f "Helvetica-Bold63" (RET)
(RET)
(RET)
CAUTION -- WET PAINT! (RET)
C-d
```

NOTE: To make a snazzier or more detailed message or sign, you would create a file in a text editor and justify the words on each line in the file as you want them to print, with blank lines where necessary. If you're getting that complicated with it, it would also be wise to use the '-p' option once to output to a file first, and preview the file before printing it (see Recipe 17.1.2 [Previewing a PostScript File], page 207).

15.2.3 Outputting Text with Language Highlighting

The **enscript** tool currently recognizes the formatting of more than forty languages and formats, from the Perl and C programming languages to HTML, email, and Usenet news articles; **enscript** can highlight portions of the text based on its syntax. In Unix-speak, this is called *pretty-printing*.

The following table lists the names of some of the language filters that are available at the time of this writing and describes the languages or formats they're used for.

FILTER	LANGUAGE OR FORMAT
ada	Ada95 programming language.
asm	Assembler listings.
awk	AWK programming language.
bash	Bourne-Again shell programming language.
c	C programming language.
changelog	ChangeLog files.
cpp	C++ programming language.

`csh`	C-Shell script language.
`delphi`	Delphi programming language.
`diff`	Normal "difference reports" made from `diff`.
`diffu`	Unified "difference reports" made from `diff`.
`elisp`	Emacs Lisp programming language.
`fortran`	Fortran77 programming language.
`haskell`	Haskell programming language.
`html`	HyperText Markup Language (HTML).
`idl`	IDL (CORBA Interface Definition Language).
`java`	Java programming language.
`javascript`	JavaScript programming language.
`ksh`	Korn shell programming language.
`m4`	M4 macro processor programming language.
`mail`	Electronic mail and Usenet news articles.
`makefile`	Rule files for `make`.
`nroff`	Manual pages formatted with `nroff`.
`objc`	Objective-C programming language.
`pascal`	Pascal programming language.
`perl`	Perl programming language.
`postscript`	PostScript programming language.
`python`	Python programming language.
`scheme`	Scheme programming language.
`sh`	Bourne shell programming language.
`skill`	Cadence Design Systems Lisp-like language.
`sql`	Sybase 11 SQL.
`states`	Definition files for `states`.
`synopsys`	Synopsys `dc` shell scripting language.
`tcl`	Tcl programming language.
`tcsh`	TC-Shell script language.

`vba`	Visual Basic (for Applications).
`verilog`	Verilog hardware description language.
`vhdl`	VHSIC Hardware Description Language (VHDL).
`vrml`	Virtual Reality Modeling Language (VRML97).
`zsh`	Z-shell programming language.

To pretty-print a file, give the name of the filter to use as an argument to the '`-E`' option, without any whitespace between the option and argument.

- To pretty-print the HTML file '`index.html`', type:

      $ enscript -Ehtml index.html (RET)

- To pretty-print an email message saved to the file '`important-mail`', and output it with no headers to a file named '`important-mail.ps`', type:

      $ enscript -B -Email -p important-mail.ps important-mail (RET)

Use the special '`--help-pretty-print`' option to list the languages supported by the copy of `enscript` you have.

- To peruse a list of currently supported languages, type:

      $ enscript --help-pretty-print | less (RET)

15.2.4 Outputting Text with Fancy Headers

To output text with fancy graphic headers, where the header text is set in blocks of various shades of gray, use `enscript` with the '`-G`' option.

- To print the contents of the text file '`saved-mail`' with fancy headers on a PostScript printer, type:

      $ enscript -G saved-mail (RET)

- To make a PostScript file called '`saved-mail.ps`' containing the contents of the text file '`saved-mail`', with fancy headers, type:

      $ enscript -G -p saved-mail.ps saved-mail (RET)

Without the '`-G`' option, `enscript` outputs text with a plain header in bold text, printing the file name and the time it was last modified. The '`-B`' option, as described earlier, omits all headers.

You can customize the header text by quoting the text you want to use as an argument to the '`-b`' option. Use the special symbol '`$%`' to specify the current page number in the header text.

- To print the contents of the text file '`saved-mail`' with a custom header label containing the current page number, type:

      $ enscript -b "Page $% of the saved email archive" saved-mail (RET)

NOTE: You can create your own custom fancy headers, too—this is described in the '`CUSTOMIZATION`' section of the `enscript` man page.

15.2.5 Outputting Text in Landscape Orientation

To output text in *landscape* orientation, where text is rotated 90 degrees counter-clockwise, use the '-r' option.

- To print the contents of the text file 'saved-mail' to a PostScript printer, with text set in 28-point Times Roman and oriented in landscape orientation, type:

      $ enscript -f "Times-Roman28" -r saved-mail (RET)

  The '-r' option is useful for making horizontal banners by passing output of the figlet tool to enscript (see Recipe 16.3.1 [Horizontal Text Fonts], page 202).

- To output the text 'This is a long banner' in a figlet font and write it to the default printer with text set at 18-point Courier and in landscape orientation, type:

      $ figlet "A long banner" | enscript -B -r -f "Courier18" (RET)

15.2.6 Outputting Multiple Copies of Text

To output multiple copies of text when sending to the printer with enscript, give the number as an argument to the '-#' option. This option doesn't work when sending to a file, but note that lpr takes the same option (see Recipe 25.1.2 [Printing Multiple Copies of a Job], page 272).

- To print three copies of the text file 'saved-mail' to a PostScript printer with the default enscript headers, type:

      $ enscript -#3 saved-mail (RET)

15.2.7 Selecting the Pages of Text to Output

To specify which pages of a text are output with enscript, give the range of page number(s) as an argument to the '-a' option.

- To print pages two through ten of file 'saved-mail' with the default enscript headers, type:

      $ enscript -a2-10 saved-mail (RET)

  To print just the odd or even pages, use the special 'odd' and 'even' arguments. This is good for printing double-sided pages: first print the odd-numbered pages, and then feed the output pages back into the printer and print the even-numbered pages.

- To print the odd-numbered pages of the file 'saved-mail' with the default headers, type:

      $ enscript -a odd saved-mail (RET)

- To print the even-numbered pages of the file 'saved-mail' with the default headers, type:

      $ enscript -a even saved-mail (RET)

15.2.8 Additional PostScript Output Options

The following table describes some of enscript's other options.

OPTION	DESCRIPTION
-*number*	Specify number of columns per page; for example, to specify four columns per page, use '-4'.
-a*pages*	Specify the page numbers to be printed, where *pages* is a comma-delineated list of page numbers. Specify individual pages by their numbers, and specify a range of pages by giving the first and last page numbers in the range separated by a hyphen ('-'). The special 'odd' prints odd-numbered pages and 'even' prints even-numbered pages.
-d*printer*	Spool output to the printer named *printer*.
-E*language*	"Pretty-print" the text written in the specified *language* with context highlighting.
-H*number*	Specify the height of highlight bars, in lines (without *number*, the value of 2 is used).
-i*number*	Indent lines by *number* characters, or follow *number* with a letter denoting the unit to use: 'c' for centimeters, 'i' for inches, or 'p' for PostScript points (1/72 inch).
-I*filter*	Pass input files through *filter*, which can be a tool or quoted command.
-j	Print borders around columns.
-L*numbers*	Specify the number of lines per page.
-u*text*	Specify a quoted string "underlay" to print underneath every page.
-U*number*	Specify the number of logical pages to print on each page of output.
--highlight-bar-gray=*number*	Specify the level of gray color to be used in printing the highlight bars, from 0.0 (gray) to 1.0 (white).
--margins=*left*:*right*:*top*:*bottom*	Adjust left, right, top, and bottom page margins; the measurements are in PostScript points, and, when specifying the values, any can be omitted. (Given on one line all as one long option.)
--rotate-even-pages	Rotate each even-numbered page 180 degrees.

15.3 LyX Document Processing

Debian: 'lyx'
WWW: http://www.lyx.org/

LyX is a relative newcomer to the typesetting and word-processing arena, and it is one of the most genuinely fresh ideas in the field: it's a kind of word processor for writing LaTeX input (see Recipe 15.4 [Typesetting with TeX and Friends], page 189). It's a visual, graphic editor for X, but it doesn't emulate the output paper directly on the display screen. In contrast to specifying exactly how each character in the document will look ("make this word Helvetica Bold at 18 points"), you specify the *structure* of the text you write ("make this word a chapter heading"). And, in contrast to the WYSIWYG paradigm, its authors call the new approach WYSIWYM—"What you say is what you *mean*."

LyX comes with many document `classes` already defined—such as `letter`, `article`, `report`, and `book`—containing definitions for the elements these document types may contain. You can change the look of each element and the look of the document as a whole, and you can change the look of individual selections of text, but with these elements available, it's rarely necessary.

Since LyX uses LaTeX as a back-end to do the actual typesetting, and LyX is capable of exporting documents to LaTeX input format, you can think of it as a way to write LaTeX input files in a GUI without having to know the LaTeX language commands.

However, even those who *do* use LaTeX and related typesetting languages can get some use out of LyX: many people find it quick and easy to create some documents in LyX that are much harder to do in LaTeX, such as multi-column newsletter layouts with illustrations.

You can also import your LaTeX files (and plain text) into LyX for further layout or manipulation.

The following recipes show how to get started using LyX, and where to go to learn more about it.

15.3.1 Features of LyX

When editing in LyX, you'll see that it has all of the commands you'd expect from a word processor—for example, some of the commands found on the `Edit` menu include `Cut`, `Copy`, `Paste`, `Find and Replace`, and `Spell Check`.

Here are some of its major features:

- Automatic generation of table of contents, nested lists, and numbering of section headings.
- Easy insertion of PostScript figures and illustrations, which can be rotated, scaled, and captioned.
- WYSIWYG construction of tables.
- Undo and redo of any operation or sequence of operations.
- All LyX functions available from both keyboard commands and pull-down menus.
- All key-presses used for commands are configurable.

15.3.2 Writing Documents with LyX

LyX runs under X, and you start it in the usual way—either by choosing it from the applications menu provided by your window manager or by typing `lyx` in an `xterm` window. (For more about starting programs in X, see Recipe 4.2 [Running a Program in X], page 54).

To start a new document from scratch, choose `New` from the `File` menu. You can also make a document from one of the many templates included with LyX, which have the basic layout and settings for a particular kind of document all set up for you—just fill in the elements for your actual document. To make a new document from a template, choose `New from template` from the `File` menu, and then select the name of the template to use.

The following table lists the names of some of the included templates and the kind of documents they're usually used for:

TEMPLATE FILE	DOCUMENT FORMAT
`aapaper.lyx`	Format suitable for papers submitted to *Astronomy and Astrophysics*.
`dinbrief.lyx`	Format for letters typeset according to German conventions.
`docbook_template.lyx`	Format for documents written in the SGML DocBook DTD.
`hollywood.lyx`	Format for movie scripts as they are formatted in the U.S. film industry.
`iletter.lyx`	Format for letters typeset according to Italian conventions.
`latex8.lyx`	Format suitable for article submissions to IEEE conferences.
`letter.lyx`	Basic format for letters and correspondence.
`linuxdoctemplate.lyx`	Format for documents written in the SGML LinuxDoc DTD, as formerly used by the Linux Documentation Project (`http://linuxdoc.org/`).
`revtex.lyx`	Article format suitable for submission to publications of the American Physical Society (APS), American Institute of Physics (AIP), and Optical Society of America (OSA).
`slides.lyx`	Format for producing slides and transparencies.

To view how the document will look when you print it, choose `View DVI` from the `File` menu. This command starts the `xdvi` tool, which previews the output on the screen. (For more on using `xdvi`, see Recipe 17.1.1 [Previewing a DVI File], page 207).

To print the document, choose `Print` from the `File` menu. You can also export it to LaTeX, PostScript, DVI, or plain text formats; to do this, choose `Export` from the `File` menu and then select the format to export to.

NOTE: If you plan on editing the document again in LyX, be sure to save the actual '`.lyx`' document file.

15.3.3 Learning More about LyX

The LyX Documentation Project has overseen the creation of a great deal of free documentation for LyX, including hands-on tutorials, user manuals, and example documents.

The LyX Graphical Tour (`http://www.lyx.org/about/lgt-1.0/lgt.html`) is a Web-based tutorial that shows you how to create and edit a simple LyX file.

LyX has a comprehensive set of built-in manuals, which you can read inside the LyX editor like any LyX document, or you can print them out. All of the manuals are available from the `Help` menu.

- To run LyX's built-in tutorial, choose `Tutorial` from the `Help` menu.

This command opens the LyX tutorial, which you can then read on the screen or print out by selecting `Print` from the `File` menu.

The following table lists the names of the available manuals as they appear on the `Help` menu, and describes what each contains:

MANUAL	DESCRIPTION
`Introduction`	An introduction to using the LyX manuals, describing their contents and how to view and print them.
`Tutorial`	A hands-on tutorial to writing documents with LyX.
`User's Guide`	The main LyX usage manual, describing all of the commonly used commands, options, and features.
`Extended Features`	This is "Part II" of the *User's Guide*, describing advanced features such as bibliographies, indices, documents with multiple files, and techniques used in special-case situations, such as fax support, SGML-Tools support, and using version control with LyX documents.
`Customization`	Shows which elements of LyX can be customized and how to go about doing that.
`Reference Manual`	Describes all of the menu entries and internal functions.
`Known Bugs`	LyX is in active development, and like any large application, bugs have been found. They are listed and described in this document.
`LaTeX Configuration`	This document is automatically generated by LyX when it is installed on your system. It is an inventory of your LaTeX configuration, including the version of LaTeX in use, available fonts, available document classes, and other related packages that may be installed on your system.

Finally, LyX includes example documents in the '`/usr/X11R6/share/lyx/examples`' directory. Here's a partial listing of these files with a description of what each contains:

DOCUMENT FILE	DESCRIPTION
`Foils.lyx`	Describes how to make *foils*—slides or overhead transparencies—with the FoilTeX package.
`ItemizeBullets.lyx`	Examples of the various bullet styles for itemized lists.
`Literate.lyx`	An example of using LyX as a composition environment for "literate programming."
`MathLabeling.lyx`	Techniques for numbering and labeling equations.
`Math_macros.lyx`	Shows how to make macros in Math mode.
`Minipage.lyx`	Shows how to write two-column bilingual documents.

`TableExamples.lyx`	Examples of using tables in LyX.
`aa_head.lyx` `aa_paper.lyx` `aas_sample.lyx`	Files discussing and showing the use of LyX in the field of astronomy.
`amsart-test.lyx` `amsbook-test.lyx`	Examples of documents written in the format used by the American Mathematical Society.
`docbook_example.lyx`	Example of a DocBook document.
`multicol.lyx`	Example of a multi-column format.
`scriptone.lyx`	Example of a Hollywood script.

15.4 Typesetting with TeX and Friends

Debian: 'tetex-base'
Debian: 'tetex-bin'
Debian: 'tetex-doc'
Debian: 'tetex-extra'
Debian: 'tetex-lib'
WWW: http://www.tug.org/teTeX/

The most capable typesetting tool for use on Linux-based systems is the TeX typesetting system and related software. It is the premier computer typesetting system   its output surpasses or rivals all other systems to date. The advanced line and paragraph breaking, hyphenation, kerning, and other font characteristic policies and algorithms it can perform, and the level of precision at which it can do them, have yet to be matched in word processors.

The TeX system itself   not a word processor or single program, but a large collection of files and data—is packaged in distributions; teTeX is the TeX distribution designed for Linux.

TeX input documents are plain text files written in the TeX formatting language, which the TeX tools can process and write to output files for printing or viewing. This approach has great benefits for the writer: the plain text input files can be written with and exchanged between many different computer systems regardless of operating system or editing software, and these input files do not become obsolete or unusable with new versions of the TeX software.

Donald Knuth, the world's foremost authority on algorithms, wrote TeX in 1984 as a way to typeset his books (http://www-cs-faculty.stanford.edu/~knuth/taocp.html), because he wasn't satisfied with the quality of available systems. Since its first release, many extensions to the TeX formatting language have been made—the most notable being Leslie Lamport's LaTeX, which is a collection of sophisticated macros written in the TeX formatting language, designed to facilitate the typesetting of structured documents. (LaTeX probably gets more day-to-day use than the plain TeX format, but in my experience, both systems are useful for different kinds of documents.)

The collective family of TEX and related programs are sometimes called "TEX and friends," and abbreviated as 'texmf' in some TEX references[1]: for example, the supplementary files included with the bare TEX system are kept in the '/usr/lib/texmf' directory tree.

The following recipes describe how to begin writing input for TEX and how to process these files for viewing and printing. While not everyone wants or even has a need to write documents with TEX and LaTeX, these formats are widely used—especially on Linux systems—so every Linux user has the potential to encounter one of these files, and ought to know how to process them.

NOTE: "TEX" doesn't sound like the name of a cowboy, nor "LaTeX" like a kind of paint: the letters 'T', 'E', and 'X' represent the Greek characters tau, epsilon, and chi (from the Greek 'techne', meaning art and science). So the last sound in "TEX" is like the 'ch' in 'Bach', and "LaTeX," depending on local dialect, is pronounced either 'lay-teck' or 'lah-teck'. Those who become highly adept at using the system, Knuth calls "TEXnicians."

15.4.1 Is It a TEX or LaTeX File?

There are separate commands for processing TEX and LaTeX files, and they're not interchangeable, so when you want to process a TEX or LaTeX input file, you should first determine its format.

By convention, TEX files always have a '.tex' file name extension. LaTeX input files sometimes have a '.latex' or '.ltx' file name extension instead, but not always—one way to tell if a '.tex' file is actually in the LaTeX format is to use **grep** to search the file for the text '\document', which every LaTeX (and *not* TEX) document will have. So if it outputs any lines that match, you have a LaTeX file. (The regular expression to use with **grep** is '\\document', since backslash characters must be specified with two backslashes.)

- To determine whether the file 'gentle.tex' is a TEX or LaTeX file, type:

      $ grep '\\document' gentle.tex (RET)
      $

In this example, **grep** didn't return any matches, so it's safe to assume that 'gentle.tex' is a TEX file and not a LaTeX file.

NOTE: For more on **grep** and searching for regular expressions, see Recipe 14.2 [Regular Expressions—Matching Text Patterns], page 166.

15.4.2 Processing TEX Files

Use **tex** to process TEX files. It takes as an argument the name of the TEX source file to process, and it writes an output file in DVI ("DeVice Independent") format, with the same base file name as the source file, but with a '.dvi' extension.

- To process the file 'gentle.tex', type:

      $ tex gentle.tex (RET)

Once you have produced a DVI output file with this method, you can do the following with it:

---

[1] The 'mf' also stands for "Metafont," the name of the font language that is part of TEX.

- Preview it on the screen with `xdvi`; see Recipe 17.1.1 [Previewing a DVI File], page 207
- Print it with `dvips` or `lpr`; see Recipe 25.2.2 [Printing with Dvips], page 274
- Convert it to PostScript with `dvips`; see Recipe 25.3.2 [Preparing a DVI File for Printing], page 276; (then, you can also convert the PostScript output to PDF or plain text)

15.4.3 Processing LaTeX Files

The `latex` tool works just like `tex`, but is used to process LaTeX files.

- To process the LaTeX file '`lshort.tex`', type:

  ```
  $ latex lshort.tex (RET)
  ```

This command writes a DVI output file called '`lshort.dvi`'.

You may need to run `latex` on a file several times consecutively. LaTeX documents sometimes have indices and cross references, which, because of the way that LaTeX works, take two (and in rare cases three or more) runs through `latex` to be fully processed. Should you need to run `latex` through a file more than once in order to generate the proper references, you'll see a message in the `latex` processing output after you process it the first time instructing you to process it again.

- To ensure that all of the cross references in '`lshort.tex`' have been generated properly, run the input file through `latex` once more:

  ```
  $ latex lshort.tex (RET)
  ```

The '`lshort.dvi`' file will be rewritten with an updated version containing the proper page numbers in the cross reference and index entries. You can then view, print, or convert this DVI file as described in the previous recipe for processing TeX files.

15.4.4 Writing Documents with TeX and LaTeX

WWW: `ftp://ctan.tug.org/tex-archive/documentation/gentle.tex`
WWW: `ftp://ctan.tug.org/tex-archive/documentation/lshort/`

To create a document with TeX or LaTeX, you generally use your favorite text editor to write an *input file* containing the text in TeX or LaTeX formatting. Then, you process this TeX or LaTeX input file to create an *output file* in the DVI format, which you can preview, convert, or print.

It's an old tradition among programmers introducing a programming language to give a simple program that just outputs the text '`Hello, world`' to the screen; such a program is usually just detailed enough to give those unfamiliar with the language a feel for its basic syntax.

We can do the same with document processing languages like TeX and LaTeX. Here's the "Hello, world" for a TeX document:

```
Hello, world
\end
```

If you processed this input file with `tex`, it would output a DVI file that displayed the text '`Hello, world`' in the default TeX font, on a default page size, and with default margins.

Here's the same "Hello, world" for LaTeX:

```
\documentclass{article}
\begin{document}
Hello, world
\end{document}
```

Even though the TeX example is much simpler, LaTeX is generally easier to use for making structured documents. Plain TeX, on the other hand, is better for more experimental layouts or specialized documents.

The TeX and LaTeX markup languages are worth a book each, and providing an introduction to their use is well out of the scope of this text. To learn how to write input for them, I suggest two excellent tutorials, Michael Doob's *A Gentle Introduction to TeX*, and Tobias Oetiker's *The Not So Short Introduction to LaTeX*—each available on the WWW at the URLs listed above. These files are each in the respective format they describe; in order to read them, you must *process* these files first, as described in the two previous recipes.

Good LaTeX documentation in HTML format can be found installed on many Linux systems in the '/usr/share/texmf/doc/latex/latex2e-html/' directory; use the lynx browser to view it (see Recipe 5.9 [Browsing Files], page 81).

Some other typesetting systems, such as LyX, SGMLtools, and Texinfo (all described elsewhere in this chapter), write TeX or LaTeX output, too—so you can use those systems to produce said output without actually learning the TeX and LaTeX input formats. (This book was written in Emacs in Texinfo format, and the typeset output was later generated by TeX.)

NOTE: The Oetiker text consists of several separate LaTeX files in the 'lshort' directory; download and save all of these files.

15.4.5 TeX and LaTeX Document Templates

WWW: http://dsl.org/comp/templates/

A collection of sample templates for typesetting certain kinds of documents in TeX and LaTeX can be found at the URL listed above. These templates include those for creating letters and correspondence, articles and term papers, envelopes and mailing labels,[2] and fax cover sheets. If you're interested in making typeset output with TeX and LaTeX, these templates are well worth exploring.

To write a document with a template, insert the contents of the template file into a new file that has a '.tex' or '.ltx' extension, and edit that. (Use your favorite text editor to do this.)

To make sure that you don't accidentally overwrite the actual template files, you can write-protect them (see Recipe 6.3.3 [Write-Protecting a File], page 87):

$ *chmod a-w template-file-names* (RET)

In the templates themselves, the bracketed, uppercase text explains what kind of text belongs there; fill in these lines with your own text, and delete the lines you don't need.

---

[2] In addition, a more advanced LaTeX style for printing many different kinds of shipping and package labels is normally installed at '/usr/share/texmf/tex/latex/labels/'.

Then, process your new file with either `latex` or `tex` as appropriate, and you've got a typeset document!

The following table lists the file names of the TeX templates, and describes their use. Use `tex` to process files you make with these templates (see Recipe 15.4.2 [Processing TeX Files], page 190).

TEMPLATE FILE	DESCRIPTION
fax.tex	A cover sheet for sending fax messages.
envelope.tex	A No. 10 mailing envelope.
label.tex	A single mailing label for printing on standard 15-up sheets.

The following table lists the file names of the LaTeX templates, and describes their use.[3] Use `latex` to process files you make with these templates (see Recipe 15.4.3 [Processing LaTeX Files], page 191).

TEMPLATE FILE	DESCRIPTION
letter.ltx	A letter or other correspondence.
article.ltx	An article or a research or term paper.
manuscript.ltx	A book manuscript.

There are more complex template packages available on the net that you might want to look at:

- Rob Rutten has assembled a very nice collection of LaTeX templates, `http://www.astro.uu.nl/~rutten/rrtex/templates/`
- The largest listing of LaTeX and TeX templates and style files is in the TeX Catalogue Online, `ftp://ftp.cdrom.com:21/pub/tex/ctan/help/Catalogue/hier.html`
- The Midnight Macros are a collection of TeX macros for printing booklets, bulk letters, and outlines, `ftp://ftp.cdrom.com/pub/tex/ctan/macros/generic/midnight/`
- Björn Magnusson's LaTeX templates for folder and register labels, `http://www.ifm.liu.se/~bjmag/latex.shtml`

15.5 Writing Documents with SGMLtools

Debian: 'sgml-tools'
WWW: http://www.sgmltools.org/

With the SGMLtools package, you can write documents and generate output in many different kinds of formats—including HTML, plain text, PDF, and PostScript—all from the same plain text input file.

SGML ("Standard Generalized Markup Language") is not an actual format, but a specification for writing markup languages; the markup language "formats" themselves are called DTDs ("Document Type Definition"). When you write a document in an SGML DTD, you write input as a plain text file with markup tags.

---

[3] The manuscript template requires that your system has the LaTeX style file called 'manuscript.sty'; most TeX distributions have this installed at '/usr/share/texmf/tex/latex/misc/manuscript.sty'.

The various SGML packages on Linux are currently in a state of transition. The original SGML-Tools package (known as LinuxDoc-SGML in another life; now SGMLtools v1) is considered obsolete and is no longer being developed; however, the newer SGMLtools v2 (a.k.a. "SGMLtools Next Generation" and "SGMLtools '98") is still alpha software, as is SGMLtools-lite (`http://sgmltools-lite.sourceforge.net/`), a new subset of SGML-tools.

In the interim, if you want to dive in and get started making documents with the early SGMLtools and the LinuxDoc DTD, it's not hard to do. While the newer DocBook DTD has become very popular, it may be best suited for technical books and other very large projects—for smaller documents written by individual authors, such as a multi-part essay, FAQ, or white paper, the LinuxDoc DTD still works fine.

And since the Linux HOWTOs are still written in LinuxDoc, the Debian project has decided to maintain the SGMLtools 1.0 package independently.

The *SGML-Tools User's Guide* comes installed with the 'sgml-tools' package, and is available in several formats in the '/usr/doc/sgml-tools' directory. These files are compressed; if you want to print or convert them, you have to uncompress them first (see Recipe 8.5 [Compressed Files], page 102).

> To peruse the compressed text version of the SGML-Tools guide, type:
>
> $ *zless /usr/doc/sgml-tools/guide.txt.gz* (RET)

- To print a copy of the PostScript version of the SGML-Tools guide to the default printer, type:

  $ *zcat /usr/doc/sgml-tools/guide.ps.gz | lpr* (RET)

15.5.1 Elements of an SGML Document

A document written in an SGML DTD looks a lot like HTML—which is no coincidence, since HTML is a subset of SGML. A very simple "Hello, world" example in the LinuxDoc DTD might look like this:

```
<!doctype linuxdoc system>
<article>
<title>An Example Document
<author>Ann Author
<date>4 May 2000
<abstract>
This is an example LinuxDoc document.
</abstract>

<sect>Introduction

<p>Hello, world.

</article>
```

A simple example document and the various output files it generates are on the SGML-tools site at `http://www.sgmltools.org/old-site/example/index.html`.

The SGMLtools package also comes with a simple example file, 'example.sgml.gz', which is installed in the '/usr/doc/sgml-tools' directory.

15.5.2 Checking SGML Document Syntax

Use **sgmlcheck** to make sure the syntax of an SGML document is correct—it outputs any errors it finds in the document that is specified as an argument.

- To check the SGML file 'myfile.sgml', type:

      $ sgmlcheck myfile.sgml (RET)

15.5.3 Generating Output from SGML

The following table lists the SGML converter tools that come with SGMLtools, and describes the kind of output they generate. All take the name of the SGML file to work on as an argument, and they write a new file with the same base file name and the file name extension of their output format.

TOOL	DESCRIPTION
sgml2html	Generates HTML files.
sgml2info	Generates a GNU Info file.
sgml2lyx	Generates a LyX input file.
sgml2latex	Generates a LaTeX input file (useful for printing; first process as in Recipe 15.4.3 [Processing LaTeX Files], page 191, and then print the resultant DVI or PostScript output file).
sgml2rtf	Generates a file in Microsoft's "Rich Text Format."
sgml2txt	Generates plain text format.
sgml2xml	Generates XML format.

- To make a plain text file from 'myfile.sgml', type:

      $ sgml2txt myfile.sgml (RET)

  This command writes a plain text file called 'myfile.txt'.

  To make a PostScript or PDF file from an SGML file, first generate a LaTeX input file, run it through LaTeX to make a DVI output file, and then process that to make the final output.

- To make a PostScript file from 'myfile.sgml', type:

```
$ sgml2latex myfile.sgml (RET)
$ latex myfile.latex (RET)
$ dvips -t letter -o myfile.ps myfile.dvi (RET)
$
```

In this example, **sgml2latex** writes a LaTeX input file from the SGML source file, and then the **latex** tool processes the LaTeX file to make DVI output, which is processed with **dvips** to get the final output: a PostScript file called 'myfile.ps' with a paper size of US letter.

To make a PDF file from the PostScript file, you need to take one more step and use **ps2pdf**, part of the **gs** or Ghostscript package; this converts the PostScript to PDF.

- To make a PDF file from the PostScript file 'myfile.ps', type:
    $ *ps2pdf myfile.ps myfile.pdf* (RET)

15.6 Other Word Processors and Typesetting Systems

The following table describes other popular word processors and typesetting tools available for Linux. Those systems not in general use have been silently omitted.

SYSTEM	DESCRIPTION
AbiWord	A graphical, WYSIWYG-style word processor for Linux systems. It can read Microsoft Word files. WWW: `http://www.abisource.com/`

groff	GROFF is the latest in a line of phototypesetting systems that have been available on Unix-based systems for years; the original in this line was `roff` ("runoff," meaning that it was for files to be *run off* to the printer). `groff` is used in the typesetting of `man` pages, but it's possible to use it to create other kinds of documents, and it has a following of staunch adherents.
	  To output the tutorial file included with the `groff` distribution to a DVI file called 'intro.dvi', type:
	    $ *zcat /usr/doc/groff/me-intro.me.gz | groff -me -T dvi > intro.dvi* (RET)
	
	Debian: 'groff'

Maxwell	A graphical word processor for use in X. WWW: `http://www.eeyore-mule.demon.co.uk/`
PostScript	The PostScript language is generally considered to be a format generated by software, but some people write straight PostScript! Recipe 15.2 [Converting Plain Text for Output], page 179, has recipes on creating PostScript output from text, including outputting text in a font. People have written PostScript template files for creating all kinds of documents—from desktop calendars to mandalas for meditation. The Debian 'cdlabelgen' and 'cd-circleprint' packages contain tools for writing labels for compact discs. Also of interest are Jamie Zawinski's templates for printing label inserts for video and audio tapes; edit the files in a text editor and then view or print them as you would any PostScript file. WWW: `http://www.jwz.org/audio-tape.ps` WWW: `http://www.jwz.org/video-tape.ps`
StarWriter	A traditional word processor for Linux systems, part of the StarOffice application suite. It can also read Microsoft Word files. WWW: `http://www.sun.com/staroffice/`

Texinfo   Texinfo is the GNU Project's documentation system and is an excellent system for writing FAQs or technical manuals. It allows for the inclusion of in-line EPS images and can produce both TeX-based, HTML, and Info output—use it if this matches your needs.
Debian: 'tetex-base'
WWW: http://www.texinfo.org/

16 Fonts

A *font* is a collection of characters for displaying text, normally in a common typeface and with a common size, boldness, and slant.

This chapter discusses the most popular kinds of fonts used on Linux systems: display fonts for use in the X Window System, fonts for use in virtual consoles, and the "fonts" often seen in Usenet and email composed entirely of ASCII characters.

Omitted are reference of the use of fonts with TeX, which are the kind of fonts you're most likely to use when producing typeset output—it is beyond the scope of this book to cover that issue with the space it needs. However, to print a text file with a font, see Recipe 15.2.1 [Outputting Text in a Font], page 180.

For more information on fonts and the tools to use them, see the *Font HOWTO* (see Recipe 2.8.6 [Reading System Documentation and Help Files], page 32).

16.1 X Fonts

You can specify a font as an option to most X clients, so that any text in the client is written in the given font. The recipe that describes how to do this is in Recipe 4.2.3 [Specifying a Window Font], page 56.

When you specify a font as an option, you have to give the X font name, which is the exact name used to specify a specific font in X. (An easy way to get the X font name is described in the first recipe in this section.) X font names consist of 14 fields, delimited by (and beginning with) a hyphen. All fields must be specified, and empty fields are permitted:

```
-fndry-fmly-wght-slant-swdth-adstyl-pxlsz
-ptsz-resx-resy-spc-avgwdth-rgstry-encdng
```

The preceding line was split because of its length, but X font names are always given on one line.

The following table describes the meaning of each field.

FIELD	DESCRIPTION
fndry	The type foundry that digitized and supplied the font data.
fmly	The name of the typographic style (for example, 'courier').
wght	The weight of the font, or its *nominal blackness*, the degree of boldness or thickness of its characters. Values include 'heavy', 'bold', 'medium', 'light', and 'thin'.
slant	The posture of the font, usually 'r' (for 'roman', or upright), 'i' ('italic', slanted upward to the right and differing in shape from the roman counterpart), or 'o' ('oblique', slanted but with the shape of the roman counterpart).
swdth	The *proportionate* width of the characters in the font, or its *nominal width*, such as 'normal', 'condensed', 'extended', 'narrow', and 'wide'.

adstyl   Any additional style descriptions the particular font takes,
                        such as 'serif' (fonts that have small strokes drawn on the
                        ends of each line in the character) or 'sans serif' (fonts that
                        omit serifs).

pxlsz   The height, in pixels, of the type. Also called *body size*.

ptsz   The height, in points, of the type.

resx   The horizontal screen resolution the font was designed for, in
                        dpi ("dots per inch").

resy   The vertical screen resolution the font was designed for, in
                        dpi.

spc   The kind of spacing used by the font (its *escapement class*);
                        either 'p' (a *proportional* font containing characters with var-
                        ied spacing), 'm' (a *monospaced* font containing characters
                        with constant spacing), or 'c' (a *character cell* font contain-
                        ing characters with constant spacing and constant height).

avgwdth   The average width of the characters used in the font, in 1/10th
                        pixel units.

rgstry   The international standards body, or *registry*, that owns the
                        encoding.

encdng   The registered name of this character set, or its *encoding*.

16.1.1 Selecting an X Font Name

X font names can be long and difficult to type; to make it easier, use the xfontsel client,
an interactive tool for picking X fonts and getting their X font names.

When you start xfontsel, it looks like this (the window frame will differ depending on
your window manager):

The row of buttons are pull-down menus containing options available on your system for
each field in the X font name. Use the mouse to select items from each menu, and the X
font you have selected is shown in the main window. Above it is written its X font name.

- To make the X font name the X selection, click the mouse on the button labeled select.

This example makes the X font name the X selection, which makes it possible to paste the X font name to a command line or into another window (see Recipe 10.4.2 [Pasting Text], page 129).

16.1.2 Listing Available X Fonts

Use `xlsfonts` to list the X font families, sizes, and weights available on your system. Supply a pattern in quotes as an argument, and it outputs the names of all X fonts installed on the system that match that pattern; by default, it lists all fonts.

- To list all the X fonts on the system, type:

    $ *xlsfonts* (RET)

- To list all the X fonts on the system whose name contains the text 'rea', type:

    $ *xlsfonts '*rea*'* (RET)

- To list all the bold X fonts on the system, type:

    $ *xlsfonts '*bold*'* (RET)

NOTE: This is not a way to *display* the characters in a font; for that, use **xfd**, described next. Furthermore, to *browse* through available X fonts, you want to use **xfontsel**, as in the previous recipe.

16.1.3 Displaying the Characters in an X Font

Use the **xfd** tool ("X font display") to display all of the characters in a given X font. Give the X font name you want to display in quotes as an argument to the '-fn' option.

- To display the characters in a medium Courier X font, type:

    $ *xfd -fn '-*-courier-medium-r-normal--*-100-*-*-*-*-iso8859-1'* (RET)

16.1.4 Resizing the Xterm Font

See Recipe 4.2.3 [Specifying Window Font], page 56 for how to specify the font to use in an **xterm** window in X. The **xterm** tool is usually used to run a shell while in X, and many people like to specify which font is used for this window.

To resize the current font when the **xterm** is running, press and hold (CTRL) and right-click anywhere in the **xterm** window. A menu will appear that gives you the size options, from **Unreadable** and **Tiny** to **Huge**. To resize the font to its original size, choose **Default**.

16.2 Console Fonts

Console fonts are screen fonts for displaying text on the Linux console (and not in the X Window System).

Console fonts are stored in the '/usr/share/consolefonts' directory as compressed files; to install new console fonts, have the system administrator make a '/usr/local/share/consolefonts' directory and put the font files in there.

These recipes show how to set the console font, and how to display a table containing all of the characters in the current font.

16.2.1 Setting the Console Font

Use `consolechars` to set the current console font; give the base file name of a console font as an argument to the '`-f`' option.

- To set the console font to the `scrawl_w` font, type:

    $ *consolechars -f scrawl_w* (RET)

Some font files contain more than one height (or size) of the font. If a font contains more than one encoding for different heights, give the height to use as an argument to the '`-H`' option. (If you try to do it without the option anyway, `consolechars` will output a list of available sizes.)

Common console font heights include 8 (for 8x8 fonts), 14 (for 8x14 fonts), and 16 (for 8x16 fonts).

- To set the console font to the 8x8 size `sc` font, type:

    $ *consolechars -H 8 -f sc* (RET)

16.2.2 Displaying the Characters in a Console Font

Use `showcfont` to display all of the characters in the current console font.

- To list all of the characters in the current console font, type:

    $ *showcfont* (RET)

16.3 Text Fonts

Text fonts are fonts created from the arrangement of ASCII characters on the screen; they are often seen in Usenet articles and email messages, included as decorative or title elements in text files, and used for printing simple banners or posters on a printer.

The making of "fonts" (and even pictures) from the arrangement of ASCII characters is known as *ascii art*. The following recipes describe methods of outputting text in these kind of fonts.

16.3.1 Horizontal Text Fonts

The `figlet` filter outputs text in a given text font. Give the text to output as an argument, quoting text containing shell metacharacters (see Recipe 3.1.1 [Passing Special Characters to Commands], page 36).

- To output the text '`news alert`' in the default `figlet` font, type:

    $ *figlet news alert* (RET)

This command outputs the following:

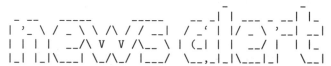

Fonts for `figlet` are kept in the '`/usr/lib/figlet`' directory; use the '`-f`' option followed by the base name of the font file (without the path or extension) to use that font.

To output the contents of a text file with a `figlet` font, use `cat` to output the contents of a file and pipe the output to `figlet`.

- To output the text of the file 'poster' in the figlet 'bubble' font, type:

      $ cat poster | figlet -f bubble (RET)

NOTE: The 'bubble' font is installed at '/usr/lib/figlet/bubble.flf'.

16.3.2 Making a Text Banner

The easiest way to print a long, vertical banner of text on a Linux system is with the old UNIX `banner` tool.

Quote a text message as an argument, and `banner` sends a large, vertical "banner" of the message to the standard output. The message itself is output in a "font" composed of ASCII text characters, similar to those used by `figlet`, except that the message is output vertically for printing, and you can't change the font. To send the output of `banner` to the printer, pipe it to `lpr`.

- To make a banner saying 'Happy Birthday Susan', type:

      $ banner 'Happy Birthday Susan' (RET)

- To print a banner saying 'Happy Birthday Susan' to the default printer, type:

      $ banner 'Happy Birthday Susan' | lpr (RET)

Unfortunately, the breadth of characters that `banner` understands is a bit limited—the following characters can't be used in a `banner` message:

      < > [ ] \ ^ _ { } | ~

To make a banner of the contents of a text file, send its contents to `banner` by redirecting standard input (see Recipe 3.2.1 [Redirecting Input to a File], page 39).

To make a banner of the contents of the file '/etc/hostname', type:

      $ banner < /etc/hostname (RET)

The default width of a banner is 132 text columns; you can specify a different width by specifying the width to use as an argument to the '-w' option. If you give the '-w' option without a number, banner outputs at 80 text columns.

- To make a banner containing the text 'Happy Birthday Susan' at a width of 23 text columns, type:

      $ banner -w 23 'Happy Birthday Susan' (RET)

- To make a banner containing the text 'Happy Birthday Susan' at a width of 80 text columns, type:

      $ banner -w 'Happy Birthday Susan' (RET)

NOTE: A method of making a horizontal text banner with `figlet` is described in Recipe 15.2.5 [Outputting Text in Landscape Orientation], page 184.

16.4 Other Font Tools

The following table describes some of the other font tools available for Linux.

TOOL	DESCRIPTION
cse	The Linux Console Font Editor, cse, is an older console font editor. WWW: http://www.ibiblio.org/pub/Linux/system/keyboards/
dtm	The Definitive Type Manager is a tool for adding and removing Adobe Type 1 fonts to and from your system. Debian: 'dtm'
fonter	Fonter is a console font editor; use it to make and edit console fonts. Debian: 'fonter'
gfont	The gfont tool creates a GIF image of text rendered in a TEX font. Debian: 'gfont' WWW: http://www.engelschall.com/sw/gfont/
gfontview	This is a tool for viewing Adobe Type 1 and TrueType fonts. Debian: 'gfontview'

PART FOUR: Images

17 Viewing Images

As with text, there are tools for both viewing and editing images. This chapter describes the various methods for viewing images; the editing of images is discussed in the next chapter). While you can view an image with an image *editor*, it is safer (and faster!) to view with a viewer when you do not intend to edit it.

17.1 Previewing Print Files

The DVI ("DeVice Independent"), PostScript, and PDF ("Portable Document Format") file formats can be generated by a number of applications. They are graphical image formats commonly used for printing; methods for previewing these files on the display screen are discussed in the following sections.

17.1.1 Previewing a DVI File

Use the `xdvi` tool to preview a DVI file in X. Give the name of the file to preview as an argument. `xdvi` will show how the document will look when printed, and let you view it at different magnifications.

- To preview the file 'gentle.dvi', type:

      $ xdvi gentle.dvi (RET)

   To magnify the view of the document, left-click any of the buttons labelled with a percentage, such as 17%; they magnify the view by that percentage.

- To magnify the view by 33%, left-click the button marked 33%.

   The following table lists some of `xdvi`'s commands.

COMMAND	DESCRIPTION
(Q)	Exit `xdvi` and stop previewing the file.
(N)	Advance to the next page.
(P)	Move to previous page.
C-c	Same as (Q).
C-d	Same as (Q).
(SPC)	Same as (N).
C-l	Redisplay the current page.
(R)	Re-read the DVI file.

17.1.2 Previewing a PostScript File

Debian: 'ghostview'
Debian: 'gv'
WWW: http://wwwthep.physik.uni-mainz.de/~plass/gv/

To preview a PostScript or EPS image file in X, use `ghostview`. It takes a file name as an argument, and it previews the contents of the file in a window, starting with its first page.

- To preview the file '/usr/doc/gs/examples/tiger.ps', type:

    $ *ghostview /usr/doc/gs/examples/tiger.ps* (RET)

Press (Q) to exit and press (SPC) to advance to the next page, if there is one.

NOTE: Some people prefer the `gv` tool as an alternate to `ghostview`; `gv` is used in much the same way, though it has a different interface.

17.1.3 Previewing a PDF File

Debian: 'xpdf'
WWW: http://www.foolabs.com/xpdf/
Debian: 'gv'
WWW: http://wwwthep.physik.uni-mainz.de/~plass/gv/

Use `xpdf` to preview a PDF file. Give the name of the PDF file to preview as an argument.

- To preview the PDF file 'flyer.pdf', type:

    $ *xpdf flyer.pdf* (RET)

To exit `xpdf`, press (Q); use the two magnifying-glass buttons to zoom the view closer in (+) or further out (-), and use the left and right arrow buttons to move to the previous and next pages, if any.

NOTE: You can also use `gv` to preview PDF files.

17.2 Viewing an Image in X

Debian: 'imagemagick'
WWW: ftp://ftp.wizards.dupont.com/pub/ImageMagick/

To view an image in X, use `display`, part of the ImageMagick suite of tools. It can recognize many image formats, including FlashPix, GIF/GIF87, Group 3 faxes, JPEG, PBM/PNM/PPM, PhotoCD, TGA, TIFF, TransFig, and XBM.

`display` takes as an argument the file name of the image to be viewed, and it displays the image in a new window.

- To view the file 'sailboat.jpeg', type:

    $ *display sailboat.jpeg* (RET)

This command displays the image file in a new window:

The mouse buttons have special meaning in `display`. Left-click on the image window to open the `display` command menu in a new window. The `display` command menu looks like this:

Menu items let you change the image size and otherwise change or transform the image display. Choose **Overview** from the **Help** menu for an explanation of the various available `display` commands.

Middle-click on the image to open a new window with a magnified view of the image centered where you click. For example, middle-clicking on the sailboat image in the previous example will open a new window that looks like this:

Finally, right-click on the image window for a pop-up menu containing a few of the most frequently-used commands; to choose one of these commands, drag the mouse pointer over the command. Commands in the pop-up menu include **Quit**, which exits `display`, and the `Image Info`, which displays information about the image file itself, including number of colors, image depth, and resolution.

The following table describes some of the keyboard commands that work when displaying an image in `display`.

COMMAND	DESCRIPTION
(SPC)	Display the next image specified on the command line.
(BKSP)	Display the previous image specified on the command line.
C-q	Quit displaying the image and exit `display`.
C-s	Write the image to a file.
<	Halve the image size.
>	Double the image size.
-	Return the image to its original size.
/	Rotate image 90 degrees clockwise.
\	Rotate image 90 degrees counter-clockwise.
?	Open a new window with information about the image, including resolution, color depth, format, and comments, if any.
h	Toggle a horizontal mirror image.
v	Toggle a vertical mirror image.

NOTE: `display` can also be used to view images on the World Wide Web—see Recipe 31.2 [Viewing an Image from the Web], page 330.

17.2.1 Browsing Image Collections in X

The `display` tool offers a feature for browsing a collection of images—give '`vid:`' as the file argument, followed by the file names or pattern to match them in quotes. `display` makes thumbnails of the specified images, and displays them in a new window, which it calls a *visual image directory*.

- To browse through the image files with a '`.gif`' extension in the '`/usr/doc/imagemagick/examples`' directory, type:

    $ *display 'vid:/usr/doc/imagemagick/examples/*.gif'* (RET)

- To browse through all image files in the current directory, type:

    $ *display 'vid:*'* (RET)

In the preceding example, only those files with image formats supported by `display` are read and displayed.

NOTE: To open an image at its normal size, right-click the image and choose `Load`; the thumbnail will be replaced by its full-size image. To return to the thumbnail directory, right-click the image and choose `Former`.

17.2.2 Putting an Image in the Root Window

One way to put an image in the root window (the background behind all other windows) is to use `display` and give 'root' as an argument to the '-window' option.

- To put the image 'tetra.jpeg' in the root window, type:

    $ *display -window root tetra.jpeg* (RET)

17.3 Browsing Images in a Console

Use `zgv` to view images in a virtual console (not in X). You can use `zgv` to browse through the filesystem and select images to view, or give as arguments the names of image files to view. It recognizes many image formats, including GIF, JPEG, PNG, PBM/PNM/PPM, TGA and PCX; one of its nicest features is that it can fill the entire screen with an image.

When you run `zgv` with no options, it displays image icons of any images in the current directory, listing any subdirectories as folder icons. You can also give the name of a directory as an argument in order to browse the images in that directory.

- To browse the images in the current directory, type:

    $ *zgv* (RET)

- To browse the images in the '/usr/share/gimp/scripts' directory, type:

    $ *zgv /usr/share/gimp/scripts* (RET)

Use the arrow keys to navigate through the file display; the red border around a image or directory icon indicates which image or subdirectory is selected. Type (RET) to view the selected image or to change to the selected directory.

You can manipulate the images you view in a number of ways—zoom the image magnification in and out, change the brightness and color, and even make automatic "slide shows" of images. The following table describes some of `zgv`'s options.

OPTION	DESCRIPTION
-c	Toggle image centering. Images are centered on screen by default; specifying this option turns off centering.
-i	Ignore errors due to corrupted files, and display whatever portion of the file is displayable.
-l	Start `zgv` in slide-show mode, where it loops through all images specified as arguments, continuously, until you interrupt it.
-M	Toggle mouse support. Mouse support is off by default; this option turns it on.
-r *integer*	Reread and redisplay every image after every *integer* seconds. Useful for viewing webcam images or other image files that are continuously changing.

17.4 Viewing an Image in a Web Browser

If you have a graphical Web browser, such as `mozilla`, you can use it to view a graphic image. While viewing images in a browser doesn't offer much flexibility (you can't zoom in on a portion of the image, or get information about the image resolution and other details), if you simply want to quickly view an image file while you are in X, and you have a Web browser running, it can be a quick and easy way to do it.

To view an image file in a Web browser, specify a `file:` URL pointing to the file name of the image in the `Location` field of the browser.

- To view the file '`/usr/share/images/mondrian-15.jpeg`', type:

    file:/usr/share/images/mondrian-15.jpeg (RET)

Notice that the given `file:` URL only has one preceding slash, pointing to the root directory, and not two, as in `http://`.

17.5 Browsing PhotoCD Archives

Debian: '`xpcd`'
Debian: '`xpcd-gimp`'
WWW: `http://user.cs.tu-berlin.de/~kraxel/linux/xpcd/`

The `xpcd` tool is an X client for viewing and browsing collections of Kodak PhotoCD images. To browse the images on a Kodak PhotoCD, mount the CD-ROM (see Recipe 24.4.1 [Mounting a CD-ROM], page 268), and then give the mount point as an argument to `xpcd`.

- To browse the images on the PhotoCD disc mounted on '`/cdrom`', type:

    $ *xpcd /cdrom* (RET)

The preceding example will open two new windows—a small `xpcd` command bar window, and a larger window containing thumbnails of all PhotoCD images on the disc.

To open a copy of an image in a new window, left-click its thumbnail image. When you do, `xpcd` will open the image at the second-smallest PhotoCD resolution, 256x384; to view it at a another size, right-click the image and choose the size to view. Once the new window is drawn, you can right-click on this new image to save it as a JPEG, PPM, or TIFF format image.

To view an individual '`.pcd`' file with `xpcd`, give the name of the file as an argument.

- To view the PhotoCD file '`driveby-001.pcd`', type:

    $ *xpcd driveby-001.pcd* (RET)

NOTE: You can also use `display` to view a '`.pcd`' PhotoCD image file (see Recipe 17.2 [Viewing an Image in X], page 208).

See Recipe 19.3 [Extracting PhotoCD images], page 232 for another recipe for extracting PhotoCD images.

17.6 Additional Image Viewers

The following table lists other tools for viewing images.

TOOL	DESCRIPTION
animate	Part of the ImageMagick suite; use **animate** to display an animated slide-show sequence of images in X. Debian: 'imagemagick' WWW: ftp://ftp.wizards.dupont.com/pub/ImageMagick/
xwud	Displays files in the special X Window Dump file format, as created by xwd. Debian: 'xbase-clients' WWW: http://www.xfree86.org/
showpicture	Views an image sent as an email attachment; requires **xloadimage**. Debian: 'metamail' WWW: ftp://ftp.bellcore.com:/pub/nsb/mm2.7.tar.Z
xli	Basic image viewer for X. Debian: 'xli'
xloadimage	Nice graphics viewer for X that contains tools for viewing images in the root window. Debian: 'xloadimage'
aview	View graphics as "ASCII art." This tool can view any image format supported by the pbmplus utility suite, and has fluid zoom in/out and all the rendering options you'd expect from a world-class viewer. Debian: 'aview' WWW: ftp://ftp.ta.jcu.cz://pub/aa

18 Editing Images

When you take an image file—such as one containing a digitized photograph or a picture drawn with a graphics program—and you make changes to it, you are *editing* an image.

This chapter contains recipes for editing and modifying images, including how to convert between image file formats. It also gives an overview of other image applications you might find useful, including the featuresome GIMP image editor.

18.1 Transforming Images

Debian: 'imagemagick'
WWW: `ftp://ftp.wizards.dupont.com/pub/ImageMagick/`

Many Linux tools can be used to transform or manipulate images in various ways. One very useful package for both transforming images and converting between image formats is the `netpbm` suite of utilities (see Recipe 19.2 [Scanning Images], page 230). Another is the ImageMagick suite of imaging tools, of which `mogrify` is particularly useful for performing fast command line image transforms; use it to change the size of, to rotate, or to reduce the colors in an image.

`mogrify` always takes the name of the file to work on as an argument, and it writes its changes to that file. Use a hyphen ('-') to specify the standard input, in which case `mogrify` writes its output to the standard output.

I'll use the image 'phoenix.jpeg' in the examples that follow to give you an understanding of how to use `mogrify`:

NOTE: You can also perform many of the image transformations described in the following sections interactively with the GIMP (see Recipe 18.3 [Editing Images with the GIMP], page 225).

18.1.1 Changing the Size of an Image

To resize an image with `mogrify`, use the '-geometry' option with the width and height values, in pixels, as an argument.

- To resize 'phoenix.jpeg' to 480x320 pixels, type:

`$ mogrify -geometry 480x320 phoenix.jpeg` (RET)

This transforms the original 'phoenix.jpeg' file to:

NOTE: Images scaled to a larger size will appear blocky or fuzzy.

When `mogrify` resizes an image, it maintains the image's *aspect ratio*, so that the ratio between the width and height stays the same. To force a conversion to a particular image size without necessarily preserving its aspect ratio, append the geometry with an exclamation point.

- To resize 'phoenix.jpeg' to *exactly* 480x320 pixels, regardless of aspect ratio, type:

  `$ mogrify -geometry 640x480! phoenix.jpeg` (RET)

This transforms the original 'phoenix.jpeg' to:

You can also specify the width or height by percentage. To *decrease* by a percentage, give the value followed by a percent sign ('%'). To *increase* by a percentage, give the value plus 100 followed by a percent sign. For example, to increase by 25 percent, give '125%'.

- To increase the height of 'phoenix.jpeg' by 25 percent and decrease its width by 50 percent, type:

    ```
    $ mogrify -geometry 125%x50% phoenix.jpeg (RET)
    ```

This transforms the original 'phoenix.jpeg' to:

NOTE: To *view* an image at a particular scale without modifying it, use `display`; when you resize its window, you resize the image on the screen only (see Recipe 4.3.2 [Resizing a Window], page 58).

18.1.2 Rotating an Image

To rotate an image, use `mogrify` with the '`-rotate`' option followed by the number of degrees to rotate by. If the image width exceeds its height, follow this number with a '>', and if the height exceeds its width, follow it with a '<'. (Since both '<' and '>' are shell redirection operators, enclose this argument in quotes, omitting either if the image height and width are the same.)

- To rotate 'phoenix.jpeg', whose height exceeds its width, by 90 degrees, type:

      $ *mogrify -rotate '90<' phoenix.jpeg* (RET)

  This transforms the original 'phoenix.jpeg' to:

NOTE: After this command, the width of 'phoenix.jpeg' now exceeds its height, so to rotate it again use '>' instead of '<'.

18.1.3 Adjusting the Colors of an Image

You can use mogrify to make a number of adjustments in the color of an image. To reduce the number of colors in an image, use the '-colors' option, followed by the number of colors to use.

- To reduce the colors in 'phoenix.jpeg' to two, type:

    $ *mogrify -colors 2 phoenix.jpeg* (RET)

This transforms the original 'phoenix.jpeg' to:

Use the '-dither' option to reduce the colors with Floyd-Steinberg error diffusion, a popular algorithm for improving image quality during color reduction.

- To reduce the colors in 'phoenix.jpeg' to four and apply Floyd-Steinberg error diffusion, type:

    $ *mogrify -colors 4 -dither phoenix.jpeg* (RET)

This transforms the original 'phoenix.jpeg' to:

Use the '-map' option with a second file name as an argument to read the *color map*, or the set of colors, from the second image and use them in the first image.

- To change the colors in the file 'rainbow.jpeg' to those used in the file 'prism.jpeg', type:

    $ *mogrify -map prism.jpeg rainbow.jpeg* (RET)

Use the '-monochrome' option to make a color image black and white.

- To make the color image 'rainbow.jpeg' black and white, type:

    $ *mogrify -monochrome rainbow.jpeg* (RET)

If you have a PPM file, use **ppmquant** to *quantize*, or reduce to a specified quantity the colors in the image—see the **ppmquant man** page for details (see Recipe 2.8.4 [Reading a Page from the System Manual], page 30).

Because of differences in display hardware, the brightness of an image may vary from one computer system to another. For example, images created on a Macintosh usually appear darker on other systems. When you adjust the brightness of an image it is called *gamma correction*.

To adjust the brightness of an image, give the numeric level of correction to apply as an argument to the '-gamma' option. Most PC displays have a gamma value of 2.5, while Macintosh displays have a lower gamma value of 1.4.

- To set the gamma correction of the image 'rainbow.jpeg' to .8, type:

    $ *mogrify -gamma .8 rainbow.jpeg* (RET)

18.1.4 Annotating an Image

Debian: 'libjpeg-progs'
WWW: http://www.ijg.org/

To annotate an image file with a comment, use **mogrify** with the '-comment' option, giving the comment in quotes as an argument to the option. This is useful for adding a copyright (or copy*left*) statement to an image, or for annotating an image file with a URL.

- To annotate the image file 'phoenix.jpeg', type (all on one line):

    $ *mogrify -comment "If you can read this, you're too close!" phoenix.jpeg* (RET)

You won't see the annotation when you view the image; it is added to the image header in the file. You can, however, read image annotations with tools that display information about an image file, such as **display** or the GIMP. To read annotations in JPEG files, you can also use the **rdjpgcom** tool—it outputs any comments in the JPEG file whose file name is given as an argument.

- To read any comments made in the image file 'phoenix.jpeg', type:

```
$ rdjpgcom phoenix.jpeg (RET)
If you can read this, you're too close!
$
```

NOTE: Another method for writing comments in JPEG files is to use **wrjpgcom**, which is distributed with **rdjpgcom** in the 'libjpeg-progs' package.

18.1.5 Adding Borders to an Image

To draw a border around an image, use **mogrify** with the '-border' option followed by the width and height, in pixels, of the border to use.

- To add a border two pixels wide and four pixels high to 'phoenix.jpeg', type:

    $ *mogrify -border 2x4 phoenix.jpeg* (RET)

This transforms the original 'phoenix.jpeg' to:

NOTE: The border is added to the outside of the existing image; the image is not cropped or reduced in size to add the border.

The '-frame' option works like '-border', but it adds a more decorative border to an image.

- To add a decorative frame eight pixels wide and eight pixels high to 'phoenix.jpeg', type:

    $ *mogrify -frame 8x8 phoenix.jpeg* (RET)

This transforms the original 'phoenix.jpeg' to:

18.1.6 Making an Image Montage

To make a montage image of other images, use `montage`. It takes as arguments the names of the images to use followed by the name of the output file to write the montage image to.

The montage image is made by scaling all of the input images to fit the largest size possible up to 120x120 pixels, and tiling these images in rows of five and columns of four.

- To create a montage from the files 'owl.jpeg', 'thrush.jpeg', and 'warbler.jpeg' and write it to 'endangered-birds.png', type:

```
$ montage owl.jpeg thrush.jpeg warbler.jpeg endangered-birds.png ⟨RET⟩
```

NOTE: In this example, three JPEGs were read and output to a PNG file; to specify the format to use in the output, give the appropriate file extension in the output file name.

18.1.7 Combining Images

Use **combine** to combine two images into one new image—give the names of the two source image files and the new file to write to as arguments. Without any options, it makes a new image file by overlaying the smaller of the two images over the larger, starting in the top left corner; if both images are the same size, only the second image is visible.

- To combine two images, 'ashes.jpeg' and 'phoenix.jpeg', into a new file 'picture.jpeg', type:

  ```
  $ combine ashes.jpeg phoenix.jpeg picture.jpeg ⟨RET⟩
  ```

You can specify the percentage to blend two images together with the '-blend' option. Give the amount to blend the second image into the first (as a percentage) as an argument to the option.

- To combine the image files 'phoenix.jpeg' and 'ashes.jpeg' so that the blended image contains 70 percent of the second image, type:

  ```
  $ combine -blend 70 ashes.jpeg phoenix.jpeg picture.jpeg ⟨RET⟩
  ```

This command combines the two images and writes a new image file, 'picture.jpeg', whose contents contain 70 percent of the first image.

NOTE: Use '-blend 50' to blend the two source files equally.

18.1.8 Morphing Two Images Together

Morphing is a method of computer imaging for finding the difference between the shapes in two images; it's often used in special effects to transform aspects of two creatures, such as the faces of a human and some other animal.

You can use **combine** to get a morph-like effect by giving the **difference** argument to the '-compose' option. When specified with two input images and an output file, this command takes the difference between corresponding pixels in the two images; the effect is like a "morphed" image.

- To make a morphed image of the files 'ashes.jpeg' and 'phoenix.jpeg', and write it to 'picture.jpeg', type:

  ```
  $ combine -compose difference ashes.jpeg phoenix.jpeg picture.jpeg ⟨RET⟩
  ```

The result in file 'picture.jpeg' is:

NOTE: 'xmorph' is a tool for morphing images; see Recipe 18.4 [Interactive Image Editors and Tools], page 226.

18.2 Converting Images between Formats

Debian: 'imagemagick'
WWW: `ftp://ftp.wizards.dupont.com/pub/ImageMagick/`

Use **convert** to convert the file format of an image. Give the name of the file to convert as the first argument, and the destination file as the second argument. When you convert a file, the original is not altered.

To specify the file type to convert to, use that file type's standard file extension in the file name of the converted file.

- To convert the JPEG file 'phoenix.jpeg' to a PNG image, type:

    $ *convert phoenix.jpeg phoenix.png* (RET)

This command converts the JPEG image 'phoenix.jpeg' to PNG format and writes it to a new file, 'phoenix.png'.

The following table lists the file extensions to use and describes their format. (The convention is to give extensions in all lowercase letters.)

FILE EXTENSION	IMAGE FORMAT
bmp	Microsoft Windows bitmap image.
cgm	Computer Graphics Metafile format.
cmyk	Raw cyan, magenta, yellow, and black bytes.
eps	Adobe Encapsulated PostScript.
fax	Group 3 fax format.
fig	TransFig image format.
fpx	FlashPix format.

gif	CompuServe Graphics Interchange Format, version GIF89a (usually pronounced "giff," rhyming with "biff").
gray	Raw gray bytes.
jpeg *and* jpg	Joint Photographic Experts Group JFIF format (usually pronounced "jay-peg").
pbm	Black and white portable bitmap format.
pcd	Kodak PhotoCD format, 512x768 pixels maximum resolution.
pcl	Page Control Language format.
pcx	ZSoft IBM PC Paintbrush format.
pdf	Adobe Portable Document Format.
pict	Apple Macintosh QuickDraw format.
png	Portable Network Graphics format (usually pronounced "ping").
pnm	Portable "anymap" format.
ppm	Color portable pixmap format.
ps	Adobe PostScript format.
rgb	Raw red, green, and blue bytes.
tga	TrueVision Targa image format.
tiff *and* tif	Tagged Image File Format (usually pronounced "tiff").
xbm	X Window System bitmap format.
xpm	Color X Window System pixmap format.
xwd	Color X Window System window "dump" file format.

When converting a file to JPEG format, be sure to use the '-interlace NONE' option to make sure the resultant JPEG image is non-interlaced—unless, of course, you *want* an interlaced image; an *interlaced* image is drawn in multiple passes, and is often used on the Web where a reader may view the low-resolution image consisting of early passes before the entire image is downloaded. A *non-interlaced* image is drawn in one single pass.

For example, use convert to convert a PNM file to non-interlaced JPEG, while sharpening it, adding a border, and adding a copyright statement.

- To convert the PNM file 'pike.pnm' to non-interlaced JPEG while sharpening the image by 50 percent and adding both a 2x2 border and a copyright comment, type:

```
$ convert -interlace NONE -sharpen 50 -border 2x2
-comment 'copyright 1999 MS' pike.pnm pike.jpeg RET
```

This command writes its output to a file 'pike.jpeg'. Notice that the options '-border' and '-comment' were previously described for the 'mogrify' tool. Some ImageMagick tools share common options, which is useful if you are making multiple changes to an image file at once; only one tool is needed for the job.

NOTE: Some image formats are "lossy," in that some image information is lost when you convert to it. For example, the JPEG format is a lossy format that is usually used for photographic images. If you convert a file from its source PNM format to JPEG and then back to PNM, the resultant PNM will not be identical to the original source PNM.

To convert image files interactively, use the GIMP to open the image, and then choose 'Save as' from the File menu, and select the file type to use; see Recipe 18.3 [Editing Images with the GIMP], page 225.

18.3 Editing Images with the GIMP

Debian: 'gimp'
Debian: 'gimp-manual'
WWW: http://www.gimp.org/

The GIMP (GNU Image Manipulation Program) is an all-encompassing image-editing and manipulation program that lets you paint, draw, create, and edit images in complex ways. Using gimp you can also convert image files, retouch and edit photographic images, and browse collections of images.

The GIMP comes with hundreds of tools, filters, fonts, and other goodies installed. Here is a partial list of its features:

- Contains a full suite of painting tools, including Brush, Pencil, Airbrush, and Clone.

- Supports custom brushes and patterns.

- Includes a full suite of image selection, transformation, and manipulation tools, including a gradient editor, color blending, and special effects.

- Includes animation support.

- Permits the use of layers and channels.

- Allows for large images, with their size being limited only by available disk space.

- Provides high-quality anti-aliasing.

- Offers full alpha-channel support.

- Supports command scripting.

- Permits multiple undo and redo, limited only by available disk space.

- Allows multiple images to be open simultaneously.

- Supports all popular file formats, including GIF, JPEG, PNG, XPM, TIFF, TGA, MPEG, PS, PDF, PCX, and BMP.

- Allows the easy addition of more than 100 plug-ins for new file formats and new effect filters.

The GIMP runs under X and is started by running `gimp` or choosing it from your window manager's menu. When started, the GIMP looks like this:

NOTE: To learn the basics of the GIMP, consult *The GIMP User's Manual* and the other documentation and resources on the Web at `http://www.gimp.org/`. You can also install the manual on your system; it comes in the Debian '`gimp-manual`' package.

18.4 Interactive Image Editors and Tools

There are all kinds of image-editing software applications available for Linux—and there are as many way to make and edit an image as there are tools to do it with.

The following table lists some other popular tools and applications for making and editing images—including CAD engineering software—that you may want to explore. It is not exhaustive.

TOOL	DESCRIPTION
bitmap	Use the `bitmap` editor to edit bitmap files, which are used for icons and tile patterns in the X Window System. Debian: '`xbase-clients`'
drgeo	`drgeo` is a program for drawing interactive geometric figures. Debian: '`drgeo`' WWW: `http://members.xoom.com/FeYiLai/dr_geo/doctor_geo.html`

dia
> Use `dia` to draw simple charts and diagrams. It saves files in its own format, but you can export files to EPS (see Chapter 20 [PostScript], page 235); if you plan on editing a diagram file again, however, be sure you keep the '.dia' file since, as of this writing, `dia` cannot import EPS files.
> Debian: 'dia'
> WWW: `http://www.lysator.liu.se/~alla/dia`

electric
> Use `electric` for designing images of electronic circuitry.
> WWW: `http://www.gnu.org/software/electric/electric.html`

freedraft
> FREEdraft is a 2-D mechanical CAD tool for precision drawing and sketching.
> WWW: `http://www.freeengineer.org/Freedraft/`

gnuplot
> `gnuplot` is a robust, non-interactive function-plotting tool. Given a data file and a formula, `gnuplot` can make charts and graphs.
> Debian: 'gnuplot'
> WWW: `ftp://ftp.gnu.org/pub/gnu/gnuplot/`

ivtools
> The `ivtools` suite of software includes `idraw`, a vector graphics editor.
> Debian: 'ivtools-bin'
> WWW: `http://www.vectaport.com/`

kali
> Use `kali` for drawing patterns and tilings, including frieze patterns and infinite or recursive tiles in the spirit of M.C. Escher.
> Debian: 'kali'

moonlight
> The Moonlight Creator is an X client for modeling, illuminating, and rendering 3-D scenes.
> Debian: 'moonlight'
> WWW: `http://www.cybersociety.com/moonlight/`

sced
> `sced` is a tool for creating 3-D scenes.
> Debian: 'sced'
> WWW: `http://http.cs.berkeley.edu/~schenney/sced/sced.html`

xfig
> Use the venerable `xfig` application for drawing figures—complex graphs, floor plans, maps, flow charts, and so forth. It saves files in its own format (giving them a '.fig' extension by default); the usual thing to do is export to EPS.
> Debian: 'xfig'
> WWW: `http://xfig.org/`

xmorph
> `xmorph` is a tool to morph (sometimes called "warp") two images together, making a new image in the process. Images must be in TrueVision Targa file format, with the same size, shape, and number of pixels in each file (also see Recipe 18.1.8 [Morphing Two Images Together], page 222).
> Debian: 'xmorph'
> WWW: `http://www.colorado-research.com/~gourlay/software/`

xpaint
          xpaint, a simple "paint" tool that predates the GIMP, contains all of the
          basic features that you would expect from a paint program. If you don't
          need the GIMP's advanced capabilities, consider using the smaller **xpaint**
          instead.
          Debian: 'xpaint'
          WWW: http://www.danbbs.dk/~torsten/xpaint/index.html

19 Importing Images

While you can always make your own images, you may sometimes want to import and use existing images from other sources. In this chapter, I'll show how to import images from scanners and Kodak PhotoCD discs. We'll begin with recipes for taking screen shots.

19.1 Taking Screen Shots

A *screen shot* is a picture of all or part of the display screen. The following recipes show you how to take screen shots in X and in the console.

19.1.1 Taking a Screen Shot in X

Debian: 'imagemagick'
WWW: `ftp://ftp.wizards.dupont.com/pub/ImageMagick/`

Use `import`, part of the ImageMagick suite, to take a screen shot in X. `import` can capture the entire screen, a single window, or an arbitrary rectangular area, taking as an argument the name of the file to save to. As with other ImageMagick tools, the image format of the output file depends on the file extension you specify: '`.eps`' for EPS, '`.tiff`' for TIFF, '`.jpeg`' for JPEG, and so on. (For a complete list, see Recipe 18.2 [Converting Images between Formats], page 223).

After you give the command, the mouse pointer changes to a set of cross-hairs. You then use the mouse to specify which window to take the shot of, as follows:

- Left-click on a window to capture it.
- Left-click on the root window to capture the entire screen.
- Left-click and drag the mouse across an area of the screen to form a rectangular selection outline; release the mouse button to capture the selected area.

When you specify a window, `import` captures only the window's contents; use the '`-frame`' option to include the window manager frame in the image.

- To capture a particular window, including its window manager frame, and write it to a PNG-format file, first type:

      $ import -frame session-1.png (RET)

- Then, left-click on the window you want to capture.

In this example, the capture is saved to a file called '`session-1.png`'.

NOTE: The system bell rings once when the screen capture starts, and twice when the captures finishes.

19.1.2 Taking a Screen Shot in a Console

To take screen shots in a virtual console, use `cat` to save the contents of the device file corresponding to that virtual console; these files are in the '`/dev`' directory, and are in the format '`vcsnumber`', where *number* is the number of the virtual console.

For example, if the target console is the first virtual console (which you would see by typing (ALT)-(F1)), the device to `cat` is '`/dev/vcs1`'.

- To take a screen shot of the fourth virtual console, and save it to a file called 'screenshot', type:

      $ cat /dev/vcs4 > screenshot (RET)

NOTE: You must have superuser privileges to access these files (see Appendix A [Administrative Issues], page 359).

Take the screen shot from a virtual console different from the one you want to take a shot of; if you try to take it from the same console you want to capture, the command line you give will be included in the shot! (Kind of like having your thumb in front of the lens while taking a photograph.)

Screenshots taken of virtual consoles, as shown here, are saved as text files; you can't take screen shots of virtual consoles when graphics are displayed.

19.2 Scanning Images

Debian: 'sane'
WWW: http://www.mostang.com/sane/

SANE, "Scanner Access Now Easy," is the de facto Linux scanner interface; use it to scan an image with a scanner and save it to a file.

SANE works with a wide array of scanning hardware, but make sure the scanning hardware you want to use is compatible by checking the Hardware HOWTO (http://linuxdoc.org/HOWTO/Hardware-HOWTO.html) and SANE's list of supported scanners (http://www.mostang.com/sane/sane-backends.html).

Once you have SANE running, you can scan images with SANE-aware applications like the GIMP (see Recipe 18.3 [Editing Images with the GIMP], page 225).

The following recipes describe use of the command-line scanimage tool, which comes with the SANE package.

NOTE: As the acronym implies, getting a scanner to work on a Linux system hasn't always been smooth going. The SANE interface is completely open, and its developers are making sure that it is generalized enough to be implementable on any hardware or operating system.

19.2.1 Listing Available Scanner Devices

Before you can use a scanner device, you need to know its device name. To get this name, use scanimage with the '--list-devices' option.

- To list available scanner devices, type:

```
$ scanimage --list-devices (RET)
device 'umax:/dev/sgb' is a UMAX     Astra 1220S      flatbed scanner
$
```

In this example, there's one scanning device on this system, a UMAX brand scanner that can be specified to scanimage by giving its device name, 'umax:/dev/sgb', as an argument to the '-d' option.

To list the available resolutions and options supported by a particular device, use the '--help' option along with the '-d' option followed by its device name.

- To list available options supported by the device listed in the previous example, type:

  $ *scanimage --help -d 'umax:/dev/sgb'* (RET)

NOTE: For all scanimage commands, specify the scanner device you want to use by including the '-d' option with the device name.

19.2.2 Testing a Scanner

To run diagnostic tests on a scanner to make sure that it can be properly read from, use scanimage with the '--test' option.

- To test the UMAX scanner listed previously, type:

  $ *scanimage --test -d 'umax:/dev/sgb'* (RET)

19.2.3 Scanning an Image

Debian: 'netpbm'
WWW: http://www.debian.org/Packages/stable/graphics/netpbm.html

Use scanimage to scan an image. Most scanners let you specify the x and y values, in pixels, for the image size to scan, starting from the top-left corner of the scanner bed. Give these coordinates as arguments to the '-x' and '-y' options. Also, give an argument to the '--resolution' option to specify the scan resolution, given in dpi ("dots per inch"). Common resolution values include 72, 120, 300, and 600 dpi; 72 dpi is the most popular resolution for use on the Web or for viewing on screen, and 204 dpi is often used for images that you want to send on a fax machine.

Scanned output is sent to standard output, so to scan an image to a file, redirect the standard output.

scanimage outputs images in the PNM ("portable anymap") formats, so make sure that you have the 'netpbm' package (installed on most Linux systems by default); it's a useful collection of tools for converting and manipulating these formats. The formats output by scanimage are as follows:

FORMAT	DESCRIPTION
PPM	Color images.
PBM	Black and white images.
PGM	Grayscale images.

Use the '--mode' option to specify the format of the output, followed by one of the following arguments: 'color' for color PPM, 'gray' for PGM grayscale, or 'lineart' for black and white PBM. Each scanner has a default mode; for most color scanners, the default mode will be 'color'.

- To make a 72 dpi scan of a color image 200 pixels wide and 100 pixels tall, using the UNIX scanner from previous examples, and writing to a file called 'scan.ppm', type:

  $ *scanimage -d umax:/dev/sgb --resolution 72 -x 200 -y 100 >*
  scan.ppm (RET)

- To make a 300 dpi scan of a black and white image 180 pixels wide and 225 pixels tall, using the UMAX scanner from previous examples, and writing to a file called 'scan.pbm', type:

```
$ scanimage -d umax:/dev/sgb --resolution 300 --mode lineart
-x 180 -y 225 > scan.pbm (RET)
```

NOTE: The command lines in this recipe are split across two lines because they're too long to fit on one, but type these commands on one long line.

Once the image has been scanned and written to a file, you can edit it just as you would any image.

19.3 Extracting PhotoCD Images

Debian: 'xpcd'
WWW: http://user.cs.tu-berlin.de/~kraxel/linux/xpcd/

There are two methods to extract an image from Kodak PhotoCD[1] ("PCD"). If you are browsing the disc with the xpcd tool, then choose an image, extract a copy at the desired resolution, and save it to a file, as described in Recipe 17.5 [Browsing PhotoCD Archives], page 212.

You can also use pcdtoppm on a PCD file directly to extract an image at a given resolution and save it to a file in PPM format. Use the '-r' option to specify the resolution to extract, given as a numeric argument from 1 (lowest resolution) to 5 (highest); if this option is omitted, a value of 3 is assumed. Also give as arguments the name of the PCD file to read from and the name of the PPM file to write to.

- To extract the highest resolution from the file 'slack.pcd' and save it to a PPM file named 'slack.ppm', type:

```
$ pcdtoppm -r5 slack.pcd slack.ppm (RET)
```

19.3.1 Converting a PhotoCD Image

Once you extract a PhotoCD image and write it to a PPM format file, use **convert** to convert it to another format and adjust or improve the image (see Recipe 18.2 [Converting Images between Formats], page 223).

To improve the image while you convert it to JPEG format, specify no interlacing with the '-interlace' option, 50 percent image sharpening with the '-sharpen' option, and add an optional border and annotation to the image with the '-border' and '-comment' options.

- To convert the file 'slack.ppm' to non-interlaced JPEG, sharpen the image, add a two-pixel by two-pixel border, and annotate the image, type (all on one line):

```
$ convert -interlace NONE -sharpen 50 -border 2x2 -comment
'Bob was here' slack.pnm slack.jpeg (RET)
```

---

[1] This is a proprietary scanned image format from Kodak, which is a current standard for scanning film images to digital.

19.3.2 Removing PhotoCD Haze

Debian: 'gimp'
WWW: http://www.gimp.org/

Extracted PhotoCD images are known to sometimes have a kind of "green haze" over
them; to remove it, open the image in the GIMP and adjust the color levels with the
Auto Levels function. This technique, adapted from a tip for using PhotoCD by Philip
Greenspun (http://philip.greenspun.com/), works well for improving any scanned or
imported image.

- To remove the "green haze" from a PhotoCD image, do the following:
  - First, open the extracted image in the GIMP (see Recipe 18.3 [Editing Images
    with the GIMP], page 225).
  - Then, click through the Image menu to the Colors submenu and then to the
    Levels submenu, and choose Auto Levels.
  - Click OK in the Levels window to accept the changes.

20 PostScript

Debian: 'gs'
Debian: 'psutils'
WWW: `ftp://www.gnu.org/pub/gnu/ghostscript/`
WWW: `ftp://ftp.dcs.ed.ac.uk/pub/ajcd/`
WWW: `http://www.cappella.demon.co.uk/tinyfiles/tinymenu.html`

PostScript is a programming language, used to describe the way a "page" (usually a physical sheet of paper) should look. PostScript files are text files containing the PostScript commands for drawing images to be printed on pages.

Like plain text files, PostScript files are commonly found on the Internet (and are used by commercial printers) because, as with plain text, they can be shared across platforms and hardware without difficulty. The same PostScript file can be output on a high-end display or printed on a low-end printer, to the best of that hardware's capability. PostScript is a compact and elegant format.

While it's possible to write directly in the PostScript language, and some people have become adept at programming PostScript, so many tools and applications convert files to and from PostScript that you don't have to. See Recipe 15.2 [Converting Plain Text for Output], page 179, for a way to convert plain text into PostScript.

Ghostscript is a free implementation of the PostScript language. The **gs** tool is a Ghostscript interpreter that is used to convert files from PostScript to other formats, usually for printing to a non-PostScript printer (see Recipe 25.3.1 [Preparing a PostScript File for Printing], page 275). The **ghostview** tool is used to preview PostScript files on the screen (see Recipe 17.1.2 [Previewing a PostScript File], page 207).

EPS, or Encapsulated PostScript, is a file format that describes the contents of a box within a page. EPS files can be embedded in the page of a PostScript file, and are therefore commonly used when inserting an illustration into a document (for example, all of the illustrations in the *Cookbook* are EPS format files). You can view and print EPS files just as you would PostScript files.

This chapter includes recipes for formatting and manipulating PostScript files. Recipes are separated according to whether they work on the individual, *logical pages* in a PostScript file (the numbered pages in the file that are not necessarily the physical pages of output), and those that work on the entire file as a whole.

Unless otherwise indicated, the tools in this chapter are part of Angus Duggan's PSUtils package. These tools can be useful for other purposes than those described below; see their respective **man** pages for more details.

20.1 Manipulating PostScript Pages

These recipes work on individual *pages* of PostScript files, and not the entire file itself.

20.1.1 Extracting DVI Pages to PostScript

To extract specific pages of a DVI ("DeVice Independent") file to PostScript, use **dvips** and give the page or hyphenated page ranges to output with the '-pp' option.

- To extract only the first page from the file 'abstract.dvi' and send the PostScript output to the printer, type:

      $ *dvips -pp1 abstract.dvi* (RET)

By default, **dvips** will output to the printer; to save the PostScript output to a file, give the file name to be used for output with the '-o' option.

- To output as PostScript the pages 137 to 146 of the file 'abstract.dvi' to the file 'abstract.ps', type:

      $ *dvips -pp137-146 -o abstract.ps abstract.dvi* (RET)

20.1.2 Extracting Pages from a PostScript File

Use **psselect** to select pages from a PostScript file; when you give an input file, it outputs a new PostScript file containing the specified pages.

Give the pages to select as arguments to the '-p' option; you can list single pages and ranges of pages separated by commas. Give ranges as two numbers between a hyphen; thus, '4-6' specifies pages four through six, inclusive. If you omit the first number in a pair, the first page is assumed, and if you omit the last number, the last page is assumed. Pages are written to the new file in the order they are specified.

To select page 47 from the PostScript file 'newsletter.ps' and output it to the file 'selection.ps', type:

      $ *psselect -p47 newsletter.ps selection.ps* (RET)

- To select the first ten pages, page 104, pages 23 through 28, and page 2 from the file 'newsletter.ps' and write it to the file 'selection.ps', type:

      $ *psselect -p1-10,104,23-28,2 newsletter.ps selection.ps* (RET)

In the preceding example, page 2 is selected twice.

Prefix a number with an underscore ('_') to indicate that the given page number is relative to the last page, counting backwards toward the first page.

- To select the second-to-last through the tenth-to-last pages from the PostScript file 'newsletter.ps' and output them to the file 'selection.ps', type:

      $ *psselect -p_2-_10 newsletter.ps selection.ps* (RET)

- To select the second-to-last through the tenth pages from the PostScript file 'newsletter.ps' and output them to the file 'selection.ps', type:

      $ *psselect -p_2-10 newsletter.ps selection.ps* (RET)

Use the '-e' option to select all even-numbered pages, and use the '-o' option to select all odd-numbered pages.

- To select all of the even pages in the file 'newsletter.ps' and write them to a new file, 'even.ps', type:

      $ *psselect -e newsletter.ps even.ps* (RET)

- To select all of the odd pages in the file 'newsletter.ps' and write them to a new file, 'odd.ps', type:

      $ *psselect -o newsletter.ps odd.ps* (RET)

Use an underscore ('_') alone to insert a blank page, and use '-r' to output pages in *reverse* order.

- To select the last ten pages of file 'newsletter.ps', followed by a blank page, followed by the first ten pages, and output them to a new file, 'selection.ps', type:

    $ *psselect -p_1-_10,_,1-10 newsletter.ps selection.ps* (RET)

- To select the pages 59, 79, and 99 in the file 'newsletter.ps', and output them in reverse order (with the 99th page first) to a new file, 'selection.ps', type:

    $ *psselect -p59,79,99 -r newsletter.ps selection.ps* (RET)

NOTE: The same result as the preceding example above could have been done by omitting the '-r' option and just listing the three pages in the reverse order:

    $ *psselect -p99,79,59 newsletter.ps selection.ps* (RET)

20.1.3 Combining PostScript Pages

Use psnup to print multiple PostScript pages on a single sheet of paper; give as an option the number of pages to be combined (or put "up") on each sheet.

- To make a new PostScript file, 'double.ps', putting two pages from the file 'single.ps' on each page, type:

    $ *psnup -2 single.ps double.ps* (RET)

To specify the paper size, give the name of a standard paper size as an argument to the '-p' option: a3, a4, a5, b5, letter, legal, tabloid, statement, executive, folio, quarto, or 10x14. You can also specify any height and width with the '-h' and '-w' options; units can be specified in centimeters (followed by 'cm') or inches (followed by 'in'). If no size is specified, psnup assumes a paper size of a4.

Use the '-l' option when pages are in landscape orientation (rotated 90 degrees counter-clockwise from portrait orientation), and '-r' when pages are in seascape orientation (rotated 90 degrees clockwise from portrait orientation).

Pages are placed in "row-major" layout in the output file, where logical pages are placed in rows across the page. Use the '-c' option to specify a "column-major" layout, where logical pages are placed in *columns* down the page. Scale the size of the pages by giving a percentage to multiply the page size by as an argument to the '-s' option; for example, '-s .5' scales pages to 50 percent of their original size.

To draw a border around each page, specify the border's width in points as an argument to the '-d' option (if no width is specified, a value of 1 is assumed).

20.1.4 Arranging PostScript Pages in Signatures

A *signature* is a group of pages in a document corresponding to sheets of paper folded and bound; these pages are normally not in sequential order in a document (for example, in a document with eight-page signatures, page 8 and page 1 might both be printed on the same sheet of paper).

To rearrange the pages of a PostScript file by signature—usually for printing the file as a book or booklet—use psbook. Give as arguments the name of the PostScript file to read from and the name to use for the output file; it reads the contents of the first, rearranges the pages, and then writes the PostScript output to the second file.

- To rearrange the pages of file 'newsletter.ps' into a signature and write it to the file 'newsletter.bound.ps', type:

      $ *psbook newsletter.ps newsletter.bound.ps* (RET)

By default, psbook uses one signature for the entire file. If the file doesn't contain a multiple of four pages, it adds blank pages to the end.

To specify the size of the signature to use—in other words, the number of pages that will appear on a single piece of paper—give the number as an argument to the '-s' option. Signature size is always a multiple of four.

- To rearrange the pages of file 'newsletter.ps' into an eight-sided signature and write it to 'newsletter.bound.ps', type:

      $ *psbook -s8 newsletter.ps newsletter.bound.ps* (RET)

20.2 Manipulating PostScript Documents

These recipes work on a PostScript document as a whole.

20.2.1 Resizing a PostScript Document

Use psresize to resize a PostScript file. It takes as arguments the file to resize and the output file to write to; you must also specify the page size of the output file, using the same format as with the psnup tool: use '-p' or '-h' and '-w' to specify the size of the output file, and use '-P' to specify the size of the input file (see Recipe 20.1.3 [Combining PostScript Pages], page 237).

- To resize the PostScript file 'double.ps' to US letter-sized paper, writing output to a new file, 'doublet.ps', type:

      $ *psresize -pletter double.ps doublet.ps* (RET)

20.2.2 Combining PostScript Documents

Use psmerge to concatenate and merge multiple PostScript files into a single file. Give the names of the files to be merged as arguments, and psmerge outputs them to the standard output in the order given. You can also specify an output file name with the '-o' option (don't put any spaces between the file name and the option).

- To merge the files 'slide1.ps', 'slide2.ps', and 'slide3.ps' into a new PostScript file, 'slideshow.ps', type:

      $ *psmerge -oslideshow.ps slide1.ps slide2.ps slide3.ps* (RET)

NOTE: As of this writing, psmerge only works with PostScript files that were made with the same application—which means, for example, that you can merge multiple files made with TeX, or multiple files made with xfig, but not a combination of the two.

20.2.3 Arranging a PostScript Document in a Booklet

To arrange the pages in a PostScript file to make booklets, rearrange the file in a signature with psbook, use psnup to arrange the pages—two to a printed page in landscape mode— and then use pstops to output first the odd and then the even pages.

The trick to doing this properly is to first determine exactly what you need to do and then calculate the proper measurements for use with **pstops**.

- To make a booklet from the file 'newsletter.ps':

  1. Rearrange the pages into a signature:

     $ *psbook newsletter.ps newsletter.signature.ps* (RET)

  2. Put the pages two to a page in landscape orientation, at 70 percent of their original size (typed all on one line):

     $ *psnup -l -pletter -2 -s.7 newsletter.signature.ps >* *newsletter.2up.ps* (RET)

  3. Output the odd pages:

     $ *pstops "2:0(1in,0in)" newsletter.2up.ps > odd.ps* (RET)

  4. Output the even pages:

     $ *pstops "2:-1(1in,0in)" newsletter.2up.ps > even.ps* (RET)

Then, to print the booklet, you send 'odd.ps' to the printer, load the printed pages in the manual feed tray and then send 'even.ps' to the printer. This prints the odd and even pages on opposite sides of the sheets.

- To make a double-sized booklet on letter-sized paper in landscape orientation, from a file using letter-sized portrait orientation, type:

```
$ psbook input.ps > temp1.ps (RET)
...processing messages...
$ psnup -l -pletter -2 -s.7 temp1.ps > temp2.ps (RET)
...processing messages...
$ pstops "2:0(1in,0in)" temp2.ps > odd.ps (RET)
...processing messages...
$ pstops "2:-1(1in,0in)" test2.ps > even.ps (RET)
...processing messages...
$
```

20.3 Converting PostScript

These recipes show how to convert PostScript files to other formats. See also the recipes for preparing PostScript files for printing, Recipe 25.3.1 [Preparing a PostScript File for Printing], page 275.

20.3.1 Converting PostScript to PDF

Use **ps2pdf**, part of the **gs** ("Ghostscript") package, to convert a PostScript file to PDF. Give as arguments the name of the PostScript file to read from, and the name of the PDF file to write to.

- To make a PDF file 'sutra.pdf' from the input file 'sutra.ps', type:

  $ *ps2pdf sutra.ps sutra.pdf* (RET)

This command writes a new file in PDF format called 'sutra.pdf'. The original file, 'sutra.ps', is not altered.

NOTE: To make proper PDF conversions, make sure that you have **gs** version 6.01 or higher installed; use the '-v' option with **gs** to output the installed version.

20.3.2 Converting PostScript to Plain Text

To convert a PostScript file to plain text, use **ps2ascii**. Give as arguments the name of the PostScript file to read from, and the name of the text file to write to.

- To make a text file, 'sutra.txt', from the input file 'sutra.ps', type:

      $ *ps2ascii sutra.ps sutra.txt* (RET)

This command writes a text file called 'sutra.txt'. The original file, 'sutra.ps', is not altered.

PART FIVE: Sound

21 Sound Files

Debian: 'alsa-base'
WWW: http://www.alsa-project.org/

This chapter covers the basic control of audio on Linux-based systems, including how to adjust the audio mixer and how to play and record sound files using basic tools. You can also play and record audio with **snd** (see Chapter 23 [Editing Sound Files], page 255) and many other sound applications.

For purposes of this discussion, I will assume you are using the ALSA sound driver on your system and that you have sound working properly; unlike the standard Open Sound System driver (OSS/Linux), the ALSA driver is made entirely of free software. It is becoming the de facto choice for musicians who use Linux.

NOTE: Most systems come configured so that you must be the superuser to be able to use sound devices, including audio CDs. If this is the case on your system, ask your administrator to give you access to these devices, typically by adding you to the **audio** group (see Recipe 6.1 [Groups and How to Work in Them], page 83).

21.1 Sound File Formats

The following table lists common audio file formats and their traditional file name extensions. You can also use **file** to determine a file's format (see Recipe 8.1 [Determining File Type and Format], page 99).

FILE EXTENSION	SOUND FORMAT
.aiff	Apple Macintosh audio file.
.au	Sun Microsystems audio file (8000 Hz, u-law compression).
.cdda *or* .cdr	Both are names for the audio compact disc format, used for burning audio CD-Rs and CD-RWs (44.1 KHz raw stereo).
.gsm	Global System for Mobile Communications (GSM) speech file format, used in some voice-mail applications.
.midi *or* .mid	The standard extensions for MIDI files.
.mod	MOD file.
.mp3	MPEG II, Level 3 file.
.ra	RealAudio file.
.raw	Raw audio data.
.sf	IRCAM SoundFile format, used by some music composition software, such as CSound and MiXViews.
.voc	SoundBlaster VOC file.
.wav	Microsoft RIFF format ("WAV").

21.2 Adjusting the Audio Controls

A *mixer* program is used to adjust various audio settings, such as volume and recording levels, and is also used for turning on or muting the microphone or other input device. You must use a mixer to adjust your audio settings before you play or record sound.

ALSA's default mixer is called **amixer**, and the following recipes assume its use. There are other mixers, and some of them are easier to use than **amixer**. If you want a graphical mixer, install the **aumix** package, or see the end of this chapter for others.

21.2.1 Listing the Current Audio Settings

To list all audio input and output devices and their settings, type *amixer* with no options.

Your sound card's components are organized in groups, from the Master group containing the master left and right volume settings to the individual groups for audio compact discs and digital sound files. (These groups have nothing to do with the file access groups described in Recipe 6.1 [Groups and How to Work in Them], page 83.)

- To peruse the current mixer settings, type:

        $ amixer | less (RET)

The following table describes some of the important sound groups that **amixer** lists.

SOUND GROUP	DESCRIPTION
Master	The master volume settings.
PCM	Digital audio for playing sound files; the first channel is group PCM,0 and the second is PCM,1.
CD	The audio compact disc player (a cable must be connected from the CD-ROM drive to the sound card).
Synth	The synthesizer device for MIDI.
Line	The sound input device (the jack on the back of the soundcard is usually labeled LINE IN).
MIC	The microphone device (the jack on the back of the soundcard is usually labeled MIC).

To list the settings for only one group, use the 'get' option followed by the name of the group you want to list. Group names are case sensitive—so giving *MIC* specifies the microphone group, while *Mic* and *mic* are not valid groups.

- To output the microphone settings, type:

        $ amixer get MIC (RET)

- To output the second PCM settings, type:

        $ amixer get PCM,1 (RET)

21.2.2 Changing the Volume Level

To change a mixer setting, give the **amixer** 'set' command as an option, followed by both the group and setting to change as arguments. To change the volume level for a device, give either a numeric value or a percentage for the volume level.

- To set the master volume to 75 percent, type:

      $ amixer set Master 75% (RET)

- To set the PCM volume to 30, type:

      $ amixer set PCM 30 (RET)

21.2.3 Muting an Audio Device

The special 'mute' and 'unmute' arguments are used for muting the volume of a given device. Before you can record something, you must unmute the input device you want to record from. Remember to also mute the microphone after you have finished recording, to avoid feedback when you turn up your speakers.

- To unmute the microphone and turn it on for recording, type:

      $ amixer set MIC unmute capture (RET)

- To mute the microphone, type:

      $ amixer set MIC mute (RET)

- To unmute the master volume and set it to 80 percent volume, type:

      $ amixer set Master 80% unmute (RET)

21.2.4 Selecting an Audio Recording Source

To select a device for recording, use set followed by the name of the device and the 'capture' argument, which designates the specified group as the one to capture sound from for recording.

- To select the LINE IN jack as the recording source, type:

      $ amixer set Line capture (RET)

- To select the microphone jack as the recording source, type:

      $ amixer set MIC capture (RET)

NOTE: You can have only one group selected for capture at a time, and when you select a group as an input source for recording, you are simply turning the microphone or other input on; recording does not occur until you use a recording tool.

21.3 Playing a Sound File

Debian: 'sox'
WWW: http://home.sprynet.com/~cbagwell/sox.html

The play tool distributed with sox (a sound file translation tool) can recognize and play many audio formats, including WAV, VOC, AU, AIFF, and SND format files, as well as audio CD-format files and various raw binary files; just about the only common audio formats it can't handle are MP3 and MIDI files, which are discussed in the sections to follow.

- To play the file 'pentastar.aiff', type:

      $ play pentastar.aiff (RET)

NOTE: Before you begin playing sound, make sure you've set the master and PCM volume levels with the mixer (see Recipe 21.2 [Adjusting the Audio Controls], page 244). The most common reason for no sound being produced when you try to play sound is not having the volume turned up!

ALSA comes with `aplay`, a tool for playing sound files that is similar to `play`, but does not recognize as many formats.

21.3.1 Playing an MP3 File

Debian: 'mpg123'
WWW: `http://mpg.123.org/`

To play an MP3 file, give its name as an argument to `mpg123`.

- To play the MP3 file 'september-wind.mp3', type:

    $ *mpg123 september-wind.mp3* (RET)

To *buffer* the audio, useful for when the system is running many processes or otherwise has a lot of activity, give a buffer size, in kilobytes, as an argument to the '`-b`' option. The default is 0 (no buffer); if you need this option, use a size of at least 1024KB (which is 1MB), or about six seconds of MP3 audio.

You can also use `mpg123` to play "streaming" MP3 audio from the Web; just give the URL of the MP3 stream as an argument.

- To play the MP3 stream at `http://example.net/broadcast/live.mp3`, type:

    $ *mpg123 http://example.net/broadcast/live.mp3* (RET)

- To play the MP3 stream at `http://example.net/broadcast/live.mp3` with a 2MB audio buffer, type:

    $ *mpg123 -b 2048 http://example.net/broadcast/live.mp3* (RET)

NOTE: There are a great many other MP3 players available; some of them are listed in Recipe 21.5 [Other Sound File Tools], page 248.

21.3.2 Playing a MIDI File

Debian: 'playmidi'
WWW: `http://playmidi.openprojects.net/`

The `playmidi` tool is for playing MIDI files; give the name of the MIDI file to play as an argument.

- To play the MIDI file 'copa-cabana.mid', type:

    $ *playmidi copa-cabana.mid* (RET)

If you have a non-MIDI sound card, you can still play MIDI files by giving the '`-f`' option, which sends the MIDI output to the FM synthesizer on the sound card, which in turn plays it using FM patches that come with the `playmidi` distribution.

- To play the MIDI file 'copa-cabana.mid' on a non-MIDI sound card, type:

    $ *playmidi -f copa-cabana.mid* (RET)

21.4 Recording a Sound File

Debian: 'sox'
WWW: http://home.sprynet.com/~cbagwell/sox.html

To record sound, first select an input device as a source for recording. Sound cards may have MIC and LINE IN jacks, as well as connections to the CD-ROM drive, all of which are sound inputs that can be recording sources. When you select a device for capture, your recording will come from this source.

Recording occurs from the currently active input, if any, which must be set with the mixer; unmute it and set its volume level before you begin recording. (Be sure to turn the volume on your speakers all the way off, or you'll get feedback.)

To record audio to a file, use the rec tool. It can write many audio file formats, either to a format you specify with the '-t' option, or by determining the format to use based on the file name extension you give the output file (see Recipe 21.1 [Sound File Formats], page 243). Type C-c to stop recording.

Give the name of the sound file to record as an argument; if a '.wav' file is specified, it records a simple monaural, low-fidelity sound sample by default.

- To record a simple WAV sample from the microphone and save it to a file called 'hello.wav', type:

      $ rec hello.wav (RET)

This command begins an 8,000 Hz, monaural 8-bit WAV recording to the file 'hello.wav', and keeps recording until you interrupt it with C-c. While the default is to make a low-fidelity recording—8,000 Hz, monaural 8-bit samples—you can specify that a high-fidelity recording be made. (But remember that high-fidelity recordings take up much more disk space.)

To make a stereo recording, use the '-c' option to specify the number of channels, giving 2 as the argument. To make a 16-bit recording, give 'w' ("wide") as the argument to the '-s' ("sample size") option.

Set the recording sample rate by giving the samples per second to use as an argument to the '-r' option. For CD-quality audio at 44,100Hz, use '-r 44100'.

Finally, to record a file in a particular format, either give the name of the format as an argument to the '-f' option, or use the traditional file name extension for that format in the output file name (see Recipe 21.1 [Sound File Formats], page 243).

- To make a high-fidelity recording from the microphone and save it to a WAV-format file called 'goodbye.wav', type:

      $ rec -s w -c 2 -r 44100 goodbye.wav (RET)

- To make a sound recording in the CD audio format, and write the output to a file called 'goodbye.cdr', type:

      $ rec goodbye.cdr (RET)

NOTE: When you're not recording sound, keep the inputs muted (see Recipe 21.2.3 [Muting an Audio Device], page 245); this way, you can have a microphone plugged in without having feedback when playing sounds. Also, make sure the volume levels are not set too high or

too low when recording; getting the right level for your microphone or other input device
may take some initial adjustment.

Like `play`, `rec` is part of the `sox` toolkit.

21.5 Other Sound File Tools

There are many mixer, playback, and recording tools available. The following table lists
some of them, giving their Debian package name and URL, where available.

TOOL	DESCRIPTION
aumix	A simple, visual audio mixer tool that can be used in X or in the console—use this if you are too frustrated by `amixer`. Debian: 'aumix'
freeamp	An MP3 player. Debian: 'freeamp' WWW: `http://www.freeamp.org/`
maplay	An MP3 player. Debian: 'maplay'
mp3asm	Use this tool to cut and paste MP3 frames and fix broken MP3 files. Debian: 'mp3asm' WWW: `http://packages.debian.org/stable/sound/mp3asm.html`
xmms	Inspired by Winamp, XMMS is a popular, comprehensive audio player for X that features an array of plug-ins. Debian: 'xmms' WWW: `http://www.xmms.org/`

22 Audio Compact Discs

Audio compact discs can be played on systems that have a CD-ROM drive and sound card installed. You can control playback of an audio CD in all the ways you can with a traditional CD player, except on a Linux system you control playback with software tools on the command line. There are tools for reading the audio data from a CD and writing it to a file (which you can later write to a CD-R disc, or convert to MP3 format).

Tools and techniques for manipulating CD-ROMs (data CDs) are in Recipe 24.4 [CD-ROMs], page 268.

22.1 Controlling CD Audio

Debian: 'cdtool'
WWW: ftp://jaka.cerl.uiuc.edu/pub/tinsel/

These recipes describe various ways to play audio CDs using the command-line tools found in the 'CDTOOL' suite. Other CD audio tools, including X clients, are listed in Recipe 22.4 [Other Audio CD Applications], page 254.

22.1.1 Playing an Audio CD

Use cdplay to play an audio CD in the CD-ROM drive; the sound is output through the speakers connected to the LINE OUT jack on your sound card. (You may need to use the audio mixer to adjust the volume level and other settings; see Recipe 21.2 [Adjusting the Audio Controls], page 244.)

- To play an audio CD, type:
      $ cdplay (RET)

To begin with a particular track, give the number of the track as an argument.

- To play an audio CD, beginning with the third track, type:
      $ cdplay 3 (RET)

To *end* with a particular track, give the number of the track as a second argument.

- To play an audio CD, beginning with the first track and ending with the fourth track, type:
      $ cdplay 1 4 (RET)
- To play only the third track of an audio CD, type:
      $ cdplay 3 3 (RET)

22.1.2 Pausing an Audio CD

Use cdpause to pause audio CD playback.

- To pause the current CD playback, type:
      $ cdpause (RET)

Use cdplay to start playback at the point where it was paused; to restart the playback from the beginning, use cdplay with 'x' as an argument.

- To restart a paused CD, type:

    $ *cdplay* (RET)

- To restart a paused CD from the beginning, type:

    $ *cdplay x* (RET)

22.1.3 Stopping an Audio CD

To stop playback of an audio CD, use `cdstop`.

- To stop the current CD playback, type:

    $ *cdstop* (RET)

22.1.4 Shuffling Audio CD Tracks

Use `cdplay` with the 'shuffle' argument to play the CD tracks in random order.

- To shuffle CD playback, type:

    $ *cdplay shuffle* (RET)

22.1.5 Displaying Information about an Audio CD

Use `cdinfo` to display information about an audio CD, including its play status and track times. With no options, it outputs the play status: 'play' if the CD is currently playing, 'paused' if the CD is currently on pause, 'no-status' if the CD is not playing, and 'nodisc' if no disc is in the drive.

- For the current status of the audio CD in the CD-ROM drive, type:

    $ *cdinfo* (RET)

In addition, `cdinfo` recognizes the following options:

OPTION	DESCRIPTION
-a	Output the absolute disc time.
-r	Output the relative track time.
-s	Output the play status (the default action).
-t	Output the current track.
-v	Output all available information: play status, current track, absolute disc time, and relative track time.

To show the lengths of all tracks on an audio CD in a directory-like format, use `cdir`. This tool will also show titles and artist names, if known, but for this to work, you must set up an audio CD database (see the `cdtool` `man` page for details—Recipe 2.8.4 [Reading a Page from the System Manual], page 30).

- To show a list of tracks, type:

```
$ cdir (RET)
unknown cd - 43:14 in 8 tracks
   5:15.00  1
   5:50.40  2
   5:29.08  3
   3:50.70  4
   4:17.00  5
   5:56.15  6
   7:13.40  7
   5:19.22  8
$
```

In this example, the CD contains eight tracks, with a total of 43 minutes and 14 seconds play time.

22.1.6 Ejecting an Audio CD

Use `cdeject` to eject the disc in the CD-ROM drive. If the disc is currently playing, play will stop and the disc will eject.

- To eject a CD, type:

      $ cdeject (RET)

NOTE: This command will also eject a CD-ROM (data CD), if the CD-ROM is not currently mounted (see Recipe 24.4 [CD-ROMs], page 268).

22.2 Sampling Sound from a CD

Debian: 'cdda2wav'
Debian: 'cdparanoia'
WWW: ftp://ftp.gwdg.de/pub/linux/misc/cdda2wav/
WWW: http://www.mit.edu/afs/sipb/user/xiphmont/cdparanoia/index.html

Two tools used for sampling (sometimes called "ripping") data from an audio CD are `cdda2wav` and `cdparanoia`. Both can retrieve single tracks or entire disks; the former is the archetypal CD audio-sampling tool for Linux, and should be used when speed is more important than sound quality. The latter does various extra checks for the paranoid, and should be used when an absolutely perfect copy is necessary—at the expense of speed. `cdda2wav` is perfectly capable of creating a digitally perfect audio sample; `cdparanoia` is useful for when your original CD may have scratches (its scratch detection capability can attempt to "hold sync" across the scratch), or for when you are using a less-than-optimal-quality CD-ROM drive.

With `cdda2wav`, you specify the track number to be retrieved as an argument to the '-t' option; use 'x' to specify a CD-quality retrieval, and give the name of the CD-ROM device with the '-D' option—unless you have multiple CD-ROM drives installed, this is almost certainly going to be '/dev/cdrom'.

By default, files are written as WAV format files; use the '-O' option followed by 'cdr' to write the files in CD audio format. '.cdr' files are useful for burning an audio CD containing the files as tracks (discussed in the following section), and '.wav' files are useful for converting to MP3 format (see Recipe 23.3.1 [Making an MP3 File], page 260). You can convert either format to the other at a later time with sox—see Recipe 23.3 [Converting Sound Files], page 259.

- To copy track seven of an audio CD to a CD-quality WAV file in the current directory, type:

    $ *cdda2wav -t7 -d0 -x -D /dev/cdrom* (RET)

- To copy all tracks on an audio CD to separate CD-quality CD audio-format files, type:

    $ *cdda2wav -D /dev/cdrom -x -O cdr -d0 -B* (RET)

For more reliable sampling, use **cdparanoia**. Give the range of audio tracks to sample as an argument (with no arguments, it samples the entire disc). Use the '-w' option to specify WAV format output.

- To sample the third track from a scratched audio CD in the default CD-ROM drive using "paranoid" data verification, and write the output to a WAV format file in the current directory, type:

    $ *cdparanoia -w 3-3* (RET)

- To sample the entire audio CD using "paranoid" data verification, type:

    $ *cdparanoia -w -B* (RET)

- To sample the entire audio CD using less-than-maximum "paranoid" data verification, without checking for scratches, and saving each song as a separate raw audio-format file in the current directory, type:

    $ *cdparanoia -B -Y -X* (RET)

NOTE: Sampling an entire audio CD can use a lot of disk space; most people delete the '.cdr' or '.wav' files as soon as they make MP3s or burn an audio CD-R from the data.

22.3 Writing an Audio CD-R

Debian: 'cdrecord'
WWW: http://freshmeat.net/projects/cdrecord/

Use 'cdrecord' to write (or "burn") audio files to a blank CD-R disc. You will need a CD-R drive[1] and the audio files must be in CD-DA CD audio format (they usually have a '.cdda' or '.cdr' file name extension).

Specify the CD-R drive with the special 'dev' argument, which is given in this form:

'dev=*scsibus*,*target*,*lun*'

where *scsibus* is the number of the SCSI bus (0 for the primary bus), *target* is the SCSI target ID (usually a number from 1 to 6), and *lun* is its LUN number (most always 0).

Use the 'speed' argument to set the speed factor for writing data: give 'speed=2' to specify double speed or 'speed=4' to specify quad speed.

Use the '-dummy' option to run with the drive laser turned off, so no actual burning takes place; this is useful when you are first using a CD-R drive and need to test your

---

[1] You can also use this tool with a CD-RW drive and write to a CD-RW disc.

configuration to make sure you've got it right. Another useful option is '-v', which gives a more *verbose* message output.

Give the names of the audio files to burn, in the order that they should appear on the disc, as arguments to the '-audio' option. The files are written in CD-DA CD audio format, and they should contain 16-bit stereo at 44,100 samples/second (the '.cdr' or '.cdda' files meet this criterion).

- To burn the file 'symphony.cdr' to the disc in the CD-R drive whose target ID is 2 on the primary SCSI bus, type:

  $ cdrecord dev=0,2,0 -audio symphony.cdr (RET)

- To burn all the files in the current directory ending with a '.cdr' extension at double speed to the CD-R drive whose target ID is 2 on the primary SCSI bus, and give verbose output, type:

  $ cdrecord dev=0,2,0 speed=2 -v -audio *.cdr (RET)

- To run a test burn of the file 'symphony.cdr' to the disc in the CD-R drive whose target ID is 6 (LUN 1) on the primary SCSI bus, type:

  $ cdrecord dev=0,6,1 -dummy -audio symphony.cdr (RET)

When you use wildcards for files, as in the second-to-the-last example, the shell expands the files in alphabetical order. To write a group of tracks in a particular order without specifying all of their names as arguments, rename them so that their names begin with numbers that correspond to the order you want to write them in (see Recipe 5.5 [Moving Files and Directories], page 76).

For example, if you have the three files 'morning-song.cdr', 'midday-song.cdr', and 'evening-song.cdr', and you want to write them in that order, rename the files to '01-morning-song.cdr', '02-midday-song.cdr', and '03-evening-song.cdr'; otherwise, if you specify them as '*.cdr', the shell will sort their names so that they will be written to CD-R in the order of 'evening-song.cdr', 'midday-song.cdr', and 'morning-song.cdr'—exactly the opposite of what was intended!

To write a disc containing both data and audio tracks, first specify the file for the data track (it should contain a filesystem image in either ISO 9660 or Rock Ridge format), and then follow it with the '-audio' option and the names of the audio tracks to use. The resulting CD-R will be both mountable as a data CD and playable on audio CD players (the first track on the disc, the data track, will be skipped when playing the audio).

- To burn the data track 'band-info' and all the audio tracks in the current directory with a '.cdda' extension to the CD-R drive whose target ID is 2 on the primary SCSI bus, type:

  $ cdrecord dev=0,2,0 band-info -audio *.cdda (RET)

NOTE: When writing an audio CD, you should have as few processes running as possible. If cdrecord has to pause even momentarily to let the system shuffle other processes, the CD-R could be ruined! For this reason, it is advisable to avoid switching between consoles—or between windows, if running X—during the CD-R burning process.

22.4 Other Audio CD Applications

The following table lists some of the other available tools and applications that work on audio compact discs.

TOOL	DESCRIPTION
dynamic	Project Dynamic is a tool for playing samples of audio CDs; it is distinctive in that it can play audio CDs *backwards*. WWW: http://www.cse.unsw.edu.au/~flatmax/dynamic/
workbone	An interactive CD player that can be used on the console or in X; it allows you to skip forward and backward through tracks as they are playing.
workman	A tool for playing audio CDs, with a graphical interface that looks like the front panel of a physical CD player.
xcdroast	XCDRoast is a graphical front-end to the cdrecord tool for use in X. WWW: http://www.xcdroast.org/

23 Editing Sound Files

All kinds of tools and applications exist to edit sound files. This chapter shows some of those tools, giving methods for for cutting and pasting sound files, applying effects and filters, and converting sound files between formats.

23.1 Working with Selections from Sound Files

Debian: 'snd'
WWW: http://ccrma-www.stanford.edu/CCRMA/Software/snd/

Snd is a sound-file editing environment for X, and aims to be for sound what Emacs is to text. (And it uses Emacs-style key bindings.)

You'll find a complete manual for it in the '/usr/doc/snd' directory; this section explains how to use Snd to work with selections from sound files.

To open a sound file in Snd, give the name of the file to be opened as an argument to snd.

- To open the sound file 'mixdown.wav' in Snd, type:

      $ *snd mixdown.wav* (RET)

This command starts Snd with a WAV file called 'mixdown.wav':

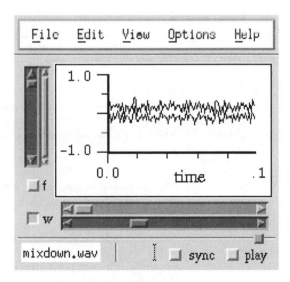

Making a selection of a sound file in snd is similar to selecting text in Emacs; you can mark a section of a sound file or recording you've made in Snd by left-clicking and dragging across the area with the mouse. The area you drag across becomes shaded and is called the *selection*. Once you select a portion of the sound, any effect you choose works on that selection. You can also cut and paste selections of the sound you are editing into other sound buffers.

The `xwave` tool (and many others, no doubt) have similar capabilities and functions (see Recipe 23.4 [Other Tools for Sound Editing], page 261).

23.1.1 Cutting Out Part of a Sound File

To cut out a portion of a sound file you are editing in Snd, first make it the selection by left-clicking and dragging, and then choose `Cut` from the `Edit` menu, somewhat like cropping an image file.

23.1.2 Pasting a Selection of Sound

Paste a cut sound selection into a different sound buffer in Snd by opening the new buffer, left-clicking in the target buffer, and then choosing `Paste` from the `Edit` menu. Your most recent selection will be pasted at the point where you clicked in the sound buffer.

23.1.3 Mixing Sound Files Together

To mix different audio files together as multiple tracks in Snd, choose `Mix` from the `File` menu and specify the files to use as the individual tracks.

23.2 Sound Effects

Debian: 'sox'
WWW: `http://home.sprynet.com/~cbagwell/sox.html`

The "Sound eXchange" tool, `sox`, is a sound sample translator. It reads sound as files or standard input and outputs the sound either to a file or standard output, while translating in between. You can use `sox` to convert sound files between formats or process sounds with special effects. This section describes some of the special effects you can apply to sound files with `sox`.

When applying an effect, the original file is never altered. You must specify an output file, or use '-' to indicate the standard output, specifying the output format with '-t'. You can only apply one effect with each `sox` command; thus, to add both echo and reverb to a sound file, you would need to issue two `sox` commands.

The amount and levels applied for each effect will vary with every situation. As such, consider the following recipes guidelines only for using the options; you will probably end up experimenting a bit to get your intended effect for any particular sound file.

Almost all of the sound effects are applied by specifying the input and output file arguments, followed by the name of the effect to use and any options the effect takes (with notable exceptions, like the '-v' option for changing the amplitude of a file).

NOTE: For more information on the effects Sox can do, see the various files in '/usr/doc/sox/', and read the `sox man` page (see Recipe 2.8.4 [Reading a Page from the System Manual], page 30).

23.2.1 Changing the Amplitude of a Sound File

To change the volume or amplitude of a sound file, use **sox** with the '**-v**' option, giving the volume level as an argument. Levels below 1.0 lower the amplitude, and higher numbers raise it.

- To raise the volume of file 'old.wav' twofold and write the output to 'new.wav', type:

    $ *sox -v3 old.wav new.wav* (RET)

- To lower the volume of file 'old.wav' by half and write the output to 'new.wav', type:

    $ *sox -v.5 old.wav new.wav* (RET)

Use **sox** with the '**stat**' option and '**-v**' to determine the largest possible value that can be used before distortion or clipping occurs (it performs a statistical analysis on the file and outputs a numeric value). This value comes in handy when you want to raise a file's volume as high as possible without ruining its fidelity.

- To raise the volume of the file '**quit.cdr**' as high as possible without distortion, type:

```
$ sox quiet.cdr loud.cdr stat -v (RET)
3.125
$ sox -v 3.125 quiet.cdr loud.cdr (RET)
$
```

The preceding example writes a new file, 'loud.cdr'.

23.2.2 Changing the Sampling Rate of a Sound File

To change the sampling rate of a sound file, use the '**-r**' option followed by the sample rate to use, in Hertz. Like the '**-v**' option, specify this option before giving the name of the output file.

- To change the sampling rate of file 'old.wav' to 7,000 Hz, and write the output to 'new.wav', type:

    $ *sox old.wav -r 7000 new.wav* (RET)

23.2.3 Adding Reverb to a Sound File

To add reverb to a sound file, use the '**reverb**' effect. '**reverb**' takes three arguments: the volume of the output (its "gain-out"), the time (in milliseconds) of reverb, and the length (in milliseconds) of delay. You can specify more than one delay; the more you specify, the more of an overlapping echo the reverb will have.

- To add a basic reverb to file 'old.wav' and write the output to file 'new.wav', type:

    $ *sox old.wav new.wav .5 1000 100* (RET)

- To add a spacey, echoing reverb to file 'old.wav' and write the output to 'new.wav', type:

    $ *sox old.wav new.wav reverb 1 1000 333 333 333 333* (RET)

NOTE: This last example makes a sound similar to some of the recordings of the band Flying Saucer Attack. You know who they are, don't you?)

23.2.4 Adding Echo to a Sound File

To add echo to a sound file, use the 'echo' effect. It takes as arguments the "gain-in" and "gain-out" volume levels, as well as the delay and decay, both in milliseconds.

- To add a 100 millisecond echo to the sound file 'old.wav' and write output to 'new.wav', type:

      $ sox old.wav new.wav echo .5 .5 100 .5 (RET)

- To add a one-second echo to the sound file 'old.wav' and write output to 'new.wav', type:

      $ sox old.wav new.wav echo .5 .5 1000 .5 (RET)

- To add a "tin-can" echo effect to 'old.wav' and write the output to 'new.wav', type:

      $ sox old.wav new.wav echo 1 .5 5 .5 (RET)

NOTE: The 'echos' effect works like 'echo', but adds a *sequence* of echos to the sound file.

23.2.5 Adding Flange to a Sound File

The 'flanger' effect adds flange to a sound file. It takes as arguments the "gain-in" and "gain-out" volume levels, as well as the delay and decay in milliseconds, and the speed of the flange, in Hertz. Specify the type of modulation with either '-s' (for sinodial) or '-t' (for triangular).

- To add an "underwater" flange to the file 'old.wav' and write the output to 'new.wav', type:

      $ sox old.wav new.wav flanger .5 .5 4 .5 1 -t (RET)

- To add flange that sounds somewhat like a "wah-wah" effects pedal to the file 'old.wav' and write the output to 'new.wav', type:

      $ sox old.wav new.wav flanger .5 .5 .5 1 2 -t (RET)

23.2.6 Adding Phase to a Sound File

The 'phaser' effect adds phase to a sound file. It takes the same arguments as the 'flanger' effect.

- To add a heavy phase to the file 'old.wav' and write the output to 'new.wav', type:

      $ sox old.wav new.wav phaser 1 .5 4 .5 1 -s (RET)

- To add a phased "breathing" effect to the file 'old.wav' and write the output to 'new.wav', type:

      $ sox old.wav new.wav phaser .5 .5 .5 .9 .5 -t (RET)

NOTE: Using a decay greater than .5 may result in feedback.

23.2.7 Adding Chorus to a Sound File

To add a chorus effect to a sound file, use 'chorus'. Its options are the "gain-in" and "gain-out" of the volume, the delay and decay in milliseconds, the speed in Hertz, and the depth of the chorus in milliseconds. Specify either '-s' or '-t' for sinodial or triangular modulation.

- To add a 100 millisecond chorus to the file 'old.wav' and write the output to 'new.wav', type:

    $ *sox old.wav new.wav chorus 1 .5 100 1 1 1 -t* (RET)

- To add a deep, "alien-sounding" chorus to the file 'old.wav' and write the output to 'new.wav', type:

    $ *sox old.wav new.wav chorus 1 .5 100 1 5 9 -t* (RET)

23.2.8 Adding Vibro-Champ Effects to a Sound File

The 'vibro' effect imitates the effect of the Fender Vibro-Champ amplifier. Give the speed in Hertz (30 maximum) as an option, and specify an optional depth value between 0 and 1 (the default is .5).

- To add a subtle Vibro-Champ effect to the file 'old.wav' and write the output to 'new.wav', type:

    $ *sox old.wav new.wav vibro 1* (RET)

- To add an effect of a maxed-out Vibro-Champ to the file 'old.wav' and write the output to 'new.wav', type:

    $ *sox old.wav new.wav vibro 30 1* (RET)

23.2.9 Reversing a Sound File

Use the 'reverse' effect to reverse the sound in a sound file.

- To reverse the sound in the file 'old.wav' and write the output to 'new.wav', type:

    $ *sox old.wav new.wav reverse* (RET)

23.3 Converting Sound Files

Debian: sox
WWW: http://home.sprynet.com/~cbagwell/sox.html

Use sox for most sound-file conversions. Give as arguments the name of the input file and the name of the output file to write to; use a file name extension specifying the sound format for the output file (see Recipe 21.1 [Sound File Formats], page 243).

- To convert the file 'new.wav' to an audio CD format file, type:

    $ *sox new.wav new.cdr* (RET)

This command writes a new file, 'new.cdr', in the audio CD format; the original file, 'new.wav', is not altered.

You may sometimes need to specify additional options, such as with raw audio files where the sampling rate and other properties must be specified.

- To convert all of the raw audio files in the current directory to audio CD format files, type:

    $ *for i in *.raw* (RET)
    { (RET)
    sox -s -w -c2 -r 44100 $i -x $i.cdr (RET)
    } (RET)

This command writes all of the '.raw' files to new files of the same name but with a '.cdr' extension. You could then use cdrecord to burn an audio CD with the '.cdr' files (see Recipe 22.3 [Writing an Audio CD-R], page 252).

To convert a file to a particular format without using the standard extension, specify the format to write to with the '-t' option.

- To convert the file 'new.wav' to the audio CD format and write output to a file named 'cd-single', type:

      $ sox new.wav -t cdr cd-single (RET)

23.3.1 Making an MP3 File

WWW: http://www.sulaco.org/mp3/

The process of making an MP3 file from a raw audio or WAV format audio file is called "encoding" an MP3 file; programs that do this are MP3 *encoders*. This is not so much a recording process as it is a *conversion* process: existing audio is converted to an MP3 file. (To make MP3 files from your own recordings, make the recording as a CD-quality WAV file, and then convert that.)

Unfortunately, the algorithm for encoding MP3 is patented, and all software which uses it must pay a license fee—including free software. This restriction makes it difficult for people to create a free software MP3 encoder, and it is the reason why some free software and open source groups advocate the development of a high-quality compressed audio format to replace MP3.[1]

A workaround is presented in the form of LAME ("LAME Ain't an MP3 Encoder"). LAME *isn't* an MP3 encoder, but it is a free software patch file (see Recipe 8.4.3 [Patching a File with a Difference Report], page 102) designed to work with the sample source code distributed by the patent holders of the MP3 encoding process.

This means that you can download both separately and combine them to get a working MP3 encoder called notlame, perhaps the fastest (yes, encoding MP3s is a slow process) encoder currently available for Linux. When you visit the LAME Project at http://www.sulaco.org/mp3/, you'll find a link to download a pre-assembled notlame binary from a site in Australia, where the patent laws do not apply.

The notlame encoder takes two arguments: the name of the input file and the name of the output file.

- To encode an MP3 file from a WAV file called 'september-wind.wav', type:

      $ notlame september-wind.wav september-wind.mp3 (RET)

It usually takes some time to encode an MP3 file; when notlame is encoding a file, it continually outputs the current percentage of completion.

NOTE: Scripts on the download site show how to encode multiple WAV files and how to decode all of the tracks on an audio CD.

---

[1] Ogg Vorbis is one such format; see http://www.vorbis.com/.

23.3.2 Converting MP3 to Another Format

Debian: 'sox'
Debian: 'mpg321'
WWW: http://home.sprynet.com/~cbagwell/sox.html
WWW: http://freshmeat.net/projects/mpg321/

To convert an MP3 file to another format, use mpg321 (or another command-line MP3 player) to play the file to the standard output, and then use sox to read the resultant raw audio and write it to another file with a specified input format.

- To convert the MP3 file 'remix.mp3' to a WAV file 'remix.wav', type:

      $ mpg321 -b 10000 -s remix.mp3 | sox -t raw -r 44100 -s -w
      -c 2 - remix.wav (RET)

23.4 Other Tools for Sound Editing

Sound software in Linux is a fast-moving target, and it is impossible for a printed volume to keep up with it; you can stay abreast of the latest developments by checking out Dave Phillips's "Sound & MIDI Software for Linux" page at http://www.bright.net/~dlphilp/linuxsound/. This page is the most comprehensive and up-to-date list of Linux-related sound software available.

As with text editors, there are all manner of sound editors, ranging from simple editors to advanced environments. The following table lists a few of the most popular ones.

SOUND EDITOR	DESCRIPTION
dap	Richard Kent's Digital Audio Processor, DAP, is a graphical tool for editing sound files. WWW: http://www.cee.hw.ac.uk/~richardk/
festival	Festival is a speech-synthesis system. It reads English (British and American), Spanish, and Welsh plain text input and outputs speech as sound. Debian: 'festival' WWW: http://www.cstr.ed.ac.uk/projects/festival/
gramofile	Use GramoFile for sampling sound from vinyl records. It can remove ticks and pops from the sound using filters and signal processing, and is frequently used to copy records onto CD-Rs. Debian: 'gramofile' WWW: http://panic.et.tudelft.nl/~costar/gramofile/
mxv	MiXViews is an advanced sound editor. Its features include cross-fades, filters, and various powerful data analysis tools. Debian: 'mixviews' WWW: http://www.create.ucsb.edu/~doug/htmls/MiXViews.html
xwave	XWave is a simple sound editor that contains the basic functions you would expect in a WAV file editor. WWW: http://www.ibiblio.org/pub/Linux/apps/sound/editors/

PART SIX: Productivity

24 Disk Storage

All files and directories on a Linux-based system are stored on a Linux *filesystem*, which is a disk device (such as a hard drive) that is formatted to store a directory tree (see Chapter 5 [Files and Directories], page 65).

There are two kinds of disk storage on a Linux system: fixed and removable. *Fixed storage* refers to a disk that is firmly attached to the computer system, and is not intended for casual removal (except when upgrading). Your hard drive (sometimes called "hard disk"), used to store the operating system, application software, and user data, is the prime example of a fixed disk.

The second kind of disk storage is *removable storage*, disks that are intended to be removed for archiving or transfer to another system. Common examples of removable storage are floppy disk (or "diskette") and CD-ROM drives, where you typically remove the storage media from its drive bay when you're done using it.

On Linux systems, disks are used by *mounting* them to a directory, which makes the directory tree the disk contains available at that given directory *mount point*. Disks can be mounted on any directory on the system, but any divisions between disks are transparent—so a system which has, aside from the root filesystem disk mounted on '/', separate physical hard disks for the '/home', '/usr', and '/usr/local' directory trees will look and feel no different from the system that only has one physical disk.

System administrators often mount high-capacity drives on directory trees that will contain a lot of data (such as a '/home' directory tree on a system with a lot of users), and for purposes of fault tolerance, administrators often use several physical hard disks on one system—if there is a disk failure, only the data in that disk is lost.

This chapter describes tools and techniques for manipulating disks and storage media.

24.1 Listing a Disk's Free Space

To see how much free space is left on a disk, use df. Without any options, df outputs a list of all mounted filesystems. Six columns are output, displaying information about each disk: the name of its device file in '/dev'; the number of 1024-byte blocks the system uses; the number of blocks in use; the number of blocks available; the percent of the device used; and the name of the directory tree the device is mounted on.

- To see how much free space is left on the system's disks, type:

```
$ df (RET)
Filesystem          1024-blocks    Used Available Capacity Mounted on
/dev/hda1                195167    43405    141684     23%   /
/dev/hda2               2783807   688916   1950949     26%   /usr
/dev/hdb1               2039559  1675652    258472     87%   /home/webb
$
```

This example shows that three filesystems are mounted on the system—the filesystem mounted on '/' is at 23 percent capacity, the filesystem mounted on '/usr' is at 26 percent capacity, and the filesystem mounted on '/home/webb', a home directory, is at 87 percent capacity.

24.2 Listing a File's Disk Usage

Use du to list the amount of space on disk used by files. To specify a particular file name or directory tree, give it as an argument. With no arguments, du works on the current directory.

It outputs a line for each subdirectory in the tree, listing the space used and the subdirectory name; the last line lists the total amount of space used for the entire directory tree.

- To output the disk usage for the directory tree whose root is the current directory, type:

```
$ du (RET)
8          ./projects/documentation
12         ./projects/source
4          ./projects/etc
24         ./projects
3          ./tmp
27         .
$
```

This example shows two subdirectories in the directory tree: 'projects' and 'tmp'; 'projects' contains three additional directories. The amount of disk space used by the individual directories is the total on the last line, 27K.

By default, output is in 1K blocks, but you can specify another unit to use as an option: '-k' for kilobytes and '-m' for megabytes.

- To output the disk usage, in kilobytes, of the '/usr/local' directory tree, type:

    `$ du -k /usr/local (RET)`
- To show the number of megabytes used by the file '/tmp/cache', type:

    `$ du -m /tmp/cache (RET)`

Use the '-s' option ("summarize") to output only the last line containing the total for the entire directory tree. This is useful when you are only interested in the total disk usage of a directory tree.

- To output *only* the total disk usage of the '/usr/local' directory tree, type:

    `$ du -s /usr/local (RET)`
- To output only the total disk usage, in kilobytes, of the '/usr/local' directory tree, type:

    `$ du -s -k /usr/local (RET)`

24.3 Floppy Disks

Before you can use a floppy disk for the first time, it must be *formatted*, which creates an empty filesystem on the disk.

To read or write files to a formatted disk, you mount the floppy on an empty directory, making its filesystem available in the specified directory. Usually, Linux systems have an empty '/floppy' directory for this purpose. (Another general-purpose directory for mounting filesystems is the '/mnt' directory.)

NOTE: While you cannot mount a filesystem on a directory containing other files, you can always create a new directory somewhere to mount a filesystem.

When you mount a disk on a directory, that directory contains all the files and directories of the disk's filesystem; when you later *unmount* the disk, that directory will be empty—all the files and directories on the disk are still on the disk's filesystem, but the filesystem is no longer mounted.

When you're done using a floppy, you must unmount it first before you remove it from the drive. If you don't, you risk corrupting or deleting some of the files on it—Linux may still be using the mounted files when you remove the disk (see Recipe 2.1.2 [Shutting Down the System], page 17).

The following sections show you how to format, mount, and unmount floppies. On many systems, you need superuser privileges to do any one of these actions.

NOTE: For recipes describing use of MS-DOS (and Microsoft Windows) formatted disks under Linux, see Recipe 26.1 [Using DOS and Windows Disks], page 279.

24.3.1 Formatting a Floppy Disk

Use mke2fs to format a floppy and make a Linux filesystem. Give the name of the device file of the floppy drive as an argument—usually the first removable disk drive, '/dev/fd0'. The floppy must be in the drive when you give the format command, and any data already on it will be lost.

- To format a floppy disk in the first removable floppy drive, type:

    $ *mke2fs /dev/fd0* (RET)

24.3.2 Mounting a Floppy Disk

To mount a floppy, use **mount** with the '/floppy' option.[1]

- To mount a floppy, type:

    $ *mount /floppy* (RET)

To mount a floppy to a specific directory, use **mount** and give as arguments the device name of the floppy drive (usually '/dev/fd0' for one-floppy systems) and the name of the directory to mount to.

- To mount the floppy in the first floppy drive to '~/tmp', type:

    $ *mount /dev/fd0 ~/tmp* (RET)

Once you have mounted a floppy, its contents appear in the directory you specify, and you can use any file command on them.

- To list the contents of the base directory of the floppy mounted on '/floppy', type:

    $ *ls /floppy* (RET)

---

[1] This works if your administrator has set up the floppy drive filesystem for user access—see Recipe A.3.2 [Letting Users Access Hardware Peripherals], page 363.

- To list the contents of the entire directory tree on the floppy mounted on '`/floppy`', type:

    $ *ls -lR /floppy* (RET)

NOTE: You can copy files to and from the directory tree that the floppy is mounted on, make and remove directories, and do anything else you could on any other directory tree. But remember, before you remove it, you must first unmount it.

24.3.3 Unmounting a Floppy Disk

Use **umount** to unmount a floppy disk, using the name of the directory it is mounted on as an argument.

- To umount the floppy that is mounted on '`/floppy`', type:

    $ *umount /floppy* (RET)

NOTE: You can't unmount a disk if your current working directory, the directory you are in, is somewhere in that disk's directory tree.[2] In this case, trying to unmount the disk will give the error that the '`/floppy`' filesystem is in use; change to a different directory that isn't in the '`/floppy`' directory tree, and then you can unmount the disk.

Sometimes when you unmount a floppy, the light on the floppy drive will go on and remain on for a few seconds after it has been unmounted. This is because Linux sometimes keeps changes to files in memory before it writes them to disk; it's making sure that the files on the floppy are up-to-date. Simply wait until the light goes off before you remove the floppy from the drive.

24.4 CD-ROMs

As with a floppy disk, before you can use a data CD (compact disc) on your system, you must first mount it on an empty directory. You then unmount it from the directory before you can eject the CD from the CD-ROM drive (you can also eject the disc using software—see Recipe 22.1.6 [Ejecting an Audio CD], page 251).

NOTE: To use audio CDs, see Chapter 22 [Audio Compact Discs], page 249.

24.4.1 Mounting a CD-ROM

To mount a CD-ROM on the system, use **mount** with the '`/cdrom`' option.[3]

- To mount a CD-ROM on the system, type:

    $ *mount /cdrom* (RET)

This command makes the contents of the CD-ROM available from the '`/cdrom`' directory tree. You can use any Linux file command on the files and directories on a CD-ROM, but you can't write to a CD-ROM—the CD-ROM format is read-only, so you can *read* the disc but not write to it.

---

[2] This is sometimes called being "under the mount point" of the disk.

[3] This works if your administrator has set up the CD-ROM drive filesystem for user access—see Recipe A.3.2 [Letting Users Access Hardware Peripherals], page 363.

Like the '/floppy' directory, the use of the '/cdrom' directory is a standard practice and convenient, but not necessary—you can mount disks in whatever empty directory you like. (You could even, for example, mount discs from the CD-ROM drive to '/floppy' and mount floppy disks to '/cdrom', but why would anyone do that!)

To mount a CD-ROM to a specific directory, use `mount` and give as arguments the name of the device file in '/dev' corresponding to the CD-ROM drive, and the name of the directory to mount to. This directory must already exist on the filesystem, and must be empty. If it doesn't exist, use `mkdir` to create it first (see Recipe 5.1.2 [Making a Directory], page 69).

Most Linux systems are set up so that the device file of the first CD-ROM drive is '/dev/cdrom', but the name of the device file may be different, especially if you have a SCSI CD-ROM drive.

- To mount the disc in the CD-ROM drive to the '/usr/local/share/clipart' directory, type:

    $ *mount /dev/cdrom /usr/local/share/clipart* (RET)

The contents of the disc in the CD-ROM drive will then be available in the '/usr/local/share/clipart' directory tree, and you can then use the files and directories on the CD-ROM as you would any other files. For example:

- To peruse a directory tree graph of the CD-ROM's contents, type:

    $ *tree /usr/local/share/clipart | less* (RET)

- To change to the root directory of the CD-ROM, type:

    $ *cd /usr/local/share/clipart* (RET)

- To list the contents of the root directory of the CD-ROM, type:

    $ *ls /usr/local/share/clipart* (RET)

24.4.2 Unmounting a CD-ROM

Use `umount` to unmount a CD-ROM; give as an argument the name of the directory it's mounted on.

- To unmount the disc in the CD-ROM drive mounted on '/cdrom', type:

    $ *umount /cdrom* (RET)

NOTE: As with unmounting any kind of filesystem, make sure that none of the files on the disc are in use, or you won't be able to unmount it. For example, if the current working directory in a shell is somewhere inside the '/cdrom' directory tree, you won't be able to unmount the CD-ROM until you change to a different directory.

25 Printing

Debian: 'magicfilter'

The usual way to print on a Linux system is to send a print job to the printer with lpr, as described below in Recipe 25.1.1 [Sending a Print Job to the Printer], page 272.

But you don't always send a file straight to the printer—sometimes you may want to add special things to it before you print it, such as headers or graphic trim. For example, you might want to split a text file into pages and add a header to the top of each page containing the file name and page number; all of this is described in Chapter 13 [Formatting Text], page 155.

Sometimes you may need to convert or otherwise prepare a file so that it can be printed on your particular printer, since not all print hardware can print the same kinds of file formats. Recipes in this chapter show how to do this, such as how to convert PostScript files so that they will print properly on a non-PostScript printer (see Recipe 25.3 [Preparing Files for Printing], page 275).

This chapter also shows how to format PostScript files for printing. To convert plain text to PostScript and enhance it for printing, by adding fonts, graphic headers, and the like, see Recipe 15.2 [Converting Plain Text for Output], page 179.

And this chapter isn't in the files section, because you can print things that aren't in a file—for example, you can pipe the output of another tool or series of tools to lpr, and it will spool that command output to the printer. This usage is actually very common.

NOTE: When a printer is properly configured on Linux, it is a pleasure to use, but a misconfigured printer can lead to all kinds of trouble—including the dreaded "staircase effect," where a text file prints with each subsequent line of output offset to the right by the length of the previous line.

If print services haven't been configured yet on your system, I strongly recommend that the 'magicfilter' package be installed; it includes filters for the automatic detection of file types—when you print a file, it automatically converts it to the proper format for your printer.

Comprehensive details on the setup of printer resources can be found in both the *Printing HOWTO* and the *Printing Usage HOWTO* (see Recipe 2.8.6 [Reading System Documentation and Help Files], page 32).

25.1 Making and Managing Print Jobs

The traditional way to print on Linux-based systems is to send a *print job* for the file or data you want to print to the *spool queue* for the printer in question. The spool queue contains all of the print jobs sent to it by all users; these jobs are released in turn to the printer device as it becomes available. In this way, Linux can handle multiple print jobs going to the same printer at once.

The following recipes show how to make and manage print jobs. In practice, you will probably send print jobs all the time—since this is the way most printing is done in Linux—and use the tools for listing or cancelling print jobs rarely. But sometimes things do go wrong, and it helps to know what to do when that happens.

25.1.1 Sending a Print Job to the Printer

Use `lpr` to send a print job to the printer—give the name of the file to print as an argument. (You can also pipe the output of a command to `lpr`.)

`lpr` writes a copy of the specified file or text to the spool queue of the specified printer, to be sent to the printer when the printer becomes available.

- To print the file '`invoice`', type:

      $ *lpr invoice* (RET)

- To type a message with `banner` and send it to the printer, type:

      $ *banner "Bon voyage!" | lpr* (RET)

- To print a verbose, recursive listing of the '`/usr/doc/HOWTO`' directory, type:

      $ *ls -lR /usr/doc/HOWTO | lpr* (RET)

If you have more than one printer connected to your system, specify the printer to send to as an argument to the '`-P`' option. (Printers have names just as user accounts and hosts do, and it is the administrator's privilege to name them; the default printer is usually called `lp`, for "line printer.")

- To send the file '`nightly-report`' to the printer called `bossomatic`, type:

      $ *lpr -P bossomatic nightly-report* (RET)

NOTE: The name of the `lpr` tool comes from "line printer," which was the kind of printer hardware in popular use back when this program was first developed.

25.1.2 Printing Multiple Copies of a Job

To print more than one copy of a print job, give the number of copies to print as an argument to the '`-#`' option of `lpr`.

- To print a dozen copies of the file '`nightly-report`', type:

      $ *lpr -#12 nightly-report* (RET)

25.1.3 Listing Your Print Jobs

To list your print jobs, use `lpq`, the "line printer queue" tool. It outputs a list of all print jobs currently in the default printer's spool queue—each on a line of its own—giving its rank in the queue, the username who sent the job, the print job number, the file names in the job, and the size of the data to be printed, in bytes.

- To view the spool queue for the default printer, type:

```
$ lpq (RET)
lp is ready and printing
Rank    Owner       Job  Files                              Total Size
active  groucho     83   cigar.ps                     1739030 bytes
1st     harpo       84   harp.ps                          499 bytes
2nd     chico       85   love.ps                        45576 bytes
$
```

In this example, there are three jobs queued for the default printer—one by user `groucho`, for the file 'cigar.ps', one by user `harpo`, for the file 'harp.ps', and one by user `chico`, who has printed a file called 'love.ps'.

The job by user `groucho` is the *active job*; this is the job that is currently printing on the printer. The other jobs must wait until this file is finished printing, and then they print in rank order.

As with `lpr`, you can specify the name of a printer as an argument to the '-P' option.

- To view the spool queue for the printer called `bossomatic`, type:

      $ *lpq -P bossomatic* (RET)

To only list the jobs for a particular user, give the name of the user as an argument.

- To list the print jobs for user `harpo`, type:

      $ *lpq harpo* (RET)

NOTE: When there are no print jobs, `lpq` outputs the text 'no entries'.

25.1.4 Cancelling a Print Job

To cancel a print job and remove it from the spool queue, use `lprm`, the "line printer remove" tool. Give as an argument the number of the print job to remove.

- To cancel print job 83, type:

      $ *lprm 83* (RET)

To cancel *all* of your print jobs in the spool queue, use a hyphen instead of the number of a print job.

- To cancel all of your print jobs, type:

      $ *lprm -* (RET)

NOTE: If you try to cancel an active job—one that has already been spooled to the printer— don't be alarmed if some pages still print; the printer probably has some of the job in its internal print buffer. To stop the printing in a case like this, take the printer offline, reset it, and then put it back online again (usually, the printer will have buttons for these commands on its front control panel).

25.2 More Recipes for Printing

Another way of printing besides making a print job is to print from within an application.

Not all applications have print controls, but some of them do—including Emacs and LyX (see Recipe 15.3 [LyX Document Processing], page 185). Their print commands essentially send the print job to the printer via `lpr`, after possibly formatting or otherwise preparing the data to print. If you are working in such an application and want to print your work, using the built-in print control can be easier than having to go to a shell to run `lpr`.

For example, to print the current document in the LyX document processing application, choose `Print` from the `File` menu; it creates the proper output for your printer and makes a print job containing this output (see Recipe 15.3 [LyX Document Processing], page 185).

Some tools, such as `dvips` and `enscript` (see Recipe 15.2 [Converting Plain Text for Output], page 179), are also configured to spool output to the printer.

You can view these print jobs in the spool queue and you can cancel them, just as you could any print job.

25.2.1 Printing in Emacs

To print the current buffer in Emacs, choose `Print Buffer` from the `Print` submenu, found off the `Tools` menu on the menu bar. Another option on the print submenu is `Print Region`, which just prints the text between point and the mark (see Recipe 10.2.1 [Getting Acquainted with Emacs], page 121). Both commands print the hardcopy output separated into pages, and with headers at the top of each page, showing the file name and current page number.

To generate and print a PostScript image of the buffer, use the `ps-print-buffer` function, which is also available on the `Print` submenu. A related function, `ps-print-region`, prints a PostScript image of the region. These commands are useful for sending the text of a buffer to a PostScript printer.

You can also run any of these functions by specifying them with the *M-x* command; additionally, the `lpr-buffer` and `lpr-region` functions send the buffer and region to `lpr` without paginating the text or inserting headers.

- To print the current buffer with page numbers and headers, type:

      M-x print-buffer (RET)

- To print the current buffer with no additional print formatting done to the text, type:

      M-x lpr-buffer (RET)

- To print a PostScript image of the current buffer, type:

      M-x ps-print-buffer (RET)

25.2.2 Printing with Dvips

You can print a DVI file directly with the `dvips` tool—omit the '`-o`' option that is used to specify an output file, and it will send the PostScript output directly to the spool queue of the default printer.

- To print the DVI file '`list.dvi`', type:

      $ *dvips list.dvi* (RET)

The following table lists some of `dvips`'s various options for controlling print output.

OPTION	DESCRIPTION
`-A`	Print only odd-numbered pages (DVI file must have been generated by TEX).
`-B`	Print only even-numbered pages (DVI file must have been generated by TEX).
`-b` *copies*	Specify the number of copies to print—useful for printing multiple copies of flyers, posters, signs, and the like.

`-k`	Print crop marks.
`-l` *last*	Specify the last page number to print.
`-m`	Use the manual feed tray.
`-p` *first*	Specify the first page to begin printing from.
`-r`	Reverse the order of the pages.
`-t` *format*	Specify paper size and format; valid options include '`letter`', '`legal`', '`a4`', and '`landscape`'. (You can use this option twice, say to specify both '`legal`' and '`landscape`').

Using the '`-m`' option and specifying landscape as the paper format with the '`-t`' option is very useful for printing on envelopes.

- To print the file '`envelope.dvi`' on an envelope loaded in the manual feed tray of the default printer, type:

      $ *dvips -m -t landscape envelope.dvi* (RET)

NOTE: You can also print DVI files with `lpr` using the '`-d`' option.

25.2.3 Printing the Contents of an Xterm Window

To print the contents of an `xterm` window, press and hold (CTRL) and left-click anywhere inside the window, and choose the `Print Window` option. This command will send a copy of all the text in the current window to the default printer.

25.3 Preparing Files for Printing

Not all printers recognize all output formats, so it's sometimes necessary to convert files before you print them.

Normally, you can print plain text on any printer. However, most graphics or image files must be converted to PostScript or EPS ("Encapsulated PostScript"). Some applications—such as TEX—produce DVI output; in this case, you convert that to PostScript for printing.

If you have a PostScript printer, you can print PostScript files directly to it. If not, you'll need to convert the PostScript output to a format your printer uses. Filter programs like '`magicfilter`' make the conversion easier by doing this work for you, but they're not a panacea, since your system may use one of a great many filters. Hence, the need for the following recipes.

25.3.1 Preparing a PostScript File for Printing

Debian: 'gs'
WWW: `ftp://www.gnu.org/pub/gnu/ghostscript/`

If you don't have a PostScript printer, you can use Ghostscript, **gs**, to convert PostScript to an output format that your printer understands.

Use the '`-?`' option to list the printers that the version of **gs** installed on your system can write output for.

- To list the available printer formats, type:

```
$ gs -? (RET)
GNU Ghostscript 5.10 (1998-12-17)
...more output messages...
Input formats: PostScript PostScriptLevel1 PostScriptLevel2 PDF
Available devices:
    x11 x11alpha x11cmyk x11gray2 x11mono lvga256 vgalib
    t4693d8 tek4696 appledmp ccr lp2563 lbp8 lips3 m8510
    oki182 okiibm la50 la70 la75 la75plus sxlcrt deskjet
    djet500 laserjet ljetplus ljet2p ljet3 ljet4 declj250
    cdeskjet cdjcolor cdjmono cdj550 cdj500 djet500c
    hpdj uniprint epson eps9mid eps9high epsonc lq850
    ap3250 ibmpro bj10e bj200 bjc600 bjc800 ljet3d faxg3
    faxg32d faxg4 dfaxhigh dfaxlow pcxmono pcxgray pbm
    pbmraw pgm pgmraw pgnm pgnmraw pnm pnmraw ppm ppmraw
    pkm pkmraw tiffcrle tiffg3 tiffg32d tiffg4 psmono
    psgray jpeg
...more output messages...
$
```

A typical **gs** installation can write to more than 100 different print devices, including HP LaserJet 4 printers ('`ljet4`'), HP Color DeskJets ('`cdeskjet`'), and Group 4 fax ('`tiffg4`'). Newer versions of **gs** will have better support for newer printers, so make sure that you have a recent version installed if you have a new model printer.

gs takes the file to convert as an argument; give the device to write output for as an argument to the '`-sDEVICE=`' option, and give the name of the file to write to as an argument to the '`-sOutputFile=`' option.

Two additional options are commonly used: '`-dSAFER`', which prevents the accidental deleting or overwriting of files, and '`-dNOPAUSE`', which turns off the pause between pages.

When the conversion is complete, you will be at the **gs** prompt; type `quit` to exit.

- To convert the file '`tiger.ps`' to a format suitable for printing on an HP Color DeskJet 500 printer, type:

  $ *gs -sDEVICE=cdj500 -sOutputFile=tiger.dj -dSAFER -dNOPAUSE*
  tiger.ps < /dev/null (RET)

This command writes the output to a file, '`tiger.dj`', which you can spool as a print job with `lpr` to print.

25.3.2 Preparing a DVI File for Printing

Debian: '`tetex-bin`'
WWW: http://www.radicaleye.com/dvips/

To convert a file from DVI format to PostScript, use `dvips`. It takes the file to convert as an argument; give the name of the PostScript file to write to as an argument to the '`-o`' option.

- To convert the file 'abstract.dvi' to PostScript, type:

      $ *dvips -o abstract.ps abstract.dvi* (RET)

This command reads the DVI file 'abstract.dvi' and writes a PostScript version of it to the file 'abstract.ps'; the original file is not altered.

To write only certain pages of a DVI file to the PostScript output, give the page or pages as arguments to the '-pp' option.

- To output only pages 14 and 36 from file 'abstract.dvi' to a PostScript file, 'abstract.ps', type:

      $ *dvips -pp14,36 -o abstract.ps abstract.dvi* (RET)

- To output pages 2 through 100 from file 'abstract.dvi' to a PostScript file, 'abstract.ps', type:

      $ *dvips -pp2-100 -o abstract.ps abstract.dvi* (RET)

- To output page 1 and pages 5 through 20 from file 'abstract.dvi' to a PostScript file, 'abstract.ps', type:

      $ *dvips -pp1,5-20 -o abstract.ps abstract.dvi* (RET)

To specify an output paper size, give it as an argument to the '-t' option; if you have a PostScript printer, you can also send the output directly to the printer (see Recipe 25.2.2 [Printing with Dvips], page 274).

- To output the file 'abstract.dvi' as a PostScript file, 'abstract.ps', with a paper size of 'legal', type:

      $ *dvips -t legal -o abstract.ps abstract.dvi* (RET)

- To print the file 'abstract.dvi' to the default printer in landscape mode, type.

      $ *dvips -t landscape abstract.dvi* (RET)

NOTE: This conversion is not only useful for print preparation. Once the DVI file is converted to PostScript, you can then convert the PostScript to other formats, such as plain text or PDF—see Recipe 20.3 [Converting PostScript], page 239.

Use the '-P' option with `dvips` to specify the printer name to write output to—use this option to make output for non-PostScript printers. For example, to convert TeX and LaTeX files to PDF, use `dvips` and give 'pdf' as an argument to the '-P' option.

- To generate a PDF file from the DVI file 'abstract.dvi', type:

      $ *dvips -Ppdf -o abstract.pdf abstract.dvi* (RET)

This command writes a new file, 'abstract.pdf', in PDF format.

25.3.3 Preparing a PDF File for Printing

Debian: 'xpdf'
Debian: 'gs'
WWW: http://www.aimnet.com/~derekn/xpdf/
WWW: http://www.cs.wisc.edu/~ghost/

There are at least two ways to convert and print a file that's in Adobe's Portable Document Format (PDF), usually marked with a '.pdf' file name extension.

The first way is to view the file in **xpdf** (the PDF file viewer), and then left-click the printer icon. This won't actually send the file to the printer, but it writes a PostScript file in the same directory, with the same base file name as the PDF file but with a '`.ps`' extension. You can then print this file with **lpr** or convert it to another format (see Recipe 25.3.1 [Preparing a PostScript File for Printing], page 275).

The second way is to use **pdf2ps**, part of the '**gs**' package, to convert the PDF file to PostScript (then print the PostScript output as described for **xpdf** above). **pdf2ps** takes two arguments: the name of the PDF file to convert, and the name of the PostScript file to write to.

- To convert the PDF file '`pricelist.pdf`', type:

    $ *pdf2ps pricelist.pdf pricelist.ps* (RET)

This command writes a PostScript file '`pricelist.ps`' in the current directory.

25.3.4 Preparing a Man Page for Printing

To convert a **man** page to output that is suitable for printing, use the '`-t`' to output PostScript, and either pipe the output to **lpr** (if you have a PostScript printer), or save it to a file that you can then convert for your printer.

- To output the **man** page for **psbook** as PostScript and send it as a print job to the default printer, type:

    $ *man -t psbook | lpr* (RET)

- To output the **man** page for **psbook** to the file '`psbook.ps`', type:

    $ *man -t psbook > psbook.ps* (RET)

In the preceding example, you can then use **gs** to convert the file to a format your non-PostScript printer understands (see Recipe 25.3.1 [Preparing a PostScript File for Printing], page 275).

NOTE: A manual "page" can actually contain more than one physical page; the output will have as many pages as necessary to print it.

26 Cross-Platform Conversions

Sometimes, it's inevitable—through no choice of your own, you must deal with a disk from another operating system, or a file with data stored in a proprietary format from one of these systems.

The recipes in this chapter are about converting data from other platforms—reading disks from DOS, Windows, and MacOS systems, and converting DOS text and Microsoft Word files.

26.1 Using DOS and Windows Disks

Debian: 'mtools'
WWW: http://mtools.linux.lu/

The `mtools` package provides a collection of tools to facilitate the manipulation of MS-DOS files. These tools allow you to use and manipulate MS-DOS disks (usually floppies, but Jaz and Zip drives are supported, too); they can handle the extensions to the MS-DOS format which are used by the different Microsoft Windows operating systems, including Windows NT.

The following recipes describe how to use some of the tools in this package to get directory listings of MS-DOS disks, copy files to and from them, delete files on them, and even format them. They're similar in use and syntax to the equivalent MS-DOS commands.

26.1.1 Listing the Contents of a DOS Disk

Use `mdir` to get a directory listing of a DOS disk. Give as an argument the "drive letter" of the disk to read, as used by DOS; for example, to specify the primary floppy drive, use 'A:' as the drive to read, and use 'B:' to specify the secondary floppy drive.

- To get a directory listing of the DOS disk currently in the primary floppy drive, type:

      $ mdir a: (RET)

26.1.2 Copying Files to and from a DOS Disk

Use `mcopy` to copy files to and from a DOS disk.

To copy a file *to* a DOS disk, give as arguments the name of the source file to copy and the "drive letter" of the disk to copy it to.

- To copy the file 'readme.txt' to the DOS disk in the primary floppy drive, type:

      $ mcopy readme.txt a: (RET)

To copy a file *from* a DOS disk, give the "drive letter" of the disk to copy from, followed by the file name to copy, and no other arguments; `mcopy` will copy the specified file to the current directory.

- To copy the file 'resume.doc' from the DOS disk in the secondary floppy drive to the current directory, type:

      $ mcopy b:resume.doc (RET)

To copy all files from a DOS disk, just give the "drive letter" without any file names.

- To copy all of the files and directories from the DOS disk in the primary floppy drive to the current directory, type:

    $ *mcopy a:* (RET)

26.1.3 Deleting Files on a DOS Disk

Use `mdel` to delete a file on a DOS disk. Give as an argument the name of the file to delete preceded by the "drive letter" of the disk to delete from.

- To delete the file 'resume.doc' on the DOS disk in the primary floppy drive, type:

    $ *mdel a:resume.doc* (RET)

26.1.4 Formatting a DOS Disk

To format a floppy disk for DOS, writing an empty MS-DOS filesystem to the disk in the process, use `mformat`. Give as an argument the name of the "drive letter" of the disk to format. (Remember, when you format a disk, any existing information contained on the disk is lost.)

- To format the floppy disk in the primary floppy drive so that it can be used with MS-DOS, type:

    $ *mformat a:* (RET)

NOTE: If you want to use a floppy disk with your Linux system and don't need DOS compatibility, don't bother using this MS-DOS format—the native Linux format is much more efficient (see Recipe 24.3.1 [Formatting a Floppy Disk], page 267). If you know how long a DOS format takes, you'll be amazed at how much faster the Linux format is, too—it will do it so fast you'll think it didn't work!

26.2 Using Macintosh Disks

Debian: 'hfsutils'
WWW: http://www.mars.org/home/rob/proj/hfs/

Apple Macintosh computers use a file system called the "Hierarchical File System," or HFS. The `hfsutils` package contains a set of tools to read and write disks in the HFS format.

The following recipes describe the use of the individual tools in this package.

26.2.1 Specifying the Macintosh Disk to Use

To use a Macintosh disk with any of the 'hfsutils' commands, you must first use `hmount` to specify the location of the HFS filesystem. Give as an argument the name of the Linux device file where the HFS filesystem exists; this virtually "mounts" the disk for use with the other 'hfsutils' described in this section.

The device file for the first floppy drive is '/dev/fd0', and for the second drive, '/dev/fd1'. Any valid device name, such as a SCSI device or Zip disk, may be given.

- To introduce the floppy disk in the first floppy drive as an HFS volume for the 'hfsutils', type:

      $ hmount /dev/fd0 (RET)

After you run this command, the other tools in the hfsutils package will work on the Macintosh disk in the first floppy drive.

26.2.2 Listing the Contents of a Macintosh Disk

Use hls to get a directory listing of the Macintosh disk currently specified with hmount (see Recipe 26.2.1 [Specifying the Macintosh Disk to Use], page 280).

- To get a directory listing of the currently specified Macintosh disk, type:

      $ hls (RET)

Give the name of a directory as a quoted argument.

- To get a directory listing of the 'Desktop Folder' directory in the currently specified Macintosh disk, type:

      $ hls 'Desktop Folder' (RET)

26.2.3 Copying Files to and from a Macintosh Disk

Use hcopy to copy files to and from the Macintosh disk currently specified with hmount (see Recipe 26.2.1 [Specifying the Macintosh Disk to Use], page 280).

To copy a file *to* a Mac disk, give as arguments the name of the source file to copy and the quoted name of the target directory on the Mac disk.

- To copy the file 'readme.txt' to the 'Desktop Folder' directory in the current Mac disk, type:

      $ hcopy readme.txt 'Desktop Folder' (RET)

To copy a file *from* a Mac disk, give the name of the directory and file to copy as a quoted argument, and the name of the target directory to copy to.

- To copy the file 'Desktop Folder:Readme' from the current Mac disk to the current directory, type:

      $ hcopy 'Desktop Folder:Readme' . (RET)

26.2.4 Deleting Files on a Macintosh Disk

Use hdel to delete a file on the Macintosh disk currently specified with hmount (see Recipe 26.2.1 [Specifying the Macintosh Disk to Use], page 280). Give as a quoted argument the path name of the file to delete. It deletes both the resource fork and the data fork of the files you specify.

- To delete the file 'Desktop Folder:Readme' on the current Mac disk, type:

      $ hdel 'Desktop Folder:Readme' (RET)

26.2.5 Formatting a Macintosh Disk

To format a disk for the Mac, writing an empty HFS filesystem to the disk, use `hformat`. Give as an argument the name of the Linux device file where the disk is at; for example, the device file for the first floppy drive is '`/dev/fd0`', and the second drive is '`/dev/fd1`'

- To format the disk in the first floppy drive with a Macintosh HFS filesystem, type:

  ```
  $ hformat /dev/fd0 (RET)
  ```

If the disk currently has a partition on it, this command won't work; use the '`-f`' option to *force* the format, thus erasing any existing partition and data the disk contains.

Give a label for the drive as a quoted argument to the '`-l`' option. The label name can't contain a colon character ('`:`').

- To format the disk in the first floppy drive with a Mac HFS filesystem, overwriting any existing Mac filesystem, type:

  ```
  $ hformat -f /dev/fd0 (RET)
  ```

- To format the disk in the second floppy drive with a Mac HFS filesystem, giving it a volume label of '`Work Disk`', type:

  ```
  $ hformat -l 'Work Disk' /dev/fd1 (RET)
  ```

When a disk has multiple partitions, give the number of the partition to format as an additional argument. To format the entire medium, give '`0`' as the partition to use.

- To format the second partition of the SCSI disk at '`/dev/sd2`' with a Mac HFS filesystem, type:

  ```
  $ hformat /dev/sd2 2 (RET)
  ```

- To format the *entire* SCSI disk at '`/dev/sd2`' with a Mac HFS filesystem, overwriting any existing Mac filesystem and giving it a label of '`Joe's Work Disk`', type:

  ```
  $ hformat -f -l "Joe's Work Disk" /dev/sd2 0 (RET)
  ```

26.3 Converting Text Files between DOS and Linux

Debian: '`sysutils`'
WWW: http://web.singnet.com.sg/~cslheng/

In all versions of DOS (and all subsequent versions of Microsoft Windows), text files are normally written with both a linefeed character and a newline, both "invisible" control characters, to signify the end of each line. In Linux and other unices, text files have only the newline character.

In either of these operating systems, text files that originated from the other may display irregularly—in DOS and Windows, the lines of a Linux text file may appear to run together; in Linux, a DOS or Windows text file may have '`^M`' newline characters at the end of each line.

To convert a text file from DOS to Linux, removing the '`^M`' newline characters in the file, use '`fromdos`'. It converts the file you give as an argument, removing the newline characters from the ends of all its lines.

To convert a text file from Linux to the convention used by DOS and Windows, use `todos`. It adds newline characters to the ends of all lines in the file you give as an argument.

- To remove the newline characters from the text file '**autoexec.bat**', type:

    $ *fromdos autoexec.bat* (RET)

- To add newline characters to all of the text files with a '**.tex**' extension in the current directory, type:

    $ *todos *.tex* (RET)

NOTE: Both commands directly write to the files you specify. To make a backup of the original file, use the '**-b**' option; before the conversion, this writes a copy of each specified file with a '**.bak**' file name extension.

26.4 Converting Microsoft Word Files

Debian: '**word2x**'
WWW: http://word2x.alcom.co.uk/

Use **word2x** to convert Word 6 files to a format you can read. It can convert files to two different formats: LaTeX and plain text.

Convert to LaTeX when the *layout* of the original document, including its formatting and font characteristics, is important. When you just need the complete *text* of the document, convert it to plain text. **word2x** can send its output to the standard output, so the latter conversion is useful for adding to a pipeline.

Word files usually have a '**.doc**' or '**.DOC**' extension, which you don't have to specify—for example, if the Word file you want to convert is called '**resume.doc**', you can simply give '**resume**' as the source file. (But if there exists another file named '**resume**' in the same directory, this trick won't work).

If you don't specify an output file, **word2x** writes its output to a file with the same base file name and an appropriate extension for the output format. This is useful for converting a lot of Word files in the same directory—specifying a wildcard such as '***.doc**' as the input and no output name will convert them all.

You can also set the maximum line width to be used in the output file; specify the width as an argument to the '**-w**' option.

The following recipes describe how to use **word2x** to convert Word files to LaTeX and plain text format.

NOTE: While **word2x** does a pretty good job of conversion, it won't convert any pictures embedded in Word documents.

Another way to read Word files is to import them into the AbiWord or StarWriter word processors (see Recipe 15.6 [Other Word Processors and Typesetting Systems], page 196).

26.4.1 Converting Word to LaTeX

To convert a Word file to LaTeX format, use **word2x** and use '**latex**' as an argument to the '**-f**' option.

- To convert the Word file '**resume.doc**' to LaTeX, type:

    $ *word2x -f latex resume.doc* (RET)

This command writes a new file, 'resume.ltx', in the LaTeX format; you can then view, print, or convert the file to other formats—see Recipe 15.4.3 [Processing LaTeX Files], page 191. The original 'resume.doc' file is unaltered.

- To convert all of the '.DOC' Word files in the current directory to LaTeX files with maximum line widths of 40 characters, type:

      $ word2x -f latex -w 40 *.DOC (RET)

26.4.2 Converting Word to Plain Text

To convert a Word file to plain text, use word2x, and use 'text' as an argument to the '-format' option.

- To convert the Word file 'resume.doc' to a plain text file called 'resume', type:

      $ word2x -f text resume.doc resume (RET)

To send a conversion to the standard output, give a hyphen character, '-', as the output file to use. This is useful for piping the plain text conversion to other tools that work on text, such as grep, a tool for searching text (see Recipe 14.1 [Searching for a Word or Phrase], page 165).

- To search the text of the Word file 'resume.doc' for the string 'linux' regardless of case, type:

      $ word2x resume.doc - | grep -i linux (RET)

These commands convert the Word file 'resume.doc' to text, and output all lines of that text, if any, that contain the string 'linux' regardless of case. The original 'resume.doc' file is unaltered.

27 Reminders

If you're working on a system on a regular basis, it can be very useful to have the system remind you when you should be doing something else. This chapter describes software tools that provide reminders—clocks, calendars, address books, and tools for tracking appointments.

27.1 Displaying the Date and Time

WWW: http://www.clock.org/
WWW: http://www.eecis.udel.edu/~ntp/

Use date to output the current system date and time.

- To output the current system date and time, type:

```
$ date (RET)
Fri May 11 11:10:29 EDT 2001
$
```

The default format of the output is to display the day of the week; the month name; the day of the month; the 24-hour time in hours, minutes, and seconds; the time zone; and the year.

Use the '-u' option to output the current date and time in Greenwich Mean Time (also known as Coordinated Universal Time, or UTC).

- To output the current date and time in UTC, type:

```
$ date -u (RET)
Fri May 11 15:10:29 UTC 2001
$
```

Use the '-R' option to output the date in the format described in RFC822 (see Recipe 11.4 [Word Lists and Reference Files], page 145): day of week followed by day of month, month name, year, time, and time zone in numeric format. This is the date format used in email messages.

- To output the current date and time in RFC822 format, type:

```
$ date -R (RET)
Fri, 11 May 2001 11:10:29 -0400
$
```

You can also use the '-d' option to specify the precise fields to output, and the order in which to output them. One useful example is given next; for more information, see the date man page (see Recipe 2.8.4 [Reading a Page from the System Manual], page 30).

To output the number of days into the year for a particular date, use '-d' with *'DD MMM'* +%j, where 'DD' is the day of month and 'MMM' is the name of month.

- To output the numeric day of the year that 21 June falls on in the current year, type:

```
$ date -d '21 Jun' +%j (RET)
172
$
```

This command outputs the number 172, which indicates that 21 June of the current year is the 172nd day of the current calendar year.

NOTE: To ensure that the time on your system clock remains as accurate as possible, your system administrator should install the 'chrony' package; it periodically adjusts the time on the system clock according to measurements obtained from other servers on the Internet via "Network Time Protocol."

27.2 Playing an Audible Time Announcement

Debian: 'saytime'
WWW: http://www.acme.com/software/saytime/

Use the saytime command to output the current system time in an audible message in a male voice. You must have a sound card installed on your system, and it must be set up with speakers or some other output mechanism at an appropriate volume level in order for you to hear it (see Recipe 21.2 [Adjusting the Audio Controls], page 244).

- To hear the current system time, type:

    $ saytime (RET)

NOTE: If you're feeling adventurous, you can record another voice—like your own—and use that voice instead of the default voice; the sound files used are Sun '.au' files and are kept in the '/usr/share/saytime' directory.

27.3 Calendars

The following recipes describe a few of the basic tools for displaying calendars in Linux.

27.3.1 Displaying a Calendar

The cal tool outputs a calendar to the standard output. By default, it outputs a calendar of the current month.

- To output a calendar for the current month, type:

    $ cal (RET)

To output a calendar for a specific year, give just the year as an option.

- To output a calendar for the year 2001, type:

```
$ cal 2001 (RET)
                              2001

        January                February                March
  S  M Tu  W Th  F  S     S  M Tu  W Th  F  S     S  M Tu  W Th  F  S
     1  2  3  4  5  6              1  2  3                    1  2  3
  7  8  9 10 11 12 13     4  5  6  7  8  9 10     4  5  6  7  8  9 10
 14 15 16 17 18 19 20    11 12 13 14 15 16 17    11 12 13 14 15 16 17
 21 22 23 24 25 26 27    18 19 20 21 22 23 24    18 19 20 21 22 23 24
 28 29 30 31             25 26 27 28             25 26 27 28 29 30 31

         April                   May                    June
  S  M Tu  W Th  F  S     S  M Tu  W Th  F  S     S  M Tu  W Th  F  S
  1  2  3  4  5  6  7        1  2  3  4  5                       1  2
  8  9 10 11 12 13 14     6  7  8  9 10 11 12     3  4  5  6  7  8  9
 15 16 17 18 19 20 21    13 14 15 16 17 18 19    10 11 12 13 14 15 16
 22 23 24 25 26 27 28    20 21 22 23 24 25 26    17 18 19 20 21 22 23
 29 30                   27 28 29 30 31          24 25 26 27 28 29 30

         July                  August               September
  S  M Tu  W Th  F  S     S  M Tu  W Th  F  S     S  M Tu  W Th  F  S
  1  2  3  4  5  6  7              1  2  3  4                          1
  8  9 10 11 12 13 14     5  6  7  8  9 10 11     2  3  4  5  6  7  8
 15 16 17 18 19 20 21    12 13 14 15 16 17 18     9 10 11 12 13 14 15
 22 23 24 25 26 27 28    19 20 21 22 23 24 25    16 17 18 19 20 21 22
 29 30 31                26 27 28 29 30 31        23 24 25 26 27 28 29
                                                  30

        October                November               December
  S  M Tu  W Th  F  S     S  M Tu  W Th  F  S     S  M Tu  W Th  F  S
     1  2  3  4  5  6              1  2  3                          1
  7  8  9 10 11 12 13     4  5  6  7  8  9 10     2  3  4  5  6  7  8
 14 15 16 17 18 19 20    11 12 13 14 15 16 17     9 10 11 12 13 14 15
 21 22 23 24 25 26 27    18 19 20 21 22 23 24    16 17 18 19 20 21 22
 28 29 30 31             25 26 27 28 29 30        23 24 25 26 27 28 29
                                                  30 31

$
```

Use the '-y' option to output a calendar for the current year.

- To output a calendar for the current year, type:

  `$ cal -y (RET)`

- So, to print out a calendar for the current year to the default printer, type:

  `cal -y | lpr (RET)`

To output a calendar for a specific month, give both the numeric month and year as arguments.

- To output a calendar for June 1991, type:

```
$ cal 06 1991 (RET)
      June 1991
 S  M Tu  W Th  F  S
                   1
 2  3  4  5  6  7  8
 9 10 11 12 13 14 15
16 17 18 19 20 21 22
23 24 25 26 27 28 29
30
$
```

27.3.2 Displaying a Calendar in Emacs

Emacs comes with its own calendar service. The `calendar` function displays a three-month calendar in a new buffer—it gives the current, previous, and next months, and it puts point on the current date. To select the month and year to display, preface the `calendar` function with the `universal-argument` command, `C-u`.

- In Emacs, to display a three-month calendar for the current month and year, type:

  `$ M-x calendar` (RET)

- In Emacs, to display a three-month calendar for August 2010, type:

  `C-u M-x calendar` (RET)

  `Year (>0): 2001` (BKSP) (BKSP) `10` (RET)

  `Month name:` *Aug* (RET)

NOTE: When you display a calendar for a specific month and year, Emacs fills in the current year in the minibuffer; in the example above, the current year was 2001, and (BKSP) was typed twice to erase the last two digits, which were replaced with '10' to make it the year 2010.

27.4 Managing Appointments

Debian: 'bsdmainutils'

The `calendar` tool is a reminder service that you can use to manage your appointments. It reads a *calendar file*, which is a text file in the current directory containing a list of appointments and reminders; then it outputs those entries from the file that have today or tomorrow's date. (On a Friday, it outputs entries for that weekend and for the following Monday.)

For example, if today is Friday, June 16, and you run `calendar` in the same directory as your calendar file, typical output might look like this:

```
$ calendar (RET)
6/16     Finish draft of book
         Party at Jack's
Fri      Lunch with Kim and Jo, 12:30
Mon      Book manuscript due
$
```

The `calendar` tool reportedly first appeared in Version 7 of AT&T UNIX, and was rewritten early on for the BSD family of Unix. While the BSD derivate is available for Debian as part of the `bsdmainutils` package, this tool isn't yet standard on all Linux distributions.

The following are recipes for writing your calendar files, including other calendar files in your own calendar file, and for automating the delivery of your reminders.

NOTE: Emacs has its own equivalent to this tool, which it calls the "Diary." See Info file 'emacs-e20.info', node 'Diary' for more information on this feature.

27.4.1 Making an Appointment File

To begin using `calendar`, you need to make a "calendar file" where you can enter your appointments. It's just a plain text file, and can be called either 'calendar' or '.calendar'; the latter makes it a "hidden" file, as described in Recipe 5.3.4 [Listing Hidden Files], page 73.

Write each appointment or calendar entry on a line by itself; blank lines in the file are ignored. The format of a calendar entry is as follows:

[date] [tab or spaces] [text of reminder itself]

Just about every common date style is recognized. For example, the following are all valid dates for the fourth of July:

```
7/4
July 4
4 July
Jul. 4
Jul 4
```

Entries aren't constrained to a single day, either; you can have entries for a day of the week or for a certain month—'Mon' or 'Monday' for every Monday; 'Jun' or 'June' for the first day of every June. You can use an asterisk as a wildcard: '*/13' reminds you of something on the thirteenth of every month. When the date is omitted on a line, the date of the preceding appointment is assumed.

For example, suppose you have a file called 'calendar' in your home directory that looks like this:

```
6/16     Finish draft of book
         Party at Jack's
6/20     Gallery reading
Fri      Lunch with Kim and Jo, 12:30
Mon      Book manuscript due
```

If the current date is 16 June, a Friday, and you run `calendar` in your home directory, you'll get the same output as in the example in the previous section, Recipe 27.4 [Managing Appointments], page 288.

NOTE: In the example above, the entry for the party doesn't have a date on it—it used the date of the preceding entry, '6/16'.

27.4.2 Including Holidays in Your Reminders

The `calendar` package comes with a collection of prepared calendar files for many kinds of holidays and other occasions, which you can reference in your own calendar file to include their entries in your own reminders.

The prepared files are stored in '`/usr/share/calendar`'. The following table gives the name of each calendar file and describes its contents.

CALENDAR FILE	DESCRIPTION
`calendar.birthday`	Births and deaths of famous people.
`calendar.christian`	Christian holidays.
`calendar.computer`	Significant dates in the history of computing.
`calendar.history`	Dates of U.S. historical events.
`calendar.holiday`	Standard and obscure holidays.
`calendar.judaic`	Jewish holidays.
`calendar.music`	Dates related to music, mostly 1960s rock and roll.
`calendar.usholiday`	U.S. holidays.
`calendar.hindu`	Hindu holidays.

To have `calendar` output dates from one of these files along with your usual appointments, put the following in your calendar file, where *file* is the name of the particular calendar file you want to include:

    #include <*file*>

For example, to output both US holidays and famous births and deaths when you run `calendar`, put these lines somewhere in your calendar file:

    #include <calendar.usholiday>
    #include <calendar.birthday>

NOTE: You can, of course, share your own calendar files with other users; this is useful for making special calendars for a group or organization. If the calendar file is in the current directory or '`/usr/share/calendar`', you can just give the file name; otherwise, give its full path name in the `include` statement.

27.4.3 Automatic Appointment Delivery

You can automate your appointment service so that your appointments and reminders are delivered each time you log in or start a new shell, or you can have the day's reminders emailed to you each morning.

Add `calendar` to your '`.bashrc`' file to output the day's appointments and reminders every time you log in or start a new shell (see Recipe 3.6.4 [Customizing Future Shells], page 47).

If you keep your calendar file in a directory other than your home directory, make sure that `calendar` (the tool) is called from that directory. For example, if your calendar file is in your '~/doc/etc' directory, you'd put the following line in your '.bashrc' file:

    cd ~/doc/etc; calendar; cd

To have the system send you the day's appointments in email, use `crontab` to schedule a daily *cron job* process which runs `calendar` and, if there is any output, mails it to you with `mail`.

To do this, add the following line to your 'crontab' file (if you don't have one, just put this line in a text file called 'crontab' somewhere in your home directory):

    45 05 * * 1-5 calendar | mail -s 'Your Appointments' joe@example.org

The '45 05 * * 1-5' specifies that these commands be run at 5:45 a.m. on every weekday. The rest of the line is the series of actual commands that are run: the `calendar` tool is run on your personal calendar file, and if there is any output, it's mailed to joe@example.org (replace that with your actual email address, or with your username on your local system if you check mail there).

Add this new `crontab` entry to the `cron` schedule by running the `crontab` tool with the name of your 'crontab' file as an argument.

- To add the new entry in the file 'crontab' to the `cron` schedule, type:

      $ crontab crontab (RET)

NOTE: The name of the command, `crontab`, is the same as the file, 'crontab'.

27.5 Contact Managers

Loosely put, a *contact manager* is a piece of software that helps you keep track of information about people you may need to contact in the future. In the past, people often called the physical embodiment of these things a "rolodex," which incidentally was a brand name for the Cadillac of such contact managers, the circular Rolodex file that sat atop the desk of every successful 20th century businessman. I hear that many people use them even today; the following recipes show how it can be done in Linux with less desk space and faster search times.

27.5.1 Keeping a Free-Form Address List

The simplest way to keep names and addresses in Linux is to keep them in a text file as a free-form address list; to find an entry, use the search capabilities of tools like `grep`, `less`, and Emacs.

This method is useful for when you need to keep track of name and address information of many parties, and don't always keep the same kind of information for each—maybe sometimes a name and phone number, sometimes just a mailing address, sometimes a name and email address. With a free-form address list, each entry contains whatever information you have in the format you want.

Separate the entries with a delimiter line of your preference. I happen to use '###', but you can use whatever characters you're comfortable with—just make it a combination that won't appear in the text for any of the entries themselves.

For example, suppose you have a text file, 'rolo', containing three entries:

```
John Dos Passos
1919 America Ave.
New York City

###

Scott F. - 602 555 1803
(don't call after 12)

###

T. Wolfe's new email has changed.
The new one is: tw@example.com
```

Notice that each entry contains varied information, and is in no particular format. That's the benefit of a free-form list—you don't have to type in the entries in any particular order, and you're not bound by a given set of "fields"; you can even cut and paste text into it from email, the Web, or other windows (see Recipe 10.4 [Selecting Text], page 128).

There are several ways to find text in such a file. Suppose, for example, you want to contact your friend Scott, and you need his telephone number.

- To output the line in the file containing the text 'scott', regardless of case, type:

```
$ grep -i scott rolo (RET)
Scott F. - 602 555 1803
$
```

This works nicely when the information you need is on the same line as the information you search for—here, the name Scott is on the same line as the telephone number; however, the output did not show the warning that appears on the next line in the file. And what about when the term you search for and the information you need are on adjacent lines?

Use the '-C' option with grep to output several lines of context before and after matched lines.

- To output the several lines around the line matching the text 'olfe', type:

```
$ grep -C olfe rolo (RET)

T. Wolfe's new email has changed.
The new one is: tw@example.com

$
```

Another way to search such a file is to open it as a buffer in Emacs and use any of the Emacs searches. The Emacs incremental-search function, *C-s*, is very useful for such files—even for very large ones. If you do such a search on a large file, and the first result doesn't turn up the right record, just keep typing *C-s* until the right one appears. If you type the letters to search for in all lowercase, Emacs matches those letters regardless of case.

- To search through the current buffer in Emacs for the first entry containing the text 'New York', regardless of case, type:

    C-s new york

- To search for the next entry containing the text 'New York', regardless of case, type:

    C-s

You can repeat the second example as many times as you wish to show all entries in the entire buffer with the text 'New York' in them. Once you reach the end of the buffer, type C-s again to loop around to the beginning of the buffer and continue the search from there. (The minibuffer will tell you when you've reached the end of the buffer, and will remind you to type this if you want to loop the search.)

NOTE: It's also useful to peruse and search through these kind of files with less—see Recipe 14.7 [Searching Text in Less], page 175.

27.5.2 Keeping a Contact Manager Database

Debian: 'bbdb'
WWW: http://pweb.netcom.com/~simmonmt/bbdb/index.html

The Insidious Big Brother Database is a contact manager tool for use with Emacs. You can use it with Emacs email and news readers, it stores contact information in records, and allows you to search for records that match a regular expression, as well as records whose particular *fields* match a regular expression (see Recipe 14.2 [Regular Expressions—Matching Text Patterns], page 166).

There are several ways to add a record to the database. Use the bbdb-create function to manually add a record (when you run this command, bbdb prompts you to enter the relevant information for each field). When in a mail reader inside Emacs, type a colon (':') to display the record for the author of the current message; if there is none, bbdb asks whether or not one should be created.

- To create a new bbdb record from scratch, type:

    M-x bbdb-create (RET)

- To add a new bbdb record for the author of the current email message, type:

    :

Use the bbdb function to search for records—it takes as an argument the pattern or regexp to search for.

- To output records containing the text 'scott' anywhere in the record, type:

    M-x bbdb (RET) scott (RET)

There are additional functions that let you narrow your search to a particular field: bbdb-name, bbdb-company , bbdb-net, and bbdb-notes, which respectively search the name, company, email address, and notes fields.

- To output records matching the regexp '*\.edu' in the email address, type:

    M-x bbdb-net (RET) *\.edu (RET)

27.6 Reminding Yourself of Things

Sometimes, it's useful to make a reminder for yourself that you'll see either later in your current login session, or the next time you log in. These recipes describe the best ways to do this.

NOTE: When you want to give yourself a reminder for a future appointment, use `calendar` (see Recipe 27.4 [Managing Appointments], page 288).

27.6.1 Sending Yourself Email Reminders

Sending yourself a short email message is often effective for reminding yourself to do something during your next workday or next time you read mail; keeping a message in your INBOX works as a constant reminder to get something done—provided you don't abuse it and fill your INBOX with lots of these "urgent" mails!

To quickly send an email reminder, give your email address (or just your username on your local system, if you check mail there) as an argument to `mail` tool. You'll be prompted to give a subject for the message, and if that isn't enough space for the reminder, you can write as many lines as you need below it as the message body text; type *C-d* on a line by itself to send the mail.

For example, if your username on your local system is `joe`, to send yourself an email reminder, you'd type:

```
$ mail joe (RET)
Subject: Bring files to meeting (RET)
C-d
Cc: (RET)
Null message body; hope that's ok
$
```

NOTE: For more about using the `mail` tool, see Recipe 30.1 [Sending Mail], page 315.

27.6.2 Reminding Yourself When You Have to Leave

Debian: 'leave'
WWW: `http://www.debian.org/Packages/stable/utils/leave.html`

Use the `leave` tool to remind yourself when you have to leave. Give as an argument the time when you have to go, using the format of *hhmm*, where *hh* is hours in 24-hour format and *mm* is minutes.

- To remind yourself to leave at 8:05 p.m., type:

    `$ leave 2005 (RET)`

When you run `leave` with no arguments, it prompts you to enter a time; if you just type (RET) then `leave` exits without setting the reminder. This method is good for adding `leave` to scripts or to your '.bashrc', so that you may interactively give a time to leave, if desired, when the script runs (see Recipe 3.6.4 [Customizing Future Shells], page 47).

NOTE: `leave` will output a reminder on the terminal screen five minutes before the given time, one minute before the time, at the time itself, and then every minute subsequently until the user logs off.

27.6.3 Running a Command on a Delay

The `sleep` tool does nothing but wait (or "sleep") for the number of seconds specified as an argument. This is useful for ringing the system bell, playing a sound file, or running some other command at your terminal after a short delay.

To do this, give the number of seconds to "sleep" for as an argument to `sleep`, followed by a semicolon character (`;`)[1] and the command(s) to run. This runs the given command(s) only after `sleep` waits for the given number of seconds.

Since the shell where you type this command will be unusable until the commands you give are executed (or until you interrupt the whole thing), type this command in an **xterm** or virtual console window (see Recipe 2.3 [Console Basics], page 20) other than the one you are working in.

- To ring the bell in five seconds, type:

      $ sleep 5; echo -e '\a' (RET)

- To announce the time in thirty seconds, type:

      $ sleep 30; saytime (RET)

You can also give the time in minutes, hours, or days. To do this, follow the argument with a unit, as listed in the following table.

UNIT	DESCRIPTION
s	Seconds.
m	Minutes.
h	Hours.
d	Days.

- To announce the time in exactly five minutes, type:

      $ sleep 5m; saytime & (RET)

---

[1] The shell command separator; see Recipe 3.1.4 [Running a List of Commands], page 39.

28 Mathematics

Tools and techniques for dealing with numbers are the subject of this chapter: listing them in sequence or randomly, calculating arithmetic, and converting between units. Larger applications, such as spreadsheets and plotting tools, are also mentioned.

28.1 Calculating Arithmetic

As you might expect, there are many tools for making arithmetic calculations in Linux. The following recipes describe how to use two of them for two common scenarios; a list of other calculator tools, including a visual calculator, appears at the end of this chapter (see Recipe 28.6 [Other Math Tools], page 302).

28.1.1 Making a Quick Arithmetic Calculation

WWW: `http://dsl.org/comp/tinyutils/`

To do a quick calculation that requires only addition, subtraction, multiplication, or division, use `calc`. It takes as an argument a simple mathematical expression, and it outputs the answer.

Use '`*`' for a multiplication sign and '`/`' for division; to output the remainder, use '`%`'. You can use parenthesis to group expressions—but when you do, be sure to quote them (see Recipe 3.1.1 [Passing Special Characters to Commands], page 36).

- To output the result of 50 times 10, type:

```
$ calc 50*10 (RET)
500
$
```

- To output the result of 100 times the sum of 4 plus 420, type:

```
$ calc '100*(4+420)' (RET)
42400
$
```

- To output the remainder of 10 divided by 3, type:

```
$ calc 10%3 (RET)
1
$
```

NOTE: This tool is useful for quickly computing a simple arithmetic equation, but it has several drawbacks: it only outputs whole integers, its operators are limited, and complex expressions must be quoted. For doing anything more than the simplest operations, see the next recipe, which describes `bc`.

28.1.2 Making Many Arithmetic Calculations

Debian: 'bc'
WWW: `ftp://src.doc.ic.ac.uk:/pub/gnu/bc-1.05a.tar.gz`

When you have a lot of calculations to make, or when you must compute numbers with decimals, use bc, a calculation language that supports arbitrary precision numbers. Type *bc* to perform arithmetic operations interactively, just like you would with a calculator.

Type each statement to evaluate on a line by itself, typing (RET) at the end the statement; the evaluation of what you type is output on the following line. Each line you type will be evaluated by bc as an arithmetic expression. To exit, type *quit* on a line by itself.

- To multiply 42 and 17, type:

```
$ bc (RET)
bc 1.05
Copyright 1991, 1992, 1993, 1994, 1997, 1998 Free Software
Foundation, Inc.
This is free software with ABSOLUTELY NO WARRANTY.
For details type 'warranty'.
42 * 17 (RET)
714
quit (RET)
$
```

In this example, bc output its version number and warranty information when it started; then, the statement *42 * 17* was typed by the user, bc output the result ('**714**'), and then the user typed *quit* to exit bc.

By default, digits to the right of the decimal point are truncated from the output—so dividing 10 by 3 would output '3' as a result, and outputting the remainder from this operation by typing *10%3* would output a '1'. However, bc is an arbitrary precision calculator, and you can give the number of digits to use after the decimal point by specifying the value of the scale variable; its default value is 0.

- To use bc to compute the result of 10 divided by 3, using 20 digits after the decimal point, type:

```
$ bc (RET)
bc 1.05
Copyright 1991, 1992, 1993, 1994, 1997, 1998 Free Software
Foundation, Inc.
This is free software with ABSOLUTELY NO WARRANTY.
For details type 'warranty'.
scale=20 (RET)
10 / 3 (RET)
3.33333333333333333333
quit (RET)
$
```

The following table describes the symbols you can use to specify mathematical operations.

SYMBOL	OPERATION
expression + *expression*	Add: output the sum of the two expressions.
expression - *expression*	Subtract: output the difference of the two expressions.
expression * *expression*	Multiply: output the product of the two expressions.
expression / *expression*	Divide: output the quotient of the two expressions.
expression % *expression*	Remainder: output the remainder resulting by dividing the two expressions.
expression ^ *expression*	Power: raise the first expression to the power of the second expression.
(*expressions*)	Group an expression or expressions together, altering the standard precedence of performing operations.
sqrt(*expression*)	Output the square root of *expression*.

28.2 Outputting a Random Number

WWW: `http://dsl.org/comp/tinyutils/`

To output a random number, use **random**. Give as an argument an integer denoting the range of numbers to be output; **random** then outputs a random number from 0 to the number you give, minus one.

- To output a random number from 0 to 9, type:

      $ random 10 (RET)

28.3 Listing a Sequence of Numbers

Use **seq** to print a sequence of numbers. This is very useful for getting a listing of numbers to use as arguments, or otherwise passing sequences of numbers to other commands.

To output the sequence from one to a number, give that number as an argument.

- To output the sequence of numbers from one to seven, type:

  `$ seq 7` (RET)

To output the sequence from one number to another, give those numbers as arguments.

- To output the sequence of numbers from two to six, type:

  `$ seq 2 6` (RET)

To specify an increment other than one, give it as the *second* argument, between the starting and ending number.

- To output the sequence of numbers from -1 to 14, incrementing by 3, type:

  `$ seq -1 3 14` (RET)

Use the '`-w`' option to pad numbers with leading zeros so that they're all output with the same width.

Specify a separator string to be output between numbers as an argument to the '`-s`' option; the default is a newline character, which outputs each number in the sequence on its own line.

- To output the sequence of numbers from 9 to 999, incrementing by 23, with numbers padded with zeros so that they're all of equal width, type:

  `$ seq -w 9 23 999` (RET)

- To output the sequence of numbers from 1 to 23, with a space character between each, type:

  `$ seq -s ' ' 1 23` (RET)

To pass a sequence of numbers as arguments to a command, pipe the output of `seq` using a space character as a separator.

- To concatenate all the files in the current directory, whose names are numbers from 25 through 75, into a new file called '`selected-mail`', type:

  `$ cat 'seq -s " " 25 75' > selected-mail` (RET)

28.4 Finding Prime Factors

The `factor` tool calculates and outputs the prime factors of numbers passed as arguments.

- To output the prime factors of 2000, type:

```
$ factor 2000 (RET)
2000: 2 2 2 2 5 5 5
$
```

NOTE: If no number is given, `factor` reads numbers from standard input; numbers should be separated by space, tab, or newline characters.

28.5 Converting Numbers

The following recipes are for converting numbers in various ways.

28.5.1 Converting an Amount between Units of Measurement

Debian: 'units'
WWW: http://www.gnu.org/software/units/units.html

Use the units tool to convert units of measurement between scales. Give two quoted arguments: the number and name of the units you have, and the name of the units to convert to. It outputs two values: the number of the second units you have, and how many of the second kind of unit can make up the quantity of the first that you've specified.

- To output the number of ounces in 50 grams, type:

```
$ units '50 grams' 'ounces' (RET)
        * 1.7636981
        / 0.56699046
$
```

In this example, the output indicates that there are about 1.7636981 ounces in 50 grams, and that conversely, one ounce is about 0.56699046 times 50 grams.

The units tool understands a great many different kinds of units—from Celsius and Fahrenheit to pounds, hectares, the speed of light, and a "baker's dozen." All understood units are kept in a text file database; use the '-V' option to output the location of this database on your system, which you can then peruse or search through to see the units your version supports.

- To determine the location of the units database, type:

```
$ units -V (RET)
units version 1.55 with readline, units database in
/usr/share/misc/units.dat
$
```

In this example, the units database is located in the file '/usr/share/misc/units.dat', which is the file to peruse to list all of the units data.

28.5.2 Converting an Arabic Numeral to English

Debian: 'bsdgames'

Use number to convert Arabic numerals to English text. Give a numeral as an argument; with no argument, number reads a numeral from the standard input.

- To output the English text equivalent of 100,000, type:
    ```
    $ number 100000 (RET)
    ```

28.6 Other Math Tools

The following table lists some of the other mathematics tools available for Linux. It is by no means a complete list.

TOOL	DESCRIPTION
calc	calc is a scientific calculator tool for Emacs. Debian: 'calc'
dc	Like bc, the dc tool is an arbitrary-precision calculator language, but it is a *reverse-polish* calculator, where numbers are pushed on a stack. When you give an arithmetic operation symbol, dc pops numbers off the stack for their operands, and then it pushes the evaluation on the stack. Debian: 'dc'
dome	Richard J. Bono's dome is a geodesic math tool for calculating the properties of a geodesic dome symmetry triangle—it can calculate chord factors, vertex coordinates, and topological abundance of various dome types, including "Buckyball" formations and elliptical geodesics. Debian: 'dome' WWW: http://www.cris.com/~rjbono/html/domes.html
gnucash	GnuCash is an intuitive personal finance application. Use it for managing finances, including bank accounts, stocks, income, and expenses; it's "based on professional accounting principles" to ensure accuracy in computation and reporting. Debian: 'gnucash' WWW: http://www.gnucash.org/
gnumeric	Gnumeric is the GNOME spreadsheet application. It is powerful, and somewhat reminiscent of Excel. Debian: 'gnumeric' WWW: http://www.gnu.org/software/gnumeric/gnumeric.html
gnuplot	The gnuplot tool can be used for data visualization, making 2-D and 3-D graphs, and plotting functions. Debian: 'gnuplot' WWW: ftp://ftp.gnu.org/pub/gnu/gnuplot/
oleo	GNU Oleo is a spreadsheet application. It can run in both X and in the console, has Emacs-like key bindings, and can generate PostScript output. Debian: 'oleo' WWW: http://www.gnu.org/software/oleo/oleo.html
sc	sc is a small spreadsheet tool that runs in the console; it provides formulas and other basic features you would expect from a minimal spreadsheet.

xcalc   xcalc is a visual scientific calculator for the X Window
                         System—it draws a calculator on the screen, and you can use
                         the mouse or keyboard to use it. It is capable of emulating
                         the TI-30 and HP-10C calculators.

xspread   xspread is the X client front-end to sc.
                         Debian: 'xspread'

PART SEVEN: Networking

29 Communications

You will almost certainly want to go "online," or otherwise communicate with other systems. Most systems today are sold with the necessary hardware that you need in order to be able to connect to other systems, such as a modem or a network card. You connect this hardware to the outside world via a telephone line or network connection.

This chapter includes recipes for connecting your Linux system to the Internet with an ISP, using fax services, and making serial connections with a modem.

For more information on this subject, see *The Linux Network Administrator's Guide* (`http://metalab.unc.edu/mdw/LDP/nag/nag.html`).

29.1 Connecting to the Internet

Debian: 'ppp'
WWW: `ftp://cs.anu.edu.au/pub/software/ppp/`

There are several ways to connect a Linux box to the Internet. Digital Subscriber Line (DSL) service, cable modems, and dial-up connections with ISDN or analog modems are currently the most popular methods. Each of these services have their own hardware and software requirements.

For up-to-date, detailed instructions for using these services on Linux-based systems, the relevant HOWTOs published by the Linux Documentation Project (`http://www.linuxdoc.org/`) remain the definitive guides (see Recipe 2.8.6 [Reading System Documentation and Help Files], page 32):

- *ISP Hookup HOWTO*, by Egil Kvaleberg
  `http://www.linuxdoc.org/HOWTO/ISP-Hookup/`

- *DSL HOWTO for Linux*, by David Fannin
  `http://www.linuxdoc.org/HOWTO/DSL-HOWTO/`

- *Cable Modem Providers HOWTO*, by Vladimir Vuksan
  `http://www.linuxdoc.org/HOWTO/Cable-Modem/`

The following recipes show how to set up and use a PPP ("Point-to-Point Protocol") dial-up connection, long the *de facto* means of connecting a computer to the Internet over a dial-up line.

29.1.1 Setting Up PPP

To configure PPP for a regular dial-up connection, where your system is assigned a dynamic IP address (the norm for home Internet access), you need to be **root** (the superuser) to edit the PPP configuration files, and you'll need the standard connection information from your ISP: the dial-up number to use, the IP addresses for their nameservers, and your username and password for accessing their system.

Use this information to customize the file '`/etc/chatscripts/provider`':

```
ABORT         BUSY
ABORT         "NO CARRIER"
ABORT         VOICE
ABORT         "NO DIALTONE"
""            "\p\p+++\p\p"
""            "at"
""            "at"
OK            "ath0"
""            atdt5551010,,
ost           ppp
ogin          smith
word          \qsecret\q
```

In this example, after eight lines of modem initialization strings, the modem is instructed to dial the ISP dial-up number, '5551010'. Some systems need one or two commas after the number to signify pauses for the modem; only do this if you can't get a good connection with just the telephone number in this space.

Next is the "host" line: this is an optional line used by some ISPs whose connection line contains a choice of services from which you must make a selection before entering your username and password (some ISPs offer SLIP and shell access along with the standard PPP, for example); customize this and the following lines as instructed by your ISP.

Finally, the username 'smith' is given, and then the password of 'secret'. The password appears between two '\q' strings, which—for security purposes—instruct ppp to display the question mark ('?') characters instead of the actual password in system log files or other places where an intruder might see it.

Next, edit the file '/etc/ppp/peers/provider' so that it contains these lines:

```
connect "/usr/sbin/chat -v -f /etc/chatscripts/provider"
defaultroute /dev/modem 115200 persist
```

The last line in this file should include the device name of the modem you are using and the maximum connect speed to try; the preceding example uses '/dev/modem' as the device name of the modem, and 115,200 bps as the maximum connect speed, which is a good value for a typical 56K modem (a rule of thumb is to use the highest connect speed your modem supports; you can always go lower when a connection is made, but you can never raise the speed above what is given here).

Finally, edit the file '/etc/resolv.conf' so that it contains the following, using the two nameserver IP addresses given to you by your ISP:

```
search .
nameserver        nameserver address 1
nameserver        nameserver address 2
```

For the two *nameserver address* values, use the IP address of the nameserver machines, as given to you by your ISP. The second is optional—most ISPs have more than one designated nameserver as a backup in the event that the first system becomes unavailable.

Make sure that your user account has membership to the dialout group; otherwise, you'll have to have the superuser account start and stop PPP, which is not recommended (see Recipe A.3.2 [Letting Users Access Hardware Peripherals], page 363).

Once you've done these things, you should be able to start and stop PPP connections to the Internet. Complete documentation for setting up PPP is in the '/usr/share/doc/ppp' directory.

29.1.2 Controlling a PPP Connection

After PPP has been installed and configured, use the **pon** tool to start a PPP connection to the Internet. It calls the number of your ISP with your modem, sends the appropriate login information, and starts the PPP connection.

- To start a PPP connection, type:

    $ *pon* (RET)

Once you have a PPP connection, you can connect to other systems on the Internet via the WWW or other network services, as described in the following chapters.

To make PPP automatically start when the system first boots, rename the file '/etc/ppp/no_ppp_on_boot' to '/etc/ppp/ppp_on_boot'. (you must be **root**, the superuser, to do this.)

To output the last few lines of the PPP log file, type **plog**. This is useful for checking the progress of your PPP connection when it first dials.

Use the **poff** tool to stop a PPP session. It disconnects your computer from your ISP and hangs up the modem.

- To stop a PPP session, type:

    $ *poff* (RET)

29.2 Faxing

Debian: 'efax'
WWW: http://casas.ee.ubc.ca/efax/

If you have a Class 1 or 2 fax modem, you can send and receive fax ("facsimile") messages with your Linux system. The following subsections show how to do this with the **efax** package, which is designed for single user systems or relatively simple fax configurations (more complicated tools for faxing exist, but they are beyond the scope of this book).

To set up **efax** for faxing, edit the file '/etc/efax.rc' (you must be **root** to do this). The important things to specify in this file are the value for 'DEV', which is the device name in '/dev' of the fax or modem device (this should almost always be 'modem'), and the values for 'FROM' and 'NAME'—the fax number and organization name to appear on outgoing faxes.

NOTE: Unless you have membership to the **dialout** group, you must ask your system administrator for access to the modem hardware before you can use it (see Recipe A.3.2 [Letting Users Access Hardware Peripherals], page 363).

More information on faxing is contained in the *Fax Server mini-HOWTO* (see Recipe 2.8.6 [Reading System Documentation and Help Files], page 32).

29.2.1 Sending a Fax

Use `efax` to send a fax. It dials the telephone number you give and faxes the contents of the file or files you specify. You can send plain text files or files in TIFF Group 3 format as they are. You can also send files in other formats, but you must convert them to 'tiffg3' first—see Recipe 29.2.4 [Converting to and from Fax Format], page 311.

Use the '-d' option to specify the full path name of the fax device (usually '/dev/modem' if you are using the modem connected to your system) and the '-t' option followed by a telephone number to specify the number you are to send the fax to. To specify DTMF tone dialing, precede the phone number with a 'T'; specify pauses in the dialing sequence with a comma (',') character—this is useful for dialing out from a PBX or office phone system.

- To fax a copy of the file 'resume.txt' to the number '555-9099', using DTMF tone dialing, type:

  $ *efax -d /dev/modem -t T555-9099 resume.txt* (RET)

To send more than one file, specify them as arguments in the order they are to be sent. You can also specify them with a wildcard character, but be careful—they are sent in the order in which the shell expands the file names, which is alphabetical order. If you have a lot of files that should be sent in a particular order, rename them so their file names begin with the number of the page they correspond to. But be sure to number them with the *same number of digits* for each file—for example, if you have eleven files to fax, don't name them '1.fax', '2.fax', and so on, to '10.fax' and '11.fax', because the shell will expand them in the order of '1.fax', '10.fax', '11.fax', '2.fax', '3.fax', and so on up to '9.fax'. In this case, you would number them as '01.fax', '02.fax', and so on, so that files one through nine contain the same number of digits in their name as do '10.fax' and '11.fax'.

- To fax all of the files with the '.fax' extension in the current directory to the number '555-9099', using DTMF tone dialing, type:

  $ *efax -d /dev/modem -t T555-9099 *.fax* (RET)

Another way to do this is to make a text file containing the list of files to fax, one file name per line, in the order you want them sent. If the files you want to send are not in the current directory, be sure to write the file names with path names relative to the current directory—so for example, if you want to send the file 'header.fax', which is in your home directory, and the current directory is '~/documents/faxes', the file should be specified as '~/header.fax'.

- To fax all of the files listed in the file 'fax.list' to the number '555-9099', dialing '9' first to obtain an outside line, and using DTMF tone dialing, type:

  $ *efax -d /dev/modem -t T9,555-9099 $(cat fax.list)* (RET)

NOTE: `efax` doesn't delete the files it faxes.

29.2.2 Receiving a Fax

To receive a fax, use `efax` with the '-w' option. You may also have to use '-iS0=1' to send an 'S0=1' command to the modem to set it to auto answer, and use '-kZ' to send an 'ATZ' reset request to the modem after `efax` exits.

As with sending a fax, specify the full path name of the device file to use with the '-d' option.

By default, **efax** outputs a "session log" to the standard error, containing information on the status of the fax messages received; use redirection to redirect it to a file (see Recipe 3.2.3 [Redirecting Error Messages to a File], page 40).

- To set up **efax** to receive an incoming fax, saving the session log to a file, '`faxlog`', type:

      $ *efax -d /dev/modem -kZ -w -iS0=1 2>&1 >> faxlog* (RET)

This command starts **efax** and sets up the modem to wait for an incoming fax. After a fax is received, **efax** exits. You can stop **efax** before it receives a fax by typing C-c or by killing the **efax** job (see Recipe 3.3.5 [Stopping a Job], page 43).

When a fax is received, it is written to a file in the current directory whose base name consists of the current numeric date and a session number generated by **efax**; each page is written to a separate file whose three-digit file extension is the page number. The received fax files are in TIFF Group 3 fax format; use **display** to view them (see Recipe 17.2 [Viewing an Image in X], page 208), or convert them to PostScript or another format for printing (see Recipe 29.2.4 [Converting to and from Fax Format], page 311).

29.2.3 Receiving Faxes Automatically

WWW: `http://dsl.org/comp/tinyutils/`

The command described in the previous recipe can only receive one fax; once the fax is received, **efax** exits. To set up your system so that you automatically receive all incoming fax messages continually, until you interrupt it, use '`faxon`', part of the **tinyutils** package. It starts **efax** for receiving an incoming fax, as explained previously, but after a fax is received, it starts **efax** again and continues until you interrupt it.

- To automatically receive any incoming fax messages, type:

```
$ faxon (RET)
efax: Wed Feb 24 08:38:52 1999 efax v 0.8a (Debian release 08a-6)
Copyright 1996 Ed Casas
efax: 38:52 opened /dev/modem
efax: 38:53 waiting for activity
```

Each time a fax is received and then saved, **efax** restarts, waiting for another fax. A session log is written to the file '`faxlog`' in your home directory.

Should an incoming facsimile message arrive, **efax** will receive it and write the message in files in the current directory, with a file name convention as described previously; then **efax** restarts, ready to receive another fax. Type C-c to stop the script and exit **efax**.

29.2.4 Converting to and from Fax Format

In order to view or print a received fax, or to fax a file that you have, you must first convert the file to or from the TIFF Group 3 ('`tiffg3`') fax format, which is the standard format for sending fax files. (You can, however, view '`tiffg3`' files with the GIMP, or with **display**—see Recipe 17.2 [Viewing an Image in X], page 208).

Use `efix` to convert (or "fix") files for faxing; it will convert a file you want to fax *to* the 'tiffg3' format. You can also use it to convert received fax files to another format you can view or print. `efax` outputs to standard output, but you can redirect its output to a file to save it.

To convert a file for faxing, type `efix` followed by the name of the file to convert, and redirect standard output to the file you want to contain your fax image. `efix` can read plain text, PBM, and TIFF files.

- To convert the file 'chart.pbm' for faxing, type:

      $ efix -i pbm chart.pbm > chart.fax (RET)

This command converts a copy of the file 'chart.pbm' to the 'tiffg3' fax format, writing it to a file called 'chart.fax'. The original PBM file is not altered.

To convert a PostScript file to fax format, use `gs` and specify `tiffg3` as the output device to write to—see Recipe 25.3.1 [Preparing a PostScript File for Printing], page 275.

- To convert the PostScript file 'resume.ps' to fax format, type:

      $ gs -q -sDEVICE=tiffg3 -dSAFER -dNOPAUSE
      -sOutputFile=resume.fax resume.ps < /dev/null (RET)

This command (typed all on one line) writes a copy of the file 'resume.ps' to the file 'resume.fax' in 'tiffg3' format, which you can then send as a fax. The original PostScript file is not altered.

To convert a received fax file to a PostScript file that you can then preview (see Recipe 17.1.2 [Previewing a PostScript File], page 207) or print (see Recipe 25.1.1 [Sending a Print Job to the Printer], page 272), use the '-o ps' option.

- To convert '19990325.001', a received fax file, to a PostScript file, type:

      $ efix -o ps 19990325.001 > received.ps (RET)

This command converts the fax file into a PostScript file called 'received.ps'.

29.3 Calling Out on a Modem

Use `minicom` to dial out with the modem and connect with another system—such as when you want to connect to a BBS ("Bulletin Board System"). It's a serial communications tool for X or the console; it resembles some of the communications tools of the DOS world, such as Telix and Procomm.

When you start `minicom`, the connection screen looks like this:

```
Welcome to minicom 1.82

OPTIONS: History Buffer, F-key Macros, Search History Buffer, I18n
Compiled on Nov  6 1998, 17:55:03.

Press CTRL-A Z for help on special keys

ATZ
OK
█
```

```
CTRL-A Z for help | 57600 8N1 | NOR | Minicom 1.82   | VT102 |     Offline
```

The bottom line contains a status bar showing a message describing how to get help, the current modem settings (in this case, 57,600 bps, 8 data bits, no parity, one stop bit), whether or not cursor keys work (the mysterious 'NOR' message), the version of the program ('1.82'), the kind of terminal emulation currently set ('VT102'), and whether or not an online connection is currently established.

To get a help menu, type *C-a z*; from this menu, you can press Ⓟ to set the communications parameters, Ⓣ to set the terminal settings, Ⓞ to configure `minicom`, or Ⓓ to enter the dialing directory.

To dial a number from the main screen, type *ATDT* followed by the number to dial.

- To dial the number '368-2208', type:

    ATDT3682208 (RET)

When you type (RET), `minicom` will begin dialing the number; type any key to interrupt the dialing and hang up the line. Once connected, type *C-a h* to hang up the line and type *C-a x* to hang up the line and exit the program.

NOTE: `minicom` isn't really a way to connect your system to the Internet; to do that, you normally start a PPP connection, as described earlier in this chapter.[1]

---

[1] Technically, you can use `minicom` to dial a computer that *is* connected to the Internet, like a local Free-Net system, but your access to the net will be restricted to inside this `minicom` window; with a traditional Internet connection, such as PPP, your whole system has direct access to the net, including your Web browsers, email software, and other networking tools.

30 Email

The primary means of sending plain-text messages (or binaries in attachment files) between users across computer networks and systems on the Internet is called electronic mail, or *email* (and more often than not these days, just "mail").

The number of email applications (called *mail user agents*, or MUAs) available for Linux is large, and you could spend endless hours exploring the details of all of them. Instead of guiding you toward this route, this chapter attempts to do three things: give a brief intro to using the default mail agent; give an overview of other well-supported mail agents, with pointers on where to go for more info; and show how you can use other tools on the system to manipulate your email.

The `mail` tool is the default mail agent on Debian and most other Linux systems. It comes without many bells and whistles that are standard with most MUAs, and any user who sends and receives email more than occasionally will certainly want to learn a more advanced system (see Recipe 30.6 [Picking the Right Mail Application], page 325).

However, `mail` is available on almost all Unix-based systems, and it works in a pinch—by learning to use it you can always send and receive email on any Linux- or Unix-based system you encounter.

NOTE: On some Unix-based systems, the name of the tool is `mailx` instead of `mail`.

30.1 Sending Mail

To send an email message with `mail`, give the email addresses to which you are sending as arguments, and then type the message proper in the lines that follow; type *C-d* on a line by itself to signify the end of the message body, and to send the message.

- To send an email message to `lisa@example.com`, type:

      $ *mail lisa@example.com* (RET)
      Subject: Hello (RET)
      Hi there, long time no talk! I'm just learning how to use (RET)
      Linux and thought I'd show you how easy it is to send email! (RET)
      C-d
      Cc: (RET)

The text you type on the 'Subject:' line is displayed as the subject of your email message, and the lines of text you type after that is the body text of the message. Type *C-d* on a line alone to end the message. Then, `mail` prompts for 'Cc:' addresses; a "carbon copy" of the email message is sent to any addresses you give here, if any (just type (RET) for none, and separate multiple addresses with commas).

When you type, `mail` just reads the standard input like any other command-line tool, so there's little direct editing capability in this basic email service—use *C-u* to erase the current line, and *C-c C-c* (that is, *C-c* pressed twice) to cancel your input and abort the message altogether.

That's it! No bells, no whistles—but no time-wasting excess, either.

30.1.1 Mailing a User on the Same System

To send an email message to another user on the same system, give their username on the system instead of an email address (technically, you *are* giving the email address, since email addresses take the form of *username@hostname*; when *hostname* is omitted, the localhost is assumed).

- To send an email message to user **mrs** on your local system, type:

```
$ mail mrs (RET)
Subject: are you going to the party tonight? (RET)
C-d
Cc: (RET)
Null message body; hope that's ok
$
```

This command sends an email message to the user **mrs** on the local system. The email message itself is empty, but the subject is a short note asking whether user **mrs** will be attending a party.

NOTE: Besides being good for sending mail to users that you might share your system with, **mail** is useful for sending *yourself* mail, as a way to give yourself a reminder at your terminal (see Recipe 27.6.1 [Sending Yourself Email Reminders], page 294).

30.1.2 Mailing a File or the Output of a Command

The **mail** tool is also useful for mailing the contents of a text file or the text output of a command. To do this, give the email addresses you want to send to as arguments to **mail**, and use the standard input redirection operators to redirect the text to use as the message body (see Recipe 3.2 [Redirecting Input and Output], page 39).

- To mail the contents of the text file 'trades' to the email address terrapin@example.com, type:

      $ mail terrapin@example.com < trades (RET)

30.1.3 Mailing the Contents of a URL

A variation on the previous recipe is to use **mail** and shell redirection to send the output of some command to some address via email. You can, for example, send the contents of a URL as an annotated text file by redirecting the output of the **lynx** Web browser (see Recipe 31.3 [Reading Text from the Web], page 330).

- To mail the text of the URL http://etext.org/ as annotated text to the email address droneon@example.com, type:

      $ mail droneon@example.com < lynx -dump -number_links
      http://etext.org/ (RET)

30.1.4 Special Mail Composition Keystrokes

The following table lists the special keystrokes that work when composing a `mail` message, and describes their functions.

KEYSTROKE	DESCRIPTION
C-c C-c	Abort the current message and exit `mail`.
. (RET) *or* C-d	On a blank line, either of these commands sends the message and then exits `mail`.
C-u	Erase the current line and move the cursor to the beginning of the line.

There are also a few special commands that you may use while composing the body of the message. They're known as "tilde escapes" because you specify them by typing a tilde character ('~').

The following table lists some of these commands and describes their functions.

COMMAND	DESCRIPTION
~!*command*	Run *command* in a shell.
~b*address*	Send a blind carbon copy to the usernames or email addresses given.
~d	Copy the file 'dead.letter' from your home directory into the message.
~e	Edit the message in the default text editor program. (When you exit the text editor, you are returned to `mail`.)
~f*number*	Insert copies of the specified received messages into the message body. Messages are specified by number or a range (for example, '2-4' inserts messages two through four inclusive); if no number is given, the current received message is inserted.
~F	Same as '~f', but reads in the messages with full headers.
~r*file*	Insert a copy of the file *file* into the message.
~w*file*	Write a copy of the body text into the file *file*.

These commands should each be typed on a line by itself.

- To insert a copy of the current mail message into the body of the message you are writing, and then open the message in the default text editor, type:

      ~f (RET)
      ~e (RET)

30.2 Receiving Mail

On Linux-based systems, the *INBOX* is a text file on the system where your incoming mail is written to. Its location is always given by $MAIL, a special shell variable (see Recipe 3.6.1 [Changing the Shell Prompt], page 46).

- To output the location of your INBOX, type:

```
$ echo $MAIL (RET)
```

Usually, the INBOX location is in the '`/var/spool/mail`' directory, and has the same name as your username—so if your username is `mrs`, your INBOX is likely '`/var/spool/mail/mrs`'.

You shouldn't directly edit this file, because doing so can inadvertently cause you to lose incoming mail.

To see if you have any mail waiting in your INBOX, type `mail`. If you don't have any mail, `mail` will indicate this and exit; if you *do* have mail waiting, `mail` outputs a list of message headers, one line per message, each containing the status of the message ('`N`' for new messages, blank for previously read messages), the message number, the name of the sender, the date and time the message was received, and the number of lines and characters in the message.

- To see if you have mail, type:

```
$ mail (RET)
Mail version 8.1 6/6/93.  Type ? for help.
"/var/spool/mail/m": 3 messages 3 new
>N  1 mrs            Mon Sep 6 17:29  13/345 "Re: A modest proposal"
 N  2 Ray            Tue Sep 7 04:20  15/694 "Latest news"
 N  3 lisa@example   Tue Sep 7 09:35  19/869 "Re: Hello"
&
```

In this example, the user has three messages waiting—one from `mrs`, one from `Ray`, and one from `lisa@example.com`.

The `mail` prompt is an ampersand ('`&`') character; from there, you can read, delete, reply to, and save messages.

When you type (RET) at the '`&`' prompt, `mail` outputs the next unread message to the screen. You can also type a number to output that message.

- To read the next unread message in `mail`, type:

    & (RET)

- To read message number three in `mail`, type:

    & 3 (RET)

There are two ways to exit `mail`: type *q* to exit `mail` and apply the deletion commands you have given, if any, to your INBOX; type *x* to exit `mail` and revert the state of your INBOX to how it was before you ran `mail`.

- To exit `mail` and revert your INBOX to its state before you started `mail`, type:

    & x (RET)

30.2.1 Deleting Mail

To delete a message in `mail`, type *d* at the '`&`' prompt after reading the message in question. You can also specify a message or a range of messages to delete as an option to *d*.

- To delete the message you just read, type:

          & d (RET)

- To delete message 3, type:

          & d3 (RET)

- To delete messages 10 through 14, type:

          & d10-14 (RET)

30.2.2 Options Available while Reading Mail

The following table summarizes the most common `mail` commands for reading mail; these commands work at the '**&**' prompt.

COMMAND	DESCRIPTION
?	Output a help menu containing a list of mail options and their meanings.
d	Delete a message. Give the number or range of the message(s) to delete as an argument.
h	Output a list of headers of mail messages. You can specify a range or the number of the message to start with.
q	Exit `mail` and apply the changes you have made in this `mail` session to your INBOX.
r	Reply to the message you last read; you can also give a message number as an argument to reply to that message number.
u	Undelete a message you have deleted in the current mail session. Give the number or range of the message(s) to be undeleted as an argument.
x	Exit `mail` and revert the INBOX to its state before this `mail` session.
s *file*	Save the message you last read to the file in your home directory specified by *file* (if the file does not exist, `mail` will ask you whether or not it should create it).

NOTE: By default, only you (and, as always, the superuser) have access to read your INBOX. While there are tools available (such as `mail`, and the other MUAs) to read this file in special ways, you can also view this file like any other text file (see Chapter 9 [Viewing Text], page 111).

30.3 Managing Mail

A *mail folder* is simply a text file whose contents consist of saved mail messages; any tool that works on text can be used on a mail folder.

The following subsections describe some of the common ways to manage and otherwise modify your saved mail.

30.3.1 Viewing a Mail Folder

Debian: 'elm-me+'
WWW: http://www.instinct.org/elm/

You can view your mail folders in `less` or edit them in a text editor, although the folder will appear as one long scroll containing all of the messages the folder contains.

You can also view them in `elm` (see Recipe 30.6 [Picking the Right Mail Application], page 325) or open them with `mail`, and they will appear in the normal way as your INBOX would appear with these tools.

To view a mail folder with `elm`, give the name of the folder as an argument to the '-f' option.

- To view the mail folder '~/email/mrs' in `elm`, type:

      $ elm -f ~/email/mrs (RET)

If you save your mail messages in a lot of separate folders, you can view a sorted list of all messages from all files by using `cat` in conjunction with `elm`. Concatenate all the folders into one with `cat` and then view that file in `elm` as you would view any folder.

- To view the contents of all of the email folders in your '~/email' directory, type:

      $ cat ~/email/* > allmessages (RET)
      $ elm -f allmessages (RET)

These commands write a new file, 'allmessages', in the current directory, containing the contents of all email folders in '~/email'; then, that file is viewed in `elm`.

NOTE: To view a list showing who all the messages in a folder are from, use `frm`; see Recipe 30.3.4 [Seeing Who Your Mail Is From], page 322.

30.3.2 Setting Notification for New Mail

Debian: 'biff'
WWW: ftp://ftp.uk.linux.org/pub/linux/Networking/
WWW: http://www.splode.com/~friedman/software/packages/index.html

The `biff` tool notifies you when new mail arrives, by printing the header and first few lines of a mail message.

To turn `biff` on, use 'y' as an option. To turn `biff` off, so that you stop being notified when new mail arrives, use 'n' as an option. `biff` options don't take a hyphen.

- To turn `biff` on, type:

      $ biff y (RET)

Some people put the above line in their '.bashrc' file so that `biff` is always set on in all of their shells (see Recipe 3.6.1 [Changing the Shell Prompt], page 46).

Typing `biff` alone with no options will tell you whether `biff` is set to 'y' or 'n'.

- To see what `biff` is set to, type:

      $ biff (RET)

A companion tool, `xbiff`, works only in the X Window System (you can use the regular `biff` in X, too). When you start it, `xbiff` draws a window containing a mailbox that looks like this:[1]

When you have mail, `xbiff` rings the system bell, the window icon reverses color, and the mailbox flag goes up:

NOTE: The original version of `biff` was named after a dog. In the early 1980s at a UC Berkeley computer lab, a girl would bring her dog, Biff, with her when she went to use the computers. Biff was known for barking at the mailman when he came in to deliver the day's mail. He was also very popular with all of the BSD UNIX hackers at Berkeley, and when one of them wrote a mail notification tool, he thought of Biff—hence the name. (Biff, the dog, died in August 1993.)

30.3.3 Counting How Many Messages You Have

Debian: 'elm-me+'
WWW: `ftp://ftp.uu.net/networking/mail/elm`

Use **messages** to count the number of mail messages in a folder or file. Give the name of a mail folder as an argument; with no arguments, it counts the mail you have waiting in your INBOX.

- To see how many email messages you have waiting, type:

---

[1] Noah Friedman has an alternate set of "Spam" images you can use, available from `http://www.splode.com/~friedman/software/packages/index.html`.

$ *messages* (RET)

- To count the number of email messages in the mail folder '~/email/saved', type:

    $ *messages ~/email/saved* (RET)

30.3.4 Seeing Who Your Mail Is From

Debian: 'elm-me+'
WWW: ftp://ftp.uu.net/networking/mail/elm

Use **frm** to output a list of sender names and subjects for your mail. Give the name of a mail folder as an option; with no options, **frm** reads your INBOX.

- To output a list showing sender names and subjects of your incoming mail, type:

    $ *frm* (RET)

- To output a list showing sender names and subjects of the mail in the file '~/email/saved', type:

    $ *frm ~/email/saved* (RET)

NOTE: An alternate tool, **from**, works in similar fashion, but it does not output subject lines; instead, it outputs the names of senders and the time that messages were received.

30.3.5 Verifying an Email Address

Debian: 'vrfy'
WWW: ftp://ftp.nikhef.nl/pub/network/

Use **vrfy** to determine whether or not a given email address works. This is useful when you are unsure whether or not you have the right email address for someone. If the address works, **vrfy** outputs a message indicating that the recipient exists; if the address is not valid, **vrfy** outputs a message saying that the user is unknown.

- To verify that the email address **user@example.edu** is valid, type:

    $ *vrfy user@example.edu* (RET)

Use the '-f' option to specify a text file containing email addresses; **vrfy** attempts to verify all email addresses contained in the file.

- To verify all of the email addresses contained in the file '**net-legends-faq**', type:

    $ *vrfy -f net-legends-faq* (RET)

NOTE: vrfy relies on the remote system to get this information; in these days of the heavily corporatized Internet, an increasing number of sites no longer supply this kind of information to the general public. However, it's still useful enough to be worth mentioning.

30.4 Mail Attachments

Debian: 'metamail'
WWW: http://bmrc.berkeley.edu/~trey/emacs/metamail.html

MIME ("Multipurpose Internet Mail Extensions") is an Internet standard for encoding and attaching files to mail messages. It's used when sending image, audio, or other non-plain-text data via email.

Normally, you read and send MIME mail with your MUA. The following recipes, which show ways to send and receive MIME mail on the command line, are useful for when you just use the mail tool to read and send occasional mail with an attachment, but the built-in methods for manipulating MIME mail in any reasonable MUA will invariably be easier and more convenient than the techniques described here (see Recipe 30.6 [Picking the Right Mail Application], page 325).

30.4.1 Reading a Mail Attachment

To read a mail attachment, write the message to a file and then run metamail with the file name as an argument. metamail lists each attachment and prompts you about whether it should display the attachment, write it to a file, or skip it.

To read a mail attachment, type:

```
$ mail (RET)
Mail version 8.1 6/6/93.  Type ? for help.
"/var/spool/mail/m": 1 messages 1 new
>N  1 Photo Dept.   Mon Feb 12 14:37   231/10980 "New Images"
& w1 image.mail (RET)
"image.mail" [New file]
& x (RET)
$ metamail image.mail (RET)
```

In this example, the mail tool was used to open the INBOX and write the message to a file called 'image.mail'; then, metamail was run with the file name as an argument.

30.4.2 Sending a Mail Attachment

To send a file as an email attachment, use metasend. It prompts for the values to use in the 'To:', 'Subject:', and 'CC:' header fields, plus the following values for each MIME attachment: its 'Content-type:' field, which describes the kind of data the attachment contains; the file name; and the type of encoding to use, if any (usually one is recommended).

- To mail the JPEG file 'dream.jpeg' in the current directory to the address dali@example.org, type:

```
$ metasend (RET)
To: dali@example.org (RET)
Subject: The image you requested (RET)
CC: (RET)
Content-type: image/jpeg (RET)
Name of file containing image/gif data: dream.jpeg (RET)
Do you want to encode this data for sending through the mail?
    1 -- No, it is already in 7 bit ASCII
    2 -- Yes, encode in base64 (most efficient)
    3 -- Yes, encode in quoted-printable (less efficient, more readable)
    4 -- Yes, encode it using uuencode (not standard, being phased out)
2 (RET)
Do you want to include another file too (y/n) [n] ? n (RET)
Delivering mail, please wait...  Mail delivery apparently succeeded.
$
```

The following table lists values to use in the MIME 'Content-type:' field for various kinds of files.

VALUE	FILE TYPE
application/gzip	File compressed with gzip.
application/zip	File compressed with zip.
application/postscript	PostScript file.
image/jpeg	JPEG image file.
image/png	PNG image file.
audio/basic	Audio file.
audio/mpeg3	MP3 audio file.
audio/wav	WAV audio file.

30.5 Making an Email Signature

Debian: 'sigrot'
WWW: ftp://metalab.unc.edu/pub/Linux/system/mail/misc/

A *signature file* (often called a "dot sig," and written as '.sig') is a text file containing text that you want to appear at the end of email messages and other online postings.

Sometimes, people put their name, email address, and a small quote, or a piece of ASCII art (such as text written in a figlet font—see Recipe 16.3.1 [Horizonal Text Fonts], page 202); once the World Wide Web became popular, many people started including the URL of their home page in their '.sig'.

The use of signatures goes in and out of vogue with the years; you can decide whether or not you want to use one, but whatever you do, be sure to keep your '.sig' at most four lines in length—to use any more is considered very bad form. A first line consisting only of '-- ' is sometimes used; many applications recognize this text as the beginning of a '.sig' when processing messages.

You create your signature file in a text editor, just like any other text file. Name the file '.signature' or '.sig', and keep it in your home directory.

If you want to use more than one signature, use sigrot to "rotate" your various signatures—every time you run sigrot, it selects one of the signature files you keep in your '.sigrot' directory and writes it to '.signature'. To change your '.signature' every time you log in, you would run sigrot in your '.bash_login' file (see Chapter 3 [The Shell], page 35).

30.6 Picking the Right Mail Application

The following table lists some of the more popular MUAs that are available for Linux, describing their special features, and listing their Debian package name and URL (when available).

APPLICATION	DESCRIPTION
balsa	A graphical email client that works in X with GNOME installed; its interface is inspired somewhat by the proprietary Eudora. Debian: 'balsa' WWW: http://www.balsa.net/
elm	A menu driven MUA, elm was popular in the early 1990s among experienced users—it has some interesting features, including ways to send mails in batch mode to many addresses at once, and a tool to send telephone messages as email messages. Interest in elm has waned somewhat over the years, and most novices are advised to try mutt instead. Debian: 'elm me+' WWW: http://www.instinct.org/elm/
gnus	The gnus newsreader for Emacs[2] can also be used to read and send mail. It has many features and should appeal to Emacs lovers—but a warning: it can be daunting to learn! Debian: 'gnus' WWW: http://www.gnus.org/
mew	mew is an Emacs mail and news facility developed in Japan. It shows promise as a fairly new MUA and has many features for handling mail in complex ways. Debian: 'mew' WWW: http://www.mew.org/
mh-e	MH-E is an Emacs front end to nmh, below. It's very powerful, yet it remains easy to use. Debian: 'emacsen-common' WWW: http://www.emacs.org/

`mozilla`   Netscape Inc.'s open source Web browser, `mozilla`, has its familiar and self-explanatory email interface that works in the X Window System.
Debian: 'mozilla'
WWW: `http://www.mozilla.org/`

`mutt`   The MUA currently in favor among many `vi` users is `mutt`; it is one of the most popular MUAs for Linux.
Debian: 'mutt'
WWW: `http://www.mutt.org/`

`nmh`   The Rand "Mail Handling" system, `mh`, is not one application but a collection of small tools for manipulating mail folders. It should appeal to those who excel at building complex commands from combinations of simple tools and operators. `nmh` is the *new* "Mail Handling" system, containing rewrites and improved versions of the `mh` tools. Most Linux systems will install this over the old `mh`.
Debian: 'nmh'
WWW: `http://www.mhost.com/nmh/`

`vm`   VM ("View Mail") is a facility for reading and sending mail in Emacs. Older than `gnus` and `mew`, it is very configurable.
Debian: 'vm'
WWW: `http://www.wonderworks.com/vm/`

`wl`   Wanderlust is a MUA for Emacs designed to facilitate reading your mail on multiple computers.
Debian: 'wl'
WWW: `http://www.gohome.org/wl/`

31 The World Wide Web

Next to email, the most useful service on the Internet is the World Wide Web (often written "WWW" or "Web"). It is a giant network of hypertext documents and services, and it keeps growing by the instant—anyone with an Internet-connected computer can read anything on the Web, and anyone can publish to the Web. It could well be the world's largest public repository of information.

This chapter describes tools for accessing and using the Web. It also describes tools for writing text files in HTML ("HyperText Markup Language"), the native document format of the Web.

31.1 Browsing the Web

Debian: 'mozilla'
Debian: 'skipstone'
WWW: http://www.mozilla.org/
WWW: http://galeon.sourceforge.net/
WWW: http://www.muhri.net/skipstone/

When most people think of browsing or surfing the Web, they think of doing it graphically—and the mental image they conjure is usually that of the famous Netscape Web browser. Most Web sites today make heavy use of graphic images; furthermore, commercial Web sites are usually optimized for Netscape-compatible browsers—many of them not even *accessible* with other alternative browsers. That means you'll want to use this application for browsing this kind of Web site.

The version of Netscape's browser which had been released as free, open source software (see Recipe 1.1.3 [What's Open Source?], page 11) in 1998 to much fanfare is called Mozilla.[1] When first released, the Mozilla application was a "developer's only" release, but as of this writing it is finally reaching a state where it is ready for general use.

Once the Mozilla browser has been installed, run it in X either by typing mozilla in a shell or by selecting it from a menu in the usual fashion, as dictated by your window manager.

Like most graphical Web browsers, its use is fairly self-explanatory; type a URL in the Location dialog box to open that URL, and left-click on a link to *follow* it, replacing the contents of the browser's main window with the contents of that link. One nice feature for Emacs fans is that you can use Emacs-style keystrokes for cursor movement in Mozilla's dialog boxes (see Recipe 10.2.2 [Basic Emacs Editing Keys], page 123).

---

[1] Netscape's browsers, from their earliest Navigator release to their later Communicator series, were always referred to by the company as *Mozilla*; this was a pun on the name Mosaic, which had been the first popular graphical Web browser in the early 1990s—Netscape's goal had been to make a *monster* Mosaic.

A typical Mozilla window looks like this:

(In this example, the URL `http://slashdot.org/` is loaded.)

A criticism of the earlier Netscape Navigator programs is that the browser is a bloated application: it contained its own email client, its own Usenet newsreader, and other functions that are not necessary when one wants to simply browse the Web. Since Mozilla is free software, anyone can take out these excess parts to make a slimmer, faster, smaller application—and that is what some have done. Two of these projects, Galeon and Skipstone, show some promise; see the above URLs for their home pages.[2]

The following recipes will help you get the most out of using a graphical Web browser in Linux.

NOTE: Mozilla development is moving very rapidly these days, and while Mozilla is continually improving at a fantastic rate, some of these recipes may not work as described with the version you have.

Another way to browse the Web is to use Emacs (see Recipe 31.4 [Browsing the Web in Emacs], page 333); more alternative browsers are listed in Recipe 31.7 [More Web Browsers and Tools], page 340.

31.1.1 Maintaining a List of Visited Web Sites

Debian: 'browser-history'
WWW: http://www.inria.fr/koala/colas/browser-history/

Use the `browser-history` tool to maintain a history log of all the Web sites you visit.

---

[2] A trimmed-down Mozilla will soon be available for Debian systems.

You start it in the background, and each time you visit a URL in a Web browser (as of this writing, works with the Netscape, Arena, and Amaya browsers), it writes the name and URL to its current history log, which you can view at any time.

- To start `browser-history` every time you start X, put the following line in your '`.xsession`' file:

    browser-history &

The browser history logs are kept in a hidden directory called '`.browser-history`' in your home directory. The current history log is always called '`history-log.html`'; it's an HTML file that you can view in a Web browser.

- To view the current history log with `lynx`, type:

    $ *lynx ~/.browser-history/history-log.html* (RET)

Past history logs have the year, month, and week appended to their name, and they are compressed (see Recipe 8.5 [Compressed Files], page 102). After uncompressing them, you can view them just as you would view the current log (if you are viewing them in Mozilla, you don't even need to uncompress them—it handles this automagically.)

You can also use `zgrep` to search through your old browser history logs. The logs keep the URL and title of each site you visit, so you can search for either—then when someone asks, "Remember that good article about such-and-such?" you can do a `zgrep` on the files in your '`~/.browser-history`' directory to find it.

- To find any URLs from the list of those you visited in the year 2000 whose titles contain the word '`Confessions`', type:

    $ *zgrep Confessions ~/.browser-history/history-log-2000** (RET)

This command searches all your logs from the year 2000 for the text '`Confessions`' in it, and outputs those lines.

NOTE: For more about `zgrep`, see Recipe 14.3.1 [Matching Lines in Compressed Files], page 171.

31.1.2 Opening a URL from a Script

To open a Web page in Mozilla from a shell script, use the '`-remote`' option followed by the text ''`openURL(`*URL*`)`'', where *URL* is the URL to open.

- To open the URL `http://www.drudgereport.com/` in Mozilla from a shell script, use the following line:

    mozilla -remote 'openURL(http://www.drudgereport.com/)'

31.1.3 Mozilla Browsing Tips

The following tips make Web browsing with Mozilla easier and more efficient.

- Many users disable Java and JavaScript altogether; most Web sites don't require their use, and they often introduce security problems or have other pernicious effects on your browsing. Just say no.
- Disabling the automatic loading of images can help if you are on a slow connection; the broken-image icons take some getting used to, but you'll be surprised at how much

more quickly pages will load! If you need to see a page's images, just left-click on the **Load Images** button. You can also right-click on the broken-image icon of the image you want to load and select **Open this Image**.

- Right-click on an image to save it to a file; you will be given a choice to either open the image in the browser window or save it to a file.

- To open a link in another browser window, middle-click on the link. Opening multiple links in their own windows saves time when you are doing a lot of "power browsing."

- If a site forces links to open in a new window, and you don't want to do that, right-click on the link you want to open, and choose **Open this Link**; the link will open in the current browser window.

- To go back to the last URL you visited, type (ALT)-(←), and to go forward to the next URL in your history, type (ALT)-(→). (These keys may not have the desired effect in some window managers; if they don't work for you, try using the (CTRL) key instead of the (ALT) key.)

- If your visited-URL history on the **Go** menu is very large, and earlier URLs are truncated, you can still visit them by doing this: left-click one of the lowest entries on the menu, and visit that; then, left-click on the **Home** button. This eliminates all the URLs in the history list that are more recent than the page you'd just visited, but all of the old pages will be back in the list.

- To open your bookmarks file in a new window, type (ALT)-*b*.

- To open a new Mozilla window, (ALT)-*n* (it's often useful to have several windows open at once).

31.2 Viewing an Image from the Web

Debian: 'imagemagick'
WWW: `ftp://ftp.wizards.dupont.com/pub/ImageMagick/`

If you just want to view an image file from the Web, you don't have to use a Web browser at all—instead, you can use `display`, giving the URL you want to view as an argument. This is especially nice for viewing your favorite webcam image, or for viewing images on `ftp` sites—you don't have to log in or type any other commands at all.

- To view the image at `ftp://garbo.uwasa.fi/garbo-gifs/garbo01.gif`, type:

      $ *display ftp://garbo.uwasa.fi/garbo-gifs/garbo01.gif* (RET)

NOTE: When viewing the image, you can use all of the image manipulation commands that `display` supports, including resizing and changing the magnification of the image. For more information about `display`, see Recipe 17.2 [Viewing an Image in X], page 208.

31.3 Reading Text from the Web

Debian: 'lynx'
WWW: `http://lynx.browser.org/`

As of this writing, the venerable `lynx` is still the standard Web browser for use on Debian systems; it was also one of the first Web browsers available for general use.[3] It can't display graphics at all, but it's a good interface for reading hypertext.

Type `lynx` to start it—if a "start page" is defined, it will load. The start page is defined in '`/etc/lynx.cfg`', and can be a URL pointing to a file on the local system or to an address on the Web; you need superuser privileges to edit this file. On Debian systems, the start page comes defined as the Debian home page, `http://www.debian.org/` (but you can change this, of course; many experienced users write their own *start page*, containing links to frequently-visited URLs, and save it as a local file in their home directory tree).

To open a URL, give the URL as an argument.

- To view the URL `http://lycaeum.org/`, type:

    $ *lynx http://lycaeum.org/* (RET)

When in `lynx`, the following keyboard commands work:

COMMAND	DESCRIPTION
(↑) *and* (↓)	Move forward and backward through links in the current document.
(→) *or* (RET)	Follow the hyperlink currently selected by the cursor.
(←)	Go back to the previously displayed URL.
(DEL)	View a history of all URLs visited during this session.
(PgDn) *or* (SPC)	Scroll down to the next page in the current document.
(PgUp)	Scroll up to the previous page in the current document.
=	Display information about the current document (like all pages in `lynx`, type (←) to go back to the previous document).
g	Go to a URL; `lynx` will prompt you for the URL to go to. Type (↑) to insert on this line the last URL that was visited; once inserted, you can edit it.
h	Display the `lynx` help files.
q	Quit browsing and exit the program; `lynx` will ask to verify this action.

The following are some recipes for using `lynx`.

NOTE: Emacs users might want to use the '`-emacskeys`' option when starting `lynx`; it enables you to use Emacs-style keystrokes for cursor movement (see Recipe 10.2.2 [Basic Emacs Editing Keys], page 123).

31.3.1 Perusing Text from the Web

To peruse just the text of an article that's on the Web, output the text of the URL using `lynx` with the '`-dump`' option. This dumps the text of the given URL to the standard output, and you can pipe this to `less` for perusal, or use redirection to save it to a file.

---

[3] Like many of my generation, it was through `lynx` that I had my first view of the Web.

- To peruse the text of `http://www.sc.edu/fitzgerald/winterd/winter.html`, type (all on one line):

    ```
    $ lynx -dump
    http://www.sc.edu/fitzgerald/winterd/winter.html | less (RET)
    ```

It's an old net convention for italicized words to be displayed in an etext inside underscores like '`_this_`'; use the '`-underscore`' option to output any italicized text in this manner.

By default, `lynx` annotates all the hyperlinks and produces a list of footnoted links at the bottom of the screen. If you don't want them, add the '`-nolist`' option and just the "pure text" will be returned.

- To output the pure text, with underscores, of the previous URL, and save it to the file '`winter_dreams`', type (all on one line):

    ```
    $ lynx -dump -nolist -underscore
    http://www.sc.edu/fitzgerald/winterd/winter.html > winter_dreams (RET)
    ```

You can do other things with the pure text, like pipe it to `enscript` for setting it in a font for printing.

- To print the pure text, with underscores, of the previous URL in a Times Roman font, type (all on one line):

    ```
    $ lynx -dump -nolist -underscore
    http://www.sc.edu/fitzgerald/winterd/winter.html | enscript -B
    -f "Times-Roman10" (RET)
    ```

NOTE: To peruse the plain text of a URL with its HTML tags removed and no formatting done to the text, see Recipe 31.6.2 [Converting HTML to Another Format], page 339.

31.3.2 Viewing a Site That Requires Authorization

To view a site or Web page that requires registration, use `lynx` with the '`-auth`' option, giving as arguments the username and password to use for authorization, separating them by a colon ('`:`') character.

- To view the URL `http://www.nytimes.com/archive/` with a username and password of '`cypherpunks`', type (all on one line):

    ```
    $ lynx -auth=cypherpunks:cypherpunks
    http://www.nytimes.com/archive/ (RET)
    ```

It's often common to combine this with the options for saving to a file, so that you can retrieve an annotated text copy of a file from a site that normally requires registration.

- To save the URL `http://www.nytimes.com/archive/` as an annotated text file, '`mynews`', type (all on one line):

    ```
    $ lynx -dump -number_links -auth=cypherpunks:cypherpunks
    http://www.nytimes.com/archive/ > mynews (RET)
    ```

NOTE: The username and password argument you give on the command line will be recorded in your shell history log (see Recipe 3.4 [Command History], page 43), and it will be visible to other users on the system should they look to see what processes you're running (see Recipe 2.7.2 [Listing All of a User's Processes], page 27).

31.3.3 Options Available while Browsing Text

The following table describes some of the command-line options lynx takes.

OPTION	DESCRIPTION
-anonymous	Use the "anonymous ftp" account when retrieving ftp URLs.
-auth=*user*:*pass*	Use a username of *user* and password of *pass* for protected documents.
-cache=*integer*	Keep *integer* documents in memory.
-case	Make searches case-sensitive.
-dump	Dump the text contents of the URL to the standard output, and then exit.
-emacskeys	Enable Emacs-style key bindings for movement.
-force_html	Forces rendering of HTML when the URL does not have a '.html' file name extension.
-help	Output a help message showing all available options, and then exit.
-localhost	Disable URLs that point to remote hosts—useful for using lynx to read HTML or text format documentation in '/usr/doc' and other local documents while not connected to the Internet.
-nolist	Disable the annotated link list in dumps.
-number_links	Number links both in dumps and normal browse mode.
-partial	Display partial pages while downloading.
-pauth=*user*:*pass*	Use a username of *user* and password of *pass* for protected proxy servers.
-underscore	Output italicized text like _this_ in dumps.
-use_mouse	Use mouse in an xterm.
-version	Output lynx version and exit.
-vikeys	Enable vi-style key bindings for movement.
-width=*integer*	Format dumps to a width of *integer* columns (default 80).

31.4 Browsing the Web in Emacs

Debian: 'w3-el-e20'
WWW: ftp://ftp.cs.indiana.edu/pub/elisp/w3/

Bill Perry's Emacs/W3, as its name implies, is a Web browser for Emacs (giving you, as

Bill says, one less reason to leave the editor). Its features are many—just about the only things it lacks that you may miss are SSL support (although this is coming) and JavaScript and Java support (well, *you* may not miss it, but it will make those sites that require their use a bit hard to use). It can handle frames, tables, stylesheets, and many other HTML features.

- To start `W3` in Emacs, type:

    `M-x w3` (RET)

To open a URL in a new buffer, type `C-o` and, in the minibuffer, give the URL to open (leaving this blank visits the Emacs/W3 home page). Middle-click a link to follow it, opening the URL in a new buffer.

- To open the URL `http://gnuscape.org/`, type:

    `C-o http://gnuscape.org/` (RET)

- To open the URL of the Emacs/W3 home page, type:

    `C-o` (RET)

The preceding example opens the Emacs/W3 home page in a buffer of its own:

The following table describes some of the various special W3 commands.

COMMAND	DESCRIPTION
(RET)	Follow the link at point.
(SPC)	Scroll down in the current buffer.
(BKSP)	Scroll up in the current buffer.
M-(TAB)	Insert the URL of the current document into another buffer.
M-s	Save a document to the local disk (you can choose HTML Source, Formatted Text, LaTeX Source, or Binary).
C-o	Open a URL.
B	Move backward in the history stack of visited URLs.
F	Move forward in the history stack of visited URLs.
i	View information about the document in current buffer (opens in new buffer called 'Document Information').
I	View information about the link at point in current buffer (opens in new buffer called 'Document Information').
k	Put the URL of the document in the current buffer in the kill ring, and make it the X selection (useful for copying and pasting the URL into another buffer or to another application; see Recipe 10.4 [Selecting Text], page 128).
K	Put the URL of the link at point in the kill ring and make it the X selection (useful for copying and pasting the URL into another buffer or to another application; see Recipe 10.4 [Selecting Text], page 128).
l	Move to the last visited buffer.
o	Open a local file.
q	Quit W3 mode, kill the current buffer, and go to the last visited buffer.
r	Reload the current document.
s	View HTML source of the document in the current buffer (opens in new buffer with the URL as its name).
S	View HTML source of the link at point in the current buffer (opens in new buffer with the URL as its name).
v	Show the URL of the current document (URL is shown in the minibuffer).
V	Show URL of the link under point in the current buffer (URL is shown in the minibuffer).

NOTE: If you get serious about using Emacs/W3, you'll almost certainly want to run the XEmacs flavor of Emacs—as of this writing, GNU Emacs cannot display images.

31.5 Getting Files from the Web

Debian: 'wget'
WWW: http://www.wget.org/

Use `wget`, "Web get," to download files from the World Wide Web. It can retrieve files from URLs that begin with either 'http' or 'ftp'. It keeps the file's original timestamp, it's smaller and faster to use than a browser, and it shows a visual display of the download progress.

The following subsections contain recipes for using `wget` to retrieve information from the Web. See Info file 'wget.info', node 'Examples', for more examples of things you can do with `wget`.

NOTE: To retrieve an HTML file from the Web and save it as formatted text, use `lynx` instead—see Recipe 31.3.1 [Perusing Text from the Web], page 331.

31.5.1 Saving a URL to a File

To download a single file from the Web, give the URL of the file as an argument to `wget`.

- For example, to download `ftp://ftp.neuron.net/pub/spiral/septembr.mp3` to a file, type:

    $ *wget ftp://ftp.neuron.net/pub/spiral/septembr.mp3* (RET)

This command reads a given URL, writing its contents to a file with the same name as the original, 'septembr.mp3', in the current working directory.

If you interrupt a download before it's finished, the contents of the file you were retrieving will contain only the portion of the file `wget` retrieved until it was interrupted. Use `wget` with the '-c' option to resume the download from the point it left off.

- To resume download of the URL from the previous example, type:

    $ *wget -c ftp://ftp.neuron.net/pub/spiral/septembr.mp3* (RET)

NOTE: In order for the '-c' option to have the desired effect, you should run `wget` from the same directory as it was run previously, where that partially-retrieved file should still exist.

31.5.2 Archiving an Entire Web Site

To archive a single Web site, use the '-m' ("mirror") option, which saves files with the exact timestamp of the original, if possible, and sets the "recursive retrieval" option to download everything. To specify the number of retries to use when an error occurs in retrieval, use the '-t' option with a numeric argument—'-t3' is usually good for safely retrieving across the net; use '-t0' to specify an infinite number of retries, good for when a network connection is *really* bad but you *really* want to archive something, regardless of how long it takes. Finally, use the '-o' with a file name as an argument to write a progress log to the file—examining it can be useful in the event that something goes wrong during the archiving; once the archival process is complete and you've determined that it was successful, you can delete the log file.

- To mirror the Web site at `http://www.bloofga.org/`, giving up to three retries for retrieving files and putting error messages in a log file called 'mirror.log', type:

      $ wget -m -t3 http://www.bloofga.org/ -o mirror.log (RET)

This command makes an archive of the Web site at 'www.bloofga.org' in a subdirectory called 'www.bloofga.org' in the current directory. Log messages are written to a file in the current directory called 'mirror.log'.

To continue an archive that you've left off, use the '-nc' ("no clobber") option; it doesn't retrieve files that have already been downloaded. For this option to work the way you want it to, be sure that you are in the same directory that you were in when you originally began archiving the site.

- To continue an interrupted mirror of the Web site at `http://www.bloofga.org/` and make sure that existing files are not downloaded, giving up to three retries for retrieval of files and putting error messages in a log file called 'mirror.log', type:

      $ wget -nc -m -t3 http://www.bloofga.org/ -o mirror.log (RET)

31.5.3 Archiving Part of a Web Site

To archive only part of a Web site—such as, say, a user's home page—use the '-I' option followed by a list of the absolute path names of the directories to archive; all other directories on the site are ignored.

- To archive the Web site at `http://dougal.bris.ac.uk/~mbt/`, only archiving the '/ mbt' directory, and writing log messages to a file called 'uk.log', type:

      $ wget -m -t3 -I /~mbt http://dougal.bris.ac.uk/~mbt/
      -o uk.log (RET)

This command archives all files on the `http://dougal.bris.ac.uk/~mbt/` Web site whose directory names begin with '/~mbt'.

To only get files in a given directory, use the '-r' and '-l1' options (the '-l' option specifies the number of levels to descend from the given level). To only download files in a given directory, combine these options with the '--no-parent' option, which specifies not to ascend to the parent directory.

Use the '-A' option to specify the exact file name extensions to accept—for example, use '-A txt,text,tex' to only download files whose names end with '.txt', '.text', and '.tex' extensions. The '-R' option works similarly, but specifies the file extensions to *reject* and not download.

- To download only the files ending in a '.gz' extension and only in the given directory '/~rjh/indiepop-1/download/' at 'monash.edu.au', type:

      $ wget -m -r -l1 --no-parent -A.gz
      http://monash.edu.au/~rjh/indiepop-1/download/ (RET)

31.5.4 Reading the Headers of a Web Page

All Web servers output special *headers* at the beginning of page requests, but you normally don't see them when you retrieve a URL with a Web browser. These headers contain information such as the current system date of the Web server host and the name and version of the Web server and operating system software.

Use the '-S' option with `wget` to output these headers when retrieving files; headers are output to standard output, or to the log file, if used.

- To retrieve the file at `http://slashdot.org/` and output the headers, type:

      $ *wget -S http://slashdot.org/* (RET)

This command writes the server response headers to standard output and saves the contents of `http://slashdot.org/` to a file in the current directory whose name is the same as the original file.

31.6 Writing HTML

Debian: 'bluefish'
WWW: http://bluefish.openoffice.nl/

Hypertext Markup Language (HTML) is the markup language of the Web; HTML files are just plain text files written in this markup language. You can write HTML files in any text editor; then, open the file in a Web browser to see the HTML markup *rendered* in its resulting hypertext appearance.

Many people swear by Bluefish, a full-featured, user-friendly HTML editor for X.

Emacs (see Recipe 10.2 [Emacs], page 121) has a major mode to facilitate the editing of HTML files; to start this mode in a buffer, type:

   M-x html-mode (RET)

The features of HTML mode include the insertion of "skeleton" constructs.

The help text for the HTML mode function includes a very short HTML authoring tutorial—view the documentation on this function to display the tutorial.

- To read a short HTML tutorial in Emacs, type:

      C-h f html-mode (RET)

NOTE: When you're editing an HTML file in an Emacs buffer, you can open the same file in a Web browser in another window—Web browsers only read and don't write the HTML files they open, so you can view the rendered document in the browser as you create it in Emacs. When you make and save a change in the Emacs buffer, reload the file in the browser to see your changes take effect immediately.

31.6.1 Adding Parameters to Image Tags

Debian: 'imgsizer'
WWW: http://www.tuxedo.org/~esr/software.html#imgsizer

For usability, HTML image source tags should have 'HEIGHT' and 'WIDTH' parameters, which specify the dimensions of the image the tag describes. By specifying these parameters in all the image tags on a page, the text in that page will display in the browser window *before the images are loaded*. Without them, the browser must load all images before any of the text on the page is displayed.

Use `imgsizer` to automatically determine the proper values and insert them into an HTML file. Give the name of the HTML file to fix as an argument.

- To add 'HEIGHT' and 'WIDTH' parameters to the file 'index.html', type:

    $ *imgsizer index.html* (RET)

31.6.2 Converting HTML to Another Format

Debian: 'unhtml'
Debian: 'html2ps'
WWW: http://dragon.acadiau.ca/~013639s/
WWW: http://www.tdb.uu.se/~jan/html2ps.html

There are several ways to convert HTML files to other formats. You can convert the HTML to plain text for reading, processing, or conversion to still other formats; you can also convert the HTML to PostScript, which you can view, print, or also convert to other formats, such as PDF.

To simply remove the HTML formatting from text, use **unhtml**. It reads from the standard input (or a specified file name), and it writes its output to standard output.

- To peruse the file 'index.html' with its HTML tags removed, type:

    $ *unhtml index.html | less* (RET)

- To remove the HTML tags from the file 'index.html' and write the output to a file called 'index.txt', type:

    $ *unhtml index.html > index.txt* (RET)

When you remove the HTML tags from a file with **unhtml**, no further formatting is done to the text. Furthermore, it only works on files, and not on URLs themselves.

Use **lynx** to save an HTML file or a URL as a *formatted* text file, so that the resultant text looks like the original HTML when viewed in **lynx**. It can also preserve italics and hyperlink information in the original HTML. See Recipe 31.3.1 [Perusing Text from the Web], page 331.

One thing you can do with this **lynx** output is pipe it to tools for spacing text, and then send that to **enscript** for setting in a font. This is useful for printing a Web page in typescript "manuscript" form, with images and graphics removed and text set double-spaced in a Courier font.

- To print a copy of the URL **http://example.com/essay/** in typescript manuscript form, type:

    $ *lynx -dump -underscore -nolist http://example.com/essay/ | pr -d | enscript -B* (RET)

NOTE: In some cases, you might want to edit the file before you print it, such as when a Web page contains text navigation bars or other text that you'd want to remove before you turn it into a manuscript. In such a case, you'd pipe the **lynx** output to a file, edit the file, and then use **pr** on the file and pipe *that* output to **enscript** for printing.

Finally, you can use **html2ps** to convert an HTML file to PostScript; this is useful when you want to print a Web page with all its graphics and images, or when you want to convert all or part of a Web site into PDF. Give the URLs or file names of the HTML files to convert as options. Use the '-u' option to underline the anchor text of hypertext links, and specify a file name to write to as an argument to the '-o' option. The defaults are to not underline links, and to write to the standard output.

- To print a PostScript copy of the document at the URL http://example.com/essay/ to the default printer, type:

    $ *html2ps http://example.com/essay/ | lpr* (RET)

- To write a copy of the document at the URL http://example.com/essay/ to a PostScript file 'submission.ps' with all hypertext links underlined, type:

    $ *html2ps -u -o submission.ps http://example.com/essay/* (RET)

31.6.3 Validating an HTML File

Debian: 'weblint'
WWW: http://www.weblint.org/

Use weblint to validate the basic structure and syntax of an HTML file. Give the name of the file to be checked as an argument, and weblint outputs any complaints it has with the file to standard output, such as whether or not IMG elements are missing ALT descriptions, or whether nested elements overlap.

- To validate the HTML in the file 'index.html', type:

    $ *weblint index.html* (RET)

31.7 More Web Browsers and Tools

Surprisingly, there are not nearly as many Web browsers for Linux as there are text editors— or even text *viewers*. This remains true for any operating system, and I have often pondered why this is; perhaps "browsing the Web," a fairly recent activity in itself, may soon be obsoleted by Web *readers* and other tools. In any event, the following lists other browsers that are currently available for Linux systems.

WEB BROWSER	DESCRIPTION
amaya	Developed by the World Wide Web Consortium; both a graphical Web browser and a WYSIWYG editor for writing HTML. Debian: 'amaya' WWW: http://www.w3.org/amaya/
arena	Developed by the World Wide Web Consortium; a very compact, HTML 3.0-compliant Web browser for X. Debian: 'arena' WWW: http://www.w3.org/arena/
dillo	A very fast, small *graphical* Web browser. Debian: 'dillo' WWW: http://dillo.sourceforge.net/
express	A small browser that works in X with GNOME installed. Debian: 'express' WWW: http://www.ca.us.vergenet.net/~conrad/express/

links   A relatively new text-only browser.
                      WWW: http://artax.karlin.mff.cuni.cz/~mikulas/links/

gzilla   A graphical browser for X, currently in an early stage of development.
                      Debian: 'gzilla'
                      WWW: http://www.levien.com/gzilla/

w3m   Another new text-only browser whose features include table support
                      and an interesting free-form cursor control; some people swear by this
                      one.
                      Debian: 'w3m'
                      WWW: http://ei5nazha.yz.yamagata-u.ac.jp/

32 Other Internet Services

There are many Internet services other than email and the World Wide Web; this chapter describes how to use many of the other popular services, including `telnet`, `ftp`, and `finger`.

32.1 Connecting to Another System

Use `telnet` to connect to a remote system. Give the name of the system to connect to as an argument, specifying either its name or numeric IP address. If that system is reachable, you will be connected to it and presented with a `login:` or other connection prompt (the network is not exclusive to Linux systems) just as if you were seated at a terminal connected to that system. If you have an account on that system, you can then log in to it (see Recipe 2.2.1 [Logging In to the System], page 18).

- To connect to the system `kanga.ins.cwru.edu`, type:

```
$ telnet kanga.ins.cwru.edu RET
Trying 129.22.8.32...
Connected to kanga.INS.CWRU.Edu.
Escape character is '^]'.


BSDI BSD/OS 2.1 (kanga) (ttypf)
```

```
                                    /\
        WELCOME TO THE...        _!  !_
                                _!__  __!_
            --                   !   !  !   !
         _!  !_                  !   !  !   !
        !     !   /\             !   !  !   !
        !     !  /  !            !   !  !    !___
        !     !  !  !            !   !  !    !   !
        !     !_!_  !            !   !  !    !   !
        !     !   !  !           !   !  !    !   !
       _!     !   !_!_  !        !   !  !_
      !       !     !_!          !     !_
     !        !                  !       !
     !     CLEVELAND FREE-NET    !
     !   COMMUNITY COMPUTER SYSTEM   !
     !_____!


              brought to you by

        Case Western Reserve University
        Office of Information Services


     Are you:
            1. A registered user
            2. A visitor
```

```
Please enter 1 or 2: 1 (RET)

Enter your user ID (in lower case) at the Login: prompt.
Then enter your password when asked.  Note that the
password will not print on the screen as you type it.

Login:
```

In this example, the user connected to the system at `kanga.ins.cwru.edu`; the bottom `Login:` prompt was the prompt of the remote system (if you are ever unsure what system you are on, use `hostname` as a shell prompt; see Recipe 2.4 [Running a Command], page 22).

To disconnect from the system, follow the normal procedures for logging out from the system you are connected to (for how to do that on a Linux system, see Recipe 2.2.2 [Logging Out of the System], page 20).

- To disconnect from a remote Linux system, type:

```
$ C-d
Connection closed.

$
```

In the preceding example, the first shell prompt was on the remote system, and the second prompt was on the local system.

32.1.1 Suspending a Connection with Another System

You can also *temporarily* escape back to the local shell by typing the *escape character*, which is a key sequence that is interpreted by `telnet` before it reaches the remote system. You will then be brought to the `telnet` command prompt, where you can suspend with the '**z**' command; to return to the remote system, bring the job back into the foreground (see Recipe 3.3.3 [Putting a Job in the Foreground], page 42).

- To temporarily return to a local shell prompt, type:

```
faraway-system$ C-[
telnet> z (RET)
[2]+ Stopped                         telnet
$
```

- To return to the remote system, type:

```
$ fg (RET)
faraway-system$
```

In the first of the two preceding examples, the escape character `C-[` was typed on the remote system, whose shell prompt in this example is '`faraway-system$`' (you don't have to type the escape character at a shell prompt, though; you can type it regardless of what program you are running or where you are on the remote system). Then, the 'z' command was given to `telnet` to suspend the `telnet` connection. In the second example, the suspended `telnet` connection to the remote system was brought back into the foreground.

NOTE: You should be aware that it's possible (though not often desirable) to "nest" multiple layers of `telnet` sessions on top of each other by connecting from one system to the next, to the next, and so on, without disconnecting from the previous system. To avoid this, make sure you know which host you're leaving when you're about to `telnet` off to another; the `hostname` tool is useful for this (see Recipe 2.2.1 [Logging In to the System], page 18).

32.1.2 Connecting to Another System with Encryption

Debian: 'kerberos4kth-user'
WWW: http://web.mit.edu/kerberos/www/
WWW: http://www.openssh.com/

On some systems, your system administrator may ask you to install and use `kerberos`, `openssh`, or some other network security tool so that you may connect to a remote system in a more secure manner than with `telnet`. These tools encrypt the data that is passed between the local and remote systems during your connect session; they're becoming very popular today among security-conscious administrators. Should you be asked to use one, follow your administrator's instructions in installing and configuring it for your system.

NOTE: In order to be of any use, the services and tools discussed in this chapter require that your system is online or otherwise connected to a network; see Chapter 29 [Communications], page 307.

32.2 Transferring Files with Another System

FTP ("File Transfer Protocol") is a way to exchange files across systems. Use the `ftp` tool to connect to another system using this protocol, giving the name or numeric IP address of the system you want to connect to as an argument. Once connected, you will be prompted to log in with a username and password (if you have one on that system).

Many systems are set up to accept "anonymous ftp" connections, where a public repository of files are available for downloading by the general public; to use this, log in with a username of `anonymous`, and give your email address for a password.

- To make an anonymous `ftp` connection to `ftp.leo.org`, type:

```
$ ftp ftp.leo.org (RET)
Connected to ftp.leo.org.
220-Welcome to LEO.ORG.
220-See file README for more information about this archive.
220-
220-Your connection class is named: The world outside Germany
220-
220-If you don't connect from inside Munich and login anonymously,
220-your data transfers are limited to a certain bandwidth.
220-
```

```
220-If you notice unusual behaviour, drop a note to ftp-admin@leo.org.
220 FTP server leo.org-0.9alpha ready.
Name (ftp.leo.org:m): anonymous (RET)
331 Guest login ok, send your email address as password.
Password: at118@po.cwru.edu (RET)
230-        _   ___ ___
230-      | | | | __|/   \         LEO - Link Everything Online
230-      | |__| _| | - |      Munich University of Technology (TUM)
230-      |___/|___|\___/       Department of Computer Science
230-
230-       This Anonymous FTP site is in Munich, Germany, Europe.
230-              It's Tue Sep 28 18:31:43 MET DST 1999.
230-    Please transfer files during non-business hours (1800-0900 CET).
Remote system type is UNIX.
Using binary mode to transfer files.
ftp>
```

Once connected and logged in, use the `cd` and `ls` commands to change directory and to list files on the remote system.

It is standard practice for public systems to have a '/pub' directory on their FTP host that contains all the files and goodies available to the general public.

- To change to the '/pub' directory on the remote system and look at the files that are there, type:

```
ftp> cd /pub (RET)
250 Directory changed to /pub.
ftp> ls (RET)
ftp> ls
200 PORT command successful.
150 Opening ASCII connection for file (918 bytes)
total 30258
-rw-rw-r--   1 ftpadmin ftpadmin 10942767 Sep 28 06:18 INDEX.gz
drwxr-xr-x   5 ftpadmin ftpadmin      512 Sep 17 18:22 comp
-rw-rw-r--   1 ftpadmin ftpadmin 9512498 Sep 28 06:40 ls-1R.gz
drwxr-xr-x   2 ftpadmin ftpadmin      512 Sep 17 18:22 rec
drwxr-xr-x   3 ftpadmin ftpadmin      512 Sep 17 18:22 science
226 Transfer completed with 918 Bytes/s.
ftp>
```

In this example, the '/pub' directory contained three subdirectories ('comp', 'rec', and 'science') and two files, 'INDEX.gz' and 'ls-1R.gz'; many public systems have files similar to these in their '/pub' directories—'INDEX.gz' is a listing of all files on their `ftp` site, with descriptions, and 'ls-1R.gz' is the output of the command `ls -1R` run on the directory tree of their `ftp` server.

The following subsections describe how to upload and download files. Use the `quit` command to exit `ftp` and end the connection to the remote system.

32.2.1 Uploading a File

Use the put command to upload a file; give the name of the file as an argument. put takes that file in the current directory of the local system, and puts a copy of it in the current directory of the remote system.

- To put a copy of the file 'thyme.rcp' from the current directory on the local system to the current directory of the remote system, type:

      ftp> *put thyme.rcp* (RET)

The current directory of the *local* system is, by default, the directory where you ran the ftp command. To change directories on your local system, use lcd; it works just like the cd command, but it changes the *local* directory.

- To change to the parent directory of the current directory on the local system, type:

```
ftp> lcd .. (RET)
Local directory now /home/james/demos
ftp>
```

In this example, the local current directory is now '/home/james/demos'.

There are other important commands for downloading files use 'i' to specify that files be transferred as *binary*; normally, the transfer is set up for text files. When you want to transfer programs, archives, compressed files, or any other non-text file, set the transfer type to 'i' first.

In recent years, most public systems have added a security measure forbidding the upload by anonymous users to anywhere but the '/incoming' or '/pub/incoming' directories.

The mput command works like put but allows you to specify wildcards. By default, mput asks you, for each file, whether to upload the file or not; to turn off this file prompting, type *prompt* before giving the mput command. This command is a toggle—type *prompt* again to turn file prompting back on for your session.

32.2.2 Downloading a File

The get command works like put, but in reverse—specify a file on the remote system, and get saves a copy to the current directory on the local system. Again, use *i* first when downloading non-text files. (You can also download text files with *i*, so it is good practice to *always* set it before you transfer files; most Linux systems are configured to set the type to 'i' immediately upon connection).

- To download the file 'INDEX.gz' in the current directory on the remote system, saving it to your '~/tmp' directory, type:

```
ftp> lcd ~/tmp (RET)
Local directory now /home/james/tmp
ftp get INDEX.gz (RET)
local: INDEX.gz remote: INDEX.gz
Transferred 10942767 bytes
ftp>
```

NOTE: The `mget` command works like `get` but allows wildcards; as with `mput`, you will be prompted to verify each file unless you use the `prompt` command first to turn this off.

32.3 Reading Usenet

WWW: `http://www.faqs.org/usenet/index.html`
WWW: `http://www.geocities.com/ResearchTriangle/Lab/6882/`

Usenet is a famous, vast collection of world-around discussion boards called *newsgroups*, where messages (called *articles*) can be read and publicly responded to. Newsgroups are named and organized by hierarchy, with each branch delineated by a period ('`.`'); for example, the '`comp.os.linux`' newsgroup is part of the '`comp.os`' branch of the '`comp`' hierarchy.

The following table lists the "Big Eight" Usenet hierarchies and give examples of some newsgroups in each one.

USENET HIERARCHY	DESCRIPTION
comp	Computing. `news:comp.os.linux.advocacy`, `news:comp.text.tex`
humanities	Humanities. `news:humanities.music.composers.wagner`
misc	Miscellaneous. `news:misc.consumers.frugal-living`
news	Newsgroups relating to Usenet itself. `news.newusers.questions`
rec	Recreation. `news:rec.music.marketplace.vinyl`, `news:rec.food.cooking`
sci	Science. `news:sci.math`, `news:sci.cognitive`
soc	Social groups and cultures. `news:soc.culture.usa`, `news:soc.college`
talk	Talk and chit-chat. `news:talk.environment`, `news:talk.politics.guns`

While there are many other hierarchies, these eight are technically the only newsgroups considered to be part of Usenet proper. While *netnews* is the term for the collection of all newsgroups including those in Usenet, these terms are often used interchangeably.

The "alternative" hierarchy, '`alt`', is perhaps the most popular hierarchy of all—just about every subject you might want to discuss has an appropriate newsgroup here, including non sequiturs. There are also hierarchies for topics concerning certain geographical areas; for example, the '`cols.`' hierarchy is for topics pertaining to Columbus, Ohio, and '`seattle`' is for Seattle, Washington. So, while 'cols.forsale' pertains to items for sale in the greater Columbus area, 'seattle.forsale' is for items for sale in and around Seattle. Hierarchies can exist also for certain organizations; for example, the 'gnu' hierarchy is for newsgroups concerning the GNU Project, and 'bit' is for newsgroup redistributions of the popular Bitnet LISTSERV mailing lists.

The following recipes describe tools for reading and posting articles to netnews.

32.3.1 Choosing a Newsreader

An application that lets you read and post articles to newsgroups is called a *newsreader*. Here are some of the best newsreaders available for Linux-based systems.

NEWSREADER	DESCRIPTION
gnus	Gnus is a very powerful and feature-full newsreader for use in Emacs. You can use it to read mail, too. Debian: 'gnus' WWW: http://www.gnus.org/
knews	A graphical newsreader for use in X. Its features include the display of article threads in a graphical tree, and options for those reading news over slow connections. Debian: 'knews' WWW: http://www.matematik.su.se/~kjj/
mozilla	Historically, commercial Web browsers also had mail and newsreaders built into them, and that capability remains in the Mozilla browser. Debian: 'mozilla' WWW: http://www.mozilla.org/
nn	The motto of nn is "No News is good news, but nn is better"; it's an older (and very popular) newsreader that was designed for reading the most news in the minimal amount of time. Debian: 'nn' WWW: http://www.math.fu-berlin.de/~guckes/nn/
pan	The "Pimp A** Newsreader" is a new-generation graphical newsreader that is designed for speed. It is meant to be easy for beginners to use, and it works in X with GNOME installed. Debian: 'pan' WWW: http://www.superpimp.org/
peruser	News Peruser is a suite of small tools for use in X that facilitate the reading and composing of news articles when you're offline—it downloads batches of news when your system is online. Debian: 'peruser' WWW: http://www.ibiblio.org/pub/Linux/system/news/readers/
slrn	Based on rn, one of the oldest newsreaders, slrn is optimized for use over slow connections (like home modem dial-ups). Debian: 'slrn' WWW: http://www.slrn.org/

32.3.2 Finding Newsgroups for a Topic

Debian: 'nn'
WWW: `ftp://ftp.uwa.edu.au/pub/nn/beta/`

Use **nngrep** to find newsgroup names that match a pattern. This is useful for finding groups on a particular topic.

- To output a list of all newsgroups that match the pattern '`society`', type:

      $ *nngrep society* (RET)

Use the '-u' option to only search through *unsubscribed* groups. This is useful if you are subscribed to a number of groups, and you are looking only for groups you aren't subscribed to yet.

- To output a list of all unsubscribed-to newsgroups that match the pattern '`society`', type:

      $ *nngrep society* (RET)

In the previous example, if you were already subscribed to the group `alt.society.neutopia`, that group will not be displayed; but other groups matching the pattern '`society`' that you are not subscribed to would be listed.

32.4 Listing Online System and User Activity

The following tools are used to list the activity of other users and systems on the Internet—showing whether or not they are currently online and perhaps displaying a little more information about them.

32.4.1 Checking Whether a System Is Online

Use **ping** to determine whether a particular system is currently connected to the Internet.

Type *ping* followed by the name or numeric IP address of the system you want to check; if your system is online and the system to be checked is also online, **ping** should continually output lines telling how long the latency, in milliseconds, is between the two systems. Type *C-c* to interrupt it and stop **ping**ing.

- To ping the host `bfi.org`, type:

```
$ ping bfi.org (RET)
PING bfi.org (209.196.135.250): 56 data bytes
64 bytes from 209.196.135.250: icmp_seq=0 ttl=63 time=190.0 ms
64 bytes from 209.196.135.250: icmp_seq=1 ttl=63 time=159.9 ms
64 bytes from 209.196.135.250: icmp_seq=2 ttl=63 time=160.5 ms
C-c
--- bfi.org ping statistics ---
3 packets transmitted, 3 packets received, 0% packet loss
round-trip min/avg/max = 159.9/170.1/190.0 ms
$
```

In this example, the host **bfi.org** was **ping**ed and a total of three **ping**s were sent and received before the user typed *C-c* to interrupt it. As long as these **ping** lines are output, you know that the other machine is connected to the Internet (or at least to the same network that your localhost is connected to).

You really don't need to analyze the information on each line of a **ping** message—the only useful information is the number at the end of the line, which tells you how many milliseconds it took to go out to the Internet, touch or "ping" that host, and come back.[1] The quicker the better—**ping**s that are four or five digits long (or greater) mean a slow connection between the two machines. When you interrupt the **ping**, some statistics are output, including the minimum, average, and maximum number of milliseconds it took to **ping** the given host. In the example above, the high was 190 and the low was 159.9 milliseconds, with an average of 170.1.

NOTE: If your own system is not online, **ping** will report that either the network is unreachable or that the host isn't found.

32.4.2 Checking Whether a User Is Online

Use **finger** to check whether or not a given user is online. Give as an argument the username of the user (if on the local system) or their email address (if on a remote system). This is called "fingering" a user.

If the system they are using has **finger** enabled (most Unix-based systems should), the command will tell you the following: the date and time when they last logged in; whether or not they are currently logged in; their full name; their office room and telephone number; their home directory; what shell they use; whether or not they have mail waiting; the last time they read mail; and, finally, their "plan," as described below.

- To finger the user **bradley@ap.spl.org**, type:

```
$ finger bradley@ap.spl.org (RET)
[ap.spl.org]
Login: bradley                          Name: Bradley J Milton
Directory: /sp1/bradley                 Shell: /bin/tcsh
Last login Wed Jan 20 16:38 1999 (PST) on ttypb from zais.pair.com
No mail.
Plan:
To learn to how use Linux and GNU software.
$
```

In this example, the user **bradley** on the system at **ap.spl.org** is not currently logged in, logged in last on 20 January, and uses the **tsch** shell.

NOTE: On Unix-based systems, you can put information in a hidden file in your home directory called '**.plan**', and that text will be output when someone **finger**s you. Some people put elaborate information in their '**.plan**' files; in the early 1990s, it was very much in vogue to have long, rambling **.plan**s. Sometimes, people put information in their '**.plan**'

---

[1] "I named it after the sound that a sonar makes, inspired by the whole principle of echo-location," said the original author of ping, Mike Muss. He died in an automobile accident in November 2000.

file for special events—for example, someone who is having a party next weekend might put directions to their house in their '`.plan`' file.

32.4.3 Listing Who Is Logged In to a System

To get a listing of *all* users who are currently logged in to a given system, use `finger` and specify the name (or numeric IP address) of the system preceded with an at sign ('`@`').

This gives a listing of all the users who are currently logged in on that system. It doesn't give each individual's '`.plan`'s, but the output includes how long each user has been idle, where they are connected from, and (sometimes) what command they are running. (The particular information that is output depends on the operating system and configuration of the remote system.)

- To output the users who are currently logged in to the system `ap.spl.org`, type:

```
$ finger @ap.spl.org (RET)
[spl.org]
Login       Name               Tty  Idle  Login Time   Office
allison     Allison Chaynes    *q2  16:23  Sep 27 17:22 (gate1.grayline)
gopherd     Gopher Client      *r4   1:01  Sep 28 08:29 (gopherd)
johnnyzine  Johnny McKenna     *q9  15:07  Sep 27 16:02 (johnnyzine)
jezebel     Jezebel Cate       *r1     14  Sep 28 08:42 (dialup-WY.uu.net)
bradley     Bradley J Milton   t2       2  Sep 28 09:35 (spl.org)
$
```

32.4.4 Finding the IP Address of a Host Name

When you know the name of a particular host, and you want to find the IP address that corresponds to it, `ping` the host in question; this will output the IP address of the host in parenthesis (see Recipe 32.4.1 [Checking Whether a System is Online], page 350).

You can also use `dig`, the "domain information groper" tool. Give a hostname as an argument to output information about that host, including its IP address in a section labelled '`ANSWER SECTION`'.

- To find the IP address of the host `linart.net`, type:

```
$ dig linart.net (RET)
...output messages...
;; ANSWER SECTION:
linart.net.              1D IN A        64.240.156.195
...output messages...
$
```

In this example, `dig` output the IP address of `64.240.156.195` as the IP address for the host `linart.net`.

32.4.5 Finding the Host Name of an IP Address

To find the host name for a given IP address, use **dig** with the '**-x**' option. Give an IP address as an argument to output information about that address, including its host name in a section labelled '`ANSWER SECTION`'.

- To find the host name that corresponds to the IP address 216.92.9.215, type:

```
$ dig -x 216.92.9.215 (RET)
...output messages...
;; ANSWER SECTION:
215.9.92.216.in-addr.arpa.   2H IN PTR   rumored.com.
...output messages...
$
```

In this example, **dig** output that the host name corresponding to the given IP address was `rumored.com`.

32.4.6 Listing the Owner of a Domain Name

An Internet domain name's *domain record* contains contact information for the organization or individual that has registered that domain. Use the **whois** command to view the domain records for the common `.com`, `.org`, `.net`, and `.edu` top-level domains.

With only a domain name as an argument, **whois** outputs the name of the "Whois Server" that has that particular domain record. To output the domain record, specify the Whois Server to use as an argument to the '**-h**' option.

- To output the name of the Whois Server for `linart.net`, type:

      $ whois linart.net (RET)

- To view the domain record for `linart.net`, using the `whois.networksolutions.com` Whois Server, type:

      $ whois -h whois.networksolutions.com linart.net (RET)

NOTE: This command also outputs the names of the nameservers that handle the given domain—this is useful to get an idea of where a particular Web site is hosted.

32.5 Sending a Message to Another User's Terminal

Use **write** to write a message to the terminal of another user. Give the username you want to write to as an argument. This command writes the message you give, preceded with a header line indicating that the following is a message from you, and giving the current system time. It also rings the bell on the user's terminal.

- To send the message '`Wake up!`' to the terminal where user '`sleepy`' is logged in, type:

```
$ write sleepy (RET)
Wake up!
C-d
$
```

The other user can reply to you by running **write** and giving your username as an argument. Traditionally, users ended a **write** message with '**-o**', which indicated that what they were saying was "over" and that it was now the other person's turn to talk. When a user believed that a conversation was completed, the user would end a line with '**oo**', meaning that they were "over and out."

A similar command, **wall**, writes a text message to all other users on the local system. It takes a text file as an argument and outputs the contents of that file; with no argument, it outputs what you type until you type *C-d* on a line by itself. It precedes the message with the text '**Broadcast message from** *username*' (where *username* is your username) followed by the current system time, and it rings the bell on all terminals it broadcasts to.

- To output the contents of '**/etc/motd**' to all logged-in terminals, type:

    $ *wall /etc/motd* (RET)

- To output the text '**Who wants to go out for Chinese food?**' to all logged-in terminals, type:

    $ *wall* (RET)
    Who wants to go out for Chinese food? (RET)
    C-d

You can control write access to your terminal with **mesg**. It works like **biff** (see Recipe 30.3.2 [Setting Notification for New Mail], page 320): with no arguments, it outputs whether or not it is set; with '**y**' as an argument, it allows messages to be sent to your terminal; and with '**n**' as an argument, is disallows them.

The default for all users is to allow messages to be written to their terminals; antisocial people usually put the line *mesg n* in their '**.bashrc**' file (see Recipe 3.6.4 [Customizing Future Shells], page 47).

- To disallow messages to be written to your terminal, type:

    $ *mesg n* (RET)

- To output the current access state of your terminal, type:

```
$ mesg (RET)
is n
$
```

In the preceding example above, **mesg** indicated that messages are currently disallowed to be written to your terminal.

32.6 Chatting with Other Users

There are several ways to interactively chat with other users on the Internet, regardless of their platform or operating system. The following recipes describe the most popular tools and methods for doing this.

32.6.1 Chatting Directly with a User

Debian: 'ytalk'
WWW: http://www.iagora.com/~espel/ytalk/

Use **talk** to interactively chat in realtime with another user. Give the username (or email address) of the user you want to chat with as an argument; a message will be sent to that user's terminal, indicating that a connection is requested. If that person then runs **talk**, giving your username as an argument, you will both be connected in a **talk** session—the screen will clear and then what you type will appear on the top of the screen; what the other user types will appear at the bottom of the screen.

- To request a chat with the user **kat@kent.edu**, type:

      $ *talk kat@kent.edu* (RET)

This command sends a connection request to the user **kat@kent.edu**. If the user is not logged on or is refusing messages, **talk** will output a message indicating such; but if that user is available, **talk** will send a message to that user asking to complete the connection, and it will tell you that it is ringing your party.

If that user then types *talk stutz@dsl.org* (if, in this example, your email address is stutz@dsl.org), then your screen will clear and you will see the following:

```
      [Connection established]
      ▮




      |_____|
```

You can then type, and what you type will appear on both your screen and that user's screen; that user, in turn, can *also* type—even while you are typing—and what that user types appears on the other half of both screens:

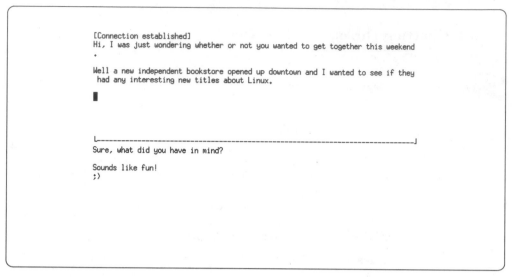

```
[Connection established]
Hi, I was just wondering whether or not you wanted to get together this weekend
·

Well a new independent bookstore opened up downtown and I wanted to see if they
 had any interesting new titles about Linux.

█



L_____J
Sure, what did you have in mind?

Sounds like fun!
;)
```

It is standard practice to indicate that you are done saying something by typing (RET)
(RET), thus making a blank line on your half of the screen. Some users, when they have
typed to the bottom of their half of the screen, sometimes type (RET) repeatedly to "clear"
their half of the screen and bring the cursor back to the top.

Type *C-c* to end a **talk** session.

When you type, both users see the characters appear in realtime; my first demonstration
of the interactive nature of the Internet, back in 1991, was when I had a live, real-time chat
with a user in Australia, on the other side of the globe—the magic felt that day has never
quite left whenever I run this command!

NOTE: A similar command, **ytalk**, allows you to connect to multiple users, and it contains
other features as well; it is generally considered to be the superior successor of **talk**, but it
is not yet available or standard on all Unix-based systems.

32.6.2 Chatting with Users on IRC

Internet Relay Chat (IRC) is a global chat system, probably the oldest and largest on the
Internet. IRC is a great way to meet and talk to all kinds of people, live on the Internet; it
has historically been very popular with Linux users.

There are several IRC networks, each with its own servers and tens of thousands of users;
to "go on" IRC, you use an IRC client program to connect with an IRC server. Like CB
radio, IRC networks have *channels*, usually based on a particular topic, which you join to
chat with other users in that channel (you can also send private messages to other users).

The following table lists some of the IRC clients available for Linux.

CLIENT	DESCRIPTION
bitchx	BitchX is an IRC client whose features include ANSI color, so it can display all of the character escape codes that are popularly used on IRC for special effects. Despite what you might gather from its name, it doesn't require X in order to run. Debian: 'bitchx' WWW: http://www.bitchx.org/
epic	EPIC is a large, feature-filled IRC client. Debian: 'epic' WWW: http://www.epicsol.org/
irssi	A modular IRC client; note that some versions can only be run in X with GNOME. Debian: 'irssi' WWW: http://irssi.org/
xchat	Xchat is a graphical IRC chat client for use in X. Debian: 'xchat' WWW: http://www.xchat.org/
zenirc	ZenIRC is a minimalist, no-frills (yet fully extensible) IRC mode for Emacs. Debian: 'zenirc' WWW: http://www.splode.com/~friedman/software/emacs-lisp/zenirc/

NOTE: If you've never used IRC before, you might want to read *The IRC Prelude*, on the Web at http://irchelp.org/irchelp/new2irc.html.

32.6.3 Chatting with Users on ICQ

WWW: http://www.portup.com/~gyandl/icq/

In the late 1990s, a company called Mirabilis released a proprietary program for PCs called ICQ ("I Seek You"), which was used to send text messages to other users in realtime. Since then, many free software chat tools have been written that use the ICQ protocol.

One nice feature of ICQ is is that you can maintain a "buddy list" of email addresses, and when you have an ICQ client running, it will tell you whether or not any of your buddies are online. But unlike `talk`, you can't watch the other user type in realtime—messages are displayed in the other user's ICQ client only when you send them.

The following table lists some of the free software ICQ clients currently available.

CLIENT	DESCRIPTION
licq	Licq is an ICQ client for use in X. Debian: 'licq' WWW: http://www.licq.org/
micq	Micq ("Matt's ICQ clone") is an easy-to-use ICQ client that can be used in a shell. Debian: 'micq' WWW: http://phantom.iquest.net/micq/
zicq	Zicq is a version of Micq with a modified user interface. Debian: 'zicq'

Appendix A Administrative Issues

Every Linux system has an *administrator*—someone who installs the hardware and software, maintains the system, and generally keeps things running smoothly. A single-user home Linux system, once installed and running, needs little administration—but the occasional upgrade or maintenance task is necessary.

This appendix exists as a reference for those users who will also be performing the administrative duties on their system. While a complete administrative guide is out of the scope of this book, the goal of this appendix is to point the new Linux administrator in the right direction, giving tips on how to choose the computer you'll use for Linux, install Debian GNU/Linux on it, and get it ready for use.

Unlike the rest of this book, this chapter contains recipes describing commands to be run by `root`, the superuser account.

If you're new to Linux administration, you may want to consult the help resources listed in Recipe 1.3 [If You Need More Help], page 16.

A.1 Linux and Hardware Compatibility

WWW: `http://www.thedukeofurl.org/`

In days gone by, Linux enthusiasts had to piece together computer systems from individual components, since the salesmen at computer stores had never even *heard* of Linux or the free software movement. But no more. Today, many dealers sell complete systems with Linux pre-installed, including corporations like Dell Computers and IBM.[1]

The Duke of URL reviews the latest hardware as it performs with Linux. His periodic "Linux Buyer's Guide" feature lists current hardware that works well on a Linux-based system, and it gives sample configurations (with prices and links to vendors) for putting together a complete system—from low-end budget system to a blazing, dual-processor rig.

Since Linux runs on many different computers and supports a wide range of hardware, and because everyone has different needs, I won't make too many recommendations as to which specific hardware to buy. (Systems change too fast for such a list to be useful, anyway.)

Before you make a hardware purchase, though, make sure that it's compatible with Linux—that bargain video-capture board will be worthless if it has a proprietary interface that only works with a certain non-free operating system.

To find out whether your hardware will work under Linux, try the following:

- Read the *Linux Hardware Compatibility HOWTO* (see Recipe 2.8.6 [Reading System Documentation and Help Files], page 32), an up-to-date list of hardware that is compatible with Linux.

- Visit the Linux Hardware Database (`http://lhd.datapower.com/`) and Linux Hardware.Net (`http://www.linuxhardware.net/`) sites, which provide reviews and information about hardware that works with Linux.

---

[1] For a complete list, visit the Linux Documentation Project (`http://linuxdoc.org/`) Web site.

- Search the Internet—particularly Usenet news and the `linux.com` site—for the hardware you intend to buy. Read any trouble reports people may have written about getting it to work with Linux, so that *you* won't be writing the next report about it.

A.2 Installing Software

All Linux distributions come with a multitude of software programs (also called "binaries"). But sooner or later, you will want to install more programs, or you will want to upgrade your existing software when newer versions are available. The following sections talk about installing the Debian GNU/Linux distribution itself, installing and upgrading software when from Debian packages, and how to install stand-alone shell scripts.

A.2.1 Getting and Installing Debian

WWW: `http://www.cheapbytes.com/`
WWW: `http://www.debian.org/`
WWW: `http://www.debian.org/releases/stable/`

You can get a copy of Debian GNU/Linux on CD-ROM from local or online vendors, or you can download the installation files from the Internet (recommended only if you have a fast Internet connection, of course).

If you choose to buy a copy of Debian in a local computer store, be sure you get the most recent version. If a store only carries an older version, the software might not work with your brand-new hardware! (Visit the Debian Web site to find the number of the latest version.)

If you'd rather buy a copy online, Cheap*Bytes sells affordable Debian GNU/Linux CD-ROMs. The Debian Project maintains a full list of vendors at `http://www.debian.org/distrib/vendors/`.

The precise details of installation are out of the scope of this book, but the Debian installation guide comes on the CD-ROM. It contains step-by-step instructions and the latest release notes.

A.2.2 Installing a Debian Package

Debian makes the software programs available in '`.deb`' *packages*, files that contain everything necessary for the installation of a given software program.

There are different methods of installing packages on a Debian system: via `dselect`, where you select packages from a menu; `dpkg`, a command-line tool for installing packages; and `apt-get`, part of Debian's new "Advanced Package Tool" system.

To install a package when you know the package name, mount your Debian distribution (for example, if you install Debian via CD-ROM, put the first Debian CD-ROM disc in your CD-ROM drive). Then run `apt-get` with the '`install`' command option, and give the name of the package to install as an argument. Should there be additional packages that must be installed first (called *dependencies*), or should the package conflict with others already installed, an action will be presented to fix this, and you will be prompted to confirm or abort the operation.

- To install the 'miscfiles' package, type:

    # *apt-get install miscfiles* (RET)

If you already have the '.deb' file, use **dpkg** to install it. Use the '-i' option and give the name of the file as an option. Any conflicts or dependencies will have to be resolved by you before the package is installed. If a problem is detected, **dpkg** will report it and exit without installing the package.

- To install the package in the 'miscfiles-1.1.7.deb' file, type:

    # *dpkg -i miscfiles-1.1.7.deb* (RET)

Finally, to peruse available packages and choose them from a menu, use **dselect**, the Debian package selection tool. A word of caution: its menu interface is different from most programs you have probably encountered, and its usage is unfortunately an acquired skill. Even the **man** page makes note of this: "The **dselect** package selection interface is confusing or even alarming to the new user."

NOTE: If you're new to Debian, I recommend consulting *Dselect Documentation for Beginners* (http://www.debian.org/releases/2.1/i386/dselect-beginner.en.html).

A.2.3 Upgrading a Debian Package

People are constantly contributing to the free software movement. This means that new software programs are constantly being added to Linux distributions, and current software programs are continually being improved—new features to match new hardware, faster program execution, security updates, and so forth. A Linux system, therefore, needs to be kept up to date in order to reap the benefits of the latest free software.

To upgrade a single package, use **apt-get** with the 'install' argument, and follow that with the name of the package to upgrade.

- To upgrade the 'sview' package, type:

    # *apt-get install sview* (RET)

This command will upgrade the 'sview' package to the most current version available, if greater than the version already installed on your system. If additional packages must be upgraded first in order for this new package upgrade to function properly, this command will fetch and upgrade those packages, too. Before downloading any packages, **apt-get** will show the list of packages that will be installed, replaced, or otherwise changed, and wait for confirmation first.

To bring your entire Debian system up to date, use the **apt-get** tool with the following command arguments. First, use the 'update' argument to update your system's list of available software packages. Then run **apt-get** again, using either the 'upgrade' argument to upgrade all of the installed packages to their most recently available versions, or use the 'dist-upgrade' argument when a new version of the Debian system is announced, to upgrade to that new version.

- To upgrade all of the software on your system to their most recent versions, type:

```
# apt-get update (RET)
...processing messages...
# apt-get upgrade (RET)
...processing messages...
#
```

- To upgrade your Debian system to the most recent release, type:

```
# apt-get update (RET)
...processing messages...
# apt-get dist-upgrade (RET)
...processing messages...
#
```

A.2.4 Installing a Shell Script

A *shell script* is a file that contains commands written in a shell command language (see Chapter 3 [The Shell], page 35). You run (or "execute") a script as you would any other command (see Recipe 2.4 [Running a Command], page 22). First, make sure that the script file is executable; if it isn't, you won't be able to execute it (see Recipe 6.3.6 [Making a File Executable], page 87).

Generally, the administrator installs new shell scripts in the '/usr/local/bin' directory. If you are on a multi-user system and you are the only user liable to run a particular script, you can put it in a special directory in your home directory tree—the '~/bin' directory is the standard recommendation here—and then add that directory to your path (see Recipe 3.6.3 [Adding to Your Path], page 47).

Not all executable script files are *shell* scripts. The first line of a script contains the full path name of the shell or other program that is to interpret and execute the script; sometimes, the path may differ on your system from the one the script was written on, and so you may have to change this line.

For example, a script may start with the following line:

```
#!/usr/local/bin/perl
```

This line means that the script is written in the `perl` language; the text after the '#!' is the full path name of the `perl` program, which in this case is '/usr/local/bin/perl'.

If you try to execute this script and the system reports an error finding the file, you'll have to change that first line to correspond to the location of the `perl` binary on your system. The `which` tool will output this location.

- To find out where `perl` is installed on your system, type:

```
$ which perl (RET)
```

If that command returns '/usr/bin/perl' or some path name other than /usr/local/bin/perl, you'll have to change the location in the first line of the script to the path name given:

```
#!/usr/bin/perl
```

NOTE: If the output of the `which` command returns nothing, that means that the `perl` program is not installed on your system at all; in that case, you should install the `perl` software.

A.3 Administrating Users

This section describes some of the things the system administrator will have to do in administrating the system's users.

All of these commands must be run by the superuser, using the `root` account—these commands edit system files.

A.3.1 Making a User Account

To make a new user account, use `adduser`. It takes as an argument the username to use for the new account. It will prompt for default setup information, including the user's full name and an initial password to use.

- To create a new user with a username of `bucky`, type:

    # *adduser bucky* (RET)

NOTE: By default, the name of the user's home directory will be the same as the username. So, for example, the user `bucky` will have a home directory of '/home/bucky'

A.3.2 Letting Users Access Hardware Peripherals

Certain hardware peripherals, like CD-ROM drives and soundcards, normally require superuser privileges in order to access them. These devices also have *groups* of their own, so a regular user can also access them by having membership to their groups (see Recipe 6.1 [Groups and How to Work in Them], page 83).

The groups that regular users might want to be part of include `floppy` (the floppy disk drive), `audio` (the soundcard), and `dialout` and `dip` (modem dial-out privileges).

Use `addgroup` to add a user to the group associated with a hardware device. Give as arguments the username to add and the name of the group to add to.

- To add the user `doug` to the `audio` group, type:

    # *addgroup doug audio* (RET)

A.3.3 Letting Users Mount Drives

The '/etc/fstab' file specifies the details about the filesystems in use on a system, including those that may be mounted by floppy or CD-ROM drive. In order to let users mount disks on these drives, make sure that there is a line in '/etc/fstab' for both the floppy and CD-ROM drives, each containing the 'user' flag:

```
/dev/fd0       /floppy      auto     defaults,noauto,user    0         0
/dev/cdrom     /cdrom       auto     defaults,noauto,user    0         0
```

A.4 Displaying Information about the System

The following recipes describe ways of displaying information about the system you are running.

A.4.1 How Long Has the System Been Up?

To find out how long the system has been running, use the `uptime` tool. When you run it as a command, it outputs the current time, how long the system has been running, how many users are logged on, and what the system "load averages" have been for the past one, five, and fifteen minutes.

- To find out how long the system has been up, type:

```
$ uptime (RET)
3:34pm  up  4:31,  4 users,  load average: 0.01, 0.05, 0.07
$
```

  To get a list of the times and dates when the system was recently rebooted, give 'reboot' as an argument to `last` (see Recipe 2.6.4 [Listing the Last Times a User Logged In], page 26).

- To output a list of times when the system was rebooted, type:
    ```
    $ last reboot (RET)
    ```

NOTE: An operating system capable of running constantly for a long time without crashes or freeze-ups is a good one, and so having a high `uptime` value is a matter of pride for many Linux users. It is not uncommon to hear of systems that have been running for months and sometimes even *years* non-stop—one Linux administrator reported on the Internet about one of his work systems, which had been running continuously without reboot for three years!

A.4.2 What Version of Linux Am I Running?

Use the GNU `uname` tool to see what version of Linux you are running. By default, it outputs the name of the operating system; the '`-r`' option outputs the operating system release number.

- To output the name of the operating system, type:
    ```
    $ uname (RET)
    ```
- To output the release number of the operating system, type:
    ```
    $ uname -r (RET)
    ```

  You can also use `uname` to output the CPU processor type of the system (such as i586, PowerPC, etc.); specify this with the '`-m`' option. The '`-a`' option is also useful; it outputs *all* information about the system that it can, including all of the mentioned options, plus the version date and number of the operating system and the machine's hostname.

- To output the CPU processor type of the system, type:
    ```
    $ uname -m (RET)
    ```
- To output all of the `uname` information for the system you are on, type:
    ```
    $ uname -a (RET)
    ```

A.4.3 What Version of Debian Am I Running?

On a Debian system, the file '`/etc/debian_version`' (see Chapter 5 [Files and Directories], page 65) contains the release name of the Debian installed.

Use `cat` to output the contents of this file (see Recipe 10.6 [Concatenating Text], page 130).

- To output the release name of the Debian system you are on, type:

      $ cat /etc/debian_version (RET)

NOTE: Debian releases have historically been named after characters from the motion picture *Toy Story*.

Appendix B Linux Resources on the Web

To get the latest news related to Linux and the free software movement, find new documentation, and keep up to date with the latest in free software, you'll want to turn to the Web.

The following table is by no means a complete list of these resources, but it gives what I consider to be the most important and useful Web resources for Linux, and free software in general. These are all sites which every avid GNU/Linux enthusiast should be aware of.

WEB RESOURCE	DESCRIPTION
http://freshmeat.net/	Freshmeat contains descriptions and links to thousands of free software packages.
http://www.gnu.org/	The GNU Project Web site lists new software packages as they become part of the GNU Project. This site is also the home of the Free Software Foundation, and is a source for both philosophical readings and news about the free software movement.
http://linux.com/	In addition to the latest in Linux news, linux.com provides feature stories, links, and a database of Linux User Groups.
http://linuxgazette.com/	The *Linux Gazette* is a monthly webzine devoted to "making Linux just a little more fun," and it has been published by SSC for years. Its "More 2-Cent Tips" column is famous.
http://linuxdoc.org/	The Linux Documentation Project manages the creation and upkeep of Linux HOWTOs and other documentation.
http://lwn.net/	Linux Weekly News contains great coverage for Linux and related free software.
http://mainmatter.com/	This site hosts the Linux FAQ.
http://sal.kachinatech.com/	SAL ("Scientific Applications on Linux") is the authoritative listing of scientific software that runs on Linux-based systems.
http://slashdot.org/	Slashdot is a popular news and discussion site for members of the Linux and free software community; many people usually check Slashdot several times daily.
http://sourceforge.net/	Sourceforge is the Internet's largest community for developers of free software; it gives free resources to developers of free software.

`http://sweetcode.org/`	Tracks free software that is *innovative*—not just the latest free clone of some old proprietary application that wasn't all that interesting to begin with.
`http://themes.org/`	A repository of GUI "themes" for your desktop.
`http://www.bright.net/` `~dlphilp/linuxsound/`	"Sound and MIDI Software for Linux" is the comprehensive guide to sound and audio for Linux-based systems.
`http://www.thedukeofurl.org/`	Provides non-partisan hardware reviews; if you are considering a new system, reading the Duke's latest "Linux Buyer's Guide" is an absolute must.

Additionally, the following table lists the primary Web sites for some of the most popular Linux distributions.

WEB SITE	LINUX DISTRIBUTION
`http://debian.org/`	Debian GNU/Linux.
`http://linux-mandrake.com/`	Linux Mandrake.
`http://redhat.com/`	Red Hat Linux.
`http://slackware.com/`	Slackware Linux.
`http://suse.de/`	SuSE Linux.

Appendix C License

Like much of the software that makes a working Linux system, including the Linux kernel itself, the text of this book is copylefted. That is, its copyright holder published it in its source form with a special kind of copyright license that has come to be known as a "copyleft" license. That does *not* mean that it has been put in the public domain; rather, the *copyleft* is a special set of terms and conditions, given by the copyright holder, that permit anyone to copy, distribute, and modify the work while all subsequent copies and derivatives retain equally open and free to anyone else. For this book those terms are described by the Design Science License, which follows.

C.1 Design Science License

TERMS AND CONDITIONS FOR COPYING, DISTRIBUTION AND MODIFICATION

Copyright © 1999–2001 Michael Stutz <stutz@dsl.org>
Verbatim copying of this document is permitted, in any medium.

0. PREAMBLE.

Copyright law gives certain exclusive rights to the author of a work, including the rights to copy, modify, and distribute the work (the "reproductive," "adaptative," and "distribution" rights).

The idea of "copyleft" is to willfully revoke the exclusivity of those rights under certain terms and conditions, so that anyone can copy and distribute the work or properly attributed derivative works, while all copies remain under the same terms and conditions as the original.

The intent of this license is to be a general "copyleft" that can be applied to any kind of work that has protection under copyright. This license states those certain conditions under which a work published under its terms may be copied, distributed and modified.

Whereas "design science" is a strategy for the development of artifacts as a way to reform the environment (not people) and subsequently improve the universal standard of living, this Design Science License was written and deployed as a strategy for promoting the progress of science and art through reform of the environment.

1. DEFINITIONS.

"License" shall mean this Design Science License. The License applies to any work which contains a notice placed by the work's copyright holder stating that it is published under the terms of this Design Science License.

"Work" shall mean such an aforementioned work. The License also applies to the output of the Work, only if said output constitutes a "derivative work" of the licensed Work as defined by copyright law.

"Object Form" shall mean an executable or performable form of the Work, being an embodiment of the Work in some tangible medium.

"Source Data" shall mean the origin of the Object Form, being the entire, machine-readable, preferred form of the Work for copying and for human modification (usually the language, encoding or format in which composed or recorded by the Author); plus any accompanying files, scripts or other data necessary for installation, configuration or compilation of the Work.

(Examples of "Source Data" include, but are not limited to, the following: if the Work is an image file composed and edited in PNG format, then the original PNG source file is the Source Data; if the Work is an MPEG 1.0 layer 3 digital audio recording made from a WAV format audio file recording of an analog source, then the original WAV file is the Source Data; if the Work was composed as an unformatted plaintext file, then that file is the Source Data; if the Work was composed in LaTeX, the LaTeX file(s) and any image files and/or custom macros necessary for compilation constitute the Source Data.)

"Author" shall mean the copyright holder(s) of the Work.

The individual licensees are referred to as "you."

2. RIGHTS AND COPYRIGHT.

The Work is copyright the Author. All rights to the Work are reserved by the Author, except as specifically described below. This License describes the terms and conditions under which the Author permits you to copy, distribute and modify copies of the Work.

In addition, you may refer to the Work, talk about it, and (as dictated by "fair use") quote from it, just as you would any copyrighted material under copyright law.

Your right to operate, perform, read or otherwise interpret and/or execute the Work is unrestricted; however, you do so at your own risk, because the Work comes WITHOUT ANY WARRANTY—see Section 7 ("NO WARRANTY") below.

3. COPYING AND DISTRIBUTION.

Permission is granted to distribute, publish or otherwise present verbatim copies of the entire Source Data of the Work, in any medium, provided that full copyright notice and disclaimer of warranty, where applicable, is conspicuously published on all copies, and a copy of this License is distributed along with the Work.

Permission is granted to distribute, publish or otherwise present copies of the Object Form of the Work, in any medium, under the terms for distribution of Source Data above and also provided that one of the following additional conditions are met:

(a) The Source Data is included in the same distribution, distributed under the terms of this License; or

(b) A written offer is included with the distribution, valid for at least three years or for as long as the distribution is in print (whichever is longer), with a publicly-accessible address (such as a URL on the Internet) where, for a charge not greater than transportation and media costs, anyone may receive a copy of the Source Data of the Work distributed according to the section above; or

(c) A third party's written offer for obtaining the Source Data at no cost, as described in paragraph (b) above, is included with the distribution. This option is valid only if you are a non-commercial party, and only if you received the Object Form of the Work along with such an offer.

You may copy and distribute the Work either gratis or for a fee, and if desired, you may offer warranty protection for the Work.

The aggregation of the Work with other works that are not based on the Work—such as but not limited to inclusion in a publication, broadcast, compilation, or other media—does not bring the other works in the scope of the License; nor does such aggregation void the terms of the License for the Work.

4. MODIFICATION.

Permission is granted to modify or sample from a copy of the Work, producing a derivative work, and to distribute the derivative work under the terms described in the section for distribution above, provided that the following terms are met:

(a) The new, derivative work is published under the terms of this License.

(b) The derivative work is given a new name, so that its name or title cannot be confused with the Work, or with a version of the Work, in any way.

(c) Appropriate authorship credit is given: for the differences between the Work and the new derivative work, authorship is attributed to you, while the material sampled or used from the Work remains attributed to the original Author; appropriate notice must be included with the new work indicating the nature and the dates of any modifications of the Work made by you.

5. NO RESTRICTIONS.

You may not impose any further restrictions on the Work or any of its derivative works beyond those restrictions described in this License.

6. ACCEPTANCE.

Copying, distributing or modifying the Work (including but not limited to sampling from the Work in a new work) indicates acceptance of these terms. If you do not follow the terms of this License, any rights granted to you by the License are null and void. The copying, distribution or modification of the Work outside of the terms described in this License is expressly prohibited by law.

If for any reason, conditions are imposed on you that forbid you to fulfill the conditions of this License, you may not copy, distribute or modify the Work at all.

If any part of this License is found to be in conflict with the law, that part shall be interpreted in its broadest meaning consistent with the law, and no other parts of the License shall be affected.

7. NO WARRANTY.

THE WORK IS PROVIDED "AS IS," AND COMES WITH ABSOLUTELY NO WARRANTY, EXPRESS OR IMPLIED, TO THE EXTENT PERMITTED BY APPLICABLE LAW, INCLUDING BUT NOT LIMITED TO THE IMPLIED WARRANTIES OF MERCHANTABILITY OR FITNESS FOR A PARTICULAR PURPOSE.

8. DISCLAIMER OF LIABILITY.

IN NO EVENT SHALL THE AUTHOR OR CONTRIBUTORS BE LIABLE FOR ANY DIRECT, INDIRECT, INCIDENTAL, SPECIAL, EXEMPLARY, OR CONSEQUENTIAL DAMAGES (INCLUDING, BUT NOT LIMITED TO, PROCUREMENT OF SUBSTITUTE GOODS OR SERVICES; LOSS OF USE, DATA, OR PROFITS; OR BUSINESS INTERRUPTION) HOWEVER CAUSED AND ON ANY THEORY OF LIABILITY, WHETHER IN CONTRACT, STRICT LIABILITY, OR TORT (INCLUDING NEGLIGENCE OR OTHERWISE) ARISING IN ANY WAY OUT OF THE USE OF THIS WORK, EVEN IF ADVISED OF THE POSSIBILITY OF SUCH DAMAGE.

END OF TERMS AND CONDITIONS

C.2 Applying Copyleft to Your Work

The underlying idea of free software is to help create a society where people are free, where we have freedom, and where we can share our work with others; but software is just one part of the digital information we work with and share in our lives.

The Design Science License is a generalized "copyleft" license that can be applied to any kind of work that is recognized by copyright law. You can use it to copyleft (make "Open Source") *any* kind of work, not just a computer software program.

In order to copyleft a work, it must exist in machine-readable form (where identical copies can be made without harm to the original), and you must be its copyright holder. If you are the author of a work, then you automatically hold its copyright; you don't need to register your work with the copyright office (`http://www.loc.gov/copyright/faq.html`).

To apply the DSL to your work, do the following:

- Use the following text for the work's copyright notice, substituting *Year* and *Author* for their appropriate values:

  ```
  Copyright © Year Your Name; this information may be copied,
  distributed or modified under certain terms and conditions, but it
  comes WITHOUT ANY WARRANTY; see the Design Science License for more
  details.
  ```

- Include a copy of the DSL with the distribution of the work.

- Include the source data of the work (see the license text itself for the precise definition) with the distribution, or make it available through postal mail for a cost not greater than storage media and postage.

  In many cases, the source data and the object form of a work will be the same—this is the case for software programs written in the Perl language, for example. But often, the source data will differ from a given object form. For example, when the object form is an MP3 format file made from a WAV format sample of an analog source, the WAV sample is the source data. For a cropped and manipulated JPEG file of a photograph obtained from a Kodak PhotoCD, the original PhotoCD file is the source data.

By copylefting your work in this manner, you can make it available for the benefit of everyone—all copies and modifications of your work remain as equally free as the original—while attribution and artistic integrity is guaranteed.

If you are interested in applying copyleft to your works, you might be interested in the following sites:

- "Copyleft and the Information Renaissance" (`http://dsl.org/copyleft/`), a general copyleft primer and collection of resources, written and maintained by the author.

- Free Music Philosophy (`http://ram.org/ramblings/philosophy/fmp.html`), on the free music movement, by Dr. Ram Samudrala.

- "What is Copyleft?" (`http://www.gnu.org/copyleft/`), an explanation of copyleft as it applies to computer software programs, by the GNU Project.

Program Index

Concept Index

391

T

LINUX MUSIC & SOUND
How to Install, Configure, and Use Linux Audio Software

by DAVE PHILLIPS

Linux Music & Sound looks at recording, storing, playing, and editing music and sound and the broad range of Linux music and sound applications. The CD-ROM includes over 100 MIDI applications, including digital audio and music notation software, games, and utilities.

2000, 408 PP. W/CD-ROM, $39.95 ($59.95 CDN)
ISBN 1-886411-34-4

THE LINUX PROBLEM SOLVER
Hands-on Solutions for Systems Administrators

by BRIAN WARD

This book is a must-have for solving technical problems related to printing, networking, back-up, crash recovery, and compiling or upgrading a kernel. The CD-ROM supports the book with configuration files and numerous programs not included in many Linux distributions.

2000, 283 PP. W/CD-ROM, $34.95 ($53.95 CDN)
ISBN 1-886411-35-2

Phone:

1 (800) 420-7240 OR
(415) 863-9900
MONDAY THROUGH FRIDAY,
9 A.M. TO 5 P.M. (PST)

Fax:

(415) 863-9950
24 HOURS A DAY,
7 DAYS A WEEK

Email:

SALES@NOSTARCH.COM

Web:

HTTP://WWW.NOSTARCH.COM

Mail:

NO STARCH PRESS
555 DE HARO STREET, SUITE 250
SAN FRANCISCO, CA 94107
USA

Distributed in the U.S. by Publishers Group West

Linux Journal's team of industry experts has put together a complete line of reference materials designed for Linux operating system users, programmers, and IT professionals. Visit your local bookstore or the Linux Journal Web site for other Linux Journal Press products. You may also request a free issue of the monthly magazine, Linux Journal, online at **http://www.linuxjournal.com.**

UPDATES

The book was carefully reviewed for technical accuracy, but it's inevitable that some things will change after the book goes to press. Visit the Web site for this book at **http://www.nostarch.com/lcbk_updates.htm** for updates, errata, and other information.

**A note on the type
in which this book is set**

The name of the font family used in this book is Computer Modern. These are free fonts designed by Donald E. Knuth for his TeX typesetting system, and are described in Volume E of the *Computers & Typesetting* series, *Computer Modern Typefaces* (Addison–Wesley, 1986).

This book was written and produced using the free software tools it describes. It was prepared with Texinfo, a system for generating both hardcopy and electronic output from a single source document. The Texinfo input files were composed in GNU Emacs, and the screen shots were taken and processed with the Image Magick suite of tools. The output was converted to PostScript for printing using Tomas Rokicki's Dvips, GNU Ghostscript, and Angus Duggan's PostScript Utilities. The system was a 100MHz 586 personal computer running Debian GNU/Linux 2.2.